Beyond Illustration: 2D and 3D Digital Technologies as Tools for Discovery in Archaeology

Edited by

Bernard Frischer
Anastasia Dakouri-Hild

BAR International Series 1805
2008

Published in 2016 by
BAR Publishing, Oxford

BAR International Series 1805

Beyond Illustration: 2D and 3D Digital Technologies as Tools for Discovery in Archaeology

ISBN 978 1 4073 0292 8

BAR Publishing is the trading name of British Archaeological Reports (Oxford) Ltd. British Archaeological Reports was first incorporated in 1974 to publish the BAR Series, International and British. In 1992 Hadrian Books Ltd became part of the BAR group. This volume was originally published by Archaeopress in conjunction with British Archaeological Reports (Oxford) Ltd / Hadrian Books Ltd, the Series principal publisher, in 2008. This present volume is published by BAR Publishing, 2016.

Printed in England

BAR
PUBLISHING

BAR titles are available from:

BAR Publishing
122 Banbury Rd, Oxford, OX2 7BP, UK
EMAIL info@barpublishing.com
PHONE +44 (0)1865 310431
FAX +44 (0)1865 316916
www.barpublishing.com

TABLE OF CONTENTS

Introduction
From digital illustration to digital heuristics

Bernard Frischer
Institute for Advanced Technology in the Humanities, University of Virginia, USA

This book is timely. As the following articles show, 2D and 3D modeling of cultural heritage is no longer used just to illustrate the location and appearance (past or present) of archaeological sites, but also as a tool to discover and recover data from archaeological remains. We have better ways of predicting where this data might be found under the surface (see **Gerlach *et al.***, **de Boer *et al.***). When applied to the legacy excavation data of a cultural heritage site—as **Lieberwirth** does in a pioneering study in this volume[1]—or when used to record the progress of a new excavation,[2] 3D modeling has the potential to mitigate the irreversible and destructive nature of archaeological excavation, an unfortunate, ironic, and unavoidable central fact of archaeology as traditionally practiced.[3] Up to now we have had, perforce, to murder to dissect. With the widespread adoption of 3D technologies to record and reconstruct archaeological sites, we can virtually preserve the site through 3D data capture as we dig it up. And, once we model the 3D data gathered in the field, we can allow our colleagues to retrace our decisions and to test the validity of our conclusions with more precision and confidence.

1. As predicted by Reilly 1991.

2. Cf. M. Bradley 2006; B. Bobowski 2007; W. Day, J. Cosmas, *et al.* 2007.

3. Cf., in general, Ananiadou *et al.* 2005; Borgman *et al.* 2005; Lord and Macdonald 2003. For the 'unfortunate irony' of archaeology, see Reilly 1989: 569.

This application of 2D and 3D digital tools in archaeology is not surprising. 2D and 3D models of cultural monuments permit us to visualize their use and evolution from inception through their latest phase. As neurobiologist Semir Zeki has emphasized, vision rarely involves mere sensation; it usually leads spontaneously to cognition as well. First we look, then we see and understand (Zeki 2003: 21, 24, 26, 93). A classic instance is Mendeleev's table of elements, whose power 'was not just that it functioned as a tool for arranging properties but that the gaps in the sequences predicted the discovery of yet *unknown* elements'.[4] A second famous case concerns John Snow's solution of the cause of an outbreak of cholera in London in 1854. By displaying all the cases on a map marked with streets and public water pumps, Snow was able to establish the likelihood that the disease had spread through water contamination at a specific pump. Its handle was removed, and the epidemic promptly ended (Tufte 1997: 27-37).

According to information scientist Colin Ware, a visualization can promote understanding in the following five ways:

- It may facilitate the cognition of large amounts of data
- It can promote the perception of unanticipated emergent properties

4. Kemp 2000: 69; for details, see Scerri 2006: 123-158.

- It sometimes highlights problems in data quality
- It makes clear the relationship of large-and small-scale features
- It helps us to formulate hypotheses (Ware 2004: 3)

The role of visualization in cognition has not yet become a major theme in discussions of 2D and 3D archaeological models. This is undoubtedly a normal case of theory-lag: since most uses of computer modeling have been for purposes of illustration, it is not surprising that theoreticians should have stressed this application. The field into which 2D and 3D modeling falls was aptly called 'virtual archaeology' by P. Reilly in 1990 (see Reilly 1991; Forte and Silotti 1995; Earl 2006). Reilly defined virtual archaeology's mission as 'enrich[ing] the perception of the material under study" (Reilly 1989), and "offer[ing]...the most faithful re-presentation of the ancient world possible: highly realistic in information and with a high scientific content' (Forte and Silotti 1997: 10). In support of this mission, theoreticians of the new field focused on such matters as what software should be used to create or view a 2D or 3D model;[5] viewshed analysis using standard GIS tools;[6] how uncertainty or degrees of probability should be represented;[7] and how 3D models could be used to improve interpretation in museums, in virtual museums, and in the classroom.[8]

5. For two early examples, see Baribeau *et al.* 1996 on 3D data capture with the use of a laser scanner; and Bloomfield and Schofield 1996 on 3D hand modeling: for an early survey of the topic with extensive bibliography, see Barcelò 2000.

6. For a survey and critique of early work see Gillings and Goodrick 1996: parts 4-4a.

7. E.g., Scagliarini Corlàita *et al.* 2003: 246-247; Frischer and Stinson 2007; Corallini and Vecchietti 2007: 19; Stinson 2007: 74-76. Note that although the last three articles cited were published in 2007, the authors presented the ideas in papers presented at conferences held in 2002. For subsequent work in this area, see Zuk *et al.* 2005 and Kozan forthcoming.

8. E.g., M. E. Bonfigli and A. Guidazzoli 2000; Loscos *et al.*, 2004; S. Pescarin *et al.* 2005; Helling *et al.* forthcoming.

That they were right to do so emerges from a quick sketch of the history of computer modeling in our field. In 1973, J.D. Wilcock set forth a prophetic vision of computer applications to archaeology at the first meeting of Computer Applications and Quantitative Methods in Archaeology. This organization—often known by the shorter name, Computer Applications to Archaeology (or CAA)[9]—was destined to become the most important in the field.[10] Wilcock predicted four main uses of the computer in our field (Wilcock 1973: 18): data banks and information retrieval; statistical analyses; recording of fieldwork; and the production of diagrams. He also had a fifth, miscellaneous category, and it is into this *omnium gatherum* that we find him talking about computer reconstructions of temples and other monuments (Wilcock 1973: 20). One thing that Wilcock failed to predict was the application of Geographic Information System software (GIS) to archaeology and historical studies generally.

In the next twelve years, most of the work presented at CAA fell into Wilcock's first three categories. Thus, E. Webb wrote in the preface of CAA 13: 'Until recently, the bulk of the papers presented were mainly concerned with the application of multivariate statistical packages to large bodies of archaeological data...on a University mainframe.... In the last few years...there has been a shift in computer-based archaeological applications from numerical analysis towards on-site recording systems and...database management systems' (Webb 1985: iii). In the same 1985 issue of CAA we find the first major article on 3D (Biek 1985). Biek wrote about the application of digital panoramic photography as a way of documenting an archaeological excavation. He was perhaps inspired by the first known large-scale digital capture of a contemporary city, the Aspen Project of 1978 (see Negroponte 1996: 65-67).[11] The

9. See http://caa.leidenuniv.nl/.

10. CAA's most recent meeting was held in Berlin in April, 2007 and attracted over 600 scholars who presented over 200 papers. See http://www.caa2007.de/.

11. For the final report, see http://www.osti.gov/energycitations/product.biblio.jsp?osti_id=5385627. Negroponte describes

first example of 3D hand-modeling of an archaeological monument followed four years later (Arnold, Huggett, Reilly, and Springham 1989).

In the early 1990s, Wilcock's prediction that computers would be used for digital reconstruction of archaeological sites started to be realized. Two early papers were published in 1992 by Reilly and by Wood and Chapman. A collection of occasional papers published by the British Museum in 1996 included four studies utilizing 3D reconstruction.[12] A well-known overview of the scene was given in 1997 in Forte and Siliotti's *Virtual Archaeology*, which looks at several dozen computer reconstructions of sites around the world. We can see that early computer models served the purpose of illustration and resulting publications tended to focus on methods and technologies supporting the creation of such illustrations. In his foreword, C. Renfrew defined the purpose of virtual archaeology as harnessing 'the power of the computer in helping us to recreate and to visualize anew the sites that archaeologists have excavated and studied' (Forte and Silotti 1997: 7). It is noteworthy that almost all the computer models described in Forte and Silotti were built by private companies and that no authorship credit was given to a professional archaeologist. By the late 1990s the situation had changed, and with the drop in the costs of creating computer models, many archaeologists started their own 3D projects. Many of these were presented at CAA 1998 in Barcelona.[13]

Looking back at Ware's list, the work done in these years can be considered examples of the first and fourth use of visualization. A computer model can help us to understand, for example, how the hundreds or thousands of fragments of an archaeological monument can be fitted back together, as well as the relationship of a single fragment to the monument as a whole. The central theoretical assumption was perhaps best articulated by Goodrick and Gillings as an exploration of reconstructed landscapes that is both embedded and embodied (Goodrick and Gillings 2000: 52).

By the late 1990s, the focus shifted from simply making models to developing and encouraging best practices. This was understood to entail not only making a model but also providing proper scientific documentation, developing a visual language to enable users to quickly distinguish between definitely attested and hypothetical elements of a model, and creation of metadata standards. This period is well represented by Frischer *et al.* (2002) and by Fernie and Richards (2003). We can see this as exemplifying Ware's third use of visualization, highlighting problems in the quality of the data.

Progress in applying the 2D technology of GIS to archaeology and historical studies generally followed a comparable trajectory. Several early papers were presented at CAA 1991 (Castleford 1991; Gaffney and Stancic 1991; Kvamme 1991a, 1991b; Rooda and Wiemer 1991; Ruggles 1991). An important article on the potential of GIS for archaeology was published in 1992 by Lock and Harris. A colloquium devoted to GIS in archaeology was held in 1996 at the XIIIth Congress of the Union Internationale des Sciences Pré- et Protohistoriques (Sept. 8-14, 1996, Forlì, Italy). In 1997, the Electronic Cultural Atlas Initiative (ECAI) was started at the University of California, Berkeley, with the mission of 'enhancing digital scholarship and cultural heritage preservation by using time and space for data sharing'.[14] In the early years of the organization's existence, ECAI members I. Johnson and A. Osmakov developed TimeMap, an important tool that adapted

the project as creation of a network of nodes covering the city. Each node was three feet from the next and at each node, a panoramic photograph was taken. The photographs were placed on a videodisc. Users had random access to the photographs and could create the illusion of moving through the city, pausing to look in any direction desired.

12. Baribeau *et al.*; Hughes; Boland and Johnson; Bloomfield and Schofield.

13. See Juan A. Barcelo, Maurizio Forte and Donald H. Sanders, eds. *Virtual Reality in Archaeology*, B.A.R. International Series 843 (2000).

14. http://h-net.msu.edu/cgi-bin/welcomeletter?list=h-ECAI.

GIS to the needs of historians.[15] In North America, the Polis Center at Indiana University has been a leader in promoting ECAI.[16] At CAA, papers using GIS were common by 1996 (Wheatley 2000), and in the current decade they have become as frequent as those dedicated to 3D modeling. A strong impetus was given by the joint meeting of ECAI and CAA in 2003 in Vienna. In general, as van Hove and Rajala (2002) noted in an important editorial in *Internet Archaeology*, in the 1990s GIS was viewed mainly as a tool for assembling and viewing digitized information about terrain and its uses,[17] but in the early years of this decade, GIS started to be seen as supporting Ware's fifth function of visualization, analysis and hypothesis formation.[18]

This historical sketch brings us to the present day and allows us to take stock of not only of which of Ware's five applications of visualization archaeologists have clearly already embraced, but also to see those that still remain to be employed, at least on a large scale, in our field. Clearly, these are the second and fifth types: promoting the perception of emergent properties; and facilitating the formation of hypotheses. This type of work does more than illustrate an archaeological monument. It helps us to respond to the often tacit assumption that 2D and 3D modeling is primarily for teaching and has little, if anything, to contribute to scholarship (cf. Kolb 1997; Earl 2006: 192-193). It also allows us to use the computer model as a research tool to generate new knowledge. The purpose of this book is to collect some of the pioneering efforts in this promising field.

In applying digital modeling, archaeologists have been recapitulating the history of physical modeling, which started no later than the fourteenth century. As noted by C. Piga, Filippo Brunelleschi (1377-1446) used physical modeling to show that his radical design for the cupola of the cathedral of Florence could function. Like the earlier architectural models of the fourteenth century, Brunelleschi's model simply operated as a means of persuasion (Piga 1996: 56, 60). But Leon Battista Alberti (1404-1472) saw the physical model as a tool to verify the correctness of an architectural design, both in terms of aesthetics and structure (Piga 1996: 68).[19] Following Alberti, the model quickly becomes a tool to

15. http://www.timemap.net/. The development of ECAI can be followed through the directors' reports, available at http://ecai.org/about/directorsRpts.html.

16. http://www.homepages.indiana.edu/021105/text/technology.shtml.

17. Hence F. Vermeulen (2002: 121) could write that 'GIS remains clearly the motor of the machine for the efficient study, rational management and attractive disclosure of the archaeological data and results'.

18. Cf. van Hove and Ryala 2002: 'In the past, there has been a tendency to use GIS solely as a tool... without any link to archaeological theory. We emphasise that although GIS are a useful tool for storage and visualisation of multiple forms of data, manipulation and analysis should take centre stage, emphasising theory driven research questions and the exploration of traditional archaeological interpretations with new research methods.... New theoretical concepts can also be tested using GIS, which might lead to the formulation of alternative theoretical perspectives to be examined further...'.

19. Cf. L.B. Alberti, 1988. *On the Art of Building in Ten Books*, translated by Joseph Rykwert, Neil Leach, and Robert Tavernor (Cambridge, MA) 33-34, 313: '...I will always commend the time-honored custom, practiced by the best builders, of preparing not only drawings and sketches but also models of wood or any other material. These will enable us to weigh up repeated and examine, with the advice of experts, the work as a whole and the individual dimensions of all the parts, and, before continuing any farther, to estimate the likely trouble and expense. Having constructed these models, it will be possible to examine clearly and consider thoroughly the relationship between the site and the surrounding district, the shape of the area, the number and order of the parts of a building, the appearance of the walls, the strength of the covering, and in short the design and construction of all the elements discussed in the previous book. It will also allow one to increase or decrease the size of those elements freely, to exchange them, and to make new proposals and alterations until everything fits together well and meets with approval. Furthermore, it will provide a surer indication of the likely costs—which is not unimportant—by allowing one to calculate the width and the height of the individual elements, their thickness, number, extent, form, appearance, and quality, according to their importance and the workmanship they require....I must urge you again and again, before embarking on the work, to weigh up the whole matter on your own and discuss it with experienced advisors. Using scale models, reexamine every part of your proposal two, three, four, seven—up to ten times, taking breaks in between, until from the very roots to the uppermost tile there is nothing, concealed or open, large or small for which you have not thought out,

stimulate the architect's creativity (Piga 1996: 56). As Baldinucci wrote in 1681, the model 'is the first and principal undertaking of the entire work.... Through it, the Craftsman achieves the summit of Beauty and Perfection. It helps the Architect determine lengths, widths, heights, and thicknesses...and to identify the diverse skills that will be needed to build the structure and to find the funds that will be needed to finance it' (*Vocabolario toscano dell'arte del disegno*, cited *apud* Piga 1996: 57 [my translation]).[20] Meanwhile, physical models of fortified cities and the surrounding territory started to be made in the sixteenth century for analogous purposes: they were a visualization tool that helped commanders to plan the defense of or attack on a fortified town (Warmoes 1999: 13). Louis XIV was the acknowledged master commissioner of city models. Of the 144 models built during his reign, thirty survive (Warmoes 1999: 8).

We digital archaeologists have been catching up with our colleagues in the physical sciences who have been using digital models as tools of discovery since at least the mid 1990s when, for example, the VR application called 'Crumbs' was developed by the National Center for Supercomputing Applications at the University of Illinois. Crumbs has been described as 'an application used for visualizing, exploring, and measuring features within volumetric data sets. Crumbs is a...tool that makes use of a variety of display paradigms and data manipulation options, allowing a researcher to explore volumetric data in intuitive and powerful ways.... The motivation for developing Crumbs [was] that many biological structures are difficult to identify and measure with traditional image analysis techniques and two-dimensional visualization interfaces' (Sherman and Craig 2003: 484). Scientists such as T. Karr of the University of Chicago have used Crumbs to measure the length of sperm tails in *Drosophila*, a very difficult task which Crumbs made easy (Sherman and Craig 2003: 506). H.E. Buhse, Jr. of the University of Illinois at Chicago used Crumbs to localize an antibody (OF-1) to the feeding apparatus of *Vorticella convolavia*. Using Crumbs, Buhse discovered that besides localizing to the feeding apparatus, the antibody localized to contractile fibers near the cell membrane (Sherman and Craig 2003: 509). This is a good example of 'promoting the perception of emergent properties that were not anticipated' (Ware 2004: 3).

By the late 1990s, such uses of visualization—whether 1D, 2D, 3D, or, indeed 4D--were common in the natural and social sciences. In a report on cyberinfrastructure commissioned by the National Science Foundation, among the major threads linking the traditional scientific disciplines today is the use of models, simulations, and visualization (Atkins *et al.* 2004: 91-11, 18, 21, 26). In 1999, Card, Mackinlay, and Shneiderman's *Information Visualization: Using Vision to Think* was published, providing a useful bibliography of more than 700 publications and an anthology of over forty classic articles.[21] In their conclusion, the editors wrote:

> [P]owerful visual tools can support discovery; Galileo's telescope enabled him to discover the moons of Jupiter, and microscopes revealed the structure of cells. Now, information visualization tools are supporting drug discovery by pharmaceutical researchers and credit card fraud detection by financial analysts. Visual data mining complements the algorithmic approaches for exploring

resolved, and determined, thoroughly and at length, the most handsome and effective position, order, and number'.

20. As Piga notes, Galileo contradicted the idea found in, e.g., Alberti and Baldinucci that architectural models can help to predict the static properties of a building since, as Galileo recognized, the static properties of a given form are not scalable but change with size (Piga 1996: 89-106). To be useful for structural engineering, physical models must have a mathematical basis, and this combination of the physical and mathematical in modeling occurred in the nineteenth and twentieth centuries (Piga 1996: 115, 141-144). One way of thinking of 3D digital models would see them as the logical climax in the merger of the physical and the mathematical approaches to representation (cf. Karasik: 118: '...3D scanners [and one might add, 3D hand-made models—*eds*] typically produce output in vector format, which is more amenable to mathematical manipulation'.

21. Stuart K. Card, Jock D. Mackinlay, Ben Shneiderman, eds. *Readings in Information Visualization. Using Vision to Think* (San Francisco 1999).

> data warehouses. Surprising patterns that appear in data sets can sometimes be found by algorithms, but visual presentations can lead to deeper understanding and novel hypotheses. These in turn can be checked with algorithmic processes such as cluster analysis, factor analysis, hierarchical decomposition, or multidimensional scaling.... The breadth of applications for information visualization is large and growing.... (Card *et al.* 1999: 625-626)

In this volume, **Gooding** gives us the 30,000-foot overview of our subject, allowing us to place visualization in the historical sciences into the broader context of science per se. **Forte** issues a manifesto calling for nothing less than a new archaeology where the bottom-up process of data collection can properly merge with the top-down process of interpreting the data and building theories around them. **Hermon** agrees with Forte that visualization technologies have been underutilized in archaeology and surveys some of the principal ways in which they can be applied to research in archaeology. On the simplest level, there is the accessing, management, interpretation, and sharing of data. Then there is the conversion of alphanumeric data to a visual display. The conversion can stimulate new understanding but also raise new questions. Moreover, the 3D visualization can be enhanced through predictive models that allow us to define and evaluate possible scenarios implied by the raw data.

In archaeology, we have thus far seen examples of Ware's second and fifth applications in two realms that could be called experimental archaeology and experimental architectural and urban history. The remaining papers in this volume exemplify what has been done to date along these lines.

In a study using a 2D approach with admittedly crude representations of the data (cf. p. 50), **Premo** shows how an agent-based model of Lower Paleolithic landscapes called SHARE ('Simulated Hominin Altruism Research Environment') can throw into question the previous explanation of archaeological features of areas of East Africa, which had been formed on the basis of analogies to modern hunter-gatherers. The agent-based approach does not necessarily result in a new explanation, but offers a tool for developing alternative explanations and testing that are more compatible with the results of fieldwork. Premo argues that when we have two or more explanations consistent with the empirical data, we should choose the simplest one, even if it is very different from the explanation derived from modern analogies.

In a second 2D study, **Indruszweski** and **Barton** use cost surface DEM modeling to reconstruct Wulfstan's late ninth-century voyage from Haidaby (Schleswig-Holstein, Germany) to Truso (near the Visula River mouth in Poland), as told in King Alfred the Great's *Orosius*. Here, interestingly enough, the goal was the opposite of what Premo had pursued: instead of questioning the validity of arguing from present analogies to lost past phenomena, Indruszweski and Barton used an actual physical reconstruction of a Viking boat and a recreation of much of Wulfstan's route to validate the itinerary suggested by application of some standard GIS least-cost analyses. Their point of departure was to dispute the correctness of an alternative reconstruction of the route by Crumlin-Pedersen (1983), which was based on depth sounding along a preselected bathymetric line. As they write, 'we can employ GIS-based simulation as a new way to develop precise and testable hypotheses about Wulfstan's sea route from the meager historical information. The simulation presented here does not operate on fictitious values, but is based on both historical information provided by Wulfstan's account and real-time data provided by experimental archaeology' (59).

Gerlach, **Herzog**, and **von Koblinski** report on work using 2D GIS and 3D terrain mapping to develop a method for distinguishing true archaeological sites from pseudo-sites in the Lower Rhine area as part of a project of the Rheinisches Amt fűr Bodendenkmalpflege in Bonn, Germany, to assess the amount of change in the natural landscape owing to modern construction work, pits, and other sources. The problem is very important: in the Lower Rhine area many pits were dug in the nineteenth and twentieth centuries in order to extract material for making bricks. Most pits were then filled in with dumps of earth and artifacts from elsewhere. In fieldwalking, the filled-in pits are indistinguishable from the rest of the terrain and hence have given rise to the discovery of false archaeological sites. By creating a digital elevation model of the region and using relief shading, the Rheinisches Amt für Bodendenkmalpflege has been able to easily identify these pits on the surrounding landscape, thus enabling it to make a much more accurate census of the area's true archaeological sites.

In a similar vein, **Lechterbeck**'s work comparing contour lines in 100-year-old historical maps of Preussische Neuaufnahme of the Rhineland against modern digital elevation models supports the use of digital GIS data when investigating archaeological sites. Changes in topography and in data collection methodology mean that the *Preussische Neuaufnahme* is not suitable for visualizing and quantifying mass movements and slope processes of the last 100 years for that region.

De Boer *et al.* show how LIDAR can provide archaeologists with 3D data needed to reconstruct historical landscapes and to trace sites. As in Gerlach *et al.*, the point of this study is to use a new approach to improve the calculation of an area's potential to contain archaeological sites, to identify specific sites, and to eliminate pseudo-sites.

As noted at the beginning of this introduction, Lieberwirth's contribution is *bahnbrechend*. She uses 3D GIS to reconstruct an archaeological site in Greece that was excavated stratigraphically more than thirty-five years ago. The model she creates of the site prior to its excavation permits her to interpret the stratigraphy independent of the explanation offered by the excavators. The result was very promising: while the excavators' interpretation was largely confirmed, important new information emerged. Much more important than the specific advances is the general point implicitly made by Lieberwirth's study that 3D software can permit us to reconstruct with great accuracy a site that has been excavated using the stratigraphic method. Much more along these lines can, and one may safely predict, will be done.

Whereas the archaeologist who uses GIS software can take advantage of a large kit of sophisticated, built-in tools (cf. the study in this volume of Indruszweski and Barton), the virtual archaeologist who creates or uses 3D models generally finds that the only tool available by default is the simple navigation tool permitting either movement of the camera or of the 3D object. Thus Lieberwirth's tools are fairly limited: the software she uses is able to spatialize legacy archaeological data, to calculate volumes of stratigraphic units and to color code them. Her methodology is thus limited to volumetric analysis and visualization of spatial (stratigraphic) relationships (which does not in any way diminish her results). She would undoubtedly be among the first to welcome software with enhanced analytical functionality. It is the merit of **Ozmen** and **Balcisoy** to begin to provide these tools. The point of departure is recognition of the important distinction between the software used to create a 3D model and that used by the end-user to visualize and explore the model. Up to now, production software (e.g., 3D Studio Max, Maya, MultiGen Creator) has had tools that permit the modeler to determine the distance between two points on an object; but standard end-user navigation software has lacked such a basic tool. Unless end-users can learn to use production software, they have been unable to unlock much of the precise data that scientific 3D models contain. Ozmen and Balcisoy argue that the solution can be found in the development of end-user software for medical applications: the software designer should provide digital tools similar to the real-world tools with which end-users are already familiar. This they have started to do with the creation of CH ('Cultural Heritage') Toolbox. This allows a user to move through virtual space, to move 3D objects found in virtual space, and finally to apply tools to the object, once it has been located and positioned for study. The tools in the early version of CH Toolbox are simple but powerful for the archaeologist: a virtual caliper and a virtual tape measure. CH Toolbox was authored in C++ using the library of OpenSceneGraph, one of the most popular open source scene graphs currently in use by virtual archaeologists.

If Ozmen and Balcisoy create two universally useful tools for archaeologists, **Johanson** and **Frischer** (who also use OpenSceneGraph) created a special virtual ephemeris tool to run a 'virtual-empirical' test of the Dearborn-Bauer thesis (Dearborn, Seddon, and Bauer 1998). This thesis entails an explanation of the positioning and alignment of two Inca towers at the north end of the sanctuary of the Sun, on the Island of the Sun in Lake Titicaca (Bolivia). According to Dearborn and Bauer, the towers in questions were not (as has sometimes been thought) tombs but markers of the position of the sun at sunset on the winter solstice. These markers functioned as a means for large-scale audience participation in the solstice ritual. The thesis was originally argued using 2D analyses on a limited subset of data. An *in situ* empirical test could only be performed at a limited time during the year (sunset on or near the June solstice), and only limited sampling of viewsheds could be examined. Furthermore, the empirical test could only be performed on partial data, since many of the critical architectural elements are only partially preserved.

The 'virtual-empirical' test undertaken by Johanson and Frischer eliminates the constraints of time and space. To conduct the test, a 3D computer model of the topography of the island and the sanctuary was built. Ephemeris data supplied by NASA's Jet Propulsion Laboratory made it possible to reconstruct the apparent course of the sun at sunset on dates surrounding the winter solstice in the year 1500 CE, the approximate date for Inca ceremonies attested by the Spanish chroniclers. Thus, using more accurate tools, the hypothesis was able to be further validated and more easily communicated to a general audience.

Karasik tackles the problem of how 3D scanning of pottery can lead not only to more accurate illustrations of the profiles of ceramics but also to new discoveries. Profiling pottery is based upon the assumption that pots are perfectly axially symmetrical, so that one profile serves for all possible profiles that might be made. But in the real world, as Karasik notes, no vessel shows perfect axial symmetry. 3D data reveals the deviations from perfection and these, in turn, can be used to determine intravessel and intervessel uniformity of pottery belonging to the same assemblage. Uniformity in this sense has never been taken into consideration in pottery studies, doubtless because without 3D vector data, it is extremely difficult to calculate. Why might uniformity be of interest to the archaeologist? As Karasik succinctly notes, 'the former [intravessel uniformity] represent[s] the quality of the production of a single vessel, and the latter [intervessel uniformity] the reproducibility of the manufacturing process.' At the end of his article, he sketches out a research program that could be based on this ability to calculate uniformity/deformation with high precision. It could lead to assessments of the motor skills of the individual potter, the ability to differentiate home-made from mass-produced pottery, the detection of individual potters' signature characteristics within a type or tradition of ceramic production that otherwise looks to very homogeneous to the naked eye; and the ability to distinguish between a fast wheel and a tournette.

If Karasik's contribution ends with a vision of possible new discoveries just around the corner as 3D scanning technologies are applied with greater frequency to the study of pottery, then **Koller** closes with some spectacular concrete results that could only have been achieved through 3D scanning. He was part of a group, led by Stanford Computer Scientist M. Levoy, that digitized and made 3D models of each of the 1200 surviving fragments of the Severan Marble Plan. This is an enormous and detailed map of Rome dating from the beginning of the third century CE. Koller played an important role on the team and wrote his dissertation on the project (Koller 2007). In his contribution in this volume, he describes the map, recounts the campaign to digitize and publish it to the Internet,[22] and reports on how he used various algorithms to find new joins

22. See http://formaurbis.stanford.edu/.

among the fragments.[23] The ability to find such joins is remarkable and represents a major early triumph for virtual archaeology: the map was discovered in the sixteenth century and for centuries has been the subject of scholarly interest, including two major monographs in the decades immediately preceding Koller's work (Carettoni *et al.* 1960; Rodríguez-Almeida 1981).

For all its strengths, Koller's study does have one major weakness: the user interface he helped create for the project does not contain the tools that he developed to achieve his results. Like most 3D user interfaces, it simply allows the user to move the fragment around on the screen. To empower the end-user, the interface would need to be enhanced with tools reflecting the searching and matching algorithms developed or used by Koller to solve the puzzle of the Marble Plan (Koller: 135-139), and it would need to support the simultaneous viewing of two or more fragments at a time, each manipulated independently so that potential joins could be virtually tested. As Koller notes, to do this now the end-user needs to load the fragments of interest into a 3D modeling software program (Koller: 134). But not all end-users have such a program, and such programs often take a great deal of training to use effectively.

Let me conclude with several observations. First, I do not mean to imply that computer models of archaeological sites do not have other legitimate uses. Illustrations, documentation, education, site presentation, etc. have become standard applications of archaeological computer models, and I certainly see nothing wrong with that. To the contrary, I predict a rosy future for such models as cities and states around the world start to create virtual cultural heritage centers.

To make progress in going 'beyond illustration', we need more tools—tools that are in part replicas within the VR interface of existing tools, such as those found in several contributions in this volume; and, of course, brand new tools. In the first category, I would put the tools created by Ozmen and Balcisoy and discussed in this volume. Into the second category, I would put tools that exploit the specific strengths of VR: for example, we need haptic tools, not just to move objects around in our illustrations, but to provide analytical data about those objects, such as their weight and other physical properties. We need tools that enable us to test lighting conditions in the virtual environments we create. A good example of the potential of this for scholarship is provided by Jabi & Potamianos. In two studies (Jabi & Potamianos 2006 and Potamianos & Jabi forthcoming), they use lighting tools to study how Anthemius of Tralles, the architect of Haghia Sophia in Istanbul, used geometrical principles to control the lighting of the apse and dome. We need sound tools, not only to populate our representations with localizable 3D sound but also to give analytical feedback about the acoustic properties of our virtual environments so that we can determine in a serious way whether, for example, the Roman Senate House with its marble floors and marble-clad walls functioned well or poorly as a place of deliberation and debate. To date, models have been used mainly to represent landscapes and built structures unenhanced by physical properties. We need to add physics engines to our 3D viewers. They will permit us to incorporate in the user interface a variety of structural engineering tools for studying the statics of our buildings, ventilation and circulation through them, and to simulate how they were subjected to damage and destruction through disasters such as fire, flood, earthquakes or by their own deficient design. Similarly, few (if any) archaeological models utilize artificial intelligence to represent the behavior of people, animals, and artifacts. The potential of doing so was recognized by the contributors to the session on 'Avatars and Virtual Humans' at VAST 2004 (cf. de Heras Ciechomski *et al.*, Gaitazes *et al.*, Ryder *et al.*) and signs of interest are scattered elsewhere throughout the scholarly literature.[24] Further progress in this direction is presented in this volume by Premo.

23. In Koller 2007 he discusses over 20 new 'highly probable' joins.

24. Balck and Keller 2004; Gutierrez *et al.* 2005; Gutierrez, Frischer *et al.* 2007; Andreoli *et al.* 2007.

Finally, we need tools that reflect the strength of digital technology generally to make links and connections. Foremost among these is the ability to link the reconstruction in the 3D scene to the underlying archaeological documentation and argumentation behind the scene. Such transparency has long been called for (see Forte 2000) and a good groundwork for how this might be done using the Resource Description Framework (RDF) encoded in the eXtensible Markup Language (XML) was laid by Ryan 2001. It should be possible for the end-user to click a key, open a window with documentation and metadata, and find out what the evidence is for each element of the 3D reconstruction in a virtual tour.

These are just some examples of the toolkit we ideally need to be creating to make our virtual environments more than pretty pictures but places where we can run experiments, collect new data, and empower the end-user to question or build on our work in a way that would simply not otherwise be possible.

Beyond tools, we need a standard user-interface that can both run the scientific cultural heritage models being made by scholars in increasing numbers and be enhanced by the new tools we need, which might be added as plug-ins. This might be a high-quality but inexpensive proprietary game engine such as Torque[25] or, perhaps, an Open Source scene graph such as OpenSceneGraph[26] or Open SG.[27] We also need an online, peer-reviewed scholarly journal in which scholars can publish their models and tool plug-ins. Up to the present, there have been very few examples in this field of fully interactive, real-time models that have been published to the Internet. Generally, scholars have only been able to publish articles about their modeling projects with, at most, several color 2D illustrations. This must change.[28]

It is not difficult to predict that 2D and especially 3D modeling of cultural heritage spaces and monuments will shortly gather momentum, especially as the tools we need and standards or best practices for creating and viewing models become available. Use of these technologies will spread through new sub-disciplines of archaeology and the humanities. In art history, for example, recent work by Dellepiane, Callieri, Fondersmith, *et al.* (2007) shows how 3D can be used in artistic attribution. The authors used 3D modeling technology to create a digital representation of a small bronze horse in the Florence Archaeological Museum. The statuette had been attributed to Benvenuto Cellini. One of the co-authors of this paper (Fondersmith) attributed the statuette to Leonardo da Vinci on the basis of a drawing of a similar horse in a Leonardo manuscript (Leonardo drawing 358, Windsor Royal Library). The drawing was digitized and then mapped to the model at the vantage points the artist could have used to draw the statuette. The digital versions of the drawing and statue could then be aligned, and the authors found that the alignments from two vantage points were very precise. Other Leonardo drawings of horses (though not of the horse depicted in the statuette) were tested, but no good alignments were found. A second horse, also in the Florence Archaeological Museum and also datable to Leonardo's lifetime (though not attributed to him) was also studied for possible alignment with the drawing. In this case, too, no good alignment was found. The authors conclude that their study may not prove that Leonardo sculpted the statuette but it does throw doubt on the attribution to Cellini.

In the field of archaeology, use of 3D has been most prevalent in Old World archaeology. But the New World is starting to shows signs of interest. Thus the 2007 annual meeting of the Society for American Archaeology had a session entitled 'Beyond Illustration: 3D Reconstructions, Virtual Reality, and Archaeological Communications in the Early 21st century', organized by graduate students D. Hixson and B. Just. If the use of

25. http://www.garagegames.com/company/.

26. http://www.openscenegraph.org/projects/osg.

27. http://opensg.vrsource.org/trac.

28. The Institute for Advanced Technology is pursuing research on a proposed new journal to fill this gap; see http://www.iath.virginia.edu/save/. For a useful survey of the current scene in electronic publication in the field of archaeology see Richards 2006. On digital scholarship generally, see Borgman 2007.

3D is spreading in space, it is also being applied to ever earlier time periods. Thus 3D technologies have recently enabled Gaffney and Thompson to succeed in the heroic task of reconstructing the submerged Mesolithic terrain of the enormous basin that is larger than the entire United Kingdom. Known as Doggerland, this landscape is presently submerged beneath the North Sea (Gaffney and Thomson 2007: 1-9). Through the use of visualization as a cognitive tool, a large area of *terra* formerly *incognita* has become *cognita.*

Looking ahead to research streams not yet represented in this volume, one can repeat the prediction made in 2000 by Goodrick and Gillings that virtual archaeology and cultural studies will intersect.[29] As they note, fundamental to this project is Tilley 1994, which introduced the powerful concept of the social construction of landscape. Tilley was himself anticipated by Berger and Luckman 1967, who wrote:

> The origins of a symbolic universe have their roots in the constitution of man. If man in society is a world-constructor, this is made possible by his constitutionally given world-openness, which already implies the conflict between order and chaos. Human existence is, *ab initio*, an ongoing externalization. As man externalizes himself, he constructs the world *into* which he externalizes himself. In the process of externalization, he projects his own meanings into reality. Symbolic universes, which proclaim that *all* reality is humanly meaningful and call upon the *entire* cosmos to signify the validity of human existence, constitute the farthest reaches of this projection (Berger and Luckman: 104)

Berger and Luckman consciously downplayed space in favor of time in their analysis of the social construction of reality.[30] Tilley redresses this imbalance, taking as his point of departure the claim that 'space is socially produced, and different societies, groups and individuals act out their lives in different spaces' (Tilley 1994: 10). The field of archaeology did not need to undergo the famous 'spatial turn'.[31] It was already, by definition, a spatially sensitive and organized discipline. But as other humanistic disciplines such as cultural studies have become spatialized, the possibility has arisen of new interdisciplinary interactions.

In a brief but striking way, Paliou and Wheatley (2007) met Goodrick's and Gillings' challenge to relate objective to subjective spatial data. They created a 3D model of two adjacent rooms in an impressive building (possibly used for public, ceremonial purposes) in Late Bronze Age Akrotiri on the island of Thera (3 and 3a of Xeste 3). Room 3a contains a long fresco known as the 'Adorants'. It is accessed through a pier and door partition in room 3. The 3D model allowed Paliou and Wheatley to see how the artist designed the fresco in room 3a to take into account the occlusions caused by the partition. These blocked the view of the entire

29. Cf. Goodrick and Gillings 2000: 52: '...there is enormous potential to use VR techniques to provide a much needed practical dimension to the more phenomenological lines of enquiry being advocated within landscape research (e.g., Tilley 1994)'. Several years earlier, the same authors had written, along similar lines: 'it is clear that if archaeologists are to utilise GIS-based approaches in their attempts to explore and articulate the archaeological record on the basis of more reflexive and experiential modes of enquiry, a more explicit discussion as to the conceptual status of the underlying space and time of the GIS is in order. The uncritically received dominance and adherence within archaeological-GIS of notions of geography and cartography as the abstract representation of the world as organised in measurable space, may have to be enriched by paying equal attention to notions of chorography, as a subject-centred sense of place.... In addition, discussions as to the role of temporality in GIS should give equal weight to more phenomenological notions of time, what Thomas refers to as "the time of the soul" (Thomas 1996: 33), as to the already prevalent Kantian notions of time as an abstracted container' (Gillings and Goodrick 1996: part 2a).

30. Cf. Berger and Luckman: 26, 'The world of everyday life is structured both spatially and temporally. The spatial structure is quite peripheral to our present considerations. Suffice it to point out that it, too, has a social dimension by virtue of the fact that my manipulatory zone intersects with that of others. More important for our present purpose is the temporal structure of everyday life'.

31. On the history of this term, see Kaufmann 2004: 3-4.

fresco for someone moving through room 3, but from most points of view in room 3 the fresco's central figure of a wounded girl could be seen. They note that this objective fact jibes well with the iconographic (and subjective) observation of art historian L. Morgan (2000) that the focal point of the painting is the central figure.

Early evidence of an even more profound confluence can be found in a collection of articles on ancient Rome edited by Larmour and Spencer (2007). Here one catches glimpses of how the gap between positivistic approach of virtual archaeologists and the phenomenological methodology of cultural studies, ultimately inspired by Berger and Luckman 1967 and Tilley 1994, might be bridged by approaches using psychogeography,[32] gaze theory,[33] Lacan's notion of *objet a*,[34] and Baktin's concept of the chronotope.[35] In Larmour and Spencer, the emphasis is on how ancient authors such as Livy, Horace, Ovid, Tacitus, Juvenal and Plutarch imagined and experienced the ancient city. At least one of the contributors uses some fairly rudimentary illustrations of the city to make her case (Spencer 2007: 98-99). Others use words to make their point, but the words almost cry out for dynamic illustration in real-time 3D imagery, as, for example, when Spencer writes:

> Physically, one **looks down** from a building or a hill, **up from** a valley, **off into** the distance or **up to** high stories from street level. Such angles of gaze, and the perceptual and cognitive possibilities that they open up, inevitably generate and respond to key sites in an urban topography. The narratives that coalesce at these conjunctions of space, place, and point of view themselves draw together further associations between people and places, personal and collective stories and myths, societal expectations and longings. Hence, at the heart of each individual's unique reading of urban topography lies a complex nexus of standpoints and angles of gaze—personal, psychological, aesthetic, mnemonic, imaginary, and experiential. Inside Augustan Rome, all of these cluster with particular urgency around the Fora, Capitoline, and Palatine.... Livy's conceptual map makes notably complex retrospective demands of his audience. It operates a space which requires that readers bring to bear a full set of urban sight/site lines even before the city proper is brought into narrative existence. (Spencer 2007: 62, 78)[36]

Equally graphic (but unillustrated) is Larmour's purely verbal analysis of the use of Roman space in the satires of Juvenal, where we would like to have not only an urban digital model but a simulation enlivened by people and their activities:

> The specific locations in the Satires appear fleetingly, flashing before us very much in the manner that sites on a museum display of Ancient Rome might do. Having surveyed them, we can say that, in the Juvenalian corpus, these locations almost always appear in the following three ways:

32. Larmour and Spencer 2007: 9.

33. Vout 2007: 305.

34. Blevins 2007: 280.

35. Banta 2007: 239.

36. Similar passages can be cited in Tilley 1994, e.g., 'Looking at the two-dimensional plane of the modern topographic map with sites and monuments plotted on it, it is quite impossible to envisage the landscape in which these places are embedded. The representation fails, and cannot substitute for being there, being *in place*. Similarly, an unfamiliar landscape remains invisible. You do not know where, or how, to look. This process of observation requires time and a feeling for the place. After being there, after making many visits to the same locales, the intensity of the experience heightens. Monuments that were initially hidden from view on a first visit to a place can now be seen, and patterned relationships between sites and their settings become apparent' (75). Of course, Tilley is talking about actual field walking, but there is no reason why such exploration cannot occur in virtual space.

> 1. They are inherently repulsive, like the Subura or the Colosseum or the Circus Maximus, places—whether a jumbled conglomeration of small buildings like the Subura district or a massive architectural expression of the desire for solidity and containment like the Colosseum or Circus—characterized by overflowing, oozing, and pollution....
>
> 2. They are important public spaces, freighted with historical and cultural significance, where repellent behavior or individuals can all too easily be witnessed—like the Forum or the Campus Martius. These public spaces, including such well-known ones as the Temple of Concord, are viewed from a 'liminal' perspective, from the position of the marginal, alienated, and about-to-depart gaze....
>
> 3. They are previously 'clean and proper' places that have become repulsive because of their penetration or contamination by outside elements. The Grove of Egeria is the most detailed description of how public space has become objectionable in various ways, but other examples include the Gallery of Triumphatores in the Forum Augusti.... (Larmour 2007: 207-208)

At times, one also can see how the 'chronotopian' method cannot simply benefit from 3D illustration so that we can see with our own eyes what the scholar has seen in his mind's eye, but how it can also offer depth and meaning to an 'objective' urban simulation that, for all its outward, physical accuracy, is lacking in cultural resonance and psychological depth. How much more meaningful from both our point of view and that of the ancient Romans to view the Capitoline Hill, dominated by the temple of Jupiter Optimus Maximus, with the following passage in mind:

> ...Tacitus offers us a richly layered narrative of the cataclysm surrounding the Capitoline Temple that exploded on a single day (19 December 69 CE), but his presentation opens up much broader temporal and textual vistas which, when viewed closely, sharpen the moralism of his account and interrogate *Romanitas* at a disastrous moment, which ultimately might have been more comfortable for his readers to forget. This is indeed a bitter and painful form of memorializing through monuments. The collective sense of *Romanitas* has, by Tacitus' own day, been progressively (if imperfectly) reconstructed, much as the Capitoline Temple itself has been restored, but a reading of *Histories* 3 shows how fragile the new 'edifice' of Roman identity remains; and even the restored temple burned down again in 80 CE.
>
> We are left with a strong sense that although the physical fabric of the city and its focal point, the Capitoline Temple, could always be reinstated (again and again, if necessary), the broader emotional fault-lines were still there in the collective memory, rendering an unexpectedly open-ended narrative for Tacitus' readers sensitive to the possibility of history repeating itself.... (Ash 2007: 236-237)

Ash's work suggests that the best examples for the merger of objective and subjective approaches under the sign of digital archaeology will come from societies like ancient Rome whose remains are both physical *and* literary. The social construction of space is almost always as peculiar and unpredictable as is Tacitus' reaction to the Capitoline Temple.[37] In this regard we may note, for

37. Cf. the Avatip on the Sepik river in northwest Papua New Guinea: 'To the villagers all land and bodies of water are fertile because they contain the rotted bodies and body-fluids of totemic ancestors. Many parcels of land are criss-cross complexes of old levees left by shifts in the course of the river; people say these have human outlines, and still bear the shapes of the ancestors who "fell down" upon them in mythical times' (Harrison 1988: 323 *apud* Tilley 1994: 58). It is noteworthy that Van Dyke and Alcock 2003 structure their anthology of phenomenological studies on world archaeology into two main

reasons observed long ago by Karl Mannheim,[38] that Tilley's analyses of contemporary small-scale societies are far more convincing than those he offers of Mesolithic and Neolithic landscapes in England and Wales, where, in discussing the original cultural significance of the physical remains, he is usually reduced to formulations such as 'I want to suggest…' (109), 'it is not hard to imagine…' (198), and 'it is not unlikely…' (200).

parts, "Memory Studies with Access to Texts" and "Memory Studies in Prehistory." Reflecting on this division, the editors write, "This is not to claim that texts 'solve' all our problems—far from it—but they unquestionably grant some richness and nuance to the relevant analyses" (7).

38. Cf. Mannheim 1971 (originally published in German in 1921): 29-30: 'That the spectator can grasp the intended expressive content of a picture is no less and no more of a miracle in principle than the general phenomenon that we can associate the sensual content of the work with any kind of meaning-function at all. Expressive meaning also is a "given"; and if interpretation of this type presents peculiar difficulties, it is only because, unlike objective meaning (such as, for example, the composition of a picture) which is self-contained and hence ascertainable from the picture alone, the expressive meaning embodied in aesthetic elements such as the subject matter, the sweep or foreshortening of a line, cannot be established without an analysis of the historic background...This difficulty, however, need not induce us to become sceptics on principle; all we have to conclude from it is that intended expressive meaning is only discoverable by factual historical research, i.e. that in investigating it we have to employ the same methods as are used in any factual historical inquiry. *That the intended expressive meaning will not remain inaccessible...is guaranteed to some extent for those periods and cultures which are in a continuity of history with ours.* The historical structure of consciousness itself is guarantee that some understanding of the intended meaning may be possible even in respect of works remote in time, the reason for this being that the range of emotions and experiences available to a given epoch is by no means unlimited and arbitrary. These forms of experience arise in, and are shaped for, a society which *either retains previously existing forms or else transforms them in a manner which the historian can observe.* Since historical consciousness can establish contact with works of the past in this fashion, the historian is able gradually to make himself at home in the "mental climate" of the work whose expressive intent he is seeking to understand; thus he secures the background against which the specific intent of the work, the unique contribution of the individual artist, will stand out in sharp detail' (my emphasis).

I conclude by expressing the hope that as virtual archaeologists are able to publish fully stocked analytical toolkits along with highly detailed 3D models of the spaces excavated by modern archaeologists or mentioned by ancient authors, cultural-studies scholars will be eager to use these resources to explore the *Schein und Sein* of 'topography…, in its broadest sense, as it (re)appears in time, space, and memory' (Larmour and Spencer 2007: ix). As this happens, chronotopians will infuse our urban simulations with historical memories and emotional associations that are every bit as indispensable to re-experiencing a lost world as are the virtual people, furnishings, and the 'bricks and mortar' themselves.

Acknowledgments

I wish to thank the Andrew W. Mellon Foundation for a grant that made it possible to write this book. For support to create the digital version, thanks are also owed to the Humanities E-Book of the American Council of Learned Societies. My own thinking about the topics treated in this book greatly benefited from what I learned from my friends Dean Abernathy, Juan Barcelò, Johanna Drucker, Ray Laurence, Franco Niccolucci, Nick Ryan, Donald Sanders, and Diana Spencer. David Koller gave me useful bibliography on the problem of the graphical representation of uncertainty in 3D models. I am grateful to all the authors who contributed to this volume for their cooperation and—in the case of those who were asked to submit their work as early as 2004—their patience. Finally, for their indispensable help in preparing a complex manuscript for publication, I acknowledge a deep debt of gratitude to our technical editor, Sarah Wells, and to my co-editor, Dr. Anastasia Dakouri-Hild, of the Institute for Advanced Technology in the Humanities at the University of Virginia.

Bibliography

Alberti, L. B. 1485. *De re aedificatoria*, Florence: Nicolaus Laurentii.

Ananiadou, S., Chruszcz, J., Keane, J., McNaught, J. & Watry, P. 2005. "The National Centre for Text Mining: Aims and Objectives", *Ariadne* 42: www.ariadne.ac.uk/issue42/ananiadou/intro.html.

Andreoli, R., De Chiara, R., Erra, U. *et al.* 2007. "An Interactive 3D Reconstruction of a Funeral in Andriuolo's Necropolis in Paestum", *CAA* 33, Tomar: CAAPortuga: 51-54.

Arnold, C.J., Huggett, J.W., Reilly, P. & Springham, C. 1989. "A Case Study in the Application of Computer Graphics", *CAA* 17, B.A.R. International Series 548, Oxford: BAR Publishing:147-155.

Ash, R. 2007. "Victim and Voyeur: Rome as a Character in Tacitus' *Histories* 3", in D.H.J. Larmour & D. Spencer (eds.), *The Sites of Rome. Time, Space, Memory*, Oxford: Oxford University Press: 211-237.

Atkins, D. E. *et al.* 2004. *Revolutionizing Science and Engineering Through Cyberinfra-structure: Report of the National Science Foundation Blue Ribbon Advisory Panel on Cyberinfrastructure*, National Science Foundation: Washington, D.C.: http://www.nsf.gov/od/oci/reports/toc.jsp.

Balck, F. & Keller, F. 2004. "Animation by Computer. A Tool for Understanding the Dynamical Behaviour of Ancient Machines," *CAA* 31, B.A.R. International Series 1227, Oxford: BAR Publishing: 359-362.

Banta, J. 2007. "The Gates of Janus: Bakhtin and Plutarch's Roman Meta-chronotope", in D.H.J. Larmour & D. Spencer (eds.), *The Sites of Rome. Time, Space, Memory*, Oxford: Oxford University Press: 238-270.

Barcelò, J. 2000. "Visualizing What Might Be: An Introduction to Virtual Reality Techniques in Archaeology", *CAA* 26, B.A.R. International Series 843, Oxford: BAR Publishing: 9-35.

Baribeau, R., Godin, G., Cournoyer, L. & Rioux, M. 1996. "Colour Three-dimensional Modelling of Museum Objects", in Tony Higgins, Peter Main & Janet Lang (eds.), *Imaging the Past. Electronic Imaging and Computer Graphics in Museums and Archaeology*, British Museum Occasional Paper 114, London: British Museum Press: 199-210.

Berger, P. and Luckman, T. 1967. *The Social Construction of Reality*, Garden City, New York: Anchor Books.

Biek, L. 1985. "LERNIE XIV: Comparology and Stereovideo", *CAA* 13, London: Institute of Archaeology: 1-35.

Blevins, J. 2007. "Staging Rome: The Renaissance, Rome, and Humanism's Classical Crisis", in D.H.J. Larmour & D. Spencer (eds.), *The Sites of Rome. Time, Space, Memory*, Oxford: Oxford University Press: 271-294.

Bloomfield, M. & Schofield, L. 1996. "Reconstructing the Treasury of Atreus at Mycenae", in Tony Higgins, Peter Main & Janet Lang (eds.), *Imaging the Past. Electronic Imaging and Computer Graphics in Museums and Archaeology*, British Museum Occasional Paper 114, London: British Museum Press: 235-244.

Bobowski, B. 2007. "Archaeoscope—Interface for 3D Stratigraphy Visualization", *CAA* 33, Tomar: CAAPortugal: 151-153.

Boland, P. & Johnson, C. 1996. "Archaeology as Computer Visualisation: 'Virtual Tours' of Dudley Castle c. 1550", in Tony Higgins, Peter Main & Janet Lang (eds.), *Imaging the Past. Electronic Imaging and Computer Graphics in Museums and Archaeology*, British Museum Occasional Paper 114, London: British Museum Press: 227-234.

Bonfigli, M.E. & Guidazzoli, A. 2000. "A WWW Virtual Museum for Improving the Knowledge of the

History of a City", *CAA* 26, B.A.R. International Series 843, Oxford: BAR Publishing: 143-147.

Borgman, C.L., Smart, L.J., Millwood, K.A., Finley, J.R., Champeny, L., Gilliland, A.J. & Leazer, G.H. 2005. "Comparing Faculty Information Seeking in Teaching and Research: Implications for the Design of Digital Libraries", *Journal of the American Society for Information Science and Technology* 56 (6): 636-657.

Borgman, C.L. 2007. *Scholarship in the Digital Age. Information, Infrastructure, and the Internet*, Cambridge, MA: MIT Press.

Bradley, M. 2006. "Archaeological Survey in a Digital World", in Thomas L. Evans & Patrick Daly (eds.), *Digital Archaeology. Bridging Method and Theory*, London and New York: Routledge: 35-49.

Card, S., Mackinlay, J. & Shneiderman, B. 1999. *Information Visualization. Using Vision to Think*, San Diego: Morgan Kaufmann.

Carettoni, G., Colini, A., Cozz, L. & Gatti, G. 1960. *La pianta marmorea di Roma antica. Forma urbis Romae*, Rome: M. Danesi.

Coralini, A. & Vecchietti, E. 2007. "L'archeologia attraverso un 3D virtual model", in A. Coralini & D. Scagliarini Corlaita (eds.), *Ut Natura Ars. Virtual Reality e Archeologia. Atti della Giornata di Studi (Bologna, 22 aprile 2002)*, Imola: University Press Bologna: 17-39.

Castleford, J. 1991. "Archaeology, GIS, and the Time Dimension: An Overview," *CAA* 19, B.A.R. International Series S577, Oxford: BAR Publishing: 95-106.

Chalmers, A. & Debattista, K., 2005. "Investigating the Structural Validity of Virtual Reconstructions of Prehistoric Maltese Temples," *The 6th International Symposium on Virtual Reality, Archaeology and Cultural Heritage, VAST*, Aire-la-Ville, Switzerland: Eurographics: 107-112.

Crumlin-Pedersen, O. 1983. "Skibe, sejlads og ruter hos Ottar og Wulfstan", in N. Lund (ed.), *Ottar og Wulfstan, to rejsebeskrivelser fra vikingetiden*, Vikingeskibshallen: Roskilde: 32-44.

Day, W., Cosmas, J., Ryan, N. *et al.* 2007. "Linking 2D Harris Matrix with 3D Stratigraphic Visualizations: An Integrated Approach to Archaeological Documentation", *CAA* 33, Tomar: CAAPortugal: 155-160.

de Heras Ciechomski, P., Ulicny, B., Cetre, R. & Thalmann, D. 2004. "A Case Study of a Virtual Audience in a Reconstruction of an Ancient Roman Odeon in Aphrodisias", *VAST* 5, Aire-la-Ville, Switzerland: Eurographics: 9-18.

Dearborn, D.S.P., Matthew, T., Seddon, M.T. & Bauer, B.C. 1998. "The Sanctuary of Titicaca. Where the Sun Returns to Earth", *Latin American Antiquity* 9, No. 3: 240-258.

Dellepiane, M., Callieri, M., Fondersmith, M., Cignoni, P., & Scopigno, R., 2007. "Using 3D Scanning to Analyze a Proposal for the Attribution of a Bronze Horse to Leonardo da Vinci," *The 8th International Symposium on Virtual Reality, Archaeology and Cultural Heritage, VAST*, Aire-la-Villa, Switzerland: Eurographics: 117-132.

During, S. 2003. *The Cultural Studies Reader: Second Edition*, London and New York: Routledge.

Earl, G. P. 2006. "At the Edges of the Lens. Photography, Graphical Constructions, and Cinematopgraphy", in Thomas L. Evans & Patrick Daly (eds.), *Digital Archaeology. Bridging Method and Theory*, London and New York: Routledge: 191-209.

Fernie, K. & Richards, J. 2003. (eds.) *Creating and Using Virtual Reality. A Guide for the Arts and Humanities*, Oxford: Oxbow Books.

Forte, M. & Siliotti, A. 1997. (eds.) *Virtual Archaeology. Re-creating Ancient Worlds*, New York: Harry N. Abrams.

Forte, M. 2000. "About Virtual Archaeology: Disorders, Cognitive Interactions and Virtuality", *CAA* 26,

B.A.R. International Series 843, Oxford: BAR Publishing: 247-259.

Frischer, B., Niccolucci, F., Ryan, N. & Barceló, J. 2002. "From CVR to CVRO: The Past, Present, and Future of Cultural Virtual Reality", in F. Niccolucci (ed.), *Proceedings of VAST 2000*, B.A.R. International Series 834, Oxford: BAR Publishing: 7-18.

Frischer, B. & Stinson, P. 2007. "The Importance of Scientific Authentication and a Formal Visual Language in Virtual Models of Archaeological Sites: The Case of the House of Augustus and Villa of the Mysteries", in *Interpreting The Past: Heritage, New Technologies and Local Development, Proceedings of the Conference on Authenticity, Intellectual Integrity and Sustainable Development of the Public Presentation of Archaeological and Historical Sites and Landscapes Ghent, East-Flanders 11-13 September 2002*: http://www.iath.virginia.edu/~bf3e/revision/pdf/Frischer_Stinson.pdf.

Gaffney, V., & Zoran, S. 1991. "Diodorus Siculus and the Island of Hvar, Dalmatia: Testing the Text with GIS," *CAA* 19, B.A.R. International Series S577, Oxford: BAR Publishing: 113-125.

Gaffney, V., & Thomson, K. 2007. "Mapping Doggerland", in Vincent Gaffney, Kenneth Thomson & Simon Fitch (eds.), *Mapping Doggerland. The Mesolithic Landscapes of the Southern North Sea*, Oxford: BAR Publishing: 1-10.

Gaitatzes, A., Chritopoulos, D., & Papaioannou, G. 2004. "The Ancient Olympic Games: Being Part of the Experience", *VAST* 5, Aire-la-Ville, Switzerland: Eurographics: 19-28.

Gillings, M. & Goodrick, G.T. 1996. "Sensuous and reflexive GIS: exploring visualisation and VRML", *Internet Archaeology*, http://intarch.ac.uk/journal/issue1/gillings/part1.html.

Goodrick, G. & Gillings, M. 2000. "Constructs, Simulations, and Hyperreal Worlds: The Role of Virtual Reality (VR) in Archaeological Research", in G. Lock & K. Brown (eds.), *On the Theory and Practice of Archaeological Computing*, Monograph No. 51, Oxford: Oxford University Committee for Archaeology: 41-58.

Gutierrez, D., Frischer, B., Cerezo, E., Gomez, I.A. & Sobreviela, E. 2005. "Virtual Crowds in a Digital Colosseum", in *Virtual Retrospect 2005. Proceedings of the Conference, Biarritz (France), November 8th-9th-10th 2005*, Bordeaux: Ausonius: 140-148.

Gutierrez, D., Frischer, B., Cerezo, E. & Serón, F. 2007. "AI and Virtual Crowds: Populating the Colosseum", in *Journal of Cultural Heritage* 8(2): 176-185.

Harrison, S. 1988. "Magical Exchange of the Preconditions of Production in a Sepik River Village", *Man* 23: 319-333.

Helling, H., Steinmetz, C., Solomon, E., & Frischer, B. forthcoming. "The Port Royal Project. A Case Study in the Use of VR Technology for the Recontextualization of Archaeological Artifacts and Building Remains in a Museum Setting", in F. Niccolucci (ed.), *CAA 32, Prato, Italy, April 13-16, 2004*: http://www.iath.virginia.edu/~bf3e/revision/pdf/FrischerFinalCAA2004Color.pdf.

Hughes, S. W. 1996. "Three-dimensional Reconstruction of an Ancient Egyptian Mummy", in Tony Higgins, Peter Main & Janet Lang (eds.), *Imaging the Past. Electronic Imaging and Computer Graphics in Museums and Archaeology*, British Museum Occasional Paper 114, London: British Museum Press: 211-226.

Jabi, W., Potamianos, I., 2006. "A Parametric Exploration of the Lighting Method of the Hagia Sophia Dome," *The 7th International Symposium on Virtual Reality, Archaeology and Cultural Heritage, VAST*, 257-265.

Kaufmann, Thomas DaCosta. 2004. *Toward a Geography of Art*, Chicago: University of Chicago Press.

Kemp, M. 2000. *Visualizations. The Nature Book of Art and Science*, Berkeley and Los Angeles: University of California Press.

Kolb, C. C. 1997. "Review of *Virtual Archaeology: Re-creating Ancient Worlds*" by Maurizio Forte & Alberto

Siliotti: http://www.h-net.org/reviews/showrev.cgi?path=2068874530446.

Koller, D. 2007. *Protected Dissemination and Computer-Aided Reconstruction of Digitized Cultural Artefacts*, unpublished Ph.D. dissertation, Stanford University.

Kozan, J. *et al.* forthcoming, "Stepping into Uncertain Worlds: Uncertainty Representation in Virtual Heritage", Proceedings of CAA 2007.

Kvamme, K. L. 1991a. "Geographic Information Systems and Archaeology," *CAA* 19, BAR International Series S577, Oxford: BAR Publishing: 77–84.

Kvamme, K. L. 1991b. "Terrain Form Analysis of Archaeological Location through Geographic Information Systems," *CAA* 19, B.A.R. International Series S577, Oxford: BAR Publishing: 127-136.

Larmour, D.H.J. & Spencer, D. (eds.). 2007. *The Sites of Rome. Time, Space, Memory*, Oxford: Oxford University Press.

Larmour, D.H.J. 2007. "Holes in the Body", in D.H.J. Larmour & D. Spencer (eds.), *The Sites of Rome. Time, Space, Memory*, Oxford: Oxford University Press: 168-210.

Lock G. & Harris, T. 1992. "Visualizing Spatial Data: The Importance of Geographic Information Systems", in P. Reilly & S.P.Q. Rahtz (eds.), *Archaeology and the Information Age: A Global Perspective*, London: HarperCollins: 81-96.

Lord, P. & MacDonald, A. 2003. *e-Science Curation Report—Data Curation for e-Science in the UK: An Audit to Establish Requirements for Future Curation and Provision,* JISC Committee for the Support of Research, Twickenham, UK: The Digital Archiving Consultancy Limited, www.jisc.ac.uk/uploaded_documents/e-scienceReportFinal.pdf.

Loscos, C., Tecchia, F., Frisoli, A. *et al.* 2004. "The Museum of Pure Form: Touching Real Statues in an Immersive Virtual Museum", *VAST* 5, Aire-la-Ville, Switzerland: Eurographics: 271-279.

Mannheim, K. 1971. "On the Interpretation of Weltanschauung," in Kurt H. Wolff (ed.), *From Karl Mannheim*, New York: Oxford University Press: 29-30.

Morgan, L., 2000. "Form and Meaning of Figurative Painting", in S. Sherratt (ed.), *The Wall Paintings of Thera. Proceedings of the First International Symposium, Petros M. Nomikos Conference Centre, Thera, Hellas, 30 August – 4 September 1997*, vol. 2, Athens: Idryma Theras: 925-945.

Negroponte, N. 1996. *Being Digital*, New York: Vintage.

Paliou, E., Wheatley, D. 2007. "Integrating Spatial Analysis and 3D Approaches to the Study of Visual Space: Late Bronze Age Akrotiri", *CAA* 33, Tomar: CAAPortugal: 307-312.

Pescarin, S., Forte, M., Guidazzoli, An., Luguori, M.C. & Felicori, M. 2005. "From GIS to Landscape VR Museums", in *The Reconstruction of Archaeological Landscapes through Digital Technologies. Proceedings of the 2nd Italy-United States Workshop, Rome, Italy, November 3-5, 2003; Berkeley, USA, May 2005*, Oxford: BAR Publishing: 229-239.

Piga, Claudio. 1996. *Storia dei modelli dal tempio di Salamone alla realtà virtuale*, Seriate (Bergamo): ISMES.

Potamianos, I., Jabi, W., forthcoming. "Interactive Parametric Design and the Role of Light in Byzantine Churches," in *Communicating Spaces, Proceedings of the eCAADe Conference, University of Thessaly, Volos, Greece, September 6-9, 2006.*

Reilly, P. 1989. "Data Visualization in Archaeology", *IBM Systems Journal* 28 (4): 569-579.

Reilly, P. 1991. "Towards a Virtual Archaeology", *CAA* 18, Oxford: BAR Publishing 133-139.

Reilly, P. 1992, "Three-Dimensional Modelling and Primary Archaeological Data", in P. Reilly & S. Rahtz (eds.), *Archaeology and the Information Age*, London: HarperCollins:147-173.

Renfrew, C. 1997. "Foreword", in M. Forte and A. Siliotti, *Virtual Archaeology: Re-creating Ancient Worlds*, New York: Harry Abrams: 7.

Richards, J.D. 2006. "Electronic Publication in Archaeology", in Thomas L. Evans & Patrick Daly (eds.), *Digital Archaeology. Bridging Method and Theory*, London and New York: Routledge: 213-225.

Rodríguez-Almeida, E. 1981. *Forma Urbis Marmorea: Aggiornamento Generale 1980*, Rome: Edizioni Quasar.

Roorda, I. M. & Wiemer, R. 1991. "Towards a New Archaeological Information System in the Netherlands," *CAA* 19, B.A.R. International Series S577, Oxford: BAR Publishing: 85-88.

Ruggles, C. 1991. "Abstract Data Structures for GIS Applications in Archaeology," *CAA* 19, B.A.R. International Series S577, Oxford: BAR Publishing: 107-112.

Ryan, N. 2001. "Documenting and Validation Virtual Archaeology", *Archeologia e Calcalatori* 12: 254-273.

Ryder, G., Flack, P., & Day, A.M. 2004. "Adaptive Crowd Behaviour to Aid Real-Tome Rednering of a Cultural Heritage Environment", *VAST* 5, Aire-la-Villa, Switzerland: Eurographics: 29-36.

Scagliarini Corlàita, D., Guidazzoli, A., Salmon Cinotti T. *et al.* 2003. "Archeologia virtuale e supporti informatici nella ricostruzione di una domus di Pompei", *Archeologia e Calcolatori* 14: 237-274.

Scerri, E. 2006. *The Periodic Table: Its Story and Its Significance*, Oxford and New York: Oxford University Press.

Sherman, W.R. & Craig, Alan. B. 2003. *Understanding Virtual Reality*, San Francisco: Morgan Kaufmann.

Sifniotis, M., White, M., Watten, P. & Mania, K. 2007. "Influencing Factors on the Visualisation of Archaeological Uncertainty", *Proceedings of VAST: International Symposium on Virtual Reality, Archaeology and Intelligent Cultural Heritage*, Aire-la-Villa, Switzerland: Eurographics: 79-85.

Spencer, D. 2007. "Rome at a Gallop: Livy, On Not Gazing, Jumping, or Toppling into the Void", in in D.H.J. Larmour & D. Spencer (eds.), *The Sites of Rome. Time, Space, Memory*, Oxford: Oxford University Press: 61-101.

Stinson, P. 2007. "Technical and Methodological Problems in Digital Reconstructions of Archaeological Sites: The Studiolo in the House of Augustus and Cubiculum 16 in the Villa of the Mysteries", in A. Coralini & D. Scagliarini Corlaita (eds.), *Ut Natura Ars. Virtual Reality e Archeologia. Atti della Giornata di Studi (Bologna, 22 aprile 2002)*, Imola: Bologna University Press: 71-79.

Thomas, J. 1996. *Time, Culture and Identity*, London: Routledge.

Tilley, C. 1994. *A Phenomenology of Landscape*, Oxford: Berg Publishers.

Tufte, E. 1997. *Visual Explanations*, Cheshire, CT: Graphics Press.

Van Dyke, R. & Alcock, S.E., 2003. *Archaeologists of Memory*, Oxford: Blackwell Publishers Ltd.: 2003.

van Hove, D. & Rajala, U. 2004. "Editorial. Introduction: GIS and Archaeological Theory", *Internet Archaeology* 16: http://intarch.ac.uk/journal/issue16/editorial.html.

Vermeulen, F. 2002. "Introduction to Symposium 2: New Technologies in Cultural Resource Management and Archaeological Presentation: G.I.S., Virtual Reality, Internet, Multimedia", *Archeologia e Calcolatori* 13: 121-123.

Vout, C. 2007. "Sizing up Rome, or Theorizing the Overview", in D.H.J. Larmour & D. Spencer (eds.), *The Sites of Rome. Time, Space, Memory*, Oxford: Oxford University Press: 295-322.

Ware, C. 2004. *Information Visualization: Perception for Design*, San Francisco: Elsevier Science & Technology Books.

Warmoes, I. 1999. *Musée des Plans-Reliefs. Historic Models of Fortified Towns*, A. Sautier-Greening (trans.), Paris: Guides Thématiques.

Webb, E. 1985. "Introduction", *CAA* 13, London: Institute of Archaeology: iii.

Wheatley, D. 2000. "Spatial Technology and Archaeological Theory Revisited", *CAA* 24, Oxford: BAR Publishing: 123-131.

Wilcock, J.D. 1973. "A General Survey of Computer Applications in Archaeology", *CAA* 1, Stratford: George Street Press: 17-21.

Wood, J. and Chapman, G., 1992. "Three-dimensional Computer Visualization of Historic Buildings—With Particular Reference to Reconstruction Modelling", in P. Reilly & S.P.Q. Rahtz (eds.), *Archaeology and the Information Age: A Global Perspective*, London: HarperCollins: 123-146.

Zeki, S. 2003. *La visione dall'interno. Arte e cervello*, Paolo Pagli & Giovanna De Vivo (trans.), Turin: Bollati Boringhieri.

Zuk, T., Carpendale, M.S.T. & Glanzman, W.D. 2005. "Visualizing Temporal Uncertainty in 3D Virtual Reconstructions", *Proceedings of the 6th International Symposium on Virtual Reality, Archaeology and Cultural Heritage (VAST 2005)*, Aire-la-Ville, Switzerland: Eurographics: 99-106.

CHAPTER 1

ENVISIONING EXPLANATION: THE ART IN SCIENCE

Visualization is the activity of making and manipulating images that convey novel phenomena, ideas and meanings. It is central to almost every area of science. It is therefore surprising that we still lack an understanding of how visual thinking works. Examples from different sciences illustrate how scientists interpret and explain new phenomena by manipulating 2D, pattern-like features of the world that lend themselves to 3D, structural representation, and vice versa. The ability to move between two, three and four dimensions structures imagination and analysis, enabling scientists to vary the complexity of each visualization as its function changes during the process of discovery and communication. This indicates a widely used visual method that relates human cognitive abilities to imaging practices and technologies shared by the sciences and the arts.

David C. Gooding

Science Studies Centre, Department of Psychology, University of Bath, United Kingdom

Just as Leonardo da Vinci attempted to capture turbulent water in a famous series of sketches, scientists and their illustrators have endeavoured to image process (Darius 1984; Ford 1992; Robin 1992). Printed images cannot display process directly to our senses as, for example, animations and simulations do. Cinematography, multimedia, and VR technologies appeal directly to the multisensory character of popular culture and are displacing the ordered unfolding of traditional narrative and discourse. The electronic revolution is transforming western culture so that the visual medium, traditionally used to illustrate texts, is becoming the dominant medium of thought (Barry 1997). There is a trend away from narrative forms of exposition, argument and intellectual comprehension and toward less structured, experiential modes of apprehending. This is reflected in the performative and experiential style of many approaches to raising public awareness of science. Are the promoters of science aping popular culture? Far from it. The sensory technologies that drive popular culture draw on features of human experience that the sciences have always exploited. These include our abilities to recognize patterns, translate sensory experience into words and pictures and to integrate these into hypotheses, models and theories about processes hidden from direct experience. Stimulating human experiential abilities has, of course, made film, multimedia, and virtual-reality technologies more appealing than the narratives and static images of printed books. We should not let this obscure the fact that the sciences have always had to push at the limitations of printed media because science is mostly about processes that we cannot experience except via technologies of animation and VR. One of the main motives of scientific enquiry is to deliver a general, intellectual understanding of the processes that produce our experience. Visualization—making and manipulating images that convey novel phenomena, ideas and meanings—is central to this intellectual objective in almost every area of science. That is

An earlier version of this paper was published in Interdisciplinary Science Reviews *29/3 (2004): 278-294. This work was supported by a Research Fellowship from the Leverhulme Trust.*

why, since the 16th century, scientists have made use of the latest visual technologies. Since the mid-20th century they have developed and exploited computer simulations and 3D modelling techniques. These are the latest developments in an enduring and fruitful interaction between the technologies of art and the creative needs of the sciences.

It is therefore surprising that we still lack an understanding of how visual thinking works. Case-studies of image-making in science display great variety in visual imagery and representational practices. In historical and cultural studies this variety identifies emerging genres, practices and consensus about representational conventions and what is depicted by them (Lynch & Woolgar 1990; Mazzolini 1993; Field & James 1998). Each style of representation, instrumentation, or argumentation defines a distinct culture. Historians have shown how modern science emerged by forging a new identity as a cultural activity distinct from the visual arts, crafts, and technology (Jones & Galison 1998). Diversification differentiates disciplines and even points to important differences within a discipline. An example is the emergence of two distinct ways of practising high energy physics according to their conflicting views about the knowledge-bearing status, respectively, of images and of measured quantities (Galison 1997). Whereas these case-studies treat diversity in the manner of natural history, scientists take a less pluralist view. This typically characterizes the sciences in terms of methods and standards for evaluating them. Robert May described a common feature of all scientific method as a means of managing complexity: 'the world is complicated but not all the complexities are important all the time' so that 'the real trick is to intuit [...] the subset of things that are important, and on this basis to formulate a tentative understanding in unambiguous terms'. You then 'pursue where that tentative understanding leads, test it against the facts, and usually circle back to refine the original assumptions'. He added that 'this basic process holds whether you are trying to understand superconductivity, or the causes and consequences of biological diversity, or how best to translate Britain's excellent science base into industrial strength' (quoted in Kelly 1995: 6). Similarly, Philip Ball remarks that 'much of the scientist's art lies in figuring out what to include and what to exclude in a model, and this ability allows science to make useful predictions without getting bogged down by intractable details' (Ball 1999: 14). Philosophers cast science more narrowly as a rational process of reasoning about facts according to logical or statistical rules of inference. Many cognitive psychologists also assume logical or statistical models of human inference. Explanations based on evolutionary principles argue that scientific methods depend on cognitive capabilities closely linked to the survival and evolutionary supremacy of humans and that these have reached their most developed form in the methods of science (Mithen 2002: 23-40).

Managing complexity: visual method in the sciences

Image manipulation is an integral part of scientific discovery and communication. Drawing on the details of case histories and the generalizing tendencies of cognitive science, I shall show that the visual strategies used in many sciences are at work in other activities as well. Although the sciences are diverse, they are not simply a panoply of local, culturally situated practices. The art historian Martin Kemp hints at this when he remarks that although 'it is inevitably the differences that most strike us, particularly as historians of culture [...] beneath the varied surface run some constant currents in our human quest for visual understanding' (Kemp 2000: 1). He argues that the most enduring of these currents is our propensity to articulate acts of seeing through 'structural intuitions'. Kemp's phrase connotes the structures both of 'inner intuitive' processes and of 'external features whose structures are being intuited'. I will elaborate both aspects of this notion with examples that identify an underlying reason for the fact that scientists vary their images. In order to articulate their intuitions scientists make representations whose complexity can be varied. They actively manage complexity by manipulating those pattern-like features of the world that lend themselves to representation in three and four dimensions. The complexity of a visualization varies according to its function at each stage in the process of discovery and of communicating about discovery. The cases which I have studied suggest a model of the process of articulating visual intuitions as visual constructs. This relates human cognitive strengths and weaknesses which are universal, to the diversity and richness of imaging practices in the sciences. These features appear wherever humans use images to discover and understand hidden structures and processes.

Visual images offer convenient windows into activities that are personal and imaginative as well as the more conventional modes of communication of the public domain. Each case is unique, yet each shares common features and similar patterns of movement between the personal, private domain of mental imagery and the public domain of communicated concepts. These patterns and features define a visual method in the play of cognition as the locus of reasoning and culture as the locus of construction of images, narratives meanings, arguments and objects. This method has its counterparts in artistic technique and—as in the graphic arts—its procedures are often embodied in new technologies.

In science, the role of an image or artefact is constantly changing: at first it conveys a tentative understanding or novel technique; later it may aid communication and the construction of arguments, and even after its publication as a phenomenon or finding, it is subject to critical reappraisal that can undermine its factual status. Alongside this dynamic of perception and acceptance is another: the generative and communicative roles of images fall away as scientists enhance their discourse with new verbal and symbolic expressions. The caption Watson and Crick gave their first published image of the double helical structure of DNA is a typical example. Extensive structural modelling had been essential to solving the problem, yet their first paper does not include an image of this model. Instead there is a diagram whose caption indicates that this image is a purely an aid to understanding a prose description that conveys the solution (Crick & Watson 1953: 737). Of course the changing role of artefacts and images follows its own pattern in each case. Nevertheless, when we look for common features in these patterns of visual inference we can see how apparently disparate elements of scientific practice—words, sketches, photographs, models, instruments, and the other traces and products of scientific activity—work together in making and communicating new knowledge. This comparative approach takes us beyond the surface history of imagery in science, allowing the visual proclivities of scientists to show us how their creativity is like that of other humans, and also how it differs. This method foregrounds visual images in order to indicate how they relate to the narrative expression of thought and to visual technologies. It does this by relating the complexity of an image to the purpose that it has at a particular time. Behind the variety is an underlying, cognitive aspect of visual thinking. Humans can do some things quickly and automatically, such as seeing patterns and comparing them. But other tasks, such as imagining how the shape of an object will change as it moves, require considerable, conscious mental effort.

We find that there is a dialectical play of simple and complex images, as scientists move from interpreting novel information through hypotheses that express its possible meanings and on to arguments that turn the information into evidence for an agreed explanation. Why is there a dialectic rather than linear progression from simple representations to more complex ones? Cutting-edge research encounters the world as a complex and often unruly affair. Abstracting from something that is too complex to interpret or communicate makes new kinds of thinking possible. A simple object is easier to manipulate in thought, by hand or by computation and it can draw on the resources of an established mode of communication. An accessible example of the problem that displays a typical solution is provided by Michael Faraday. Like the other scientists described in this chapter he wrestled with the related difficulties of interpreting and communicating novel phenomena. Between 1821 and 1831 he adapted the existing discourse of 'lines' and 'curves' used in areas as diverse as electromagnetism, descriptive geometry and geomagnetism, developing it into a powerful visual language for his electromagnetic theory (Gooding

1989). Faraday knew well that simple representations leave out features that later prove to be important. By 1832 his intimate, experiential knowledge of the interactions of electricity, magnetism and motive force far exceeded the descriptive capabilities of his earlier attempts. So he devised a structural model which he sketched in the margin of his laboratory diary (Martin 1932: 425). This model combines word and image to express the observed relationships between these three 'powers' (Gooding 1992) **[Fig. 1]**. Faraday's innovation is that the forces act not between magnets, charges or other active objects, but between lines that visualize electric, magnetic and motive action.

This succinct visual-verbal statement typifies how scientists build simple descriptions into representations of complex experiences. The 'convergent', integrating function of such images has been noted by historians (Gooding 1990; Tweney 1992; Trumpler 1997). The more complex a representation is, the greater its power to integrate different kinds of information derived from various sources. But increasing its complexity makes a representation more difficult to think about. This leads to new simplification in a further cycle of abstraction, which often draws on mathematical expressions and computer-based models. I shall illustrate this by examples from three areas—the reanimation of fossils, reconstructive visualization in hepatology and stereographic projection in early X-ray crystallography. What these disparate fields have in common suggests widespread use of a distinctive, visual method of thinking in the sciences.

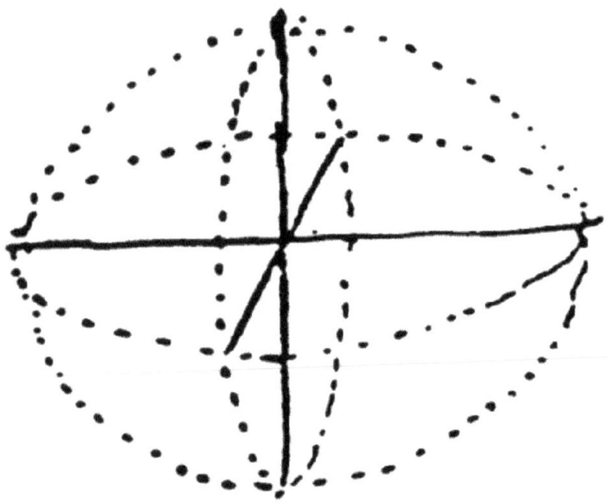

Fig. 1. *Faraday's sketch of March 1832. The text shows how to animate the 3D image as a 4D process model which expresses Faraday's discovery of the three-way mutuality of electric, magnetic and motive actions (Martin 1932: 425).*

The cognitive need to vary the complexity of images also explains an important group of technologies—the many artefacts and procedures scientists have devised to manage visualization and to communicate its emergent meanings. Contemporary 3D digital technologies are the latest addition to this group of technologies that organize information into a visual product. We can understand this continuity by drawing an analogy between visualization in science and the use of the drawing frame. Illustrated in a famous engraving by Albert Dürer, this device was designed to reproduce a perspective drawing on a flat surface. It does so by structuring and disciplining the actions of a human observer (Alpers 1983: 43; Veltman & Keele 1986: 108; Ferguson 1992: 80-82). It requires a technique that orders discrete acts of perception (looking through the drawing frame at objects at different distances from the eye) into acts of depiction (marking paper or canvas), thus integrating them into a single image. Many scientific technologies develop out of similar procedures that organize human agency. Some of these technologies dispense with the human observer altogether. For example, functional magnetic resonance (FMR) images of the brain display a cross-section of neuronal activity everywhere at once. They are produced by computer programs that organize vast quantities of numerical data that is collected by instruments having special sensors. The drawing frame analogy captures this procedural aspect of visualization. A more recent example from art takes the analogy further. Picasso's early experiments with photography show that ordering can be applied to the very medium in which an image is fixed. Picasso made photographs of his paintings at various stages of completion. The images were fixed on glass plates. There is evidence that during the first decade of the 20th century he superimposed images of his paintings by projecting light through stacks of photographic plates, creating the multifaceted images that characterize early cubist art (Miller 2001: 119-120). As we shall see, scientists use very similar methods of 'stacking' images to make structures visible to the eye or to display new properties. Picasso's stacked negatives have their counterparts in sciences from X-ray crystallography and virology to tissue engineering, where 3D printing technologies originally designed to make images of complex objects like organic molecules are now used to construct live tissue. These 'printers' build up cell tissue by printing complex patterns of living cells into a matrix, layer by layer (Choi 2003: 16). Where 16th century craftsmen used the drawing frame to arrange pencil marks in a grid drawn on a single sheet of paper, these 21st century devices arrange different kinds of material (including live cells) in layers, according to patterns that scientists have elicited from real tissue. Archaeology provides a third example. In the field of osteoarcheology, computerized tomography (CT) scanners are used to create a 3D representation of the hidden, internal structure of ancient, fragile bones. The 3D computer image can be viewed from any angle and manipulated, for example, to separate soil from bone. It can be used to guide lasers fired into a liquid photosensitive polymer resin to create physical 3D replicas of the bone and can even fabricate models of the hidden structure of bones. Internal investigation by dissection normally destroys an archaeological find but this method is non-invasive (Lynnerup *et al.* 1997: 91-94). All these technologies depend on a basic human ability to organize information visually into patterns and structures. The following three examples show how scientists do this.

Reanimating extinct organisms

The distorted, fossilized remains of organisms offer glimpses into the long history of life. To contribute to the story each fossil is reconstructed as a plausible model of a living organism. To be plausible it must be identified as an instance of either a known species or of a new one. The fossils of the Burgess shales of British Columbia are unusual in that many are complete and even traces of soft parts and internal organs are preserved (Briggs & Conway Morris 1979; Conway Morris 1979; Bruton 1981). But the identity of a fossil impression cannot be 'read off' the rock. Fixing its identity is complicated by several factors. Sedimentary rock splits along cleavage planes to reveal a fossil imprint. The matching positive and negative imprints ('part' and 'counterpart') are dispersed by geological process and by human disturbance and often end up in different geological collections. Organisms are trapped at many angles by sediment, so the cleavage planes 'cut' the flattened organisms at different angles. Given difficulties such as these, fossil imprints are interpreted by analogy to the morphology of modern counterparts. However, most Burgess shale organisms became extinct and have no modern analogues (Briggs & Conway Morris 1979: 227-231; Gould 1989). How did paleontologists get from the barest hints of structure in pieces of rock to working models of novel organisms? They reasoned with sketches, diagrams and drawings and they manipulated physical models to produce new images.

A reconstruction is considered plausible if it produces a model of an organism that could have lived. Reconstructing Burgess shale animals from fossil imprints involved creating images of the traces of an organism from the rock using a camera lucida (Briggs & Williams 1981; Hammond & Austin 1987; Collins 1988). These 2D images diagram features whose function and relation to the anatomy remains conjectural. The diagrams are simplified, provisional interpretations of the complex phenomenology of the 'raw' fossil imprints. Features are labelled to indicate structures that could represent a plausible anatomy (Briggs & Williams 1981; Briggs & Collins 1988) **[Fig. 2]**. Of course, expert knowledge about possible structures influences the selection of features in the diagram. The camera lucida diagram generated from the photograph guides morphological interpretation of the photograph. The diagram mediates between flattened features extracted from the photographic image and an emerging, 3D model of a possible organism **[Fig. 3]**. To be identified as a section of a particular organism, each impression must be associated—via its camera lucida

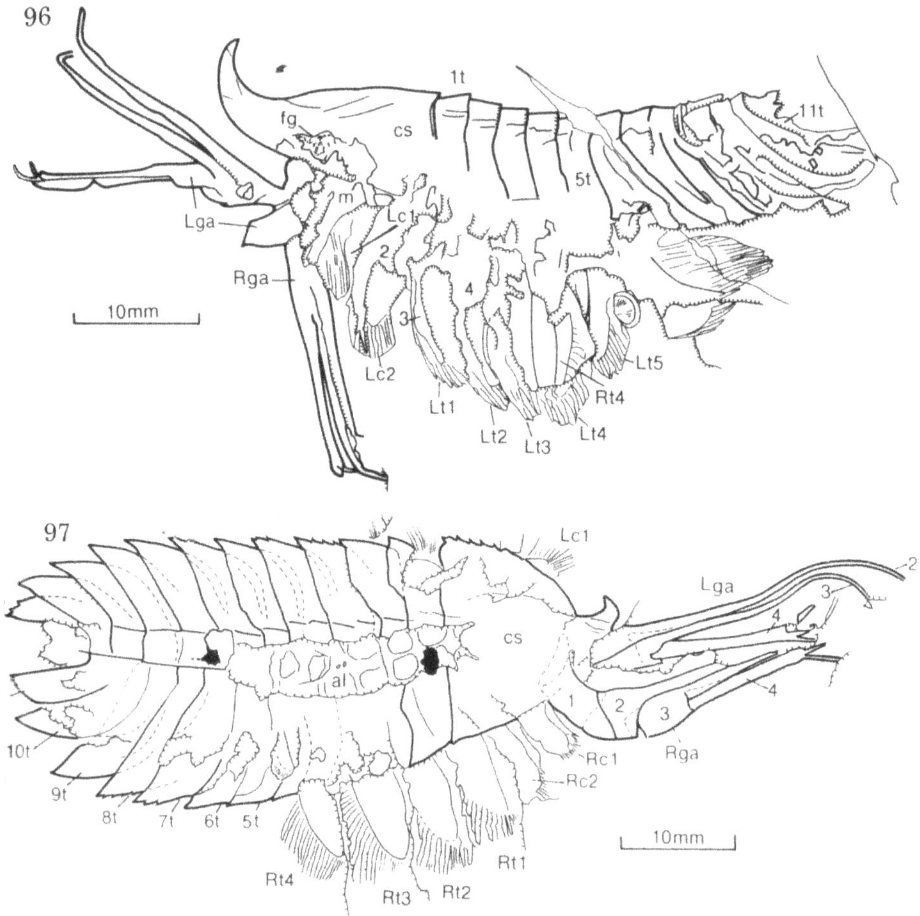

Fig. 2. *Camera lucida drawings of two specimens of* Leanchoilia superlata *(after Bruton & Whittington 1983: figs. 96 and 97; reprinted by permission of the Royal Society of London).*

diagram—with other impressions that could be images of the same animal captured in different orientations, but may turn out to be images of completely different animals. Painstaking, image-based searches for visual matches are made to reduce the number of possible matches. Failure to recognize the effects of variable orientation in the shale can lead to misidentification so every fossil impression must be re imaged mentally, as if from several points of view (Briggs & Williams 1981: 157). These mental images are sketched or modelled as sections. Each one of these images is then evaluated as a possible match for other known impressions.

One investigator, Simon Conway Morris, reports drawing specimens found in various orientations, then passing countless hours 'rotating the damned thing in [his] mind' from the position of one drawing to the different angle of another, until every specimen 'could be moved without contradiction from one stance to the next' (quoted in Gould 1989: 92). His phrase 'without contradiction' hints at informal, implicit rules for transforming and comparing mental images. Variability between different individuals' ability to generate sketches of images produced by mental rotation compounds the problem of variable orientation. The use of informal procedures leads to variable results. To remove this, scientists develop imaging techniques that give a constant result. In this case scientists made 3D models of the conjectured organism **[Fig. 3]** and, by projecting the changing shapes of shadows cast by sections of these models, replaced the laborious image-based 'thought experiments' by systematic, model-based transformations. Once a set of patterns from

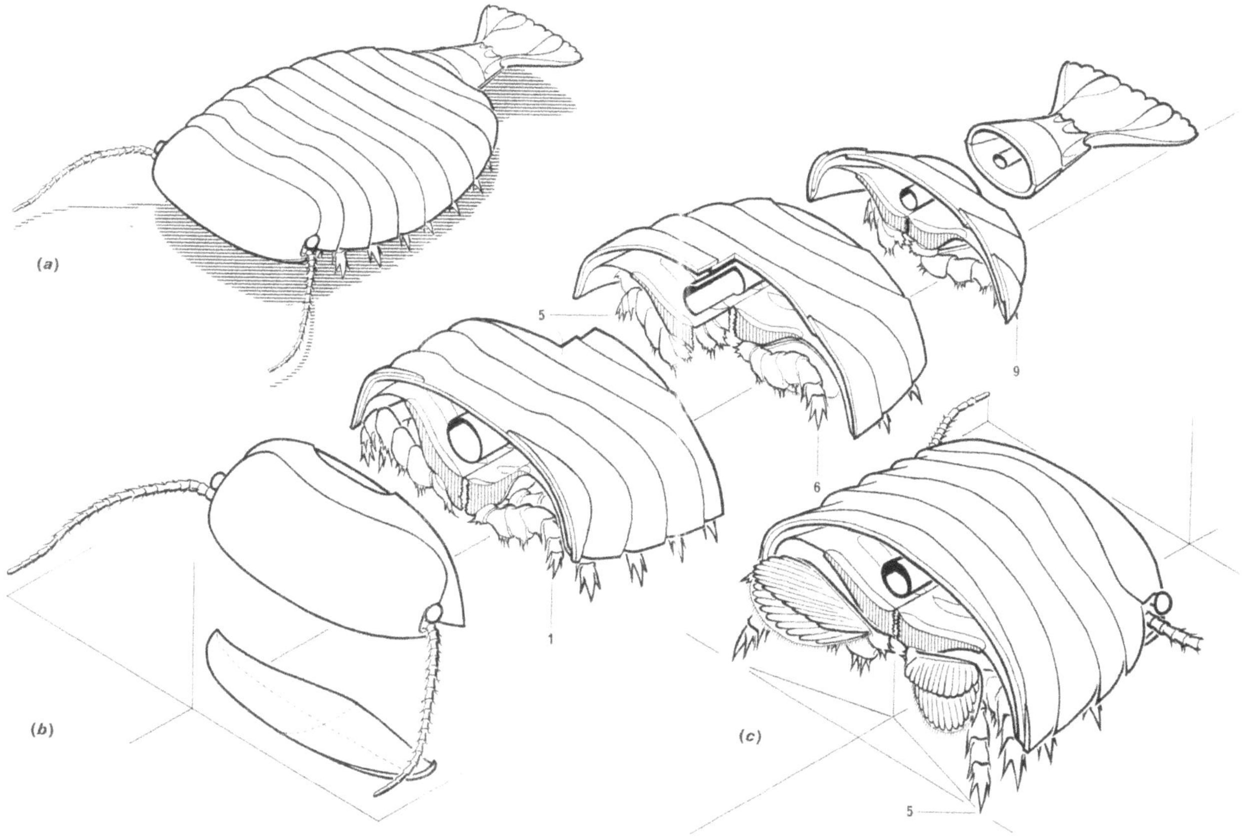

Fig. 3. *Reconstruction of the arthropod* Sidneyia inexpectans *as a 3D model built in sections derived from camera lucida drawings such as those in Fig. 2 (after Bruton 1981: fig. 107; reprinted by permission of the Royal Society of London).*

different fossil imprints is associated with an organism, each image in this set can be treated as a 2D section of the 3D structure that represents the morphology of that organism. Those diagrammed imprints of the organism that cannot be made to fit sections of known animals are anomalies. They suggest that a new 3D structure be conjectured.

So far the process of identifying imprints has involved a dialectical play between 2D photographic images of fossils, 2D diagrammatic images of fossils, 2D images of 3D structures, actual 3D structures and their 2D shadow-projections, and the 'animation' of these structures as living organisms. The 3D visual model generated from the set of matches or correlated 2D impressions integrates several different types of information. It must be consistent in a cognitive sense with a large set of mental and physical images and be consistent in a conceptual sense with expert knowledge about the morphology of similar organisms. This must in turn be compatible with other kinds of knowledge about life processes such as the animal's ecology (food sources, predators and so on) and the behaviours afforded by its environment, given its anatomy. The 3D model is repeatedly tested in two ways. The first involves showing that a living organism that had the postulated structure would, when buried in sediments and subjected to known geological, chemical and mineralization processes, produce the fossil impression(s) from which the original diagrams were abstracted. Thus the camera lucida diagram is used both as an interpretative source of possible models and as an empirical check on animated versions of their structural projections. The second type of test involves creating a life-process (or 4D) model that integrates information from disciplines such as ecology, anatomy, physiology, and evolutionary biology so as to evaluate the 3D structure as a model of

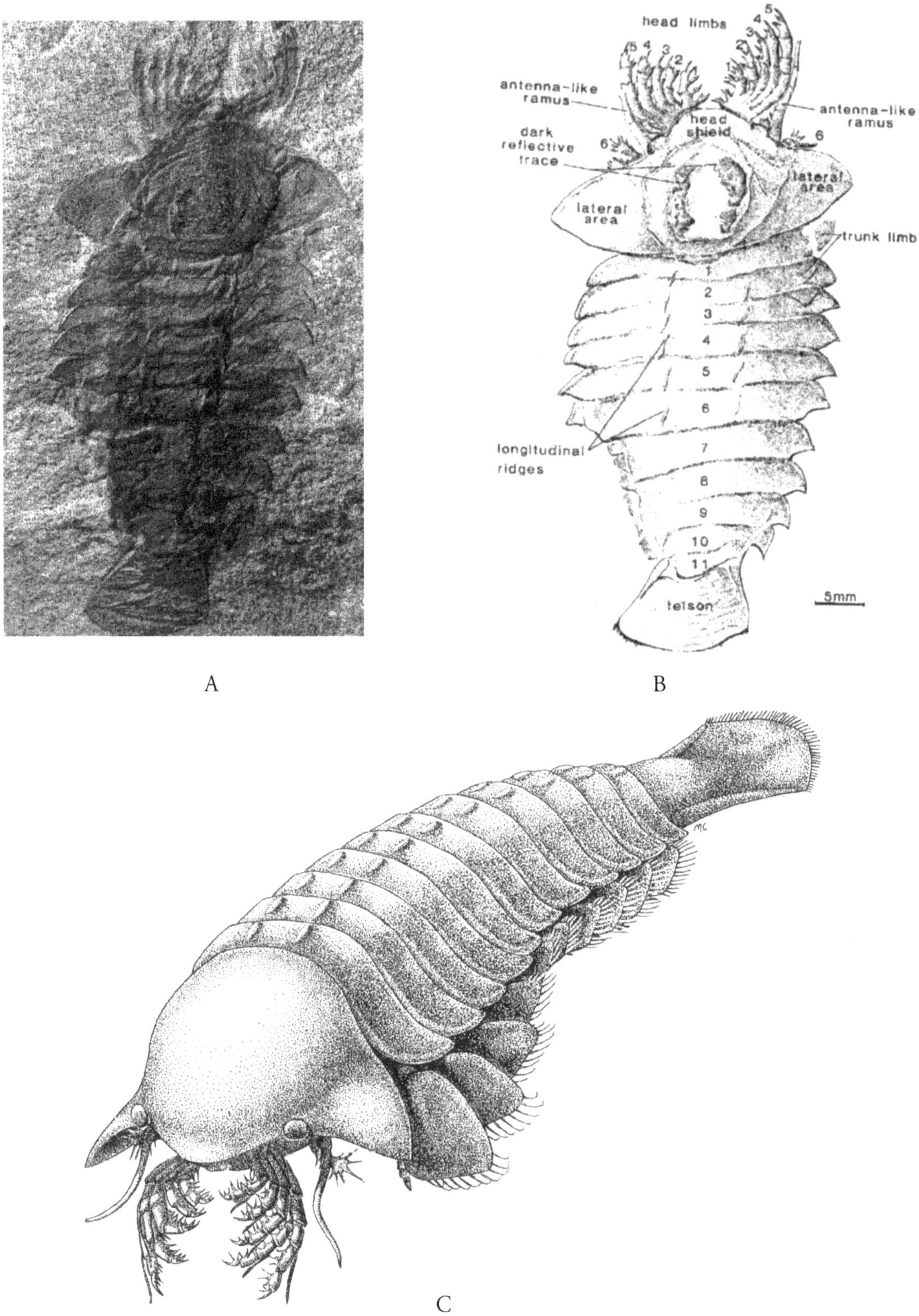

Fig. 4. *A selection of images from the reconstruction of the arthropod* Sanctacaris uncata*: A. Photograph of a counterpart (dry specimen, dorsal view); B. Labelled drawing based on the photograph; C. Reconstruction drawing based on several fossil 'sections' (after Briggs & Collins 1988: text-fig. 1B, pl. 71, fig. 3, and text-fig. 6; copyright of the Palaeontological Association).*

such an animal. This illustrates how structure models such as the one shown **[Fig. 3]** mediate between images of patterns and theories about process.

The interpretations of a few investigators must be evaluated by a wider group of experts. For use in the public forum of negotiation and argument the fossil photographs are retouched to highlight features selected as significant by a provisional identification. The diagrams are also redrawn as 'reconstructions' that include features that can be inferred even though they are missing from the original images. These are shown in drawings of the organism from various views. **Fig. 4** sets out a sequence of images from the reconstruction of another organism, *Sanctacaris uncata* (Briggs & Collins 1988; see also Whittington 1985: esp. figs. 4.40, 4.50). In publications each photographic image is paired with a labelled camera lucida diagram and text. This shows readers how to interpret the 2D images in terms of the 3D reconstruction described in the paper. Using these shared objects of discussion readers can reenact the play of images of flattened layers, diagrams and structures.

How pattern and structure elucidate process

This example illustrates features of visual thinking that are found throughout the sciences:

- There is a dialectical play of personal and public representations (Goldschmidt 1991).
- Diagrams select and highlight certain features of the 'raw' (uninterpreted) imprint.
- A technology (the camera lucida) is used to produce abstractions which scientists then work with, using techniques devised to reduce the variability and difficulty of mental tasks such as working out 2D projections of complex 3D structures (Briggs & Williams 1981). Since the 1970s, computational methods have also been used (Doveton 1979).
- The selected features are used to construct a 3D model that can integrate information from diverse knowledge domains.
- Information-rich, integrated representations are developed into process models that can explain both the original 2D imprints and the 3D anatomical features that they are now shown to display.
- The complex models are evaluated by abstracting simpler visualizations from them and comparing these to the source patterns.

This set of strategies is motivated by the key aim of the sciences: starting from complex experience produced by hidden processes, to explain visualized experience of patterns and structures in terms of process (Ball 1999). In paleontology the physiology and life process cannot be presented directly to the mind's eye. They are reconstructed verbally and pictorially by the informed, guided use of imagination, like Faraday's verbal instructions for animating his structural model of electricity, magnetism and motive force **[Fig. 1]**. Similarly, a geological block diagram is a 2D (printed) image of a 3D (structural) model designed to explain a lengthy geological process (Gooding 2004). In block diagrams texture and colour identify different types and states of rock. Signs such as arrows indicate the need to iterate versions of the imaged model through a series of steps. Thus, time (a non-spatial dimension) is represented by a symbol which is read as an instruction to follow a procedure. Mathematical equations and operators such as integral signs are 'read' in a similar way. In visualizations such as data plots, time is represented spatially rather than by symbols. I refer to images and composite visual-symbolic representations that include indicators of process as 4D. By analogy uninterpreted 'sources' such as fossil imprints or 'raw' numerical data would have zero dimensionality.

Visualization is a process that involves varying the dimensions of these objects of thought, talk and action. The ability to move easily between visualizations of differing complexity is a very important feature of scientific thinking. Why should this be? In each of the

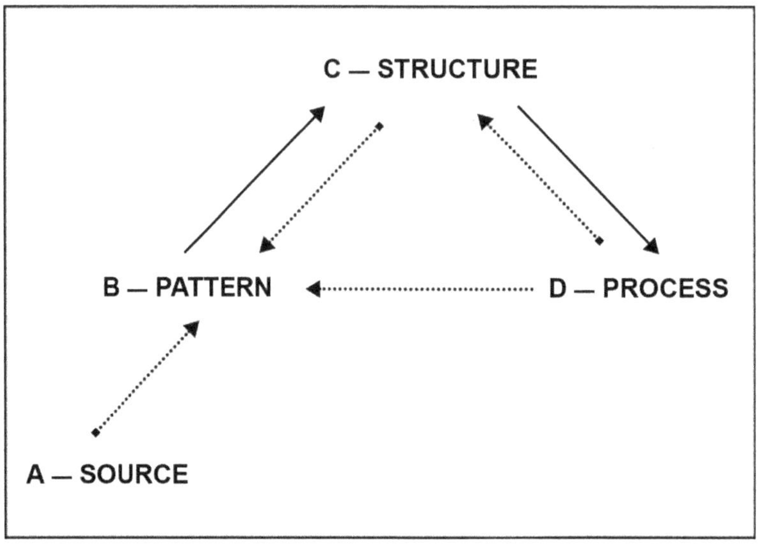

Fig. 5. *A depiction of types of visual inference showing four main transformations. Moves from pattern to structure (arc BC) and from structure to process (CD) are generative and expand information content. Moves from unresolved phenomena to a pattern (arc AB), from process to structure or from structure to pattern (CB, DC, DB) are also generative but reduce the information content of an image.*

examples in this chapter, every transformation increases or decreases the complexity of the new visualization it produces. Each new visualization is a response to the constraints and opportunities posed at the point at which it is invoked in the problem-solving process. The information content of a representation is broadly related to the number of dimensions that it has and to whether it combines different modes of representation (e.g. image, text, symbols, animation, sound). The unlabelled photograph in **Fig. 4A** and the drawing in **Fig. 4C** are 2D and unimodal. The labelled diagrams in **Fig. 2** and **Fig. 4B** are 2D and bimodal, while Faraday's diagram in **Fig. 1** is 3D and bimodal. Animating it according to his instructions (say, in a computer graphic) would make it trimodal and 4D (albeit viewed on a 2D screen). Pattern-matching requires representations having only two dimensions whereas creative inferences require representations that are multidimensional and multimodal. By adding dimensions and modalities scientists increase the capacity of a representation to convey meaningful information. However, this also increases its complexity. This usually reduces its transparency because greater mental or computational effort is needed to manipulate the information conveyed consistently and to understand what it means. So there is a trade-off: increased interpretation and explanatory power require the increased information content of more complex representations, while transparency, accessibility and ease of communication require the reduced complexity of simpler representations. This dynamic drives the invention of imaging techniques and technologies that both simplify and regulate moves between images and models of different complexity.

Changing representational demands produce the changes in complexity that we see in every case of scientific problem-solving. The diagram in **Fig. 5** captures just one aspect of this, the dimensionality of visual representations. Each of the four nodes (labelled A-D) denotes representations having a different number of dimensions. The arrows denote manipulations that transform simpler into complex, and vice versa. A manipulation may be conducted mentally (as in Conway-Morris' mental rotations) or by techniques such as rotating a 3D physical model to study its 2D shadow projections. At node A is the unresolved, complex phenomenology (of zero dimensionality); at B, we have 2D, bimodal images (sketches or diagrams) that abstract features from A and provide resources for 3D, bimodal structural models at C. Visualizations at nodes B and C also provide a framework for integrating other kinds of knowledge into a 4D process model at node D. Computer animations typically make it easy to move between nodes C and D. This schema also shows how images are used in testing visual models: structure and process models are validated when source information as imaged at B can be re-derived from C or from D, along with new patterns or structures. This diagram allows us to situate some of the images, objects and processes that contribute to the variety of visual imaginings in science.

The sequence of images, objects and inferences is unique to each case. It reflects contingent factors which influence stylistic and other features of the representations. Yet the types of transformation shown in **Fig. 5** occur wherever visual images are used in science. This scheme shows that visualizations bear a distinct, inferential relationship to each other, relating each occurrence of an image or model to the larger context of observation, experimentation, modelling, dissemination and argument in which it is used. It therefore offers a basis for the systematic comparison of episodes of scientific discovery as well as a more general understanding of visual technologies.

Visualizing vascular structures

The liver regulates the level of glucose in the blood, responding to fluctuations in the nutritional supply and demand. Opposing systems of enzymes act to release glucose or to reduce its uptake into the blood. The enzyme chemistry that balances supply and use of blood sugars is well understood. But for some mammalian livers there is a long-standing puzzle about the physiology that supports the biochemical function. In some mammals dissection does not support structural hypotheses because structures which must exist cannot be observed by the usual method of visually inspecting sections. As in the previous example the problem is to find a physiologically plausible structure, but here visual inspection of tissue sections provides few clues. Harald Teutsch (2004) and his collaborators solved this by envisioning the structures supporting the process. This involved making spatially distributed sets of measurements. From these they produced a functional

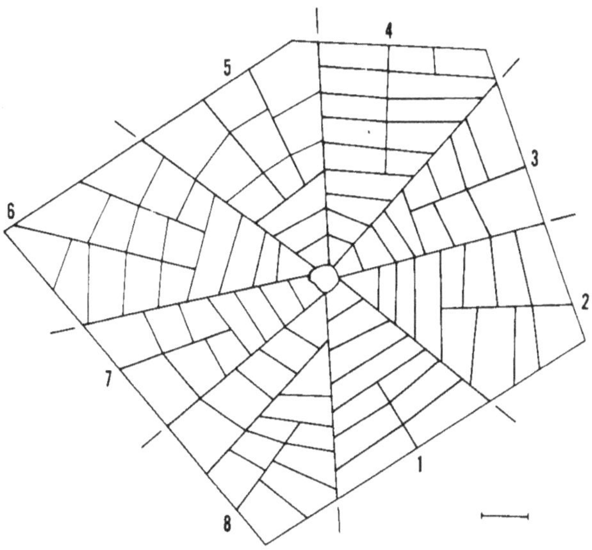

A

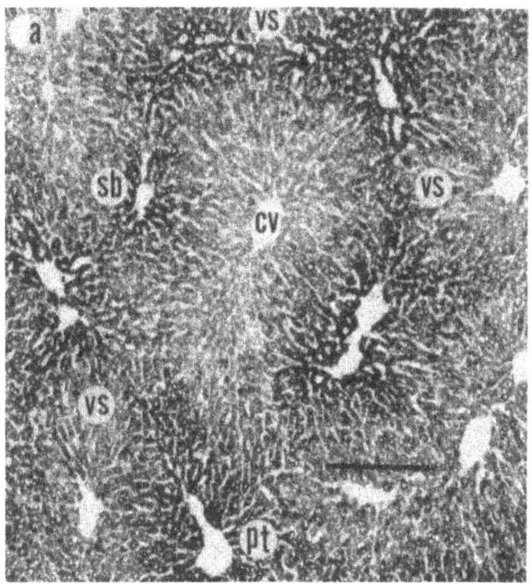

B

Fig. 6. Maps that organize numerical data: A. Micro-dissection map showing subdivision of a liver lobule cross-section into eight adjacent sectors; B. Histochemically stained sections guide this subdivision. The abbreviated labels indicate sections of entities such as a central venule (labelled 'CV'). This structure will emerge (approximately) perpendicular to the plane of the imaged section as data is processed and imaged (after Teutsch 1988: figs. 1 and 2; copyright of J. Wiley & Sons, Inc.).

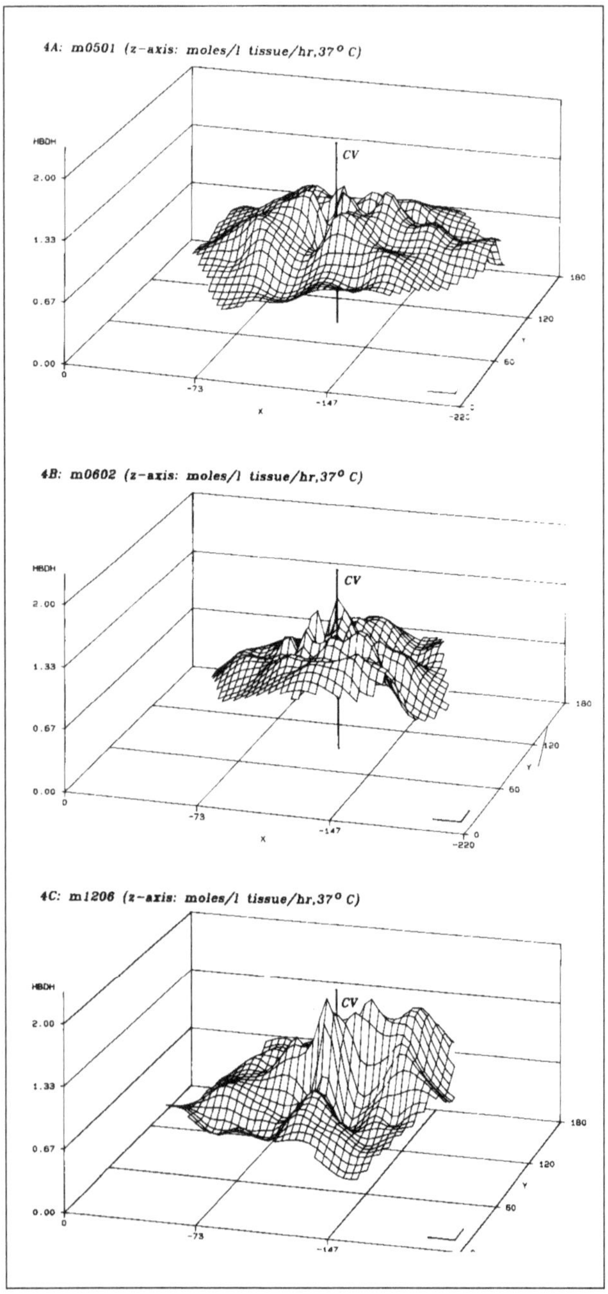

A

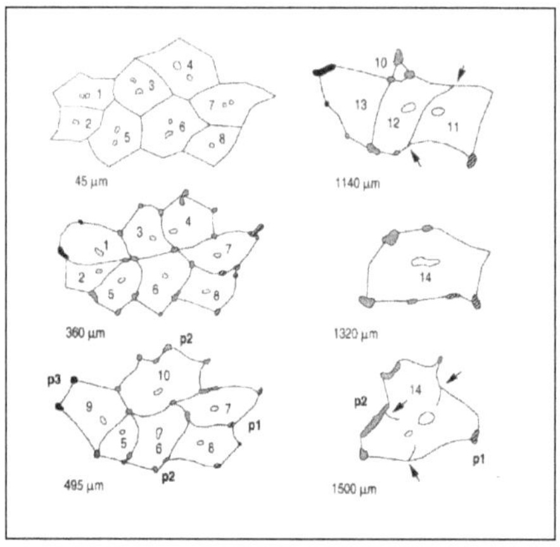

B

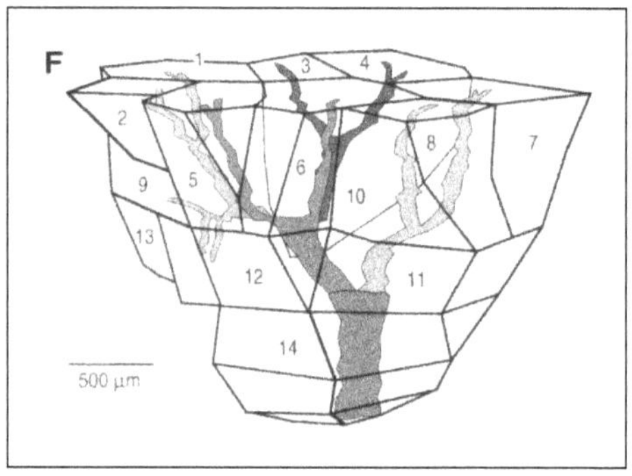

C

Fig. 7. *A. Plots of the distribution of enzyme activity over cross-sections of a primary modular structure of rat liver, reconstructed as 3D surfaces. The central vertical line denotes the location of the central venule, labelled 'CV' in Fig. 6B (after Teutsch* et al. *1992: fig. 4; reproduced by permission of the Histochemical Society); B-C. A few of the 146 drawings of cross-sections of a secondary unit showing segments of the portal tracts and septa, from which a 3D structure—shown at right, C—was constructed (after Teutsch* et al. *1999: figs. 3 and 6; copyright of J. Wiley & Sons, Inc.).*

model of the elusive primary and secondary vascular structures.

Teutsch and his team needed to develop an empirical method that could decide between different models of the relationship between liver function and its structure. They organized a numerical data set measuring biochemical processes in dissected livers first into 2D and then into 3D arrays. Sections are mapped and imaged as in **Fig. 6**. But they needed to make the opposed catalytic actions of the enzymes visible. To achieve a spatial separation of these actions they made a closer study of rates of glucose uptake and release in frozen slices (cryosections) of rat livers. Further visualizations plot the gradients of enzyme activity rather than discrete values **[Fig. 7]**. Increasing the quantity of data improved the 'resolution' of these plots, making it possible to infer the sub-modular structures consisting of populations of cells that had eluded visual inspection (Teutsch 1988).

Teutsch demonstrated modularity and vascular structure by constructing 3D images from virtual 'stacks' of images of very thin cryosections (Teutsch *et al.* 1992). A sample from a much larger set of drawings of these is shown in **Fig. 7B**. A particular structure of the modules and of the ducts that supply and drain them was produced, consisting of a set of 3D drawings, some of which are shown in **Fig. 7C**. The final result of the reconstructive method is a 4D or process model that provides the physiological explanation of the source images of visualized data. This was validated by creating a physical representation using 3D image-printing technology (Teutsch *et al.* 1999). The 3D blocks of 2D sections guided further construction of colour-coded models in paste and plastic **[Fig. 8]**. Actual construction is needed to work out particular features, such as how modular structures incorporate portal and venal ducts. Teutsch presented this method of reconstructive visualization as demonstrating the existence of complex vascular structures. These are now considered as facts established by 3D reconstruction. Both their meaning and their factual status emerge from this method of visual modelling.

Reconstructive visualization combines veridical images, sketches, schematic images, 2D and 3D plots of numerical data, 3D stacks of 2D plots and physical models. 3D-printing technology automates the process of assembling a 3D structure from a large set of data-generated 2D section plots. Just as drawing directs attention to surface features, physical modelling checks the efficacy of a structure with regard to function, as we saw in the case of the Burgess shale fauna, or to phenomenology—as will be shown in the next example, X-ray crystallography. This conjunction of images, models, instruments and theories shows how diverse kinds of artefact extend the range of what can be visualized in a creative yet systematic manner.

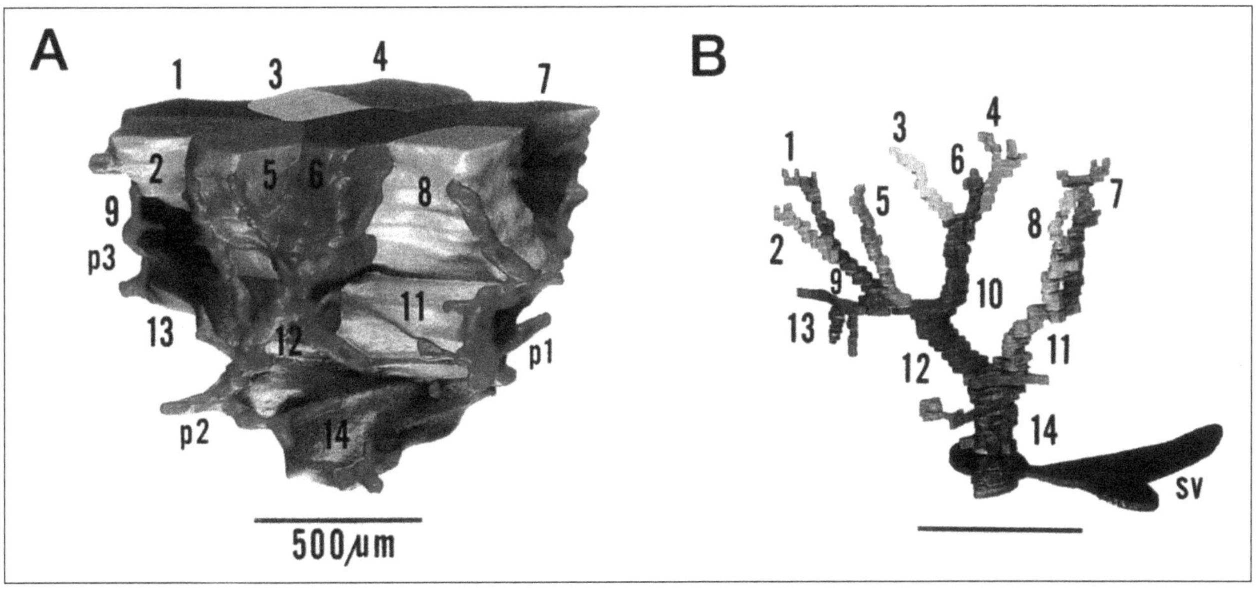

Fig. 8. *Images of a model that is also an artistic reconstruction comparable to* Sanctacaris *in Fig. 4C. A is the front view of a secondary parenchymal unit (left) and B shows the central venular tree that drains it. In the original, colour coding is used to differentiate the primary units of which the whole is composed. This coding is lost in monochrome reproductions (after Teutsch* et al. *1999: fig. 4; copyright of J. Wiley & Sons, Inc.)*

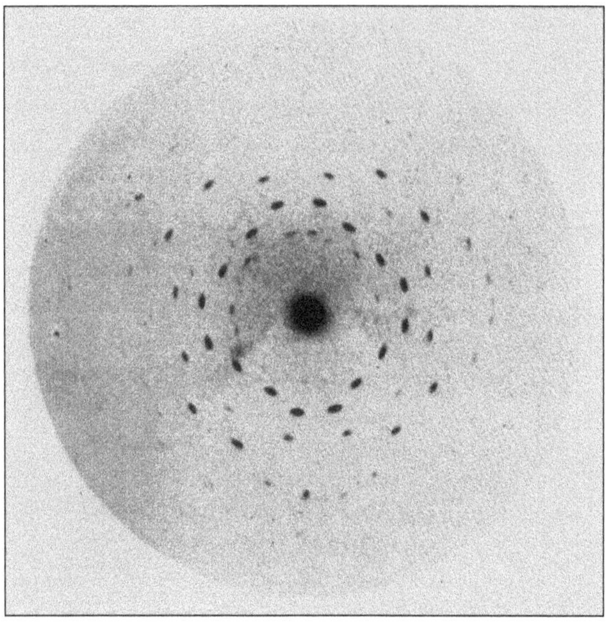

A

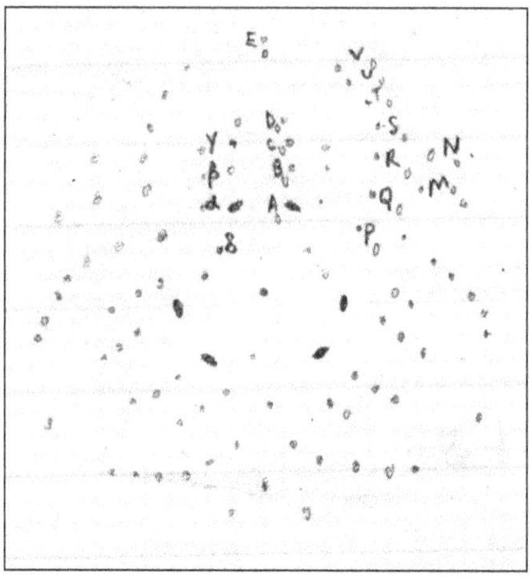

B

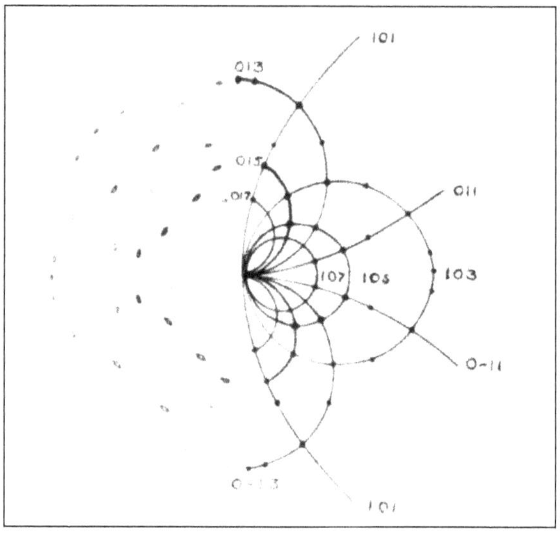

C

Fig. 9. *From patterns to crystal structure: A. Photograph of pattern produced by diffraction of X-rays by a crystal lattice (after Bragg 1913: fig. 3); B. Excerpt from a notebook entry showing the pattern and size of spots being abstracted from an X-ray image (courtesy of the Royal Institution of Great Britain, W. L. Bragg Papers, RI MS WLB 86); C. Pattern of ellipses drawn to indicate stereographic projection (after Bragg 1913: fig. 4).*

Stereographic projection of crystal structure

In 1912 Max von Laue published images formed on a photographic plate by X-rays passing through a crystal **[Fig. 9A]**. He surmised that if the wavelength of the X-rays is of the same order of magnitude as the distance between atoms in the crystal, then the crystal will act on the X-rays in the same way that a diffraction grating affects light waves. Each plane in the crystal will deflect the incident ray at a slightly different angle, splitting it into interfering rays. But this process is happening in three dimensions, not just the two dimensions that frame the patterns displayed on the plates. Inspired by von Laue's 'intricate geometrical patterns', W. L. Bragg published the first of his papers on crystal structure in the same year. These papers established a method of inferring crystal structure from features of the pattern of spots produced by the X-rays (Bragg 1913A). These features include symmetry, actual position, the size of each spot, and—it would soon emerge—points at which spots are not actually visible. The variable size of the spots led Bragg to surmise that—contrary to von Laue—any wavelength can be dispersed by a crystal but that as each successive plane deflects the rays, there is interference between rays only when some relationship between wavelength and inter-atomic distance is satisfied.

Symmetry is to be expected if crystals behave like 3D diffraction gratings. The position and magnitude of each spot as well as points where spots are absent provide clues to the relative positions of the planes in which atoms of the crystal might lie. The spots appear where there is positive interference between the rays. So, thinking in three dimensions, a spot indicates an intersection between adjacent cones that represent the maximum dispersion of each set of rays. An array of spots thus defines sets of intersections of conical pencils of rays whose origins should be in the crystalline plane in which the atoms that are deflecting the beams lie. The cones are geometrical constructs that turn the 2D pattern into a 3D set of pointers that locate the planes in which the atoms lie.

Bragg learned to produce his own X-ray photographs. He transformed these into diagrams by pricking through the photos onto paper on which he then marked the size of the spots. He then drew ellipses through them **[Fig. 9C]**. The ellipses represent sections of the conical pencils of rays that converge inside the crystal at a point where the atoms lie. Bragg realized that by varying the distance of the plate from the source he could also work out the geometry of the action of the crystal on the X-ray beam **[Fig. 10A]**. Similarly, varying the angle of incidence by moving the crystal produced displacements and distortions which could, when actively 'read' in terms of this geometry, provide additional information about the relative positions of the crystal planes (Bragg 1914A: 9).

Bragg subsequently called this 'the method of stereographic projection' because the 2D pattern of spots is reconstructed as a 3D system of cones. Each cone points back into the photographic plate to atomic points in intersecting planes of the crystal. This reconstruction turns a pattern of dots on the plate into a representation of a 3D structure of X-ray beams created by two physical processes, diffraction of the X-rays by the crystal lattice and subsequent interference between diffracted rays. He went on to develop a method of measuring the intensity of the deflected rays producing each spot by adapting an optical spectrometer that deflected X-rays to ionize gas in a chamber connected to an electroscope. Ionizing action was measured as electrostatic charge, quantifying the action produced by a specific ray. This established a relationship between the beam intensity and the angle of deflection (Bragg 1913B; 1914B). The X-ray spectroscope substituted a precise measure of intensity for Bragg's estimated spot magnitude. This precision enabled him to calculate distances between planes and from these, relative positions of atoms in the crystal planes (Bragg & Bragg 1913). Here the physical meaning of the measured quantities is given by a simplified, visualized process model of how an X-ray interacts with and is dispersed by a crystal lattice. The accuracy of the X-ray spectrometer method allowed Bragg to narrow possible lattices down to two or even one structure. Nevertheless, he preferred the stereographic method because the data produced, like the spots in the X-ray patterns, have physical meaning only in the context of the patterns (Bragg 1933: 30).

This model is based on the original analogy between a lattice and a diffraction grating but the full explanation combines several distinct models: geometrical constructs which define crystal types (according to the type of symmetry they display), geometrical constructs which describe how the X-rays will behave in the crystal, mathematical models of the interference of deflected rays and further geometrical constructs which relate the phenomenology (patterns of spots and sizes of spots expressed as measured intensities) to the diffraction grating model, via the model of interference. Given this complexity, it is not surprising that Bragg devised a simple way of demonstrating these relationships. He simulated the optical process postulated by the theory using polished, reflecting rods arranged symmetrically around but diverging from a central axis (Bragg 1933: 25, fig. 19). As can be seen in **Fig. 10B** the rods deflect light to form shadow patterns similar to those in the X-ray images. Like the paleontologists' shadow-projection method and Teutsch's liver-process simulation, Bragg's device makes it easy to conduct and to understand complex transformations between 2D patterns and 3D models of processes that produce those patterns. As he moved from an interpretation of the phenomenology of von Laue's X-rays toward a coherent explanation of key features of those patterns, Bragg moved back and forth between simple and complex visualizations and

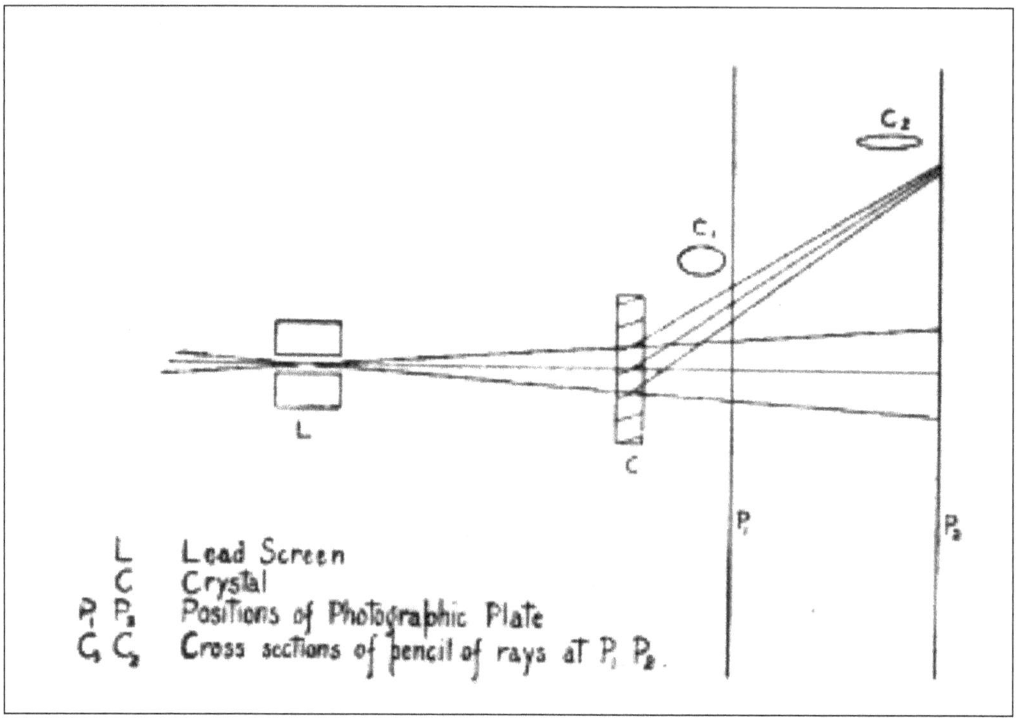

A

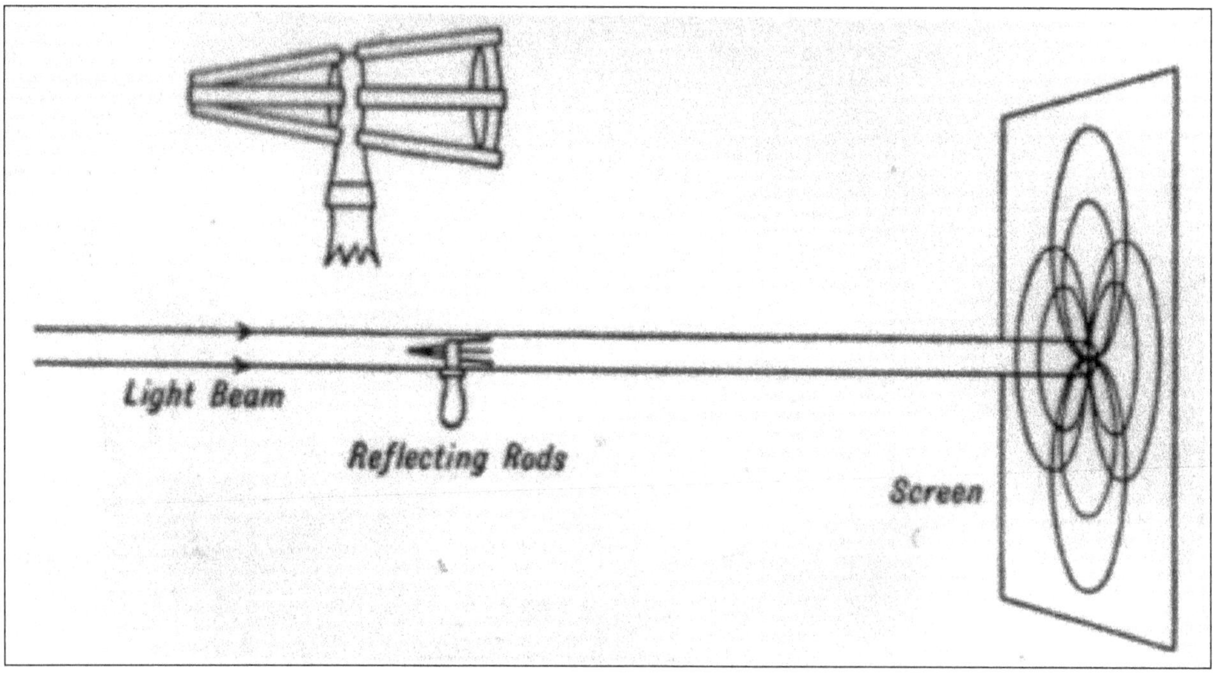

B

Fig. 10. *A. Bragg's earliest diagram of the diffraction of X-rays by a crystal (after Bragg 1913: fig. 2); B. The model demonstrating how diffraction can produce the elliptical patterns that correspond to positions of spots on the X-ray photographs such as 9A (after Bragg 1933: fig. 19).*

between mental and physical representations, in the same way that we have seen in the other cases.

Conclusion

David Hockney (2001) recently revived the thesis that the graphic arts owe much to imaging techniques developed in other contexts. By demonstrating how light rays reconstruct on the retina an exact (albeit inverted) replica of an external scene, the camera obscura became far more than an imaging technology. It has dominated science and philosophy as an explanation of how the external world is known to the mind's eye (Alpers 1983; Baxandall 1985), an epistemological engine which placed the viridicality of mental images beyond question for several centuries (Ihde 2000). The optical metaphor of the camera obscura still lends credibility to processes of visualizing hidden structures as diverse as of crystals, visceral organs and extinct arthropods. Biologists and chemists modelling complex molecules still quote da Vinci's observation that 'the eye [...] is the chief means whereby the understanding may appreciate the works of nature' (Olson & Goodsell 1992: 44). Despite the continued appeal of visual perception as a metaphor for intellectual comprehension, the camera obscura fails as an explanation of how 'nature' gets into 'the mind's eye' because it bypasses two key features of our use of visual imagination. One is the active, dynamic character of perception, much studied by psychologists. This chapter has focused on the other key feature: our use of many objects, procedures and technologies to image our experience and communicate what we imagine. Attending to the function of different kinds of visual object shows how these techniques relate visual, verbal and other aspects of the problem of envisioning an explanation. I suggested earlier that Albert Dürer's drawing frame offers a better understanding of what is required for visualization because it reminds us that we design and use technologies to order and inform our perception. Thus, projecting shadows of 3D fossil models to verify informal 'mental' projections made in constructing 3D model from patterns (as in **Fig. 3A** and **Fig. 3B**) has its counterpart in Bragg's physical illustration of the analogy between light and X-rays **[Fig. 10B]**. Cognitive artefacts such as these make features of creative visual thinking accessible to us. These same features are exploited by contemporary computer visualization methods.

The way in which a science is practised reflects our cognitive makeup just as it reflects our social, political and other propensities. By comparing methods across domains we have identified some features of human reasoning that combine visual with non-visual elements. These include 2D images such as photographs, visualizations of phenomena (diagrams, plots, graphs) and visual representations of theories about the phenomena (3D structures such as physical stacks of data plots and physical models). All are visual, yet each is a very different type of thing. A diagrammatic abstraction from a photograph (whether of a fossil or an X-ray) is a move from a barely interpreted source to an informative construct. This 'move' is motivated by the desire to understand. It is informed by expert (often tacit) knowledge about indicative features which need to be preserved or highlighted in the diagram. My examples show that integrating many images into structural and process models overcomes spatial or temporal discontinuity and sometimes both together. The ability to move between two, three, and four dimensions is what structures the play of interpretation and explanation in many scientific fields. Diagrams and process models also combine different sensory modalities and symbol systems, through the use of labels, colours, legends, or index numbers. These objects cannot be purely visual (as photographs are) because their role is to introduce and integrate several kinds of knowledge in order to produce an explanation. Examples are Bragg's analogy between X-ray diffraction by a 3D crystal and optical diffraction by a 2D grating and, in paleontology, knowledge about the anatomy and physiology of known life forms. These examples show that visual inference itself has a patterned character. This suggests a profound similarity between art and science. The methods of structuring perception in science guide visual imagination rather than the artist's hand yet they, too, inform and discipline perception in order to convey understanding.

Bibliography

Alpers, S. 1983. *The Art of Describing*, Chicago: Chicago University Press.

Ball, P. 1999. *The Self-Made Tapestry: Pattern Formation in Nature*, Oxford: Oxford University Press.

Barry, A. M. 1997. *Visual Intelligence: Perception, Image and Manipulation in Visual Communication*, Albany: SUNY Press.

Baxandall, M. 1985. *Patterns of Intention*, New Haven: Yale University Press.

Bragg, W. H. & Bragg, W. L. 1913. "The reflection of X-rays by crystals", *Proceedings of the Royal Society of London, Series A* 88: 428-438.

Bragg, W. L. 1913A. "The diffraction of short electromagnetic waves by a crystal", *Proceedings of the Cambridge Philosophical Society* 17: 43-57.

Bragg, W. L. 1913B. "The structure of some crystals as indicated by their diffraction of X-rays", *Proceedings of the Royal Society of London, Series A* 89: 248-277.

Bragg, W. L. 1914A. "X-rays and crystals", *Journal of the Roentgen Society* 10: 1-12.

Bragg, W. L. 1914B. "The analysis of crystals by the X-ray spectrometer", *Proceedings of the Royal Society of London, Series A* 89: 468-489.

Bragg, W. L. 1933. *The Crystalline State: a General Survey*, London: Bell.

Briggs, D. & Collins, D. 1988. "A Middle Cambrian chelicerate from Mount Stephen, British Columbia", *Palaeontology* 31: 779-798.

Briggs, D. & Conway Morris, S. 1983. "New Burgess shale fossil sites reveal middle Cambrian faunal complex", *Science* 222: 163-167.

Briggs, D. & Williams, S. H. 1981. "The restoration of flattened fossils", *Lethaia* 14: 157-164.

Bruton, D. L. 1981. "The arthropod Sidneyia inexpectans, Middle Cambrian, Burgess Shale, British Columbia", *Philosophical Transactions of the Royal Society of London, Series B* 295: 619-656.

Bruton, D. L. & Whittington, H. B. 1983. "Emeraldella and Leanchoilia, two arthropods from the Burgess Shale, British Columbia", *Philosophical Transactions of the Royal Society of London, Series B* 300: 553-585.

Choi, C. 2003. "Replacement organs, hot off the press", *New Scientist* 180 (25 January): 16.

Conway Morris, S. 1979. "Middle Cambrian polychaetes from the Burgess shale of British Columbia", *Philosophical Transactions of the Royal Society of London, Series B* 285: 227-274.

Crick, F. & Watson, J. 1953. "Molecular structure of nucleic acids", *Nature* 171 (25 April): 737-739.

Darius, J. 1984. *Beyond Vision: One Hundred Historic Scientific Photographs*, Oxford: Oxford University Press.

Doveton, J. H. 1979. "Numerical methods for the reconstruction of fossil material in three dimensions", *Geological Magazine* 116: 215-226.

Ferguson, E. S. 1992. *Engineering and the Mind's Eye*, Cambridge: MIT Press.

Field, J. V. & James, F. A. J. L. 1998 (eds.). *Science and the Visual*, British Journal for the History of Science 31, London: The British Society for the History of Science.

Ford, B. 1992. *Images of Science: a History of Scientific Illustration*, London: British Library.

Goldschmidt, G. 1991. "The dialectics of sketching", *Creativity Research Journal* 4: 123-143.

Gooding, D. C. 1992. "Mathematics and method in Faraday's experiments", *Physis* 29: 121-147.

Gooding, D. C. 1989. "Magnetic curves and the magnetic field: experimentation and representation in the history of a theory", in D. C. Gooding, T. Pinch & S. Schaffer (eds.), *The Uses of Experiment*, Cambridge: Cambridge University Press: 183-223.

Gooding, D. C. 1990. *Experiment and the Making of Meaning*, Dordrecht: Kluwer Academic.

Gooding, D. C. 2004. "Cognition, construction and culture: visual theories in the sciences", *Journal of Cognition and Culture* 4: 551-593.

Gould, S. 1989. *Wonderful Life: the Burgess Shale and the Nature of History*, London: Penguin.

Hammond, J. H. & Austin, J. 1987. *The Camera Lucida in Art and Science*, Bristol: Institute of Physics and Hilger.

Hockney, D. 2001. *Secret Knowledge: Rediscovering the Lost Techniques of the Old Masters*, London: Thames and Hudson.

Ihde, I. 2000. "Epistemology Engines", *Nature* 406 (6 July): 21.

Jones, C. & Galison, P. 1998 (eds.). *Picturing Science: Producing Art*, New York and London: Routledge.

Kelly, M. 1995. "Whitehall's superconductor", *Times Higher Education Supplement* (September 29): 6.

Kemp, M. 2000. *Visualisations: the Nature book of Art and Science*, Oxford: Oxford University Press.

Lynch, M. & Woolgar, S. 1990 (eds.). *Representation in Scientific Practice*, Cambridge: MIT Press.

Lynnerup, N., Hjalgrim, H., Nielsen, L., Gregersen, H. & Thuesen, I. 1997. "Non-invasive archaeology of skeletal material by CT scanning and three-dimensional reconstruction", *International Journal of Osteoarchaeology* 7: 91-94.

Martin, T. 1932 (ed.). *Faraday's Diary*, vol. 1, London: Bell.

Mazzolini, R. 1993 (ed.). *Non-verbal Communication in Science Prior to 1900*, Florence: Olschki.

Miller, A. I. 2001. *Einstein-Picasso: Space, Time and the Beauty That Causes Havoc*, New York: Basic Books.

Mithen, S. 2002. "Human evolution and the cognitive basis of science", in P. Carruthers, P. Stich & M. Siegal (eds.), *The Cognitive Basis of Science*, Cambridge: Cambridge University Press: 23-40.

Olson, A. & Goodsell, D. 1992. "Visualizing biological molecules", *Scientific American* 267: 44-51.

Robin, H. 1992. *The Scientific Image from Cave to Computer*, New York: Abrams.

Teutsch, H. 1988. "Regionality of glucose-6-phosphate hydrolysis in the liver lobule of the rat", *Hepatology* 8: 311-317.

Teutsch, H. 2004. "Modular design of the liver of the rat", in G. Malcolm (ed.), *Multidisciplinary Studies of Visual Representations and Intrepretations*, Amsterdam: Elsevier: 63-67.

Teutsch, H., Shuerfeld, D. & Groezinger, E. 1999. "Three-dimensional reconstruction of parenchymal units in the liver of the rat", *Hepatology* 29: 494-505.

Teutsch, H., Altemus, S., Gerlach-Arbeiter, S. & Kyander-Teutsch, T. 1992. "Distribution of 3-hydroxybutyrate dehydrogenase in primary lobules of rat liver", *Journal of Histochemistry and Cytochemistry* 40: 213-219.

Trumpler, M. 1997. "Converging images: techniques of intervention and forms of representation of sodium-channel proteins in nerve cell membranes", *Journal of History of Biology* 30: 55-89.

Tweney, R. 1992. "Stopping time: Faraday and the scientific creation of perceptual order", *Physis* 29: 149-164.

Veltman, K. H. & Keele, K. D. 1986. *Linear Perspective and the Visual Dimensions of Science and Art*, Munich: Deutscher Kunstverlag.

Whittington, H. B. 1985. *The Burgess Shale*, New Haven: Yale University Press.

Chapter 2

Virtual archaeology: communication in 3D and ecological thinking

In the digital global era, the quantity of information surrounding us is constantly increasing. In a similar vein, 3D models in archaeology are becoming more and more complex, confronting archaeologists with an enormous amount of information. This paper discusses the process by which analogical information deriving from archaeological fieldwork is transformed into digital information after excavation. 3D information is regarded as the core of the knowledge process, because it creates feedback, then cybernetic difference, among the interactor, the scientist and the ecosystem. It is argued that Virtual Reality (both offline and online) represents the ideal ecosystem, which is able to host top-down and bottom-up processes of knowledge and communication.

Maurizio Forte

Istituto per le Tecnologie Applicate ai Beni Culturali, Consiglio Nazionale delle Ricerche, Italy

Introduction

> Information presupposes something unexpected and thus is directly connected to the improbable. In other words, information is inversely proportional to probability (Taylor 2005: 41).

In the era of digital globalization and of postmodernism, the daily bombardment of information has reached unimagined levels. We are surrounded by information that generates noise first, and then (if we are lucky) understanding. This dramatic growth of information generates greater complexity as 'mind is distributed in the world' (Taylor 2005: 295). It is not clear that an excess of information existing on the margins of chaos can create understanding, and, if it does, we must create a suitable mechanism for its communication. 'Without context, there is no communication,' as Bateson (1972: 402) taught us; and without communication, there can be no understanding. The sciences of antiquity cannot escape from this dynamic of complexity. On their own margins of chaos they must find an interdisciplinary way to transmit and communicate knowledge. If the process from understanding/research to communication becomes fragmented or starts to evolve on parallel tracks, we inevitably lose information on the way, and we weaken the social impact of research.

I believe that this epistemological consideration applies just as well to archaeology as to any other field. In archaeology the research path (typically starting with fieldwork) results in the publication of only a small part of what has been studied and, measured in terms of understanding, even a smaller fraction. To this problem may be added the scant 'transparency' of the analytical process of study, or the difficulty of making information available which has contributed to the final interpretation. It is clearly important for

This paper is the result of theoretical research by the team of the Virtual Heritage Lab, which I am fortunate to direct. I hereby express my thanks to the entire staff, including: Carlo Camporesi, Marco Di Ioia, Fabrizio Galeazzi, Alessia Moro, Augusto Palombini, Sofia Pescarin, Eva Pietroni, Bartolomeo Trabassi, Valentina Vassallo, and Lola Vico. The translation from the Italian is by Bernard Frischer.

interpretation to validate the pathway understanding-communication; and it is equally important to create a cybernetic syntax, step-by-step, ideally from one digital ontology to another. We may also note that the mere digitization of archaeological research does not lead to miraculous results, nor should it give rise to exaggerated expectations (the so-called 'cool' factor). But it remains a fact that we must soon expect to have information that is many times greater than that seen in recent decades. More information means more complexity, more complexity means more steps in arriving at understanding. So what should we expect the future to bring the field of archaeology?

The speed at which technology evolves is often greater than the methodological progress of many disciplines, especially those in the humanities. This means that those responsible for undergraduate and graduate studies find it hard to keep pace with the multidisciplinary use of digital technologies, and this causes a certain lack of coordination between methodologies and digital technologies.

If we consider this quantitative and qualitative jump in information, in archaeology the highest percentage is alphanumeric, next come 2D maps and surfaces, and 3D data make up the smallest percentage. It is useful to recall how in the 1980s and 1990s academic archaeologists put up great resistance (in part still active today) to modelling and visualization of 3D data and contexts, as if the third dimension represented some kind of aesthetic fantasy and information that is basically superfluous and dispensable for scientific use. In our opinion, people holding this point of view have been led astray by some out-of-date commonplaces: a 3D model can lead to a certain aesthetic inventiveness to the detriment of content; the techniques of 3D modelling/reproduction in the past were very expensive; the technology policies of some multinational software companies were, with a few notable exceptions, based on the assumption that the market niche of 3D (one thinks here of GIS, for example) was small and large investments were thus unattractive. Finally, 3D reconstruction was thought appropriate for didactic applications, or better it was interpreted as part of the process of dissemination, not discovery, of information. 3D was thus relegated to the task of illustrating knowledge already gained once serious scientific investigation had been concluded. It is no accident that a high percentage of the reconstructions using computer graphics in the 1990s were created without taking into account detailed spatial and philological data.

When the term 'virtual archaeology' was introduced and popularized (Forte 1996), most academics reacted to it with extreme caution, lack of understanding, or with hostile polemics, both for terminological reasons and, especially, because of the difficulty (which one could, indeed, sympathize with) of imaging the scientific (and not just the didactic) potential of 3D worlds, both those reconstructed *ex novo* ('virtual antiquity') and those documenting the current state of archaeological remains ('observed antiquity'). I believe that this diffidence was motivated by the difficulty of imagining the 3D model as an interactive, a multimodal, and—especially—a holistic container of information, a whole greater than the sum of its parts. Indeed there is no doubt that a 3D model, be it of a landscape or of a monument, can add information and thus insight to what we already know, at least if the model is correctly built. In **Plate 1**, for example, is shown the cybermap of the Virtual Reality (hereafter VR) system of the Scrovegni Chapel in Padua. This 3D navigable map represents the georeferenced information provided by the model. The 3D geometric model of the cybermap shows by means of different forms and colours the relationships that develop at every multimedia node/theme within the system: iconography, style, light, colour, composition, and space (Forte *et al.* 2002). In this case, the cybermap seeks to demonstrate that information, if associated with conceptual-spatial models, is a better instructional tool than are traditional means (scholarly lectures, papers, textbook descriptions, etc.). That is to say, in a VR system of this kind, the interaction occurs in x, y, z coordinates and this leads to the creation of a mental map of the monument which subsequently grows upon contact with the actual monument. The cybermap demonstrates in an eloquent way how the third dimension permits us to build a new cognitive geometry of the cultural artefact, especially if, as in this case, it is associated with narrative and communicative sequences.

The balance sheet of the last 20 years of archaeological research on the application of the third dimension as a research tool is fairly depressing: the use of 3D representations has been completely random and thus has not had a great impact on the development of research methodologies and protocols. Only rarely is adequate time and attention paid to them in university courses and programs of study. There are, of course, a few courageous exceptions, but to the extent that 3D has made it into the curriculum, it has been at the level of short, postgraduate training courses. As for fieldwork, here the picture is much the same: the use of 3D technologies for data capture, analysis, and reconstruction is still considered experimental and is thus still quite rare. In the best of circumstances, 3D is used to represent data collected by hand and in two dimensions and/or integrating spatial information that is either not correct or simply invented. This leads to a first and complete separation between knowledge acquisition and knowledge communication, a sequence we hold to be the cybernetic vehicle necessary for cultural transmission. If the 3D world constructs its own holistic models based on unreliable or hard-to-test information, then the result in archaeological methodology is a lack of transparency as well as a lack of semiotic superpositioning of the sources of knowledge. To give one example, it is one thing to create a 3D model of a site drawn manually on a plan, and it is quite another to do so on the basis of a corresponding point cloud of data points collected by a laser scanner or by some other digital technology.

The issue is not trivial because the ontology of archaeological information, or the cybernetics of archaeology, refers to all the interconnective relationships which the datum produces, the code (or the 'map', as Bateson [1972], calls it) of transmission, and its transmittability. Because it depends on interrelationships, by its very nature information cannot be neutral with respect to how it is processed and perceived. It follows that the process of knowledge and communication have to be unified and represented by a single vector. Thus, from the first phases of data acquisition in the field, the technical methodologies and technologies that we use, influence in a decisive way all the subsequent phases of interpretation and communication. In the light of these considerations, what is the relationship between information and representation? How much information does a digital model contain? What sorts of and how many ontologies ought to be chosen to permit an acceptable transmittability? These and many other questions on related topics take on a certain urgency because they relate directly to the loss of information from understanding, learning, and the transmittability of culture.

Indeed, our ability to transmit culture depends on a model which combines on the same axis processes of understanding and communication. Thus, the questions which we pose in a phase of bottom-up knowledge (for example, in an archaeological excavation) will influence the top-down phases of interpretation, or the mental patterns (for example, a comparative analysis and reconstruction of models). From this derives the need to interconnect the top-down processes with the bottom-up in accordance with a reciprocal systemic interaction, for example in a virtual space where both sequences can coexist. If we peremptorily separate knowledge and communication, we risk losing information along the way, reducing the relationships that are constructed between acquisition/input and transmission/output.

Archaeological communication ought to be understood as a process of validation of the entire cognitive process of understanding and not as a simple addendum to research, or as a dispensable compendium of data. But the methodological tradition which we inherit has almost always separated the realm of fieldwork, reports, and publications from the realm of cultural communication, which is too often popularized and marginalized under the vague term 'didactic'. To the contrary, the grand challenge posed by digital technologies is to integrate the ontologies of data into a single process: digital acquisition, digital processing, digital communication (online and offline). Every conceivable segmentation of this process leads to a loss of data and of knowledge and to a diminution of the social impact of research: what is not perceived cannot be communicated. Moreover, communication often is marginalized precisely because it ought to face the difficult challenge of proposing hypotheses of reconstructing the ancient world, harmonizing the observed and observable data within models that seem to be arbitrary. The lack of scientific communication causes the discipline of archaeology to have less social import than it might otherwise have, causing a sort of cultural solipsism and low level of transmittability.

Once the phase of the technological 'wow factor' has passed—i.e. the moment in which the aesthetics of models seemed to have a higher priority than the accuracy and quantity of the information they conveyed—we enter into the current phase in which researchers must raise epistemological questions to enable their discipline to advance methodologically. The quantity of models (geometric, epistemological, cultural, spatial, etc.) which digital technologies have been able to produce is impressive and grows at a constantly increasing rate. This phenomenon cannot be culturally digested without suitable methodological and theoretical reflections. It is the purpose of this paper to offer a sketch of a possible starting point for such reflections.

Methodology of archaeological research

One of the indisputable results of multidisciplinarity in archaeology is the continual posing of new questions about research methodology and the use of applied technologies. It is difficult to construct complex ontologies of data if research does not ask new questions. Information per se does not create knowledge, but it constitutes its precondition in accordance with a process of selection: 'selection filters the noise and reveals at the same time the information, channeling it into patterns that will result in understanding' (Taylor 2005: 261). The path from understanding to communication is thus selective regarding information and propaedeutic regarding the dissemination and transmission of culture. To select information we must process it in accordance with a valid sequence of acquisition, modelling, representation, and communication. In this sense it is useful to distinguish between accumulated (i.e. not selected) knowledge and the quality of perceived (selected) information. The indiscriminate accumulation and growth of databases, catalogues, and geometric data (one thinks of the millions of points in point clouds created by laser scanners) present serious problems of information management and of knowledge which concern the relationships between data and perceptions.

In the archaeology of landscapes, for example, the reconstruction of the ancient landscape presents a focal and often unsolved problem precisely because the data are too sketchy and the analysis of the territory does not pose questions appropriate to the study of ecosystems but remains limited solely to human activities. In contrast, if one analyzes the landscape as an organism, relationships and activities come to light which would have otherwise not appeared in other contexts. If we do not raise the 'right' research questions, it is obvious that we do not have data which are adequate to create reconstructive models.

So, what happens to the pathway leading from archaeological knowledge to communication? If in the phase of input/research the right questions are not asked, the phase of output/communication will necessarily be lacunose and will not support an adequate monitoring of the path of understanding, following the progressive transformation of the various ontologies of information. Here we will discuss briefly these issues in relation to some themes treated elsewhere in this volume: the relationship between knowledge and communication, the third dimension and learning through virtual technology, and the relationship between 3D digital technologies and methodologies of archaeological research.

In the history of archaeological research and, for instance, in the context of Italian cultural policy (see Settis 2002) we always encounter a clear-cut distinction between what is considered a process of research/understanding and a process of communication. The

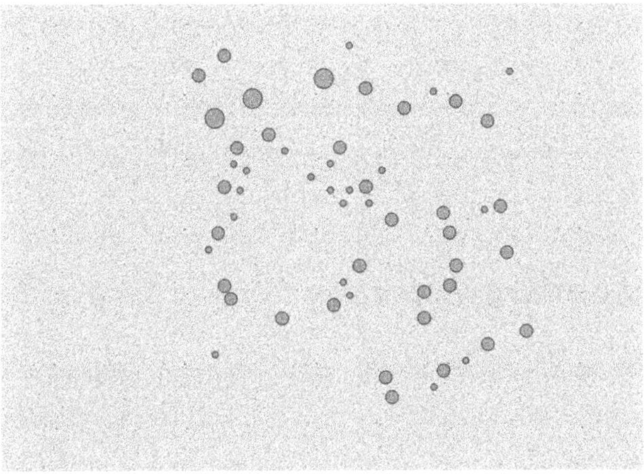

Fig. 2. *Excavation plan of a structure with stake holes attributable to a hut (bottom-up phase).*

processes of understanding have been considered the basis of scientific research and include the interpretative phase and the phase in which information is processed. The modes of acquiring and processing of data influence, in a systematic way, the rules of understanding and contribute to the dialectic of knowledge. But cultural policies aiming to clearly differentiate the realms of understanding and communication are doomed to failure, and we have seen examples of this recently.

Bottom-up and top-down

The activity of archaeological research follows rules of the types bottom-up and top-down. In fieldwork, the activity of understanding starts from the lowest level (bottom-up) insofar as precognitive perception is addressed in the identification of forms, patterns, crop-marks, structures, etc., which come to light in the course of archaeological investigation. The bottom-up process follows rules of 'pattern recognition', i.e. it identifies borders, forms, and outlines in such as way as to unite mentally the residual traces on the ground to the point where a (stratigraphic, structural, taxonomic etc.) map can be created **[Figs. 2-3]**. This activity produces discrete (topographical, excavation etc.) maps, basically composed of vectors, lines, and polylines which presuppose interpretative actions and logics of perception. In contrast, the process of interpretation, which follows top-down rules, functions from high to low, according to the mental patterns which our cognitive experience uses as elements of comparison. For example, in **Fig. 2** we have the plan of circular forms which, in the bottom-up phase are correlated to cultural forms in order to be later represented and reconstructed (top-down). In **Fig. 3**, as a result of the top-down phase (which affects mental models) the morphology of the structure is identified according to two possible interpretations: two huts with different shapes, or a single rectangular structure with an entrance oriented to the northeast. The bottom-up phase of research, especially in the case of archaeological research, is very delicate because it results in the first set of information (often with destructive consequences for the stratigraphy) and hence is propaedeutic to understanding. It extrapolates from the chaos/noise of the information a cybernetic pattern which becomes fundamental for the top-down phase. Next follows the bottom-up phase of survey which should be as careful as possible and concerned to show and validate all the relationships useful for creation of the mental map.

From this discussion we can infer that archaeological understanding is a process of interaction between bottom-up and top-down rules. The construction of cybernetic maps as a result of this interaction constructs codified information which, in the end, can be transmitted. The transmission then takes place through publication tools that are both linear (books, paper, exhibitions etc.) and non-linear or reticular (multimedia, web, VR). In the process of standardization of archaeological data destined to be published, there is no doubt that a hiatus is created between what we call knowledge (or the scientific knowledge codified for a few experts) and that which we call communication (information shared by and codified for the public). The problem with digital artefacts, as has been correctly seen by Settis (2002), is that starting from the second half of the 1980s, they have been used in attempts to resolve the problem structurally with an exaggerated technological inventiveness which has not led to positive results. Digital artefacts have mainly been created purely with the goal of archiving knowledge (but in a retrograde and only pseudo-standardized way) and not with the aim of the multidisciplinary virtualization of information. Thus, on the one hand researchers have undertaken the creation of enormous databases, but, on the other hand, they have delegated to multimedia the task of transmitting cultural information that has been 'popularized' for didactic use. Here, again, we find the two realms of knowledge and communication to be distinct. The multimedia products have too often followed the model of linear media, translating into digital format the semiotic formulae of print media with little added value from the digital per se.

It is clear at this point that the above mentioned problem of digital artefacts has generated no little confusion: in what way, then, do we ask of archaeological communication that it provide the information gathered from research? Is a strict line of demarcation really needed between knowledge and communication? To have concrete and far-reaching results from the application of digital technology to archaeology, it is indispensable to launch a new cultural policy and a new policy for scientific research. The methodology of research ought to offer an important space for discussion to cybernetic archaeology, in the etymological sense of the term. Without adequate epistemological reflection, there can be neither a methodology incorporating a theory of information nor an absolute cognitive value of technology. According to Bateson's cybernetics, context does not exist without communication, without an exchange of information. We must thus create new codes, new maps, new itineraries of knowledge. The factor of transmittability of culture will depend in a massive way on digital technologies.

The third dimension

Three-dimensionality is the geometric property to represent and describe space with three coordinates: the perception of volumes, the scope and depth of field indicate the properties of the environment that we want to describe. Our mind interprets the world in three dimensions by means of a system combining perception and sensation.

> The senses, as Locke well knew, are without doubt the gates and windows of our mind through which passes each new piece of information; there exist no thoughts, ideas or concepts that do not originally come from the sensory stimuli of our body. (Humphrey 1998: 77).

Studies of the multisensory nature of the human body have amply demonstrated that the perception of three-dimensionality involves not only vision (Humphrey 1998: 77), but that vision can even be absent. In this context two opposite situations have been

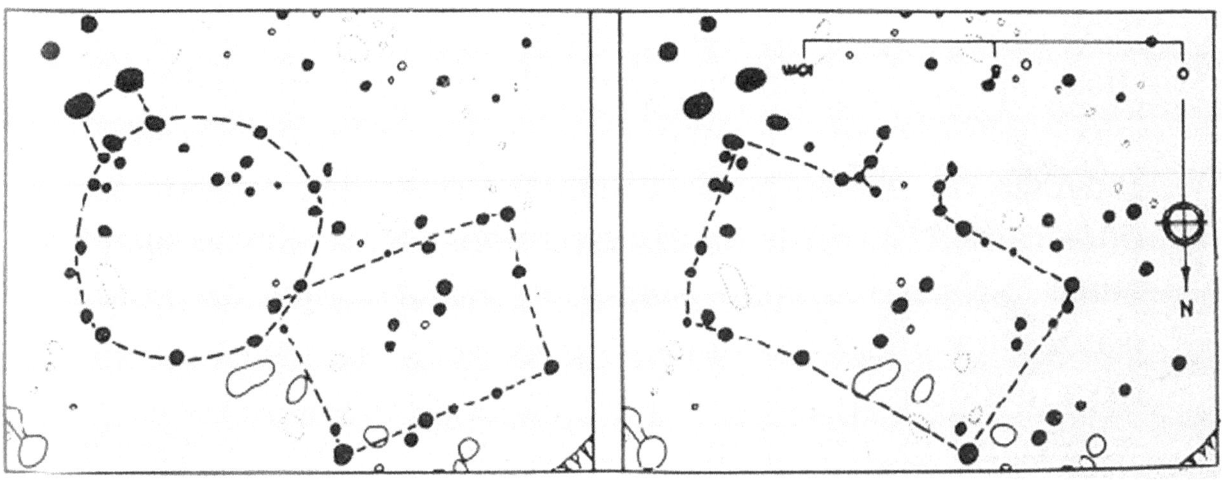

Fig. 3. *Possible interpretations of the structure in Fig. 2 correlated to two different forms of huts (rectangular and circular) or to a single hut with a small access dromos (top-down phase).*

distinguished: normal vision and cutaneous vision. The latter is possible only through vibrations on the skin (Humphrey 1998: 90-91). Experiments undertaken on blind subjects have shown that they can gather detailed information about external space and achieve 3D perception (Humphrey 1998). This research shows how essential three-dimensionality is for our understanding of the external environment, even in the absence of sight. Our system of interpreting the world is based on rules that are experiential, genetic, and illusory in terms of mental reassembly in which the depth of space and its volumes constitute the main feature.

If our more profound knowledge of the environment starts from the perception of the spatial coordinates and from the third dimension, a digital 3D ecosystem able to simulate these rules ought to be able to communicate more information and, especially, ought to accelerate the process of learning. The modes of perception and mental representation of models contribute to the construction of our knowledge of the world.

If very sophisticated instrumentation, such as laser scanners, captures thousands of points per second, are we really able to perceive this enormous quantity of information? And do these models communicate knowledge because they have a geometry made of millions of faces or because their representation stimulates the construction of mental maps? Or because of both? In **Plates 4-5** we have represented two versions of the 3D model of a wall of the Roman imperial period: to the left is the geometry of 46,145 polygons created by a point cloud captured with a laser, while on the right is the geometry of the model reduced to 1,237 polygons, with the aid of normal mapping.

Visual perception of the two models is practically identical, given the fact that we construct a mental map without any significant differences. If, on the other hand, we wanted to make a detailed analysis of the geometry of the model (structural calculations, statics etc.) we would have to make use of the more complex version generated by the laser scanner. The normal map is a map of RGB colour which defines for each point the effects of the reflection of light on the surface (by means of the normals). 'Normal' in this sense refers to normal mathematics, which defines the direction of a vector. This involves techniques frequently used in videogames and VR applications: first, one creates a very detailed model using a large number of polygons. Then, one passes to a simplified model with far fewer polygons. The differences between the two models are calculated and transformed into a texture (the normal map) which incorporates a good part of the detail which is lost in the simplification of the original model. The normal map is then applied to the simplified model, and the final result is very similar to the model with more polygons. In conclusion, the normal maps simulate the impression of a 3D surface, such as a relief.

This relief will not project any shadow and will not cover other objects. If the angle of the camera is too flat on the surfaces, one will note that the surfaces are not really in relief. This example is useful for understanding that the transfer of digital information depends both on the techniques of representation/processing and on the use of the model itself, insofar as no communicative model exists a priori. If we increase the interactivity of the model we will have an experiential cognition determined by feedback, given the fact that coherent cognitive interpretation depends in good part on rules of illusion that are spatial, perceptual, and visual. But why is it useful to project information into a 3D space? A 3D model offers a holistic perspective of the world because it synthesizes different qualities of information into a whole that is greater than the sum of its parts. In 2000-2001 we created the prototype of a VR system dedicated to information relating to the preservation and restoration of the House of the Vettii in Pompeii. The connectedness of the data (microscopic, archaeometric, thermographic, wear-and-tear analysis etc.) allowed the researcher to interact with the data in a 3D space. In this way, all the data were entirely spatialized and usable in real time. The future scope of projects such as this that collate information in 3D space will help restorers, conservators, and archaeologists. It will enable them to make their diagnoses after having visualized and spatialized all the knowledge collected about the monument and its genetic-archaeometric structure.

In conclusion, we see the following as the main foci of 3D cybernetics:

Difference. Representation in three dimensions produces great difference in a cybernetic sense, i.e. interacting with 3D data we develop a greater exchange with the cybernetic ecosystem. According to the principles of cybernetics, learning arises through difference.

Spatial relationships. 3D space visualizes, models and develops relationships not otherwise obvious.

Multi-commensurability. 3D modes of interaction induce our cognitive system to adapt itself to spatial reference coordinates, assimilating scale and proportions to them.

Light. Movement in three dimensions brings a change of the state of luminosity and shadowing. Different conditions of light give rise to a more complex reading of information and increase our faculties for learning about an environment.

Geometry. The greater geometric complexity of a space determines a more advanced analytical faculty.

Transparency. The reconstructive process of information can be illustrated and refuted by a sequence of 3D worlds and maps superimposed over each other.

Multimodality. A 3D world is suited to a multimodal and multisensorial form of interaction. The modes of perception, sensation and interaction determine learning.

Connectivity. Each piece of information spatialized in three dimensions multiplies its own model of communication in a conceptual network of associations.

Eureka!

A 3D model, be it individual or belonging to a VR system, ought also to be considered a dynamic process, i.e. dependent on interaction and feedback: in action and in 3D behaviour we increase the 'difference' in a cybernetic sense, thus we learn more and faster. The exchange between mind and model represents the key moment of interpretation: the image re-projected onto the retina is coded and interpreted by the mind; and it is in this precise instant that we become aware of it. In the top-down phase, mental processing classifies the interpretation with respect to experience and contextualizes it on the basis of our cultural background. In the dynamic characterization of a 3D model is thus implied, as noted above, an acquisition of a greater amount of information, a structured whole, a whole greater than the sum of its parts.

Learning is a process that is essentially dynamic (i.e. an exchange between the learner and his environment), and interpretation results from the dynamic between interaction and the recognition of information. In this regard we recall a paradigmatic experience: working on the reconstruction of the archaeological landscape of Aksum (CNR Project 2000), we used a panchromatic aerial photograph dating from the 1960s which we superimposed onto the digital terrain model. The same aerial photograph was systematically used by the archaeologists who worked for years on the ground and who had already identified numerous features that could be understood as possible ancient anthropic modifications of the terrain. Superimposing the photo in texture mapping the DTM, we simulated in real time a flight at low altitude. This simulation, through the dynamics of interaction, allowed the archaeologists to recognize some new anthropic features of the landscape which up to that moment they had not noticed or reported. Whence came this additional information, given the fact that the photograph remained the same? Can we speak of something the archaeologists had simply missed or of their insufficient experience in reading aerial photographs? Such reasons certainly would not be applicable in this case since the archaeologists had been working at Aksum for many years (M. Forte *et al.* 2001). The catalyst was identified as the 3D dynamic visualization, the multiple points of view offered by the simulation, and by the simulation of light and shadow in the virtual flight. The thus the difference in a cybernetic sense was determined by the dynamic nature of the model and by the process of interaction, from the holistic relationships of the model with the landscape and especially with the overlaid elements.

Another example of 3D cybernetic exchange was tried in the creation of a VR system of the Scrovegni Chapel (Forte *et al.* 2002), where a 3D cybermap was projected with the goal of representing the information and behaviour of the VR system, following an interface that was basically aniconic, i.e. the space without the images that characterize and contextualize it. In the case of the Scrovegni Chapel, the pictorial registers of Giotto which make up the monument's palimpsest of images constitute the primary source of literacy and learning both in the real world and in the virtual. If, in contrast to this, we use as metaphors of navigation the geometrical solids of the cybermap, we enter into intra-informational behaviour, i.e. we move in cybernetic hyperspace, in relationships that each feature of the map produces. The cybermap seeks to simulate, even if in a completely approximate way, the behaviour of the mind which proceeds by means of associations, hypertexts, cross-references etc.: each element of 3D space is interconnected and transmits the codes of the context to which it belongs.

From what we know about the activities of mirror neurons, the imitative process is a fundamental part of the dynamic of learning and refers to the way in which the mental images that we perceive take shape. The consciousness of action elsewhere produces an induced mental effect and from this the beginnings of knowledge arise. The awareness and the consciousness of information are key elements which distinguish the evolution of the human mind from that of the Neanderthals. We might call it the 'cognitive big bang', because it revolutionizes thought and from it presumably arises the aesthetic principle which constitutes the artefact. The mind of *Homo sapiens* in fact represents *in toto* all the faculties of knowledge, consciousness and transmittability of information and of codes. A recent book, *The Mind in the Cave* (Wilson-Lewis 2002), draws attention to the cognitive revolution brought about by prehistoric cave painting. Wilson-Lewis posits a vigorous aesthetic action in cave painting, aimed at reproducing 3D immersive effects that increase the perceptual feedback of those who are admitted to the rite or to its transmission/reprocessing. The cavern becomes the 3D projection of shamanic vision, the immersive world of experience codified by means of symbols of cultural transmission. The extraordinary examples of Lascaux, Altamira and of other African caves offer the traces of the first cognitive experiments in the translation of artistic codes and symbolic complexes, perhaps the world's first system of the symbolic construction of knowledge and of learning from structured iconic models. The environment of the cave was presumably chosen for its immersiveness, its elite status and for its ability to produce feedback, experiential narrative, 3D communication, relation affordances (see below for the meaning of this term). Here the relationships are not evoked to demonstrate the supernatural character of the experience but to understand the physical world by means of hyperreality, an informational increase in what is real. Understanding of the world occurs through a process of intermediation, the shaman, and the visionary representation of relationships not yet codified in the real world. The prehistoric pictures thus become the map of the natural world, the catalyst of new forms of knowledge and learning.

VR and learning

According to Fry, the great works of art attract us both at the dramatic or psychological level—for their figurative and narrative content—and on the plastic level or through their aesthetic content tied exclusively to the combination of forms and colors. But these two aspects, maintains Fry,

> [...] are often in competition, to the point where we are forced to focus on them separately [...]. In fact, it happens that we continually shift our attention forwards and backwards from one to the other so that the painting becomes familiar and then 'psychological factors become

> secondary and the plastic quality emerges in its fullness (Humphrey 1998: 74).

Learning and mental maps are thus created by exchanging information of difference with the environment and, in the case at hand, between the semiotics of the object and its formal properties: this exchange of information multiplies the feedback relationships (something Gibson [1998] calls 'affordance'). To study the dynamics of learning by means of VR systems could represent one of the grand challenges of the neurosciences and of new cultural media, but perhaps we do not yet know enough to formulate precise answers. But, first of all, what is VR? And what role might it play in the thread connecting knowledge and communication? Is it, then, the elusive map which corresponds to the territory? Does it constitute that which Bateson (1972; 1979) calls 'deutero-learning', the ability to learn to learn?

VR is generally defined as having the following essential properties: inclusiveness, interactivity, three-dimensionality, and movement in real time. We have already discussed elsewhere the epistemological relationship between the virtual, ecosystems, and cultural property (Forte 2000; 2003; Forte & Siliotti 1997). Here we will only add that the creation of a system of VR does not have as its primary objective the simulation of the real but a representation of knowledge by means of a multiplicity of relationships, of which reality is only one part (on the false distinction between the real and the virtual, see Levy 1995; 1998; 2001). In this sense, photorealism is also not considered by researchers to be an imitation of the real but as a perceptual-evocative catalyst. A photorealistic quality can increase our capacity to learn because it influences mental patterns through affordance (Gibson 1999), not because it is a replica of the real. One final consideration is that virtual space can host artificial life, and is thus for all intents and purposes an ecosystem in which the whole is greater than the sum of the parts, where information can become alive, autopoetic and self-organizing (Annunziato & Pierucci 2002; Maturana & Varela 1980). On the basis of this, VR constructs relationships or affordances (Gibson 1998). According to Gibson, affordance means the relational property entrusted to objects.

> For Gibson, information is already present in the stimulus array, in the stimulus as it presents itself directly to the subject. And information can be directly received by the subject without recourse to computational systems, information flows, or representational structures. Information makes sense for the organism that collects it directly from stimulus (there is a reference here to the theory of direct perception) in the form of affordances (Bozzi & Luccio in Gibson 1999: 13-14).

The concept of affordance seems to us to be able to designate rather well the feedback relationships suggested by the objects themselves, which can be experienced in the act of knowing the environment. An affordance could have a spatial, temporal, typological, functional, or behavioural relationship.

Can we thus imagine VR as a catalyst of learning or the cybernetic map of that territory of information so dear to Bateson (1972: 79)? How do we perceive information in a virtual space? These and many other questions are not easily answered, but they may have an initial explanation in some recent discoveries of neuroscience. The discovery of mirror neurons in the frontal lobes of macaques is one of the most important of the last decade; it has radically modified our understanding of the mind. It was discovered that the mirror neurons are active when the primates pursue certain tasks, but they are also activated when they observe another member of their group doing the same thing (Rizzolati *et al.* 1996; 2001). It was subsequently shown that a similar imitative system of observation/action exists in human beings: the mirror system might represent the primitive version or perhaps precursor in phylogeny of a heuristic simulation which could be the basis of 'mindreading'. The mirror neurons have played a fundamental role in the evolution of language, empathy and self-consciousness. Starting from the principle of imitative learning, the system of mirror neurons has contributed to the rapid transmission of cultural innovations, leaving out of consideration evolution that is solely genetic. Indeed, human social cognition contemplates the ability to read the mind which, in turn, constitutes a fundamental passageway of communication. Expressed in cybernetic terms, the activity of the mirror neurons produces a 'difference', i.e. the mind acquires information by means of a process of learning the difference between itself and its environment, in accordance with an ecology of thought. According to Bateson, the capacity of learning to learn can be defined as deutero-learning, while the construction of a map (in the cybernetic sense) is fundamental for codifying and understanding a territory (Bateson 1972; 1979).

Since VR represents an artificial environment of simulation and learning, is it possible to obtain the same behaviour of the mirror neurons in a virtual space? Through VR, can one imagine imitative behaviours able to accelerate or modify the dynamics of learning? What is the scientific basis for validating and judging the potential of VR to transmit information? For these and other questions we do not yet have a definite answer from neuroscience, but it is possible to hypothesize that in the future by increasing the level of immersive behaviours in the virtual sphere and by the development of artificial life, VR can constitute a very advanced domain of learning, communication, and the transmission of cultural codes. Our minds are essentially machines constructed of models and are thus capable of creating virtual simulations of the world. An increased connectivity of neurons permits greater communication between different mental systems (internally and reciprocally), making possible more elevated symbolic representations of sensory input. Moreover, if we augment the involvement/embodiment of our senses, we increase the difference between us and our environment in such as way as to acquire greater information. In theory, it should be possible to reproduce in the virtual sphere the same conditions of 'mindreading' identified in the mirror neurons. In this context various scientific projects have been launched, including 'MIRRORS: Mirror Neurons and the Execution/Matching System in Humans' (Agus *et al.* 2001), which aims at verifying the behaviour of mirror neurons through artificially simulated environments.

So what does the future hold in store for us? VR, for now mainly offline, but destined to migrate and settle permanently on the web, constitutes the concluding segment of the process mentioned above of knowledge-communication, precisely because it is able to produce first difference, then knowledge and communication. 'If information is a "difference that produces difference,"then the domain of information is balanced between too much and too little difference. On the one hand, information is difference and thus where there is no difference, there is no information; on the other hand, information is a difference which produces a difference' (Taylor 2005: 41).

Accuracy, precision, information

Up to now, we have tried to describe a 3D model that can communicate by itself and (at least theoretically) carry a greater quantity of information. How does one describe such a model? To what extent must it be accurate and precise?

Accuracy, in this context, means the degree to which the theoretical datum, taken from a series of measured values, corresponds to the real datum. Precision refers to the degree to which the data converge on an average value within the series to which they belong.[1] From this it follows that a model may be very precise and not at all accurate, or vice versa. In each variant (precise and accurate; accurate and not precise, precise and not accurate) information is transmitted that is quantitatively and qualitatively different. To these objective and analytical factors one may add the perceptual factor, when the model can be cognitively acquired. A reconstruction model of a monument can be very detailed because it assimilates thousands or millions of polygons and points, but it can still be imprecise because it is not in scale or has erroneous proportions.

1. See 'Accuracy and Precision', 2006, http://en.wikipedia.org/wiki/Precision_and_accuracy (seen December 29, 2006).

In models made by photogrammetry or laser scanning **[Plate 9]**, we know that the geometry of the monument can be better grasped if the textures are removed. In the same way, mapping and colour, superimposed onto the geometry can give additional information about the relationships between the model and chromatic and material qualities of the original. In the creation of a model, we need to take into account both the input (documentation/acquisition, **[Plate 9]**) and the output (the representation **[Plate 10]**). With the most advanced techniques of 3D representation we can obtain exact geometric data which depend on the instruments of acquisition: for example, a model generated by a laser scanner is highly accurate but necessitates a long phase of post-processing before it becomes usable. In contrast, a model generated by the techniques of computer vision is not as accurate but can be immediately experienced and communicated. Computer vision uses algorithms that reconstruct the movement of the digital camera calibrated in the third dimension, starting from the equation of projection which ties points of 3D space to the 2D points of the image. For this purpose, 3D patterns are used whose positions in space are known. Generally these objects ought to have the property of facilitating the recovery of the positions of characteristic points. To judge the accuracy and precision of techniques of computer vision, it is indispensable to make calibration tests. Even if the results obtained thus far are not statistically significant, the experiments are very encouraging, especially in view of their speed at which such models can be processed.

An interesting example is an experiment in survey and 3D representation of a monument which has recently been undertaken using the techniques of computer vision. The experiment was done with the help of the prototype software known as Epoch 3D, developed by a team under the direction of Luc Van Gool through the Epoch project sponsored by the European Union.[2] The system includes client software that can be installed on any personal computer as well as server software. Epoch 3D works as follows. The user takes a series of photographs of a side of an object. These pictures are shot with the same view of the object in the viewfinder but from varying points of view along an approximate semicircle (which need not be at all accurately measured). The resulting series of digital photographs are next loaded onto the client PC and uploaded to the server at the University of Leuven. The server processes the pictures and by means of calibrating the photographs to each other and then constructs the 3D geometry of the object photographed, applying the photographs to the model as textures. In **Plate 7** we see the survey (model plus textures) of the Maya Tempio del los Mascarones created with a digital camera, which took 14 shots at a distance of *ca.* 3 m. The geometric results (or mesh) of the model are seen in **Plate 8** in which one can sense the large quantity of information captured and conveyed by the 47,484 polygons of the model. The model is accurate but not precise, at least in an absolute sense. It shows a considerable ease of communication and could easily be inserted into a virtual environment. This example shows clearly that, besides commensurability, accuracy and precision, each 3D model has a significant communicative and evocative power which can easily be integrated with a top-down approach. If we will increase the 3D graphic libraries (for example, **Plates 9-10**), we will in time launch diversified interpretative and refutable processes from the stage of fieldwork to that of virtual reconstruction, from how the monument is today **[Plate 9]** to how it once appeared **[Plate 10]**.

Conclusion

The extraordinary growth of information and digital technologies in archaeology raises urgent new questions about research methodology, knowledge and the dissemination of culture. In particular, the technologies of 3D acquisition and representation such as computer vision, photogrammetry, and laser scanning, create information that has a complexity unimaginable a few years ago and whose codes of representation still must be defined and investigated. We do not adequately understand the cognitive processes which connect the geometric complexity of models with their representation. The key element on which we construct

2. See http://www.epoch-net.org/.

our codes, our maps, is the perception which first selects what is high-priority information and then transforms it into knowledge.

Thus, we do not know the cybernetic geometry of models and the related autopoetic and self-communicative capacity, but we do know that each model contains a universe of discrete information which, when inserted into a digital ecosystem, is able to develop relationships, retroactions, and interactions that were not suspected in advance and which modify our level of eco-informational knowledge. We also know that VR is destined to become a living organism made of artificial life and of spontaneous movement: it is not accidental that the concept of digital biology has already been theorized. The methodological itinerary connecting knowledge and communication is a univocal process and ought to be inserted into a digital ecosystem, from bottom-up digital input (the methodologies of acquisition and post-processing) to top-down digital output (the mental patterns and comparative analysis). In archaeology, in the phases of input we include the technologies of 3D documentation and modelling; in the output, the technologies of offline and online VR (from the Web 3D GIS to virtual communities).

From this point of view it is clear that, if, first, information and, secondly, the process of understanding, are maintained within a sequence of integrated digital protocols we have more opportunities not to lose data. In this methodological sequence learning occurs by difference, by means of cybernetic maps defined by transmission codes—something that Bateson describes as deutero-learning, or teaching how to learn to learn.

In conclusion, the theses discussed in this paper can be summarized as follows:

- The thread connecting knowledge and communication is a univocal process, one that is unilinear (albeit able to be segmented into separate actions) and multidisciplinary. To separate the two domains means, in fact, to lose information, to atomize the incremental value which derives from the feedback of learning in the cybernetic process.
- This thread is indeed a cybernetic process because it selects information and produces knowledge and communication.
- The thread is also an analytical process 'by means of transparency', in the sense that it determines the visibility of the processes that have been investigated and reconstructed.
- Information loses its neutrality as soon as it is constructed. From this it follows that the tools of digital acquisition determine the first informational geometry.
- In archaeology, the greater part of information still follows a route from the analogue (documentation in the field) to the digital (post-processing).
- The division of data into analogue and digital is doomed to introduce great error and arbitrariness into the knowledge-communication thread.
- If the passage between data not selected (pre-knowledge) and selected information (knowledge) is from digital to digital, we can increase the quantitative and qualitative standards of information and its representation.
- The bottom-up and top-down processes ought to be integrated into one space of shared interaction.
- 3D interaction is an integral part of the knowledge process because it increases informational value, produces feedback (i.e. cybernetic difference) between the interactor (i.e. the scientist) and the ecosystem.
- 3D models which respect the refutability of bottom-up and top-down become holistic models and develop new feedback and communication processes.
- VR (offline and online) constitutes the ideal ecosystem to host top-down and bottom-up

processes of knowledge and communication. A VR environment is much greater than the sum of its parts.

Finally, the discovery of mirror neurons opens a promising opportunity to validate cognitive behaviours for VR and for the dynamics of learning in the 3D world. If this happens, VR would be peremptorily the cybernetic map of Batesonian territory, that deutero-learning which has so fascinated students of the ecology of mind.

Bibliography

Agus, M., Bettio, F., Gobbetti, E. & Fadiga, L. 2001. "An integrated environment for stereoscopic acquisition, off-line 3D elaboration, and visual presentation of biological actions", in J. D. Westwood, H. M. Hoffmann, G. T. Mogel, D. Stredney & R. A. Robb (eds.), *Medicine Meets Virtual Reality 2001 - Inner Space, Outer Space, Virtual Space*, Amsterdam: Ios: 23-29.

Annunziato, M. & Pierucci, P. 2002. "Relazioni emergenti: experiments with the art of emergence", *Leonardo International Journal* 35/2: 147-152.

Bateson, G. 1972. *Steps to an Ecology of Mind*, San Francisco: Chandler Press.

Bateson, G. 1979. *Mind and Nature: a Necessary Unit*, New York: Dutton.

Bozzi, P. & Luccio, R. 1999. "Introduzione all'edizione italiana", in J. J. Gibson, *Un approccio ecologico alla percezione visiva* (Italian translation): Bologna: Il Mulino: 11-25.

Forte, M. & Siliotti, A. 1997 (eds.). *Virtual Archaeology: Re-creating Ancient Worlds*, New York: Abrams.

Forte, M. 2000. "About virtual archaeology: disorders, cognitive interactions and virtuality", in J. A. Barceló, M. Forte & D. H. Sanders (eds.), *Virtual Reality in Archaeology*, B.A.R. International Series 843, Oxford: BAR Publishing: 247-263.

Forte, M., Bard, K., Fattovich, R., Foccillo, M., Manzo, A., Perlingeri, C. 2001. "The Aksum project (Ethiopia): GIS, Remote Sensing applications and Virtual Reality", in Z. Stančič & T. Veljanovski (eds.), *Computer Archaeology for Understanding the Past (CAA 2000, Proceedings of the 28th Conference, Ljubljana, April 2000)*, B.A.R. International Series 931, Oxford: BAR Publishing: 214-251.

Forte, M., Pietroni, E. & Rufa, C. 2002. "Musealising the virtual: the Virtual Reality project of the Scrovegni Chapel of Padua," in *Creative and Digital Culture: Proceedings of the International Society for Virtual Systems and Multimedia 2002 (Gyeonggju, Korea, 25-27 September 2002)*, Seoul: VSMM 2002 Organization: 43-52.

Forte, M. 2003. "Mindscape: ecological thinking, cyber-anthropology, and virtual archaeological landscapes", in M. Forte & P. R. Williams (eds.), *The Reconstruction of Archaeological Landscapes through Digital Technologies: Proceedings of the 1st Italy-United States Workshop (Boston, Massachussets, USA, November 1-3, 2001)*, B.A.R. International Series 1151: Oxford: BAR Publishing: 95-108.

Gibson, J. J. 1999. *Un approccio ecologico alla percezione visiva*, Bologna: Il Mulino.

Harrison, S. & Dourish, P. 1996. "Re-place-ing space: the roles of place and space in collaborative systems", in *Proceedings of the ACM 1996 Conference on Computer Supported Cooperative Work (Boston, MA., United States)*, New York: ACM Press: 67-76.

Horgan, J. 1999. *The Undiscovered Mind: How the Human Brain Defies Replication, Medication, and Explanation*, New York: The Free Press.

Humphrey, N. 1998. *Una storia della mente*, Turin: Instar Libri.

Korzybski, A. 1941. *Science and Sanity*, New York: Science Press.

Lévy, P. 1995. *Qu'est-ce que le virtuel?*, Paris: Editions la Découverte.

Lévy, P. 1998. *Becoming Virtual: Reality in the Digital Age*, New York: Plenum.

Lévy, P. 2001. *Cyberculture*, Minneapolis: University of Minnesota Press.

Manghi, S. 1998 (ed.). *Attraverso Bateson: ecologia della mente e relazioni sociali*, Milan: Cortina.

Maturana, H. R. & Varela, F. J. 1980. *Autopoiesis and Cognition: the Realization of the Living*, Boston Studies in the Philosophy of Science 42, Boston: Springer.

Rizzolatti, G., Fadiga, L., Gallese, V. & Fogassi, L. 1996. "Premotor cortex and the recognition of motor actions", *Cognitive Brain Research* 3: 131-141.

Rizzolatti, G., Fogassi, L. & Gallese, V. 2001. "Neurophysiological mechanisms underlying the understanding and imitation of action", *Nature Neuroscience Reviews* 2: 661-670.

Settis, S. 2002. *L'Italia S.p.A. L'assalto al patrimonio culturale*, Turin: Einaudi.

Taylor, M. C. 2005. *Il momento della complessità. L'emergere di una cultura in rete*, Turin: Codice.

Wilson-Lewis, D. 2002. *The Mind in the Cave: Consciousness and the Origin of Art*, London: Thames and Hudson.

Chapter 3

Reasoning in 3D: a critical appraisal of the role of 3D modelling and virtual reconstructions in archaeology

This article discusses the use of 3D modelling techniques and virtual reconstructions in archaeology, arguing that, while they are widely used for broadcasting a tangible cultural heritage to both specialized users and the general public, they are not often used for digital, virtual conservation of objects or monuments, and are even less often employed in the reasoning process of archaeological scientific research, despite the fact that a great deal of archaeological work is often invested in building 3D models and the virtual objects/worlds. Consequently, here we present basic concepts of 3D modelling and virtual reconstructuctions and their potential use in archaeological research, mainly as part of the process of investigating and interpreting data; more precisely, as part of the process of turning data into information and into knowledge. By building a 3D model and a VR world, archaeologists can uncover new scientific questions and problems that might be otherwise missed through traditional research.

Sorin Hermon

Virtuale Archeologia e Scientifica Territoria Laboratorio, Polo Ingegneria, Università di Firenze, Italy

Introduction

Early VR and 3D modelling projects involving archaeological data began as early as the late 1980s and early 1990s (for an extensive survey of the history of VR, see Frischer *et al.* 2002). At about the same time, there were proposals of possible applications of VR and 3D modelling techniques for solving archaeological problems (Reilly 1989; Reilly & Shennan 1989; Sims 1997). The field gradually advanced, and new models and projects virtually reconstructed archaeological sites, monuments, and artefacts. By the end of the 1990s, several major publications summarized theoretical aspects and practical work in virtual archaeology (Forte & Siliotti 1997; Barceló *et al.* 2000; Niccolucci 2002). These years also saw the first attempts to establish standards and propose methodologies for the use of VR and 3D modelling techniques in archaeology, especially for communicating data by means of these techniques (Ryan 1996). Others explored the historical credibility of the VR and 3D products, the accuracy of the products from an archaeological point of view (Kanter 2000; Frischer *et al.* 2000), and the need for transparent data (Forte 2000).

The use of VR projects is constantly increasing, as can be seen in the annual Computer Applications in Archaeology (CAA) conferences, a major stage for presenting innovative projects related to VR. The 2001 conference featured five lectures concerning VR (cf. Burenhult & Arvidsson 2002). By 2004, almost three dozen papers on VR topics were presented. A clear trend can be seen towards two major subjects: communicating cultural heritage to the public and presenting new methods for improving the quality of the VR product, whether from an artistic or computer graphics point of view (a 'pitfall', at least from a strict archaeological point of view, already pointed out by Ryan 1996). If we include presentations at VAST conferences from 2000 to the present (e.g. Arnold *et al.* 2003; Chrysanthou *et al.* 2004), there is a large bulk of information, more than a hundred articles, dealing with various aspects of VR and archaeology. Most of these papers are concerned with different aspects of computer graphics innovations and educating the public about cultural heritage artefacts and sites through VR and 3D models. Very few examine the methodological and theoretical aspects of VR and 3D modelling applications in archaeology (e.g. Vatanen 2004) or use these tools as an investigative aid for archaeological problems (e.g. Beex & Peterson 2004). Therefore, after a five-year boom in VR and 3D modelling archaeological projects, hardly any of these projects have impacted or changed archaeology.

Several questions arise at this point: should archaeologists bother at all with VR and 3D? Beyond an occasional consultation on the 'credibility' of the VR model, they become no more than authentication tools—'is the model archaeologically proven'? And does VR actually benefit the field? More strongly emphasized, why should archaeologists spend the time and effort that VR requires? Why not leave it to computer graphic specialists? An immediate answer is that any research result must be communicated to the public, and VR and 3D modelling has proven itself as a most efficient tool for education and communication of cultural heritage. More importantly, the research process can benefit from these tools in the investigation of human past activity and its context. They can also be linked to a more general issue regarding the archaeologist's goals (beyond the obvious—excavating is fun!) of reconstructing human history and daily life from cultural remains and their natural context. It is precisely here that VR and 3D modelling can make a great contribution, by visually expressing alphanumeric data and by graphically expressing thoughts and ideas, and translating 'empirical phenomena into geometric language' (Frischer *et al.* 2002: 11). This point has also been made by Niccolucci (2002: 3):

> [...] since interpretation, explanation and communication involve reasoning, Virtual Archaeology can provide virtual creations to organize and synthesize known facts, showing them with greater clarity to others or to one's 'inner eye', or virtual substitutes of physical objects.

The following paragraphs will present some basic VR and 3D modelling concepts and how they can contribute to the archaeological scientific process.

VR and 3D models: basic definitions and applications in archaeology

A simple and comprehensive definition of VR is the simulation of a real or imagined environment, experienced visually in three dimensions (cf. Jones 1996; Rosenblum & Cross 1997). In order to understand and analyze the complexity of the real world, people draw pictures or build abstract descriptions or models. By focusing on selected details and relevant factors, we can build models that explore a particular problem or predict the behaviour of a particular phenomenon. A model has value, however, only when it can provide insight to some situation or answer a specific question, and the model can be analyzed, i.e. is accessible to critical evaluation (Jones 1996).

Thus we see VR's potential. In order to understand a past human activity, we must imagine it and thus reconstruct its context, whether environmental, anthropogenic, or social. Once this context is made visual, it becomes mobile, immutable, and reproducible (Latour 1986). Researchers in cognitive psychology have found a positive relationship between the ability to visualize (to manipulate or transform an image of spatial patterns into other arrangements; cf. Ekstrom *et al.* 1976) and the use of visualization tools (Sein *et al.* 1993). The implication is that the better the visual tool, the better the explanation and the comprehension of information. VR and 3D visualization of concepts, objects or spaces and their contextualization provide a visual framework in which data is displayed. The example in **Fig. 1** demonstrates the difference between a traditional and a 3D presentation of data. Being interactive, the 3D model can be rotated. All of its views can be captured and analyzed as in a traditional presentation. But additional data are added and made available for interpretation. A quick glance at building heights and tower shapes and heights make clear the visual range of soldiers on guard. The 3D visualization of the military camp also helps estimate its spatial organization, such as efficiency of movement in case of emergency: the model could be populated with soldiers running from barracks, climbing the ladders, and readying for battle, to see how easy it would be move about under different circumstances.

3D visualization is also an invaluable method for turning data obtained during the excavation, survey or investigation of the archaeological site into information that is available for further study and investigation, as well as generating a portable form of the elaborated data. VR enables interaction with data organized on three dimensions, facilitating the interaction between human, data, and information (cf. Stone 1998; Warwick *et al.* 1993). There are increasingly large amounts of information being generated by all scientific fields, and visualization helps to access, manage, interpret and share all of this data (Tufte 1990). The displayed environment shown in **Fig. 2** is based on the results of several otherwise disparate fields of enquiry. Geomorphological studies estimated the erosion degree and thus the shape of the valley where the habitation is located. Palynological work studied fossilized pollens and spores, and paleobotanical and paleoclimate studies examined plant life and climate in the area. Finally, human habitations in the area were recontructured from ethnographic and architectural work on human remains. All this information was used to estimate changes in the environment's ecology over a given period of time, as estimated by radiometric dating methods.

Fig. 1. *A. Plan of the military camp at Avdat, Israel; B. VR view of the same military camp (after Hermon & Fabian 2002).*

Moreover, 3D visualization allows experiments or simulations (based on scientific rules and constraints). The interpretation of accurate predictions or numerical simulations (Silver 1995), in turn, permits the investigation of new phenomena. For instance, **Fig. 2** could be used to simulate available land for agriculture, and the amount of labour invested in deforestation could enable an estimate of the population of the archaeological site under research and its subsistence economy.

Fig. 2. *Reconstruction of the environment of an archaeological site (after Negroni Catacchio & Cardosa 2001).*

Fig. 3. *Virtual reconstruction of Porsenna's mausoleum.*

Fig. 2 demonstrates another aspect of 3D visualization, which is the conversion of data from an alpha-numeric to a visual display. In other words, VR transforms information, making it more accessible to the human eye and more easily perceptible (Friedhoff & Benzon 1989; Brown 1997). The two methods contain the same information, but the visual display translates a table of palynological data into a realistic representation of vegetation. This stimulates new questions regarding the relationship between the human settlement and its environment, such as catchment analysis, how exposed the habitation areas were, how close they would have been to forests, and so on. **Fig. 3** further exemplifies the capability of 3D visualization to enhance perception in the context of scientific interrogation. Pliny the Elder, quoting an earlier historical source (Marcus Terentius Varro), describes a mausoleum apparently built by Lars Porsenna, last of the Etruscan kings and ruler in Clusium (present-day Chiusi, Tuscany).[1] The mausoleum was apparently destroyed by an earthquake in the 5th century BC. All traces were erased in Pliny's time (1st century BC). A virtual reconstruction of the mausoleum and its scientific analysis would therefore clarify many aspects of the historical text. The accuracy of Pliny's description, with all details and parts of the mausoleum accurately provided (including sizes and raw materials), enables the detailed virtual reconstruction of the monument. The model can be subjected to architectural analysis (static and dynamic laws) to test whether it is structurally feasible. Alternatively, it can be used to posit other possible models, taking into account the soil characteristics, building materials and engineering knowledge of the period, and possible location.[2] Needless to say, there are certain requirements for building a scientifically valid 3D model. The resources and assumptions upon which it is based should be explicitly presented (Allen 1998) and open to evaluation, while alternate reconstructions should be made available to the user (Roberts & Ryan 1997).

Moreover, 3D visualization can be enhanced (as 4D) through predictive models, evaluating scenarios, alternative versions of past events. In this sense, VR allows archaeologists and the public alike to view the past in a more experiential way, from within a certain time or place.

The process of 3D modelling

A virtual representation of an archaeological entity is based on data originating from various sources, such as historical records of graphical nature (ancient maps, drawings, paintings, mosaics etc.), texts, archaeological field investigation (surveys, soundings or excavations), comparative studies, and, last but not least, the modeller's informed imagination. **Fig. 4** shows the typical stages of 3D modelling and its basic components, which can also be expressed as an equation where the various kinds of data are the variables **[Fig. 5]**. It should be stressed that these variables are in turn informed by further, usually unrelated to each other, variables (e.g. accuracy of measurements, reliability of historical texts, ancient maps etc.).

1. '*Namque et Italicum (labyrinthum) dici convenit, quem fecit sibi Porsenna rex Etruriae sepulcri causâ, simul ut externorum regum vanitas quoque ab Italis superetur. Sed cum excedat omnia fabulositas, utemur ipsius M. Varronis in expositione ejus verbis: Sepultus est, inquit, sub urbe Clusio; in quo loco monumentum reliquit lapide quadrato: singula latera pedum lata tricenûm, alta quinquagenûm; inque basi quadratâ intus labyrinthum inextricabilem; quo si quis improperet sine glomere lini, exitum invenire nequeat. Supra id quadratum pyramides stant quinque, quatuor in angulis, in medio una: in imo latae pedum quinûm septuagenûm, altae centum quinquagenûm: ita fastigatae, ut in summo orbis aeneus et petasus unus omnibus sit impositus, ex quo pendeant exapta catenis tintinnabula, quae vento agitata, longe sonitus referant, ut Dodonae olim factum. Supra quem orbem quatuor pyramides insuper, singulae exstant altae pedum centenûm. Supra quas uno solo quinque pyramides; quarum altitudinem Varronem puduit adjicere*' (C. Plinius Secundus, Naturalis Historia 36.18,4).

2. The Latin text above states that the monument was 'under the city of Chiusi'. There are legends of labyrinths and hidden treasures in the many underground passages that still exist today in the city's old centre. However, a monument of such size—an estimated 190 m in height—would be by far the largest monument in antiquity and was most probably located outside the city, e.g. in a nearby valley. The 3D visualization in **Fig. 3** allows us to put the historic source to the test, in terms of whether the monument described is structurally feasible.

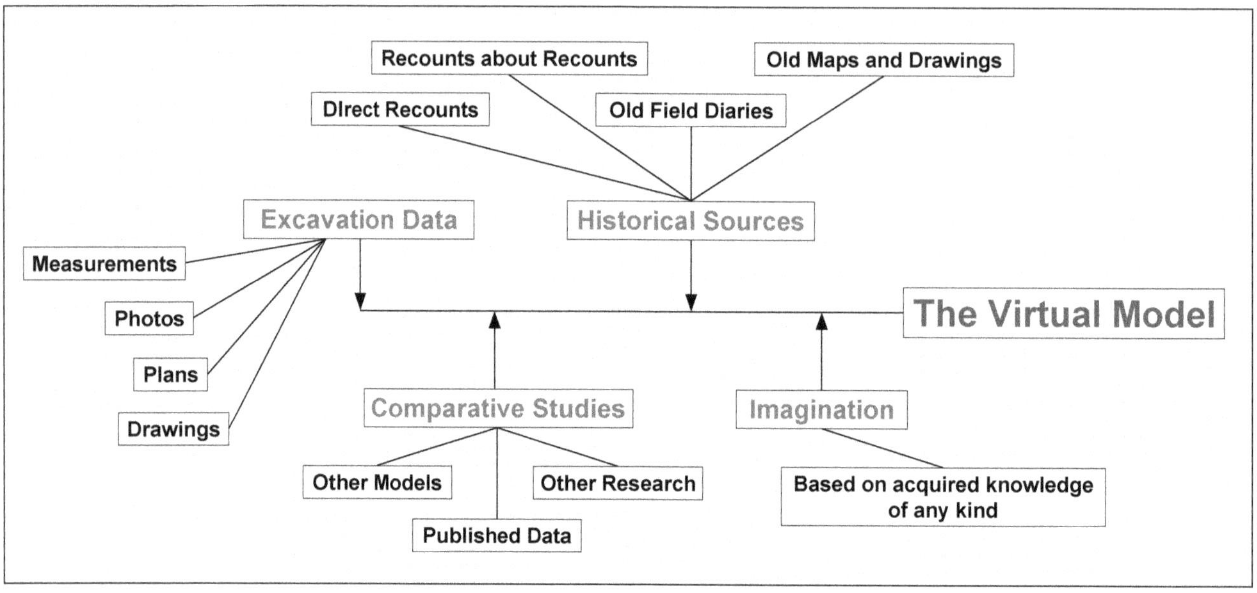

Fig. 4. *Schematic diagram of 3D modelling stages (after Niccolucci & Hermon in press).*

In order to evaluate the model's reliability and allow its (virtual) deconstruction, various steps need to be taken to arrive to the final (M_n) and alternative (M') models, from the first draft (M_0) **[Fig. 6]**. After examining the surviving building, any collapsed elevation material around the tower, any existing parallels (in this case, a church tower bell of the 12th century), as well as the relevant historical sources, a first reconstruction can be attempted (M_0). On this basis, it is then possible to create two further models: a version of the building with defensive elements (M_n), and a version that features a bell-tower (M'). An oblique line clearly distinguishes the actual, surviving features from the reconstruction. At each step of the reconstruction process, metadata are generated (for more on sources and their reliability, Niccolucci & Hermon in press). This permits data transparency and satisfies scientific requirements for the model. The relationship between archaeology and VR should be explicitly stated, for instance through a slider interface on the display system that allows the user to choose what data is displayed (e.g. ranging between archaeological reality, '1', to conjecture, '0'). Unreliable data or conjectural elements should be displayed as 'ghosts', i.e. alternative models in fainter colours.

Visualization tools and basic requirements

Visualization tools can be divided into two main groups: interpretative and expressive (Gordin *et al.* 1996; Nielson *et al.* 1997). The former help users to view and manipulate visuals, extracting meaning from the information being visualized; they help clarify difficult and/or abstract concepts (Levin *et al.* 1987). One such use of 3D visualization is exemplified in **Fig. 7**, showing a vertical cross-section of the old centre of the town of Chiusi, in southern Tuscany. The large building is a 16th century palace. The cellars, some of them of Medieval date, provide access to a series of underground tunnels and a complex water system from the Etruscan period. Users can investigate the superimposition of the various strata and follow Chiusi's urban development. Information about the Etruscan

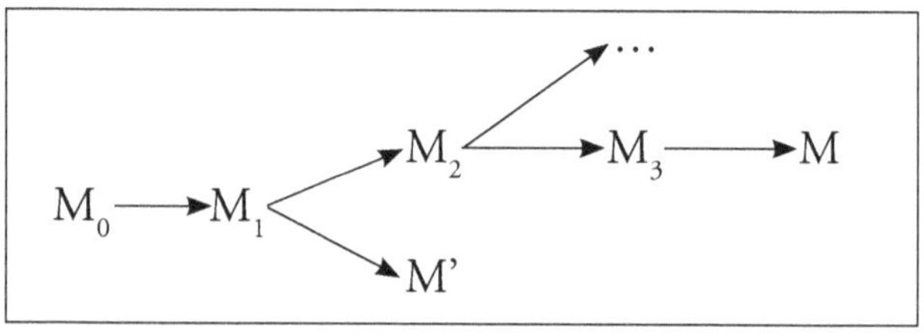

Fig. 5. *Schematic representation of the process of 3D modelling.*

Fig. 6. *3D model and alternative model (after Niccolucci & Hermon in press).*

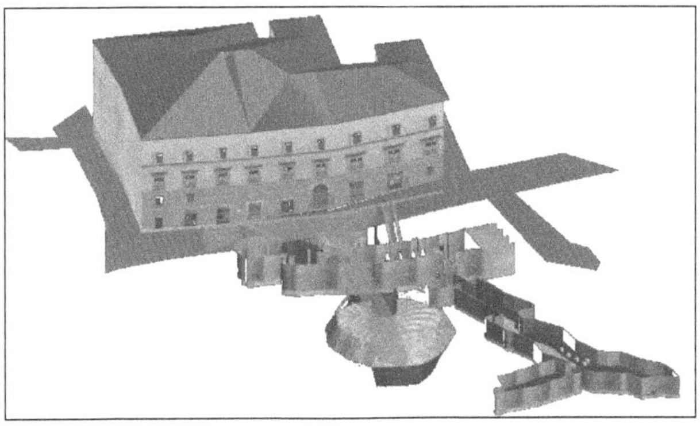

Fig. 7. *Virtual reconstruction of the underground Etruscan water system at Chiusi, Tuscany.*

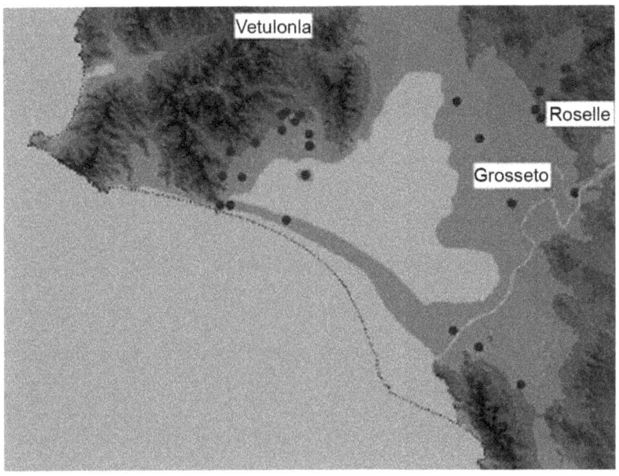

Fig. 8. *3D model of Tuscan coast temporal development and settlement pattern (Niccolucci* et al. *2001).*

water system, its tunnels, and the subterranean lake can be used to study water systems in later periods and technical development over time. Using the same data, the model can also aid the study of the Etruscan water-supply system, by simulating the process of tunnel-digging, and showing the tunnels' inclination, probable length and height, as well as the amount of accumulated water in the cistern. The user gains a realistic impression of the underground system and is able to select parts of the conduit, or the entire complex, for viewing from a number of angles.

Expressive tools, on the other hand, visually convey sets of beliefs, cuing and accelerating comprehension through visual coding. **Fig. 8**, a screenshot from a digital elevation model (DEM), shows part of the Tuscan coast that endured major changes through the Quaternary. These changes culminated in modern times in the formation of a lake, Prile, where there was once an open sea and a bay. The model shows the relationship between the changing landscape and the human settlement pattern and the inhabitants' subsistence economy. The modern coastal line is displayed as a line connecting the two parts of the former bay. Human occupation sites are represented by dots, which are colour-coded to indicate particular historical periods ranging from the Upper Paleolithic to the Roman periods.

Among the various methods available for data manipulation and information creation, selective emphasis allows the user to detect, identify and visualize hidden patterns by highlighting or hiding parts of the visualized data (Erickson 1993). **Fig. 9** illustrates this application. To evaluate the regularity of the edges of a flint tool, an important attribute for classifying these objects (cf. Hermon *et al.* 2001), the tool's contour can

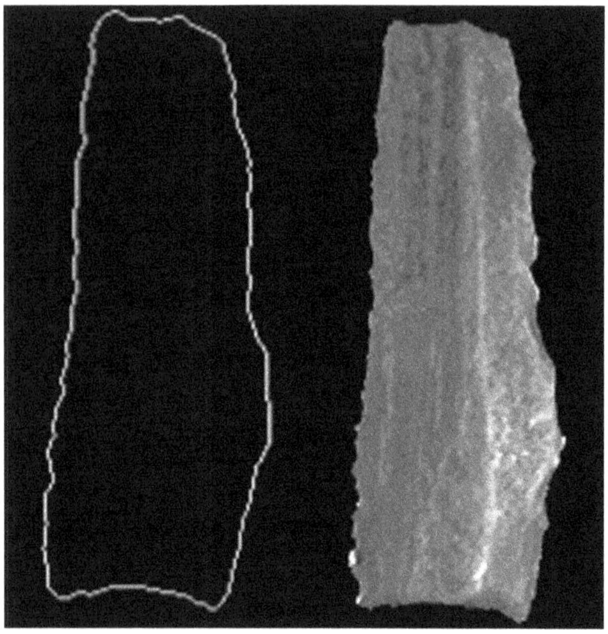

Fig. 9. *Flint tools and selective contour (after Hermon* et al. *2001).*

be selectively visualized and subsequently processed into a mathematical formula, enabling fast and reliable classification based on predefined criteria. This process, when done by hand, is not only time-consuming but also less reliable than the automated application of a priori classificatory criteria (see also Karasik *et al.* 2004; Karasik this volume, for a similar approach to automatic classification of pottery).

The transformation of non-visual data to an image can clarify the former and allow for new interpretations (cf. Risch *et al.* 1996; van Teylingen *et al.* 1997; Freeman *et al.* 1998; Herman *et al.* 1998). And, contextualization provides a visual framework within which data are displayed and investigated (Erickson 1993). Looking back at **Fig. 2**, for example, shows how human social interaction affects the settlement pattern and its relationship with the surrounding environment, as well as the subsistence economy.

Summary and conclusions

The last decade has witnessed a growth in VR and 3D modelling in archaeology. However, despite VR's great potential as a research tool and the fact that it has already been used in many disciplines, it has had little impact on archaeological scientific research, in the sense that the 3D modelling and VR toolkit has not been fully adapted to the archaeological reasoning process. There is too much emphasis on artistic, instead of intellectual, aspects; typically, archaeologists are concerned with how accurately a VR model represents archaeological entities, not how it can enhance an understanding of the past. Nevertheless, VR can greatly contribute to archaeology, its ideal place on the archaeological *chaîne ópertoire* being perhaps after data classification and before data dissemination. It enables the visual expression of numerical data as well as abstract notions, serves as a platform for hypothesis-testing, aids the integration of various kinds of data in a visual form. It permits not only reconstruction, but also deconstruction and alternative interpretations. Evading language barriers, visualization fosters inter-cultural communication in the scientific community and the public. The dissemination of both the reasoning process and the final results in planned and intuitive fashion encourages the transmission and understanding of information. Therefore, VR facilitates the transformation of data into information and knowledge.

Bibliography

Allen, W. J. 1998. *Levels of Archaeological Evidence Illustrated in Three-Dimensional Computer Models*, unpublished M.A. thesis, Mississipi State University.

Arnold, D., Chalmers, A. & Niccolucci, F. 2003 (eds.). *Proceedings of the 4th International Symposium on Virtual Reality, Archaeology and Intelligent Cultural Heritage (VAST 2003, Brighton, November 5–7, 2003)*, Aire-la-Ville: Eurographics Association.

Barceló, J. A., Forte, M. & Sanders, D. H. 2000 (eds.). *Virtual Reality in Archaeology*, B.A.R. International Series 843, Oxford: BAR Publishing.

Beex, W. & Peterson, J. 2004. "The Arminghal henge in space and time: how virtual reality contributes to research on its orientation", in *Enter the Past–the E-Way into the Four Dimensions of Cultural Heritage (CAA 2003 Proceedings, Vienna, 8-12 April 2003)*, B.A.R. International Series 1127, Oxford: BAR Publishing: 490-493.

Burenhult, G. & Arvidsson, J. 2002 (eds.). *Archaeological Informatics: Pushing the Envelope (CAA 2001, Proceedings of the 29th Conference, Gotland, April 2001)*, B.A.R. International Series 1016, Oxford: BAR Publishing.

Brown, J. R. 1997. "Visualization and scientific applications", in R. Earnshaw, J. Vince & H. Jones (eds.), *Visualization and Modeling*, London: Academic Press: 1-13.

Ceccarelli, L. & Niccolucci, F. 2003. "Modelling time through GIS technology: the ancient Prile lake (Tuscany, Italy)", in M. Doerr & A. Sarris (eds.), *The Digital Heritage of Archaeology (CAA 2002, Proceedings of the 30th Conference, Heraklion, Crete, April 2002)*, Athens: Archive of Monuments and Publications, Hellenic Ministry of Culture: 133-138.

Chrysanthou, Y., Cain, K., Silberman, N. & Niccolucci, F. 2004 (eds.). *Proceedings of the VAST 2004 Conference*, Aire-la-Ville: Eurographics Association.

Ekstrom, R. B., French, J. W. & Harman, H. H. 1976. *Manual of Kit of Factor-Referenced Cognitive Tests*, Princeton: Educational Testing Service.

Erickson, T. 1993. "Artificial realities as data visualization environments: problems and prospects", in A. Wexelblat (ed.), *Virtual Reality Applications and Explorations*, Cambridge: Academic Press Professional: 1-22.

Forte, M. 2000. "About virtual archaeology: disorders, cognitive interactions and virtuality", in J. A. Barceló, M. Forte & D. H. Sanders (eds.), *Virtual Reality in Archaeology*, B.A.R. International Series 843, Oxford: BAR Publishing: 247-259.

Forte, M. & Siliotti, A. 1997 (eds.). *Virtual Archaeology: Great Discoveries Brought to Life Through Virtual Reality*, London: Thames and Hudson.

Freeman, C. L., Webster, C. M. & Kirke, D. M. 1998. "Exploring social structure using dynamic three-dimensional color images", *Social Networks* 20/2: 109–118.

Friedhoff, R. M. & Benzon, W. 1989. *Visualization: the Second Computer Revolution*, New York: Abrams.

Frischer, B., Abernathy, D., Favro, D., Liverani, P. & De Blaauw, S. 2000. "Virtual reality and ancient Rome: the UCLA Cultural VR Lab Santa Maria Maggiore project", in J. A. Barceló, M. Forte & D. H. Sanders (eds.), *Virtual Reality in Archaeology*, B.A.R. International Series 843, Oxford: BAR Publishing: 155-162.

Frischer, B., Niccolucci, F., Ryan, N. S. & Barceló, J. A. 2002. "From CVR to CVRO: the past, present, and future of cultural virtual reality", in F. Niccolucci (ed.), *Virtual Archaeology, Proceedings of the VAST Conference, Arezzo, Italy*, B.A.R. International Series 834, Oxford: BAR Publishing: 7-18.

Gording, D. N., Edelson, D. C. & Gomez, L. 1996. "Scientific visualization as an interpretive and expressive medium", *Proceedings of the International Conference on the Learning Sciences, Charlottesville, Association for the Advancement of Computers in Education*, Evanston: International Society of the Learning Sciences: 409-414.

Herman, I., Delest, M. & Melancon, G. 1998. "Tree visualisation and navigation clues for information visualisation", *Computer Graphics Forum* 17/2: 153–165.

Hermon, S., Petrone, M. & Calori, L. 2001. "An experimental method for the analysis of attributes of flint artefacts using image processing", in Z. Stančič & T. Veljanovski (eds.), *Computing Archaeology for Understanding the Past (CAA 2000, Proceedings of the 28th Conference, Ljubljana, Slovenia, 18-21 April 2000)*, B.A.R. International Series 931, Oxford: BAR Publishing: 91-98.

Hermon, S. & Fabian, P. 2002. "Virtual reconstruction of archaeological sites—some archaeological scientific considerations", in F. Niccolucci (ed.), *Virtual Archaeology, Proceedings of the VAST Conference, Arezzo, Italy*, B.A.R. International Series 1075, Oxford: BAR Publishing: 103-118.

Jones, C. V. 1996. *Visualization and Optimization*, Boston: Kluwer Academic Publishers.

Kanter, J. 2000. "Realism vs. reality: creating virtual reconstructions of prehistoric architecture", in J. A. Barceló, M. Forte & D. H. Sanders (eds.), *Virtual Reality in Archaeology*, B.A.R. International Series 843, Oxford: BAR Publishing: 47-52.

Karasik, A., Sharon, I., Smilansky, U. & Gilboa, A. 2004. "Establishing optimal core sampling strategies: theory, simulation and practical implications", in G. Burenhult & J. Arvidsson (eds.), *Archaeological Informatics: Pushing the Envelope (CAA 2001, Proceedings of the 29th Conference, Gotland, April 2001)*, B.A.R. International Series 1016, Oxford: BAR Publishing: 472-477.

Latour, B. 1986. "Visualization and cognition", *Knowledge and Society: Studies in the Sociology of Culture Past and Present* 6: 1-40.

Levin, J. R., Anglin, G. J. & Carney, R. N. 1987. "On empirically validating functions of pictures in prose", in D. M. Willows & H. A. Willows (eds.), *The Psychology of Illustration*, New York: Springer: 51-85.

Negroni Catacchio, N. & Cardosa, M. 2001. "Imago Etruriae, una reconstruzione 3D del paessagio antico in Etruria, il caso di Sovana", in F. Niccolucci & S. Hermon (eds.), *Multimedia Communication for Cultural Heritage, Budapest*, Budapest: Archeolingua: 127-134.

Niccolucci, F. & Hermon S. in press. "A fuzzy logic approach to reliability in archaeological virtual reconstructions", in F. Niccolucci & S. Hermon (eds.), *Beyond the Artifact: Digital Interpretation of the Past (CAA 2004, Proceedings of the 32nd Conference, Prato, Italy, 13-17 April 2004)*, Budapest: Archeolingua.

Nielson, G., Hagen, H. & Müller, H. 1997. *Scientific Visualization*, Washington: Institute of Electrical and Electronics Engineers Computer Society.

Reilly, P. 1989. "Data visualization in archaeology", *IBM Systems Journal* 28/4: 569-579.

Reilly, P. & Shennan, S. 1989. "Applying solid modeling and animated three-dimensional graphics to archaeological problems", IBM UK Scientific Centre (Winchester) Technical Report UKSC 209.

Risch, J. S., May, R. A., Dowson, S. T. & Thomas, J. J. 1996. "A virtual environment for multimedia intelligence data analysis", *Institute of Electrical and Electronics Engineers, Computer Graphics and Applications* 16/6: 33–41.

Roberts, J. C. & Ryan, N. S. 1997. "Alternative archaeological representations within virtual worlds", in R. Bowden (ed.), *Proceedings of the 4th UK Virtual Reality Specialist Interest Group Conference - Brunel University*, Uxbridge: 179-188.

Rosenblum, L. J. & Cross, R. A. 1997. "The challenge of virtual reality", in R. Earnshaw, J. Vince & H. Jones (eds.), *Visualization and Modeling*, London: Academic Press: 325-339.

Ryan, N. S. 1996. "Computer-based visualisation of the past: technical realism and historical credibility", in P. Main, T. Higgins & J. Lang (eds.), *Imaging the Past: Electronic Imaging and Computer Graphics in Museums and Archaeology*, British Museum Occasional Papers 114, London: The British Museum: 95-108.

Sein, M. K., Olfman, L., Bostrom, R. P. & Davis, S. A. 1993. "Visualization ability as a predictor of user learning success", *International Journal of Man-Machine Studies* 39: 599-620.

Silver, D. 1995. "Object-oriented visualization", *Institute of Electrical and Electronics Engineers, Computer Graphics and Applications* 15/3: 54-62.

Sims, D. 1997. "Archaeological models: pretty pictures or research tools?", *Institute of Electrical and Electronics*

Engineers, Computer Graphics and Applications 17/1: 13-15.

Stone, R. J. 1998. "Virtual reality: definition, technology and selected engineering application overview", *Mechatronics Forum Paper* (May).

Tufte, E. R. 1990. *Envisioning Information*, Cheshire: Graphics Press.

van Teylingen, R., Ribarsky, W. & van der Mast, C. 1997. "Virtual data visualizer", *Institute of Electrical and Electronics Engineers, Transactions on Visualization and Computer Graphics* 3/1: 65-74.

Vatanen, I. 2004. "Argumentation paths in information infrastructure of the archaeological virtual realities", in G. Burenhult & J. Arvidsson 2002 (eds.), *Archaeological Informatics: Pushing the Envelope (CAA 2001, Proceedings of the 29th Conference, Gotland, April 2001)*, B.A.R. International Series 1016, Oxford: BAR Publishing: 494-499.

Warwick, K., Gray, J. & Roberts, D. 1993. *Virtual Reality in Engineering*, London: Institute of Electrical and Electronic Engineers.

Chapter 4

Exploring behavioural *terra incognita* with archaeological agent-based models

Agent-based models are of the greatest utility when employed as behavioural laboratories in which archaeologists can explore the non-linear dynamics of artificial societies and their depositional processes by experimenting with a wide range of initial conditions and alternative histories. This approach differs from that which employs agent-based models as simulators, which paradoxically attempt to emulate the very behavioural processes under study. After discussing three deficiencies of the emulation approach, a few lessons are drawn from an ongoing project that employs an agent-based model strictly as an exploratory tool for learning more about Lower Paleolithic archaeological landscape formation from the 'null-up'. One lesson learned from this heuristic modelling research is that, even in cases where hominin agents lack the ability to transport food resources to central places, ecological patchiness can structure their simple foraging behaviours such that the artificial archaeological landscapes they create display the same spatial signature that characterizes Oldowan archaeological landscapes.

Luke S. Premo
Max-Planck-Institut für evolutionäre Anthropologie, Abteilung für die menschliche Evolution, Germany

More than a decade ago, agent-based models found their way from computer scientists who were interested in artificial life to archaeologists who were interested in understanding the past. Since then, the technique has been used in a wide variety of archaeological applications, ranging from East African Plio-Pleistocene hominids (Premo 2005; 2006) to small-scale agriculturists in the U.S. Southwest (Dean *et al.* 2000; Kohler *et al.* 2000).[1] For the most part, the archaeological community has met this initial round of agent-based applications with a healthy mix of enthusiasm and skepticism, but unfortunately many archaeologists still view agent-based models as a hybrid of Virtual Reality and role-playing video games (Bawaya 2006). I fear that, if left uncorrected, this misperception might lead to a consensus that, while agent-based models might be useful for illustration, they cannot be trusted for enquiry-based exploratory research, when in reality nothing could be further from the truth. This paper explains why archaeological agent-based models should be used principally for exploration and not for illustration, and it provides an example of how this kind of research can be done.

As the name implies, agent-based models make use of software objects called agents. Agents are specified by means of object-oriented programming languages (Java, Objective-C, etc.). These autonomous software entities are equipped with limited means to both perceive and react to aspects of their environment on an individual and usually goal-directed basis. Each agent 'decides' when and how to act by continually

1. See Kohler & Gumerman 2000, and Beekman & Baden 2005 for many other examples.

This research was supported in part by an Emil W. Haury Graduate Fellowship, awarded by the Department of Anthropology at the University of Arizona, and by the Max Planck Society. I thank Steve Kuhn and Steve Lansing for their help with SHARE. Jonathan Scholnick provided comments on an earlier draft that significantly improved this paper. The source code for SHARE is freely available upon request.

comparing the values of its internal state variables to desired, optimal, or ideal values. Because internal values are derived from physical and social environmental surroundings, agents' actions are ultimately a response to their environment. Agents also communicate with each other via messages.

In some agent-based models, a single agent interacts with an environment through simulated time (Brantingham 2003; 2006). In others, hundreds, thousands, or even millions of agents interact with an environment and with each other, thereby forming an artificial society (Epstein & Axtell 1996; Lansing 2002; Kohler *et al.* 2005). Whereas the conditional rules that each agent follows may be quite simple (e.g. if body temperature exceeds an acceptable threshold, then move to a cooler locale as efficiently as possible), the aggregate outcome of a population of agents may be difficult to predict (e.g. the migration of a group of agents to a cooler locale might take a direction not allowed to any individual agent). Such emergent properties are generated from the bottom-up in agent-based models. They arise from individual agents' actions just as the global properties of an actual society emerge from the actions of, and interactions between, individual persons. Artificial societies often exhibit emergent collective properties that can be strikingly similar to those displayed by real societies. The ability to study non-linear dynamics generated from the bottom-up not only distinguishes agent-based models from top-down, deterministic models, but it also makes them especially attractive to social scientists (Epstein & Axtell 1996).

Archaeology has had a long, fruitful relationship with deterministic formal models. For example, linear programming models were once very popular among those interested in modelling hunter-gatherer foraging decisions (Reidhead 1979). However, most agent-based models are fundamentally different from deterministic mathematical models because a) they allow for populations of heterogeneous agents, b) they can be spatially explicit, and c) they incorporate stochasticity and historical contingency, so that one can study behavioural tendencies rather than laws (Kohler 2000; Premo 2006). The most important and unique features of the methodology can be summarized in one brief sentence: agent-based models make possible the study of non-linear cultural dynamics that emerge from historically contingent actions of heterogeneous agents interacting in space. Thus, one can use them to explore the kinds of biocultural evolutionary dynamics that are of ultimate interest to archaeologists of all stripes.

A tale of two approaches: emulation and exploration

'Simulation' is a synonym for 'imitation'; to simulate is to mimic. However, while the terms 'computer simulation' and 'simulation model' are freely used in archaeological literature, no computer model truly imitates, mimics, or emulates every detail of reality. This limitation can be used to an advantage. Models encode our simple concepts about how the world works. This allows us to explore systematically our ideas about the past, independently of the empirical archaeological data against which we must continuously test theory (van der Leeuw 2004). Despite the fact that this built-in exploratory lever is inherent to all agent-based models, there is a strong temptation for archaeologists to emulate only those scenarios which they think were most likely responsible for the formation of empirical archaeological datasets, often at the expense of looking for other plausible alternatives.

There are many uses for models that simulate real phenomena (i.e. simulators), but such models include two important caveats. First, simulators work well only if one knows almost everything there is to know about the phenomenon of interest *a priori*. For example, the extremely realistic flight simulators used to train new pilots are effective because they incorporate so many of the details that are known to be involved in flying an airplane. The same cannot be said of our simulation models of past behaviours and environments, because our prior knowledge of important variables is at best terribly incomplete. Obviously, it is impossible to create a model that accurately emulates something one does not completely understand. I cannot precisely emulate *Homo habilis* behaviours in the same sense that Wilbur and Orville Wright could not possibly have created a usable flight simulator for an F-16 fighter pilot. In both cases, we simply lack the knowledge needed to provide an accurate imitation.

Second, simulators are usually employed as teaching devices, not as discovery tools. In the example above, flight simulators are employed to teach less experienced pilots what other pilots have already learnt about flying airplanes. In archaeology, however, the function of simulation is often just the opposite. Our best simulation models function as a heuristic devices, designed to help one learn more about the deficiency of one's ideas about an unknown phenomenon or systemic process, or, as Zubrow (1981: 143) put it over a quarter of a century ago, 'not to solve problems but to create new problems and view old ones in new and interesting ways'. However, if the main goal of an archaeological agent-based model is to reproduce some characteristic of an archaeological assemblage (i.e. to act as a simulator), it cannot help but reiterate what one already 'knows'. As a result, simulators will reinforce a small subset of ideas about the past without first testing them against empirical data or comparing their expectations to those of simpler alternatives, and they will rarely illuminate new problems or cast old ones in a new light.

The emulation approach to archaeological agent-based modelling suffers from at least three serious logical deficiencies. First, although one might create a model with the good intention of making it as 'realistic' or as well-supported by ethnographic observations as possible, the fact remains that an infinite number of conceptual models can reproduce important characteristics of any archaeological phenomenon. In most cases, many different models can yield nearly identical outcomes, each of which matches the empirical expectation equally well. This many-to-one relationship is due to the principle of equifinality, which states that, in open systems, any given final state, or 'result', can be reached via more than one possible path and/or from more than one set of initial conditions, or 'starting points'. Equifinality prompts a difficult question: when the observed outcomes (i.e. simulated data) of several different models match the expected outcome (i.e. empirical data), which is the preferred model for explanation? One answer to this question is 'none', because they are all equally relevant. Another common answer is the model that explains the greatest amount of variation in the empirical data. I think a better answer than either of these is the simplest model, because it provides the best place to start the heuristic process. It is best to start this process with simple models because they include far fewer of the unnecessary assumptions that plague more complicated explanations. This does not mean that the simplest model will always provide the most comprehensive, or even the most accurate, explanation possible; Ockham's razor is not a magic wand. For this reason, one should not stop the heuristic process after only one model. Alternative versions will vary both in the complexity and the number of assumptions they include. Not only is this acceptable, it is to be expected. However, the decision to use more complicated versions to inform archaeological interpretation should be based not on the perception that they are 'more realistic', but on the fact that they provide hypotheses that cannot be disproved by empirical data when those provided by the simpler version can be. Finally, we need to keep in mind that, unless alternative models are created systematically from a null or neutral version, the task of deciphering which is simpler is non-trivial.

Second, the act of tuning variable values to match the conditions of just one scenario can lead to a false sense of explanation by emergence, which I call the Sirens of Titan fallacy. Kurt Vonnegut, Jr. explores the notion of free will in his second novel, *The Sirens of Titan*. One of its main characters, named Winston Niles Rumfoord, has been cursed to a life of unrest: he and his dog are beamed across the solar system and through time at just a moment's notice. During the course of his travels, Rumfoord meets an interesting robot named Salo, who has been marooned on Titan for over 200,000 years. From back on his home planet of Tralfamadore, Salo's superiors have repeatedly assured the shipwrecked voyager that the small part needed to repair his hobbled space ship is on its way. However, they communicate with Salo in a most unusual way:

> It was through his viewer that [Salo] got his first reply from Tralfamadore. The reply was written on Earth in huge stones on a plain in what is now England. The ruins of the reply still stand, and are known as Stonehenge. The meaning of Stonehenge in Tralfamadorian, when viewed from above is: 'Replacement part being rushed with all possible speed'. Stonehenge wasn't the only message old Salo had received (Vonnegut 1959: 271).

In this story, many of humankind's architectural achievements—the Great Wall of China ('Be patient. We haven't forgotten about you.'), the Golden House of Nero ('We are doing the best we can.'), and the Palace of the League of Nations in Geneva ('Pack up your things and be ready to leave on short notice.')—were actually intergalactic messages to a stranded alien (Vonnegut 1959: 271-272). Even more disturbing is that human behaviour had been 'scripted', or determined from the top-down, by the Tralfamadorians, who had both the will and the power to influence occurrences on Earth.

Until Rumfoord discovered Salo's deep secret, only one party (the Tralfamadorians) was privy to the fact that human behaviour was being 'tuned' from the top-down. To any other intergalactic observer, the development of human civilizations would have looked like an interesting emergent property. Those observers would have been fools, however, because the Tralfamadorians kept their human agents to a deterministic script. Unfortunately, the same can be true of agent-based models designed to emulate one preconceived notion of what happened in the past. In many of these cases, it is impossible for casual observers to discern between two possible explanations for the observed outcome: a) the collective behaviour of interest is predetermined by a small set of 'tuned' variables, or b) the collective behaviour of interest emerges from interactions of individuals who make their decisions independently of any script. As a general rule, one should avoid models that make possible the interpretation that important collective behaviours are emergent when they are in fact predetermined.

Third, emulation is not explanation. Engineers have built bipedal robots that are capable of moving about an arena on two 'legs'. Some of these engineers might argue that the process of constructing these robots has taught them something new about bipedalism, but far fewer would argue that by simply emulating a form of bipedalism with machines, they have gained a suitable explanation for how and why the earliest hominins evolved their unique bipedal gait. The same is true if one merely emulates preconceived notions of past behaviours in agent-based models. Simply emulating a particular view of the past *in silico* does not an explanation make. Further, very little new knowledge is gained from an agent-based model built expressly to imitate an archaeological outcome. Such exercises may demonstrate programming skill, but they will rarely teach us anything new about the behavioural processes of interest. Much like the engineer, who cannot be certain that her mechanical solution in any way 'explains' something about how bipedalism evolved in hominids millions of years ago, a programmer cannot be certain that any single simulation run—especially one designed to replicate a particular set of archaeological data (i.e. a simulator)—explains anything at all about the real biosocial processes that played some part in the formation of a real archaeological landscape. Do not despair, for it does not have to be this way. In my opinion, archaeologists interested in using agent-based models as tools to better inform their interpretations should refrain from attempting to explain the past by simply emulating processes which they do not fully understand; instead, they should employ an exploratory experimental design—one which allows them to replay the so-called 'tape of history' (Gould 1989) as they explore how a wide range of plausible environmental and behavioural scenarios affects the distribution and composition of artificial archaeological assemblages over the course of thousands of simulation runs.

In discussing the importance of contingency in understanding evolutionary history, the late Stephen J. Gould proposed an interesting thought experiment (Gould 1989). Imagine being able to pick any point in the past—the Cambrian explosion, the last glacial maximum, etc. History could be restarted and certain subjects observed from that point. One could then watch different plots unfold, depending on the contingencies of history. Gould notes that

> [...] the divine tape player holds a million scenarios, each perfectly sensible [...] the slightest early nudge contacts a different groove, and history veers into another plausible channel (1989: 320-321).

Unlike a videotape of *The Natural*, which repeatedly and faithfully depicts an injured Roy Hobbs launching an improbable home run into the stadium lights and rounding the bags one final time under a cascade of sparks and cheers, the divine tape player can show different evolutionary outcomes, depending on both the sequence and the types of unique historical events (e.g. changes in climate, meteorites, epidemics, off-speed pitches, etc.). Thus, if *The Natural* were replayed in Gould's cosmic tape player, Hobbs might strike out.

Gould's thought experiment illustrates the importance of historical contingency, a component of cultural and biological evolution that is often downplayed by those concerned with uncovering universal laws. But it also introduces a novel research methodology to everyone involved in the historical sciences. Archaeologists are interested in retracing the trajectories of past societies, in hopes that a better understanding of past cultures will ultimately contribute to a more nuanced appreciation of our own species' place in the natural world, as well as how our decisions will affect the future. In this endeavour, we have access to two types of empirical data sets. The first is an exceedingly incomplete and biased subset of all of the physical matter (fossils, stone tools, ancient DNA, etc.) deposited during the one and only run of the tape of history. The second is composed of that which we can observe in the current (unique) outcome of the evolutionary tape of history—the details of life as it exists today.

Considering these remains and the selective forces that operated on the organisms responsible for them prompts an important question: how likely is the current scene—life as we witness it today—given all reasonable historical possibilities? For instance, given our empirical observations of the current scene, we know that humans are bipedal. But what is the likelihood that bipedalism would have evolved in our lineage given a slightly different historical scenario, perhaps one that involved a slightly different climate? Of course, archaeological landscapes are also open to the same kinds of questions. For example, how do qualitatively different behaviours affect the spatial distributions of cultural material, and would the archaeological patterns that we exhume have been sensitive to small changes in these behaviours? Answers to these questions lie in discovering the likelihood that currently observable 'outcomes' would also occur in other plausible social and biological environmental settings. This is impossible to do in reality because the real tape of history cannot be re-run. However, this feat can be realized by looking for regularities in the behaviour of agent-based models of complex adaptive systems under a variety of experimental conditions (Lansing 2002; Premo 2006).

In summary, emulation *in silico* cannot prove that our ideas about the past are correct. To believe otherwise is to fall victim to the silicon siren's song. But, by allowing the user to control initial conditions while playing out multiple alternatives—to replay Gould's tape of history hundreds or thousands of times—agent-based simulation can provide a way to explore the archaeological implications of a wide range of plausible scenarios and alternative histories. This is not to say that such exploratory models can be used to support any interpretation, regardless of how far-fetched or divorced from empirical data that interpretation might be. To the contrary, one is able to eliminate unfit propositions using this modelling approach precisely because it allows one to test often ill-defined alternatives in a more rigorous setting. This approach also allows us to see when common assumptions and expectations lead to implausible archaeological outcomes. This experimental design yields fruitful models that permit the exploration of multiple 'what if' scenarios, which Gould (1989) calls 'plausible channels' and Gumerman & Kohler (2001) call 'alternative cultural histories'. By contrast, the emulation approach yields models that are engineered to produce the outcomes to which we are predisposed and, as a result, stands to teach us very little that we did not already 'know' to be true.

Exploring behavioural terra incognita in the Lower Paleolithic

> [...] in pursuing the archaeology of the very remote past we are exploring behavioural *terra incognita*. If we are to avoid simply creating our origins in our own image, we have ruthlessly to expose all important propositions, however obvious seeming to potential falsification (Isaac 1983: 16).

This candid statement by Glynn Isaac outlines a simple, yet under-appreciated, approach to Paleolithic archaeology. Following this advice, I have reported elsewhere on a recent attempt to falsify some fundamental assumptions concerning the formation of Plio-Pleistocene archaeological landscapes (Premo 2005; 2006). In the spirit of experimentation and exploration, I used a null model to question whether some previously held behavioural assumptions are logically necessary to produce spatial signatures in artificial archaeological landscapes that are similar to those documented empirically in East Africa. Of particular interest is whether food sharing at central places was necessary for the formation of the so-called 'scatter and patches' archaeological landscapes that are characteristic of the Lower Paleolithic record in East Africa (Kroll & Isaac 1984). Many early studies relied heavily upon observations of living humans to address early hominid food sharing, but extant and historically documented hunter-gatherer groups represent a small subset of possible forager societies, each bound by its own historical, economic, and political contexts. Equally important is the fact that modern hunter-gatherers are members of an entirely different hominid species than those living during the Plio-Pleistocene. For these reasons, the referential method of using modern hunter-gatherer behaviours as direct analogues for those displayed by earlier hominids has fallen out of favour with many paleoanthropologists.

In contrast to previous referential studies, I employed an agent-based model, called the Simulated Hominid Altruism Research Environment (hereafter SHARE),[2] as a behavioural laboratory to investigate how a wide range of experimental behavioural and ecological scenarios affect artefact clustering in artificial archaeological landscapes. SHARE's behavioural assumptions are much simpler than those of earlier explanatory frameworks, many of which presumed that Plio-Pleistocene hominids habitually employed central place foraging techniques (Leakey 1971; Isaac 1978; Lovejoy 1981; but see Binford 1981; 1987; Isaac 1983; Potts 1988 for some earlier examples of those that did not). Central place foraging, which is commonly observed among contemporary hunter-gatherers, involves delaying consumption of procured foodstuffs until they have been transported back to a prearranged meeting place, where they are often shared with others who have congregated there. This modern human behaviour was often attributed to early hominins as a way to explain the formation of the 'scatter and patches' distribution of Oldowan material. Although subsequent research has tempered the precocious interpretation that 'patches' of Oldowan artefacts are the by-products of hominin activities centred on central places, this notion has been very influential in prior Lower Paleolithic reconstructions, despite the lack of empirical archaeological evidence that independently demonstrates that central place foraging was employed regularly by hominins during the Oldowan.

With SHARE, I am using a bottom-up model as a behavioural laboratory. More specifically, SHARE is a spatially-explicit agent-based model that explores how 'scatter and patches' archaeological landscapes could have been produced by Plio-Pleistocene hominins under various behavioural and ecological conditions. The hominins in the model are independent agents that can be equipped with different behaviours and dropped in a

2. SHARE is programmed in Objective-C, and makes use of Swarm libraries (see http://www.swarm.org).

range of ecologically patchy food resource distributions. It is important to emphasize that SHARE is neither VR nor a role-playing video game. What little SHARE has in the way of visualization is highly effective, but laughably crude **[Plate 1]**. In fact, it would not be an exaggeration to say that, beyond serving a valuable use in visual debugging (Grimm 2002), SHARE's visual interface is completely superfluous (this statement certainly is not true of VR). But this is of little concern to my behavioural research agenda, because eye-popping visual effects are far less important than the artificial archaeological data collected during each simulation run. The raw spatial data describing artefact density across space—not fancy visual displays—can be used to address the research question concerning the extent to which resource patchiness affects the spatial structure of an artificial archaeological landscape.

SHARE's results demonstrate the powerful role that resource patchiness can play in structuring the archaeological remains of a population of socially inept foragers who do not employ central place foraging techniques of any kind or share food with others

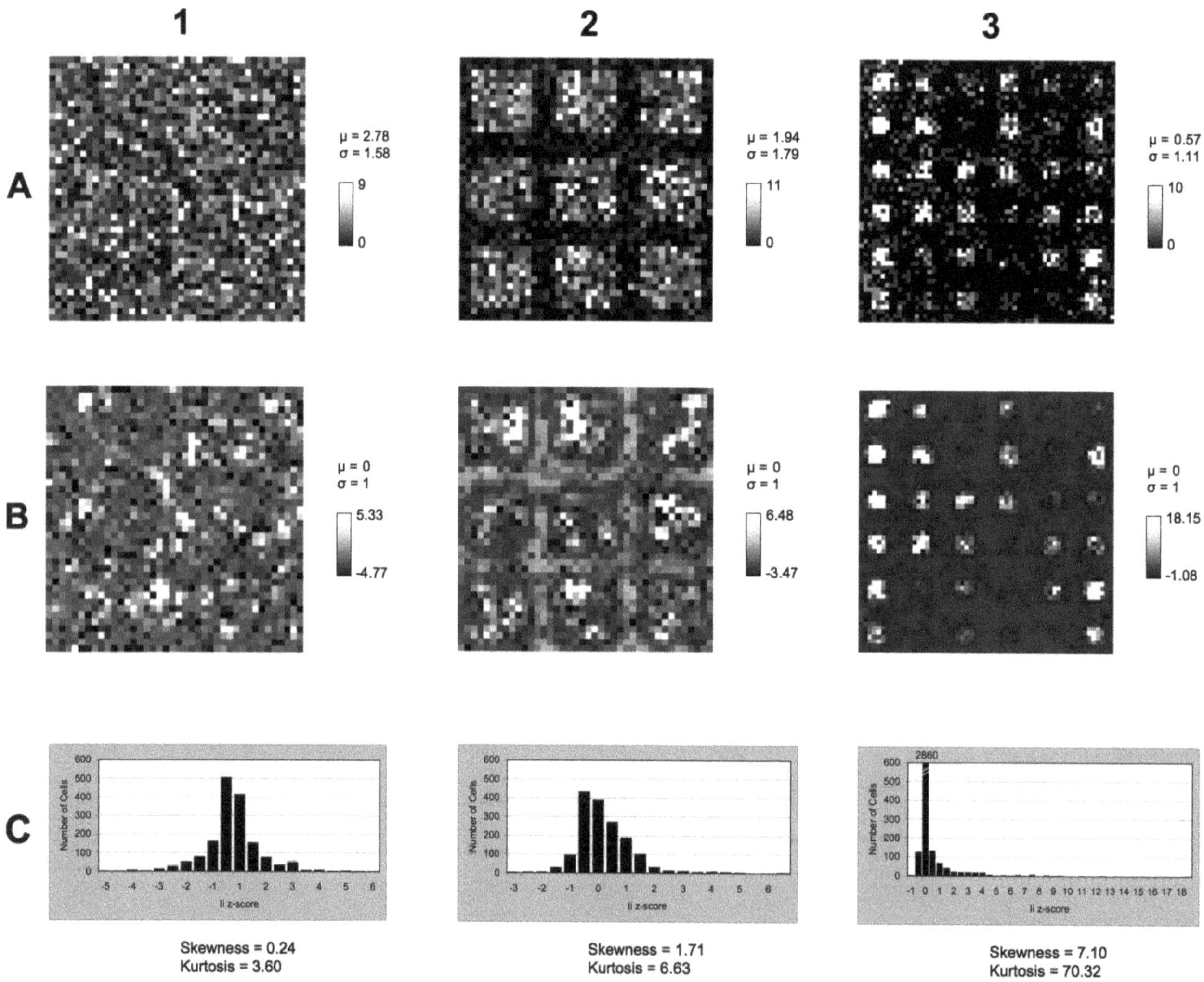

Fig. 2. *Local Moran's Ii quantifies the effect of ecological patchiness on the spatial structure of archaeological landscapes. Each column presents three looks at the spatial structure of a different artificial assemblage: A. raw number of artifacts per cell, B. Ii z-scores, and C. histogram of Ii z-scores. Note that each appears with some summary statistics. Underlying ecological patchiness increases from left to right: 1. patch size 42, gap size 0; 2. patch size 10, gap size 4; and 3. patch size 4, gap size 6.*

in need. **Fig. 2** presents the artificial archaeological landscapes of three different simulation runs at three different levels of ecological patchiness, ranging from one megapatch on the left (not patchy) to a very patchy environment on the right. The integers in the raster surfaces presented in Row A of **Fig. 2** represent the number of artefacts deposited per cell.

Using only the naked eye one can detect the patterning in archaeological assemblages that is caused by increasing ecological patchiness. But to analyze this clustering quantitatively, local spatial statistics are required. Elsewhere, I have introduced archaeologists to local spatial autocorrelation statistics, including local Moran's I (I_i) (Premo 2004). Local Moran's I can be used to identify localized hotspots of similar values, whether low or high. Positive I_i z-scores indicate that the target cell is similar to its spatial neighbourhood, whereas negative scores indicate that it is very different from its neighbours; a value near 0 means that there is no spatial autocorrelation at that scale. Although the raster maps of the standardized z-scores [**Fig. 2**, row B] seem to reflect an obvious trend from less to more patchy assemblages from left to right, the more reliable evidence for this trend comes in the form of quantitative measures of skewness and kurtosis [**Fig. 2**, row C]. Skewness characterizes the degree to which values are asymmetrically distributed around their mean. Positive skewness indicates a right-skewed distribution, which has an asymmetric tail extending toward positive values; while negative skewness indicates a left-skewed distribution, which has an asymmetric tail extending into negative values. Kurtosis, on the other hand, characterizes the relative flatness (or evenness) of a distribution as compared to a normal, bell-shaped distribution. Positive kurtosis indicates a relatively peaked distribution in which many values are concentrated in just a few bins. Negative kurtosis indicates a relatively flat distribution in which values are more uniformly distributed across the entire range.

When foraging in a large, homogeneous resource distribution, hominin agent movements yield a diffuse scatter of artefacts [**Fig. 2**, column 1]. Note that in this scenario, I_i scores are distributed normally about 0. These are the very results one would expect to see under the assumption of a homogeneous archaeological distribution, one which lacks localized concentrations of artefacts. However, the other columns demonstrate that as food resource patchiness increases, so too does the structure of the resulting archaeological assemblages. As many generations of hominid agents search for energy via simple (i.e. not central place) foraging strategies, a consistently patchy resource distribution influences the spatial structure of the resulting archaeological landscape such that concentrations of artefacts accumulate in the vicinities of diachronically reliable food sources. As a result, the histograms in columns 2 and 3 are quite different from that in column 1. First, unlike the normally distributed I_i z-scores of column 1, the histograms in the others are right skewed. Whereas the homogeneous spatial distribution yields relatively equal numbers of scores on either side of the mean and, as a result, a correspondingly low skewness value, the patchy spatial distributions produce far more positive I_i scores than negative ones. This trend towards positive skewness is just what we would expect to see when archaeological distributions possess localized concentrations of similar values (i.e. patchiness). Second, as archaeological landscapes become patchier, one should expect their I_i scores to be less evenly distributed across the range of possible values, a quality which can be assessed via a measure of kurtosis. As expected, the kurtosis value calculated for the z-scores of the patchiest spatial distribution [**Fig. 2**: 3C] is more than an order of magnitude greater than those calculated for either of the more diffuse spatial disctributions.

So, how does this agent-based exploration better inform our ideas about Lower Paleolithic archaeology and Plio-Pleistocene hominin behaviours? For starters, it demonstrates that ecological patchiness can structure hominin agent behaviour such that artificial archaeological assemblages display the characteristic 'scatter and patches' distribution in lieu of central place foraging. Indeed, spatial data collected from a number of artificial assemblages created in different ecological scenarios demonstrate that foragers living in patchy environments need not display central place foraging strategies in order to leave behind equally patchy archaeological landscapes (Premo 2006). Note that, if this agent-based model had merely emulated Lower Paleolithic archaeological landscapes with central place foraging agents, this finding could not have been reached, even though such a model probably would have yielded similar spatial data.

SHARE teaches us that in some ecological settings we may jettison some of the central assumptions of our highly detailed referential models without sacrificing much of their explanatory power. The spatial results demonstrate that, if minimal assumptions are made from the outset, many of the behavioural assumptions that have accompanied previous reconstructions are not necessary to explain the archaeological phenomenon of interest—at least in patchy 'mosaic' environments representative of those that become more prominent in East Africa throughout the Pliocene (Levin *et al.* 2004; Quade *et al.* 2004). According to this theoretical work, ecological patchiness alone can have a significant impact on the structure of the archaeological record left by solitary foragers. SHARE's artificial archaeological results imply that in cases where Plio-Pleistocene hominins inhabited patchy ecological settings, it may not be necessary to invoke the more complicated behavioural explanations that involve central place foraging, division of labour, and male provisioning of nuclear families to explain the characteristic 'scatter and patches' archaeological landscapes they leave behind. Whether this simpler, theoretically derived alternative can be falsified requires that we return to the archaeological data, this time with different questions in mind and new hypotheses to test. This recursive movement between theory and data is the cornerstone of any heuristic modelling approach.

Conclusion

Exploratory models like SHARE force us to rethink the validity of our highly detailed behavioural reconstructions and their relationship to empirical archaeological data. SHARE does not 'prove' that central place foraging had no influence on the formation of empirical archaeological landscapes. However, it demonstrates that in certain ecological scenarios even simple foraging strategies, which do not include food-sharing at central places, can yield patchy archaeological distributions. The take-home message here is not that Plio-Pleistocene hominids were asocial, solitary foragers (itself, a tactful assumption made for the sake of the null model). Rather, it is that previous paleoanthropological reconstructions probably include a number of behavioural assumptions that are not necessary to explain important spatial signatures of Lower Paleolithic archaeological landscapes in patchy environments. If we avoid making these assumptions, at least until systematic testing has proven them necessary, we might allow ourselves to find empirical archaeological support for simpler alternatives that otherwise would not receive consideration.

Incorporating a more rigorous, theoretical modelling program in paleoanthropology—one that is founded on Glynn Isaac's advice to expose our propositions to potential falsification—will prove enormously fruitful. One major goal of such a program is to build archaeological inferences of Lower Paleolithic behaviour from the 'null-up' via systematic experimentation with artificial societies. This approach provides a significant departure from that which borrows inferences from ultimately unrepresentative sources in hopes that they will apply in some essential way to hominins that lived over two million years ago. Agent-based models, designed with exploration and experimentation—not emulation—in mind, provide powerful tools for theory-building and, ultimately, for explanation, as researchers in other disciplines have already noted (Grimm *et al.* 2005). After all, interesting discoveries about the past are made possible by exploring different plausible behavioural and environmental scenarios and by testing new hypotheses, not by imitating the *status quo in silico*.

Bibliography

Bawaya, M. 2006. "Digital digs", *Nature* 440/27: 1106-1107.

Beekman, C. S. & Baden, W. W. 2005. *Nonlinear Models for Archaeology and Anthropology*, Hampshire: Ashgate.

Binford, L. R. 1981. *Bones: Ancient Men and Modern Myths*, New York: Academic Press.

Binford, L. R. 1987. "Searching for camps and missing the evidence: another look at the Lower Paleolithic", in O. Sofer (ed.), *The Pleistocene Old World: Regional Perspectives*, New York: Plenum Press: 17-31.

Brantingham, P. J. 2003. "A neutral model of stone raw material procurement", *American Antiquity* 68/3: 487-509.

Brantingham, P. J. 2006. "Measuring forager mobility", *Current Anthropology* 47/3: 435-459.

Dean, J. S., Gumerman, G. J., Epstein, J. M., Axtell, R., Swedlund, A., Parker, M. & McCarroll, S. 2000. "Understanding Anasazi culture change through agent-based modeling", in T. A. Kohler & G. J. Gumerman (eds.), *Dynamics in Human and Primate Societies: Agent-Based Modeling of Social and Spatial Processes*, Oxford and New York: Oxford University Press: 179-206.

Epstein, J. M. & Axtell, R. 1996. *Growing Artificial Societies: Social Science from the Bottom-up*, Washington DC and Cambridge: The Brookings Institution Press and MIT Press.

Gould, S. J. 1989. *Wonderful Life: the Burgess Shale and the Nature of History*, New York: Norton.

Grimm, V. 2002. "Visual debugging: a way of analyzing, understanding and communicating bottom-up simulation models in ecology", *Natural Resource Modelling* 15/1: 23-38.

Grimm, V., Revilla, E., Berger, U., Jeltsch, F., Mooij, W. M., Railsback, S. F., Thulke, H., Weiner, J., Wiegand, T. & De Angelis, D. L. 2005. "Pattern-oriented modeling of agent-based complex systems: lessons from ecology", *Science* 310: 987-991.

Gumerman, G. J. & Kohler, T. A. 2001. "Creating alternative cultural histories in the prehistoric Southwest: agent-based modeling in archaeology, a progress report", in D. A. Phillips & L. Sebastian (eds.), *Examining the Course of Southwest Archaeology: the Durango Conference, September 1995*, Albuquerque: New Mexico Archaeological Council: 113-124.

Isaac, G. L. 1978. "The food sharing behaviour of protohuman hominids", *Scientific American* 238/4: 90-108.

Isaac, G. L. 1983. "Bones in contention: competing explanations for the juxtaposition of Early Pleistocene artefacts and faunal remains", in J. Clutton-Brock & C. Grigson (eds.), *Animals in Archaeology*, vol. 1, B.A.R. International Series 163, Archaopress: Oxford: 3-19.

Kohler, T. A. & Gumerman, G. J. 2000 (eds.). *Dynamics in Human and Primate Societies: Agent-Based Modeling of Social and Spatial Processes*, Oxford and New York: Oxford University Press.

Kohler, T. A., Gumerman, G. J. & Reynolds, R. G. 2005. "Simulating ancient societies", *Scientific American* 293/1: 76-83.

Kohler, T. A., Kresl, J., van West, C., Carr, E. & Wilshusen, R. H. 2000. "Be there then: a modeling approach to settlement determinants and spatial efficiency among Late Ancestral pueblo populations of the Mesa Verde region, U.S. Southwest", in T. A. Kohler & G. J. Gumerman (eds.), *Dynamics in Human and Primate Societies: Agent-Based Modeling of Social and Spatial Processes*, Oxford and New York: Oxford University Press: 145-178.

Kroll, E. M. & Isaac, G. L. 1984. "Configurations of artefacts and bones at early Pleistocene sites in East Africa", in H. J. Hietala (ed.), *Intrasite Spatial Analysis in Archaeology*, Cambridge: Cambridge University Press: 4-31.

Lansing, J. S. 2002. "Artificial societies and the Social Sciences", *Artificial Life* 8: 279-292.

Leakey, M. D. 1971. *Olduvai Gorge: Excavations in Beds I and II, 1960-1963*, vol. 3, Cambridge: Cambridge University Press.

Levin, N., Quade, J., Simpson, S. W., Semaw, S. & Rogers, M. 2004. "Isotopic evidence for Plio-Pleistocene environmental change at Gona, Ethiopia", *Earth and Planetary Science Letters* 219: 93-110.

Lovejoy, C. O. 1981. "The origin of man", *Science* 211: 341-350.

Potts, R. 1988. *Early Hominid Activities at Olduvai*, New York: de Gruyter.

Premo, L. S. 2004. "Local spatial autocorrelation statistics quantify multi-scale patterns in distributional data: an example from the Maya Lowlands", *Journal of Archaeological Science* 31/7: 855-866.

Premo, L. S. 2005. "Patchiness and prosociality: an agent-based model of Plio/Pleistocene hominid food sharing", in P. Davidsson, K. Takadama & B. Logan (eds.), *Multi-Agent and Multi-Agent-Based Simulation*, Lecture Notes in Artificial Intelligence 3415, Berlin: Springer: 210-224.

Premo, L. S. 2006. "Patchiness and prosociality: modeling the evolution and archaeology of Plio-Pleistocene hominin food sharing", unpublished Ph.D. dissertation, University of Arizona.

Quade, J., Levin, N., Semaw, S., Stout, D., Renne, P., Rogers, M. & Simpson, S. 2004. "Paleoenvironments of the earliest stone toolmakers, Gona, Ethiopia", *Geological Society of America Bulletin* 116/11-12: 1529-1544.

Reidhead, V. A. 1979. "Linear programming models in archaeology", *Annual Review of Anthropology* 8: 543-578.

van der Leeuw, S. E. 2004. "Why model?", *Cybernetics and Systems* 35: 117-128.

Vonnegut, Jr., K. 1959. *The Sirens of Titan*, New York: Dell.

Zubrow, E. 1981. "Simulation as a heuristic device in archaeology", in J. Sabloff (ed.), *Simulations in Archaeology*, Albuquerque: University of New Mexico Press: 143-188.

Chapter 5
Cost surface DEM modeling of Viking Age seafaring in the Baltic Sea

Inferences in nautical archaeology about sailing routes in northern Europe are based today almost entirely on historical information coupled with results from experimental archaeology. The authors propose here a third method, which combines computer simulation with the aforementioned information sources. Digital bathymetric models (DBMs) of the Baltic seafloor, wind, current, and other real sailing parameters are used to create cost surfaces for modelling early Medieval seafaring. Real sailing data from 2004 sailing voyage of an early Medieval replica, the Ottar, is used to model sea routes in the Baltic Sea. Both GIS-Esri and GRASS GIS are compared as modelling tools and used in least-cost path and anisotropic spread analyses to simulate sea routing in prehistoric land- and seascapes across which humans travelled a thousand years ago.

George Indruszewski† & C. Michael Barton•

† Vikingeskibshallen, Roskilde, Denmark

• School of Human Evolution and Social Change, Center for Social Dynamics and Complexity, Arizona State University, USA

Introduction

Maritime archaeology, especially historical research dealing with Viking Age seafaring, has tried for a long time to decipher the reasons behind the choice of specific sea itineraries connecting Medieval trading centres in the Baltic realm. The problem is complex, because explicit itineraries from that period do not actually exist and because the literates who laid them on the parchment for the posterity used their epoch's writing style and conventions. This is the case with King Valdemar's early 13th century journey from Utlängan (Sweden) to Reval (Estonia), where the route follows the Swedish coastline in earnest (Varenius 1995: 189-194). Adam of Bremen's late 11th-century ecclesiastic history, on the other hand, lists just the main descriptive elements of a sea voyage: the departure point, the destination, and the time spent in reaching the destination (Schmeidler 1917: 80).

The situation becomes even more difficult in the Viking Age (8th to 11th century AD). Very few written sources are available for the interested scholar. One such source is Wulfstan's late 9th century account of his sea voyage, included in the Orosian history of King Alfred the Great. Wulfstan sailed for seven days and nights from Haidaby, in the lower Schlei Fjord (in today's Schleswig-Holstein, Germany), to Truso, near the Vistula River mouth (identified archaeologically with Janowo Pomorski located about 4 km south of Elbląg in eastern Pomerania, Poland) **[Plate 1]**. During the voyage, Weonodland was on his starboard side (that is the Land of the Wends in the southern Baltic), and islands under Danish overlordship (Langeland, Lolland,

The authors wish to thank the Vikingeskibshallen (Viking Ship Museum) for supporting this research initiative, Arleyn Simon from the Arizona Research Institute (Arizona State University) who generously provided ArcView GIS resources and research space, and the GRASS international development team for making open source GIS available to everyone. We also offer our thanks to Steve Schmich for his helpful insights.

and Falster), followed by Bornholm, Möre, Blekinge, Öland, and Gotland (the latter belonging to the Svear) were off to port.

The text is important for several reasons. Its briefness, composition, and informal content point to a description of a sea voyage that happened sometime in the second half of the 9th century, and it is one of the very few surviving sailing narrations of the Viking Age Baltic Sea. Furthermore, it describes sea travel between two archaeologically significant trading centres in the Baltic: Haidaby (Haithabu) and Truso. Last but not least, the text provides us with clues about contemporary navigational methods. The author displays a geographical knowledge in employing a maritime orientation system that uses the ship as the central point. That is, he does not orient the coastlines and islands in relation to each other, but in relation to the sailing ship. This contrasts with the orientation system(s) used in Alfred's Orosius (Korhammer 1985: 251-269), and is also unique among historical sources in general. Paradoxically, but not unexpectedly, it is the least ambiguous in terms of cardinal directions. When Wulfstan says that the islands under Danish suzerainty were on the port side and that Weonodland was on starboard all the way until the mouth of the Vistula, it is clear that his ship sailed on a general course from west to east.

The research issue

Nevertheless, that is all that the text explicitly indicates. Specific routing is left to more speculative hypotheses, such as the one envisioned by Crumlin-Pedersen (1983: 32-44). Relying upon iconographic evidence from the Bayeux Tapestry and other Medieval historical sources, Crumlin-Pedersen pioneered a novel conceptual approach to early Medieval Norse navigation that emphasized the importance of depth sounding. He suggested that Wulfstan used soundings to follow a preselected bathymetric line (he proposed using the –10 or –20 m depth lines) running along the southern Baltic coastline, from the mouth of the Schlei to the mouth of the Vistula (Crumlin-Pedersen 1983: 42-43). In other words, Crumlin-Pedersen argued that the primary orientation system for the Viking Age navigator was below the waterline and not above it, and that coastal sailing was the main type of navigation knowledge for that period. Besides relying on iconographic and historical sources that are post-Viking Age, the proposed construct conflicts with the Wulfstan's textual information as well as the character of his voyage. His sea voyage was a routine journey, which required neither sounding navigation nor coastal sailing. This is supported not only by the text but also by the following arguments:

- Sounding as a method of orientation at sea was known since Herodotus' times in the Mediterranean region and was documented in northern Europe later in the Middle Ages. But when documented it is mentioned only in relation to landing or approaching a coastline.
- Wulfstan's route could not have followed a specific isobathic line, since a high resolution bathymetric chart (DBM) of the Baltic Sea bottom clearly shows the sinuosity of these lines. In fact, the route that Crumlin-Pedersen proposed crosses several of these isobaths representing some tens of meters variation in depth—an unlikely route for a navigator following a constant depth.
- Crumlin-Pedersen's route also puts an important island, Fehmarn, on the port side. But this is not mentioned in the Wulfstan text. Fehmarn was a part of the Wendland until the mid-12th century, but was not mentioned with the other portside isles under Danish suzerainty. In the last decades of the 11th century, Adam of Bremen considered Fehmarn an integral part of the Wendish lands: '*Quarum prima Fembre vocatur. Haec opposita est Wagris, ita ut videri posit ab Aldinburg, sicut illa, quae Laland dicitur. [...] Ambae igitur hae insulae pyratis et cruentissimis latronibus plenae sunt, et qui nemini parcant ex transeuntibus. Omnes enim, quos alli vendere solent, illi occidunt*' (Schmeidler

1917: 113).[1] It seems unlikely that Wulfstan would not have included it in his list.

- Land was in view but sufficiently far away all the way up to Arkona and Bornholm that soundings were not necessary for orientation, even during night sailing.
- Wulfstan's voyage did not have an exploratory character and would follow established routes.
- Wulfstan underlines in his account non-stop navigation both day and night, which implies sailing away from the coastline. Sailing close to the coastline at night and without navigational aids holds considerable risks even today, because while most of the Baltic Sea bottom is covered by 'till' (boulder clay) and sand, it has stony grounds. This, plus the presence of strong coastal currents that endanger even modern coastal navigation (especially on the long flat Polish coast), would have given Wulfstan little chances for reaching his destination if he used the coastal routing.[2]

Wulfstan sailed non-stop for seven days and nights, and the shortest linear distance between his departure and arrival points is 390 nautical mi (Nmi). Therefore the average minimum speed of his vessel was 2.3 kn (or 55 Nmi every 24 hours). The more the vessel departed from this straight-line route, the longer the distance it would travel and the greater the average speed required to make the voyage in the recorded seven days. We do not know Wulfstan's actual travel speed or his routing, but the historical account provides a set of geographical and temporal constraints within which the voyage took place. Thus, the northern sailing boundary is defined by the southern limits of the Danish archipelago and the southern sailing boundary follows the southern coastline of the Baltic, including its affiliated islands. In navigational parlance, the Danish isles must remain on port while the Wendish (Slavic) lands stay on the starboard side. This means that the historical voyage was of a 'corridor-sailing' type, at least for the western Baltic portion (up to Cape Arkona, the northeasternmost tip of the Rügen Island; for details, see Indruszewski & Godal in press).

In order to go beyond the basic understanding of the text, and also to keep highly speculative constructs at bay, we can employ GIS-based simulation as a new way to develop precise and testable hypotheses about Wulfstan's sea route from the meagre historical information. The simulation presented here does not operate on fictitious values, but is based on both historical information provided by Wulfstan's account and real-time data provided by experimental archaeology. In order to use the data provided by experimental archaeology, sailing voyages replicating Wulfstan's routing have to fulfill several strict conditions, such as natural propulsion (wind, currents, human power); a route from Haithabu to Janowo Pomorski; non-stop sailing during day and night; and no modern navigational aids (including sea charts and a compass). An earlier attempt to sail a hypothetical route of Wulfstan's voyage, by the Danish Marine cutter Barsø in 1993 cannot be used for our simulation since it did not fulfill any of the above mentioned conditions.

In the summer of 2004, a replica of the 11th century Skuldelev 1 vessel, the Ottar, reached Gdańsk, Poland from Schleswig, Germany, after sailing a total distance over ground of 390 Nmi in a little over four consecutive days and nights (A. Englert and W. Ossowski, official communication Wismar 28 September 2004). Although this voyage did not fulfil most of the conditions required of a real experimental voyage (the crew used modern navigational aids, the ship was sailed under motor in the Schlei and in Gdańsk and also stopped at anchor

1. For early Medieval Slavic settlements and artefact distribution see Hucke 1938: 4-43; Harck 1988: 299-314.

2. 'With persistent winds a rate of about 2 kn (100 cm/s) may be experienced, being strongest about 4.5 Nm offshore. With onshore winds and a swell from the NW, a dangerous S set may prevail. Statistics over the last 60 years demonstrate that 25% of all incidents involving vessels grounding offshore, particularly between Świnoujście and Jaroslawiec, about 87 miles NE, were caused by lack of appreciation and allowance for currents. With onshore winds it is advisable to keep well offshore until the weather improves before attempting a landfall' (United Kingdom Hydrographic Office, Baltic Pilot volume II – South part of Baltic Sea and Gulf of Riga, Taunton, 2002: 337). And this advice is for modern ships.

for the first night of the voyage etc.), the Ottar's real-time sailing data, its open sea routing, and the wind and current conditions were used in our GIS-based simulations to emulate the conditions from the real-world of sailing, inasmuch as the sailing capabilities of the vessel and the crew were the closest approximation one can presently get for replicating Wulfstans' sailing itinerary. The Ottar voyage was carried out as a result of a larger research project directed by G. Indruszewski at the Vikingeskibshallen and aimed on the theoretical and practical reconstruction of Wulfstan's voyage. The initial plan of sailing from Haithabu to Janowo Pomorski with a small-size historical replica was cancelled because of the crew's psychological and physical lack of preparation to endure the sailing conditions characteristic of 9th century navigation.

Replicated voyages and computer simulation have been used in other settings to develop and test proposed hypotheses about sea voyages in a systematic way (e.g. Heyerdahl 1950; Levison 1973; Irwin *et al.* 1990; Irwin 1992). While our focus here is on computer simulation, both methods have been applied to developing a more accurate reconstruction of Wulfstan's voyage and more generally for studying Viking seafaring. Through this chapter, we suggest an alternative and complementary means of testing and generating hypotheses about ancient sea voyages through computer simulation modelling. While this has generally been done through customized software, it could be more widely employed by archaeologists and historians if easily available 'off-the-shelf' packages could be used. Modern GIS software includes tools for simple modelling of movement across space. Here we present the initial results of using two types of such GIS tool sets to simulate Viking seafaring, using Wulfstan's voyage as a test case. Real-time sailing data, including routing and wind conditions collected during the Ottar's replicated voyage in 2004, were used to evaluate the GIS-based simulations. We compare sailing routes generated by a least-cost path (henceforth LCP) routine in ArcView 3.1 and an anisotropic spreading routine (hereafter AS) in GRASS 6 GIS (open source) with both the historical information and the real-time data from the replica voyage from Schleswig to Gdańsk.

Research methods

As already mentioned, we employ two GIS methods for modelling movement across surfaces to simulate Viking Age sailing, and for both modelling tests, we focus on wind intensity (velocity) and direction as the primary drivers of a sailing vessel. Currents, although relatively weak in the southern Baltic, would have also affected sailing routes in that period. At this point, however, we chose not to include currents in our simulation. The main reasons for this decision were that we do not have clear information about currents affecting Ottar's voyage in 2004 as we do for wind and, more importantly, the algorithms used in each GIS method of computation do not permit the incorporation of a second force vector to drive movement (though either method could be extended to do so). Below is a brief overview of each simulation method.

LCP modelling has been used extensively in GIS applications for identification of optimal routing based on user-defined criteria. Optimal routing seeks to minimize travel costs between an origin point and destination point across a terrain where movement can be affected (encouraged or impeded) by variables such as slope, vegetation, urban attributes, and water vicinity. In applying LCP to a sailing voyage, a trailing wind is treated conceptually like going downslope on a topographically variable terrain, while a headwind is treated like travel upslope. In brief, the LCP procedure, as implemented in GIS, involves the following steps:

- Create one or more cost surface raster grids, where the value of each grid cell represents the absolute or relative costs of (or resistance to) movement at every location in the research area. In our case this is derived from wind velocity.
- Create an accumulated cost distance grid, where each cell represents the total costs of travel (based on the combination of all relevant cost surfaces)

from a starting location (source or origin point) to all other locations in the study area.

- Optionally, create a backlink grid (cost-direction-surface) from the accumulated cost surface that indicates the directionality of travel costs in each grid cell (e.g. it costs more energy to travel upslope than downslope). We use wind direction in this calculation (i.e. a tailwind decreases movement costs while a headwind increases them).
- Calculate a path that minimizes total costs from the source to a desired end location (the destination) across the accumulated cost surface. This path is the modelled sailing route.

AS is less well-known than the LCP analysis. It models the spread of a phenomenon across a terrain from a point of origin. Perhaps the most common usage of AS procedures in GIS is in modelling the spread of wildfires. The rate and extent of spread for a wildfire can be affected by topography and forces that have both intensity and direction (such as wind), causing it to spread unequally in different directions (e.g. faster downwind and uphill). It might seem odd, at first, to use modelling algorithms most widely used for fire to simulate travel across water. However, in some ways, it may be more realistic than LCP. Conceptually, a vessel is treated as a specific point on a fire front that is driven by wind of variable velocity and direction, over a given time period. The AS routine also can calculate back from any given point on a fire front to its point of origin, tracing the route it took under variable environmental (i.e. wind) conditions.

The AS routine in GRASS is optimized to model the behaviour of wildfires (Jianping 1994). Hence, as input, it requires information about parameters that commonly affect wildfires: the speed and direction of the wind, the slope and aspect of the topography, and characteristics of the vegetation that is burning. In order to use this routine to model a wind-driven sailing vessel traversing the Baltic Sea, we used a level plane 'topography' and chose grassland for vegetation. In spite of waves at local scale, the sea approximates much more closely a plane than a hilly or mountainous terrestrial landscape. Fire spreads variably across space in forest and woodland, depending on such parameters as moisture content, the amount of downed wood, and the relative densities of arboreal and shrub vegetation. Grass, on the other hand, burns quickly and evenly in all directions across a level plane, except as influenced by the wind, as would be expected for wind blowing unimpeded across the sea surface. As developed in GRASS, AS modelling involves three major steps:

- Using a series of raster maps that represent the parameters which influence the spread as values for each grid cell (e.g. maps of wind direction and wind velocity), to create three raster maps showing: 1) the maximum rate of spread (henceforth ROS) in the primary direction of spread (i.e. downwind, in our case); 2) the direction of the maximum ROS; and 3) the ROS perpendicular to the primary direction of spread (this has no impact in our example here, but is required for subsequent steps).
- The three ROS maps produced in the first step are then used to model the spread phenomenon (in this study, wind-driven sailing routes). This second step produces a graphic simulation of the AS, as well as a map of the cumulative duration of spread and a map containing the backlink information.
- In the third step, the backlink map is used to calculate the most probable spread path from the origin point to the destination. This is the modelled sailing route for the example presented here.

In order to make our simulations more realistic, we constrained them to the possible water routes that Wulfstan could have taken. We set all land areas—island and continental—to null value masks so that the costs surface for LCP and spread maps for AS routines would be limited to the grid cells over water and extending eastward from the western coast of Denmark to east of the Vistula River mouth. We used wind data encountered by Ottar during its 2004 Baltic voyage for this test of GIS-based simulation methods. Wind speed and direction measurements were collected for every 10' of latitude and longitude across the Baltic Sea between 54° and 56° N and 10° and 20° E for the duration of the Ottar's voyage **[Plate 1]**. These measurements were then reprojected to UTM Zone 32 and interpolated to continuous raster grids of wind speed and direction at a 1-km resolution **[Plates 2-3]**, using Regularized Spline Tension in GRASS 6 (Mitas & Mitasova 1999; Hofierka *et al.* 2002), that were subsequently used for LCP and AS modelling.[3]

The AS sailing simulation in GRASS

The AS routine models the spread of phenomena over a given surface during a given period of time, taking into account the effects of spatial heterogeneity in local conditions on the unevenness of spreading (i.e. anisotropy) in different directions. Here, relevant spatial heterogeneity included wind velocity, wind speed, and the distribution of land and water. As described above, wind data collected during the Ottar's voyage were interpolated to raster maps of wind speed and wind direction. The interpolated raster maps of wind speed and direction extended to a 20-km buffer beyond the original data grid to minimize edge effects in subsequent models. A digital elevation model (DEM) of the Baltic area, interpolated in GRASS from a file of elevation points for the region (Seifert *et al.* 2001), was then used to mask out the land area from the wind speed and wind direction raster grids. In this manner, all modelling was restricted to those parts of the Baltic Sea relevant to the voyage.

The simulation was done in three major steps, as noted above, using the AS module for wildfire modelling in GRASS 6. For surface topography, we created a level plain DEM to represent the Baltic Sea surface. Wind velocity had to be converted from minute/second to feet/minute for the modelling routine. For the required vegetation input, we empirically tested several U.S. Forest Service fuel models (Rothermal 1983) before settling on a grassland model, as noted above. The fuel models are based on the burning parameters of different categories of vegetation, including the mass of fuel per unit area (fuel loading), fuel depth, fuel particle density, and the heat of burning for each fuel. We tried timber, brush, chaparral, and tall grass. We used default USFS values for fuel moisture in dead and live vegetation in different vegetation communities. Slower burning models (e.g. timber) spread more evenly in all directions and are not driven by the primary wind direction and speeds, as were vessels like the Ottar. Many of these models failed to spread across the Baltic Sea to the eastern edge of the study region, even when we weighted the primary ROS before using it in the spread simulation analysis. Faster burning fuel models (e.g. tall grass) spread most rapidly in the main wind direction, mimicking a sailing ship being driven by wind, and were better able to spread across the entire study region. The fuel model we used had the fuel source input as a constant across the whole study region (rather than as a map of spatially varying vegetation).

The most successful simulation used the tall grass fuel model with standard values of 3% for one hour fuel moisture and 0% for live fuel moisture **[Plates 4-6]**. However, it was still necessary to multiply the maximum ROS and base ROS by ten in order to create a model that would spread across the entire Baltic study area, a much larger area than that of a normal wildfire **[Plates 7-9]**. These issues are related to the specific wildfire implementation of the AS routine in GRASS rather than considerations about the usefulness of the underlying AS algorithm. The starting point of the anisotropic spread was set at the mouth of the Schlei

3. The following data sources were used in this analysis: 1) Sea bottom data: Seifert et al. 2001; Bundesamt für Schiffahrt und Hydrographie 3021/3022 (2003/2004) Charts; Deutsches Hydrographisches Institut, Die Ostsee mittlerer Teil (1930). 2) Wind data: M. Ketzel, Danish Meteorological Institute, Risø, Denmark (pers. comm. Roskilde 2005); Denmark Meteorological Institute, http://www2.dmu.dk/AtmosphericEnvironment/thor/metindexdk.html; Air Resources Laboratory, NASA, http://www.arl.noaa.gov/ready/amet.html; Jet Propulsion Laboratory, NASA, http://poet.jpl.nasa.gov; WindData.com, http://130.226.17.201/site_distrubutions.php?site_code=roedsand&country=Denmark. 3) Sea current data: Bundesamt für Schiffahrt und Hydrographie, http://www.bsh.de/aktdat/modell/stroemungen/Modell1.htm9; and Meteomedia Wetterstationen, http://wetterstationen.meteomedia.de/messnetz/.

Fjord in northern Germany at 54° 41 latitude north, 10° 02 longitude east. By setting all input variables except wind to constants, the GRASS wildfire routine produced a resultant raster grid of the spread and associated backlink grid based on the wind velocity and direction in the study area. This approximates the likely paths taken by a simple sailing vessel outward from Schlei Fjord given the weather conditions recorded during the Ottar's voyage in 2004.

The LCP sailing simulation in ArcView

The LCP simulation was more difficult because ArcView normally requires a single DEM of topography, from which it calculates cost intensity and cost distance from the slope, and cost direction from the aspect. We tried various methods to combine wind speed and direction into a single DEM of sailing conditions, without success. On the other hand, multiple cost variables or cost direction variables can easily be combined. For example, combining wind direction and current direction produced apparently meaningful results **[Plate 10]** from the mouth of Schlei Fjord eastward across the Baltic. This avenue deserves more research in order to be used in subsequent simulations and to model more accurately the parameters affecting sailing.

Fortunately, it is possible to input two separate grids representing cost intensity and cost direction into ArcView. We followed this approach, setting wind strength as the cost intensity (equivalent to slope calculated from a DEM) and wind direction as cost direction (equivalent to aspect calculated from a DEM). As with the AS analysis in GRASS, we set all land grid cells equal to null so that the LCP analysis would only take place on sea grid cells **[Plate 11]**. ArcView calculated an accumulated cost distance map from wind velocity without difficulty **[Plate 12]**. However, using wind direction as cost direction **[Plate 13]** was considerably more problematic.

Intuitively, wind direction values should be 180° from an aspect value in a DEM needed for LCP analysis. This is because a wind from the west will reduce the cost of a vessel travelling towards the east, equivalent to travelling downslope on an east-facing slope. Surprisingly, creating a cost direction grid in this way did not have the desired result but instead produced completely meaningless LCPs, such that no path from Schlei Fjord to the Vistula River mouth could be calculated. After additional testing, we discovered if we used a normal wind direction raster map and allowed ArcView to create a cost direction grid from this map (i.e. another cost direction grid) and this direction grid was combined with the cost distance map created from wind velocity, we were able to achieve a meaningful LCP **[Plate 14]**.

The results of the LCP analysis closely match both the AS analysis and the actual path of the Ottar, suggesting that they are correct if wind velocity and direction are the primary variables influencing the route. However, the final cost direction grid used in the LCP analysis was created automatically from the input cost direction grid (i.e. wind direction) by an undocumented ArcView routine. Because the software is proprietary (produced and distributed by ESRI) and the underlying code is not accessible to users, leaving us uncertain about the wider applicability of this particular approach. There is no documentation in ArcView as to the kinds of values needed for a valid cost direction grid. We tested various possible combinations of values for cost direction and all except the method described here gave spurious results. Hence, we recommend caution when using this routine until it has been tested further or properly documented.

Discussion

The final step in both GRASS AS and ArcView LCP analyses was calculating a probable sailing route from Schlei Fjord, Germany to Janowo Pomorski, Poland as an anisotropic least-cost path in the GIS routines. These routes are shown in **Plate 15**, along with the route of the 2004 Ottar voyage. Both simulations closely match the Ottar's actual route, navigating off the southern coastlines of Lolland and Langeland, southern tip of

Falster, and around Bornholm's southern shores, before heading eastward across the open Baltic.

The AS routine in GRASS 6 seemed to track more closely a sailing route influenced mainly by wind conditions than did the ArcView LCP routine. The change in wind direction at the foot of the Hel Peninsula caused the path to veer towards the northeast, which would be normal for a ship propelled primarily by the prevailing wind and whose skipper is sufficiently skilled to forecast the subsequent wind change. In spite of the cautions expressed above, the ArcView-generated LCP also matched closely Ottar's voyage from Schleswig, Germany to Gdańsk, Poland, although it seems somewhat less sensitive to shifts in wind direction than the AS routine. The fact that both routines produced similar results that closely match a real voyage suggests that GIS-based simulation has considerable potential for modelling ancient sailing routes.

As noted previously, three routes have been proposed for Wulfstan's 9th century voyage: 1) a route developed on the basis of historical and archaeological considerations (the O. Crumlin-Pedersen 1983 line in **Plate 16**, marked OCP 1983); 2) an actual coastal voyage carried out in 1993 by the Danish Navy cutter Barsø (marked Barsø 1993), which attempted to recreate the Crumlin-Pedersen's hypothetical route; and 3) the early Medieval ship replica Ottar's open sea voyage (marked Ottar 2004). The next stage of our GIS modelling of Viking seafaring will be to simulate sea routes based on monthly and seasonal average weather conditions in the eastern Baltic in order to better evaluate which of these (or other) routes are more likely. We also hope to be able to incorporate sea current data into our simulation in the future to better account for the combinations of wind and current conditions that affected Viking seafaring. GIS-based modelling is a promising means of recreating the spatial and temporal dynamics of ancient societies from the static remains that make up the archaeological record.

Bibliography

Bately, J. in press. *Wulfstan: Text, Translation, and Notes*, Ohthere Seminar Proceedings, Roskilde: Vikingeskibshallen.

Crumlin-Pedersen, O. 1983. "Skibe, sejlads og ruter hos Ottar og Wulfstan", in N. Lund (ed.), *Ottar og Wulfstan, to rejsebeskrivelser fra vikingetiden*, Roskilde: Vikingeskibshallen: 32-44.

Harck, O. 1988. "Zur spätslawisch-frühmittelalterlichen Besiedlung auf den Ostseeinseln Rügen und Fehmarn, Offa—Berichte und Mitteilungen zur Urgeschichte", *Frühgeschichte und Mittelalterarchäologie* 45: 299-314.

Heyerdahl, T. 1950. *Kon-Tiki: Across the Pacific by Raft*, New York: Pocketbooks.

Hofierka, J., Parajka, J., Mitasova, H. & Mitas, L. 2002. "Multivariate interpolation of precipitation using regularized spline with tension", *Transactions in GIS* 6: 135-150.

Hucke, K. 1938. *Tonware und Siedlung der Slawen in Wagrien*, Vor- und frühgeschichtliche Untersuchungen aus dem Museum vorgeschichtlicher Altertümer in Kiel (Neue Folge) 3, Neumünster, Holstein: Wachholtz.

Indruszewski, G. & Godal, J. in press. "The art of sailing like Wulfstan in Wulfstan's Voyage–New light on Viking-Age seafaring within the ethnic geography of Mare Balticum", *Proceedings of the International Seminar in Wismar September 2004*, Vikingeskibshallen/ Archäologisches Landesmuseum, Mecklenburg-Vorpommern.

Irwin, G. 1992. *The Prehistoric Exploration and Colonization of the Pacific*, Cambridge: Cambridge University Press.

Irwing, G., Bickler, S. & Quirke, P. 1990. "Voyaging by canoe and computer–experiments in the settlement of the Pacific-Ocean", *Antiquity* 64/242: 34-50.

Jianping, X. 1994. "Simulating the spread of wildfires using a geographic information system and remote sensing", unpublished Ph.D. dissertation, Rutgers University.

Korhammer, M. 1985. "The orientation system in the Old English Orosius: shifted or not?", in N. Lapidge & H. Gueuss (eds.), *Learning and Literature in Anglo-Saxon England: Studies presented to Peter Clemoes*, Cambridge: Cambridge University Press: 251-269.

Levison, M. R., Ward, G. & Webb J. W. 1973. *The Settlement of Polynesia: a Computer Simulation*, Minneapolis: University of Minnesota Press.

Mitas, L. & Mitasova, H. 1999. "Spatial interpolation", in P. Longley, M. F. Goodchild, D. J. Maguire & D. W. Rhind (eds.), *Geographical Information Systems: Principles, Techniques, Management and Applications*, Hoboken: Wiley: 481-492.

Rothermal, R. C. 1983. "How to predict the spread and intensity of forest and range fires", National Wildfire Coordinating Group PMS-436-1, NFES 1573.

Schmeidler, B. 1917. *Adam von Bremen*, Hannover/ Leipzig: Hamburgische Kirchengeschichte.

Seifert, T., Tauber, F. & Kayser, B. 2001. "A high resolution spherical grid topography of the Baltic Sea—revised edition", *Proceedings of the Baltic Sea Science Congress (25-29 November 2001)*, Stockholm: Stockholms Marina Forskningscentrum: 25-29.

Varenius, B. 1995. "The Baltic itinerary of Codex Holmiensis A41", in O. Olsen, J. Skamby-Madsen & F. Rieck (eds.), *Shipshape*, Roskilde: Vikingeskibshallen: 189-194.

Chapter 6
Visualizing DEMs: the significance of modern landscape modifications in the distribution of archaeological finds

On a standard DEM map of an agricultural region in the Rhineland, we detected pits which were not created by geological processes but resulted from human activity. This paper will examine (i) who created these pits (ii) the DEM method that can best be employed to detect them and (iii) the other sources we use to map as many pits and heaps as possible. Many of these pits destroyed archaeological features in a significant percentage of the Rhineland and other regions that were densely populated during the past two centuries.

Renate Gerlach, Irmela Herzog & Julia von Koblinski
Rheinisches Amt für Bodendenkmalpflege, Landschaftsverband Rheinland, Germany

Introduction

The Rhineland Commission for Archaeological Monuments and Sites (Rheinisches Amt für Bodendenkmalpflege) in Bonn, Germany, undertakes archaeological work in the Rhineland and is responsible for a densely populated (about 9,600,000 inhabitants) area of approximately 12,600 square km. The favourable climatic conditions and natural resources attracted many settlers during archaeological and historical periods. Therefore, not only the population density but also the number of archaeological sites is high. Modern construction work causes destruction of cultural heritage predominantly in urban areas, and archaeologists are aware of this threat. It is often assumed that the archaeological sites are well preserved in agrarian landscapes. Though densely populated, about half of the Rhineland is used for agricultural purposes. Erosion and ploughing are considered to be the main problems in these areas. It is the aim of the Rheinisches Amt für Bodendenkmalpflege to preserve these sites and to document archaeological features before they are destroyed by building activities.

On a standard digital elevation (DEM) map covering a 4 square km quadrangle of an agricultural region in the Rhineland near Erkelenz in the western part of the federal state North Rhine-Westphalia **[Plate 1]**, we detected pits that were not created by geological processes (Herzog 2001, 2002). Later, we found these pits on many other DEMs covering 4 square km in this region. The pits were mostly a product of the brick making industry and its precursors in the 19th and 20th century.[1] Why are these pits important? Let us consider a site with a few small pits containing artefacts, and the topmost layer of the pit fill has been distributed on the field as a result of ploughing. A brickearth pit is dug and the site is partly destroyed. Some of the topsoil is deposited nearby. Later, the pit is refilled with humic

1. There was a high density of brickyards in the area close to the Rhine and in the western parts of the Rhineland (Momburg 2000:76).

Thanks go to Ulla Ullrich-Wick for the total station measurements and for acquiring the more accurate DEM test data, to Jutta Lechterbeck for the error calculations which form part of Table 1, to Reiner Lubberich and Alexander Thieme who digitized the pits from historical and modern maps, to colleagues of the Landesamt für Statistik in North-Rhine Westphalia for reliably supplying the 10-m grid DEM data, and to Günter Merboth for correcting our English.

topsoil and material from somewhere else, possibly containing objects from another site. In field-walking surveys, these pseudo-sites can hardly be distinguished from authentic sites. However, in many cases the pits are not completely refilled and can still be detected via DEM visualization **[Fig. 2]**. Most of these pits have diameters of 50-200 m, but their depth is often less than 2 m. Frequently, they are rectangular and aligned along modern roads or farm tracks. Sometimes a DEM will even show an access path to the pit.

Creating the DEM image

The basis of the DEMs are data from the Ordnance Survey in North Rhine-Westphalia, made available to our institution free of charge.[2] Different methods were employed to create the data sets: digitizing of contour lines can still be found in forest areas, while photogrammetry and laser scanning prevail in the rest of the Rhineland. Currently, we work mainly with the 10-m grid. Given pit diameters of 50 m or more, the Ordnance Survey's 10-m DEM grid meets the Nyquist Limit, which determines the maximum permissible distance between grid points forming the DEM.[3]

Elevation data is delivered in form of an ANSI list of x-,y-,z-values with 40,000 points per 2x2 square km quadrangle. We used GIS applications MapInfo 6.0 and Vertical Mapper 3.0 to visualize the DEM data. MapBasic, the programming language for MapInfo operations, was used to convert coordinate lists to MapInfo points. Inverse Distance is the only interpolation method supported by MapInfo 6.0; Vertical Mapper offers a wider range of methods, but we found that Inverse Distance was fast and created reasonable results with the 10-m grid data. Trial and error led to a standard search radius of 20 m. With relief shading, the pits become more clearly visible, and the shading properties are preferably adjusted for each individual DEM separately.

Several visualization techniques were tested to identify the best method for detecting refilled pits and manmade heaps. **Plate 3** shows a thematic map of the elevations with additional contour lines. The green areas are the lowest whereas brown denotes the most elevated parts of the map. Small contour line circles, with the interior below the contour line, indicate pits. Pits on different elevation levels are represented with different colours in this visualization, but it is difficult to detect pits on sloping terrain. The pits can be discerned more easily with a smooth colour profile and omitting the contour lines, but the image appears blurred **[Plate 1]**. Our preferred method is relief shading with different shades of gray **[Fig. 2]**. The absolute differences in elevation are no longer visible, but relative differences stand out more clearly.

The accuracy of the DEM grid

According to Ordnance Survey information available on the Web, the accuracy of the DEM is +/-0.5 m. However, some obvious errors in the DEM grid made us wonder how accurate the data are. For example, **Plate 5** shows small bumps in the south-north and east-west axes. Comparing neighbouring profile lines on grid points, with one line on the bumps and the adjacent line at 10 m distance, we found that in most cases the bumps are on one profile line only and that the bulk of the errors is within a tolerable range of 20 cm.

Another way to test the grid is to compare it to our own total station measurements of finds in the field. We selected five data sets with fairly equally distributed finds. With the Point Inspection function of Vertical Mapper we estimated the elevation of the find locations based on the DEM grid and then compared these estimated elevations with the true values **[Table 1]**. In some cases all the points were below the estimated elevations (or vice versa). We compensated for that by subtracting the average point difference. The resulting relative differences are relevant for detecting pits. The examples show that in most cases the proportion of

2. http://www.lverma.nrw.de

3. 'The maximum distance between two points should be 0.25 the size of the area/shape of a feature to be detected' (Beex 2004:240-241).

Fig. 2. Shaded relief map of the DEM shown in Plate 1.

	1	2	2a	3	4	5
Size (ha)	34.49	29.64	7.70	37.40	2.3	2.2
Test point nos.	1763	1286	847	2771	951	524
Max. height difference (m)	6.5	3.07	2.23	7.40	0.76	3.56
Mean difference, DEM/point data (m)	0.09	0.44	1.08	0.92	0.09	0.07
Max. error (m)	1.06	0.72	0.82	2.25	0.30	0.28
% of errors, -0.1 to 0.1 m	40.34	85.88	76.32	53.21	78.34	76.91

Table 1. Comparison of total station measurements versus estimated elevation of locations based on the DEM grid.

points with an error of less than molehill size (i.e., 10 cm) is above 50%.

We recently purchased more accurate test data in order to detect smaller features and to compare the results. The laser-scanning data sets consist of points which are distributed fairly regularly at a distance of 2 m or less. The official accuracy is +/-0.3 m. Visualizing these elevation data with the Inverse Distance method and a search radius of 5 m, even World War II bomb craters can be detected. The diameter of these bomb craters is typically 8-15 m. Burial mounds in forests with similar diameters are also visible on these more accurate DEMs.

According to the Ordnance Survey, the 10-m grid data are calculated from laser scanning data, whenever available. We tested the accuracy of this process using a 2 x 2 km test area that had a maximum elevation difference of more than 60 m. Whereas the 10-m grid includes 40,000 points, the laser scanning data consists of 1,428,865 points. Using the 10-m grid and the Point Inspection function, we estimated the elevation of the original laser scanning points. The average error was 11 cm, for 56% of the points the difference between the estimated value and the laser scanning height did not exceed 10 cm and for 14% of the points the difference was greater than 20 cm. The points where the difference exceeds 1 m can mainly be found in a narrow trench and in the bomb craters, and only 0.06% of all points fall into this category.

A GIS of pits and heaps

Our aim throughout this process has been to detect as many pits and heaps as possible so that pseudo-sites could be identified and field walking could be directed to other places. Several sources are being used and the results stored in a GIS format (Gerlach 2001; Eckmeier, Gerlach 2002). Historical and modern topographic maps often represent these refilled pits by closed contour lines with an arrow pointing to the interior; these outlines of the pits were digitized. Another source was soil maps used for tax purposes. On these maps, areas of disturbed soil are designated with a U. Aerial photographs may also show traces of refilled pits. Sometimes, old aerial photographs depict pits which are no longer visible at all, or track the development of a brickyard and its pits. Finally, the DEM data was analyzed, as described above.

Three test areas in different landscapes

Three 4 x 4 km test quadrangles in three different landscapes of the Rhineland were analyzed taking all the sources listed above into account. One quadrangle is near Goch situated on a lower terrace and part of a flood plain landscape. The second is from a loess landscape near Erkelenz (close to the area shown in **Plates 1-3**). The third quadrangle is from the area east of the river Rhine between Bonn and Cologne and is on a lower terrace with a non-active river system.

The area near Goch is characterized by the lower terrace with a flood plain that was covered mainly by meadows during the past few centuries **[Plate 4]**. The historical map and the modern topographic map document old clay and gravel pits. The soil map plays the most important role in this case, since it shows that the abandoned branches of the river Niers have been refilled. So we can demonstrate that at least 5% of the area is either covered with soil from somewhere else or the top level soil was removed and not replaced. It should be noted that this image is based only on the sources described above, and additional investigations will certainly show that much more of the area is affected.

The loess landscape in the second quadrangle is gently sloped and used for intensive farming **[Plate 5]**. In this case the data have the bump problem discussed above, but the DEM shows that many of the pits which are visible on the topographic map are in fact bigger than the contour lines suggested. In this case, at least 7.7% of the area is affected. Once again, this is only the tip of the iceberg, since completely refilled pits have good chances to remain undetected.

The lower terrace in the third quadrangle was formed during the last ice age. The abandoned non-active river system dates back to this period, but in general the area is fairly flat [**Plate 6**]. The pits created by industrial activities can be easily identified. All pits together cover at least 16% of the area. Overlaying the GIS layer containing the archaeological sites and monuments recorded at our institution on the layer of pits and heaps, reveals that some of the site locations are quite close to the pits and therefore it is likely that theses locations are pseudo-sites with relocated finds.

Modern features mould the terrain

Plates 6-7 suggest that a map can be drawn based on the DEM data alone. **Plate 7** shows a valley, a motorway and another main road, and three bridges. Slope and aspect maps can be easily calculated using this data, but the results are of no use for predictive modelling. It is not easy to erase the modern features from the DEM in trying to reconstruct the landscape of historical periods. However, when overlaying the DEM with the topographic map we found that the crossing in the south-western area does not correspond to a map feature, but is actually a sunken road crossing. In a few years' time these differences in elevation will no longer be visible because ploughing will finally fill the sunken road trenches with eroded material from the fields nearby. Therefore, we search the DEM and maps for sunken roads as well and incorporate these features into our GIS project. With the more accurate DEM, we are able to detect abandoned tracks in the loess area, these tracks can be considered small-scale sunken roads.

Conclusion

Refilled pits and trenches as well as heaps pose a problem because archaeological finds may be re-deposited this way. Open pits and heaps can be easily detected, but refilled pits are nearly invisible except on appropriate DEMs with relief shading. The problem is not restricted to the Rhineland, since brickearth and other bulk material pits were dug and refilled in many other industrialized European countries. The Netherlands are as densely populated as the Rhineland, suitable brickearth can be found in many regions, and therefore the brickearth industry was very busy during the 19th and 20th century. Similarly, Great Britain has a long and active history of brick production, going back to Roman times.[4] A single brick factory, Faversham Bricks, produced 100,000 bricks a day in the 1830s.[5] Refilled gravel and sand pits pose the same problem if their location has not been recorded.

In the Rhineland, brickearth pits are the main cause of pseudo-sites: it has been shown that more than 16% of an area characterized by a mix of agrarian and industrial activities is affected. This is only the portion which can be identified based on our sources—the true amount is definitely larger. In the Rhineland we are addressing this problem by developing a GIS system that can keep track of as many pits and heaps as possible. It has been demonstrated that DEM visualization with relief shading is an effective tool to detect the pits.

Bibliography

Beex, W. 2004. "Use and abuse of digital terrain/elevation models", in *Enter the Past–the E-Way into the Four Dimensions of Cultural Heritage (CAA 2003 Proceedings, Vienna, 8-12 April 2003)*, B.A.R. International Series 1127, Oxford: BAR Publishing: 240-242.

Eckmeier, E. & Gerlach, R. 2002. "Achtung: Löcher in der Landschaft. Die Materialentnahmegruben-Datenbank", *Archäologie im Rheinland* 2001: 155-157.

Gerlach, R. 2001. "Keinesfalls Ausnahmen. Materialentnahmegruben als Befundzerstörer", *Archäologische Informationen* 24/1: 29-38.

Herzog, I. 2001. "Ehemalige Material entnahmegruben erkennen-Auswertung von Höhendaten", *Archäologische Informationen* 24/1: 39-43.

4. http://www.tegula.freeserve.co.uk/BRICMAK.HTM

5. http://www.faversham.org/pages/standard.aspx?i_PageID=15796

Herzog, I. 2002. "Materialentnahmegruben in digitalen Geländemodellen erkennen", *Archäologie im Rheinland* 2001: 155-157.

Momburg, R. 2000. *Ziegeleien überall. Die Entwicklung des Ziegeleiwesens im Mindener Lübbecker Land*, Mindener Beiträge 28, Minden: Bruns.

CHAPTER 7

THE POTENTIAL OF ANCIENT MAPS FOR QUANTIFYING SLOPE PROCESSES – COMPARISON OF HISTORICAL AND MODERN ELEVATION MODELS

Slope processes are of great importance for the development and preservation of archaeological sites. Archaeological sites could already be eroded in the upper part of the slope and buried under colluvial deposits at the bottom, which form favorable conditions for preservation. It would be of great interest for the cultural heritage management to know the amounts of these mass relocations in different landscapes. Here, direct approach was tested and 100-year-old maps of the Preussische Neuaufnahme (PN) of the Rhineland were compared to modern elevation models. The aim was to detect differences in the relief and further calculate the mass relocations. On the whole, this project shows that the contour lines of the historical map are not suited to visualizing and quantifying mass movements and slope processes of the last century. The aberrations of the map are far too great and too unsystematic to carry out detailed analyses on the basis of this map. This paper is the first attempt to evaluate the accurateness of the "Preussische Neuaufnahme" and is thus a contribution to source critique.

Jutta Lechterbeck
Institut für Ur- und Frühgeschichte der Universität zu Köln, Germany

Slope processes are of great importance for the development and preservation of archaeological sites. Archaeological sites could already be eroded in the upper part of the slope and buried under colluvial deposits at the bottom, which form favorable conditions for preservation. It would be of great interest for the cultural heritage management to know the amounts of these mass relocations in different landscapes. Different models exist to simulate erosion (Ducke 2004), but these methods are far too generalizing and speculative. Furthermore historical amounts of erosion are difficult to reconstruct, because the different parameters (such as steepness) are unknown. Here, a more direct approach was tested: the approximately 100-year-old maps of the Preussische Neuaufnahme of the Rhineland **[Fig. 1]**, which is in the western part of Northrhine-Westfalia, were compared to modern elevation models. The aim was to detect differences in the relief. All analyses were carried out with MapInfo and Vertical Mapper.

Fig 1. *Localization of the Rhineland.*

Material and Methods

As a first step, five areas were chosen for analysis **[Table 1]**. An important criterion was that these five areas lie in different landscapes of the Rhineland. For every area there is a digital and straightened map, on a 1:25,000 scale, of the *Preussische Neuaufnahme* (PN). The PN was

Name	number TK25 sheet	area (km^2)	max. height (m)	min. height (m)	height difference
Kleve	4202 Kleve	2.72	77.88	32.11	45.77
Bell	4804 Mönchengladbach	1.90	88.59	53.05	35.54
Genhülsen	4804 Mönchengladbach	1.34	85.05	68.99	16.06
Willich	4304 Xanten	3.44	23.62	18.13	5.49
Siebengebirge	5309 Königswinter	2.70	162.79	421.14	258.35

Table 1. *Overview of the areas analyzed.*

begun in 1892 in the territory of today Northrhine-Westfalia. It was the first systematic attempt in Germany to measure heights and to display the relief as isolines on a map.

Further height information for this work was taken from the German topographic map 1:25,000 (TK25). Additionally a digital elevation model on the scale 1: 5,000 exists for all analyzed areas. This model consists of geodetic points in a 10 m grid (DGM5). The DGM5 has been available area-wide for the whole of Northrhine-Westfalia since 2002. The points of the grid were gained by three different methods: beside airborne laser scanning of the earth's surface, stereoscopic measurements of aerial photographs were made. Large parts of the DGM5 were constructed by digitizing the contour lines of the *Deutsche Grundkarte 1:5,000.* (Landesvermessungsamt NRW 2004) All maps, grids and point measurements were available in digital form at the Rheinisches Amt für Bodendenkmalpflege in Gauss-Krüger projection. The maps were georeferenced scans of printed maps. To obtain digital elevation data from these, elevation points were set along the contour lines. The resulting elevation model could then be compared with the elevation model of the DGM5. This technique is problematic with the TK25 because the original contour lines are often destroyed and disrupted by added areas of newly constructed buildings, roads and railways. Such areas were excluded from the originally rectangular investigation areas. The achieved point densities reach from 1092 points per km^2 to 280 points per km^2.

From these points elevation models for both topographic maps were constructed. The next step was to assign a height on the PN and the TK25 to every point of the DGM5. Thus the respective differences between the DGM5, the PN and the TK25, could be calculated.

Results and Discussion

The differences between the elevation models were mapped **[Plate 2]**. Areas in which the DGM5 is higher are displayed in brown, areas in which the DGM5 is lower are displayed in green. **Table 2** shows the maximal differences in height between the elevation

Name	height-differences DGM5-PN (m)		height-differences DGM5-TK25 (m)	
	max.	min.	max.	min.
Kleve	9.80	-5.48	3.20	-4.40
Bell	7.63	-26.10	26.29	-28.15
Genhülsen	8.13	-4.92	11.92	-16.50
Willich	2.86	-4.16	2.70	-3.20
Siebengebirge	41.56	-17.79	40.76	-22.83

Table 2. *Maximal height differences between DGM5 and PN and topographic map 1 : 25000 (TK25).*

	Single finds area 1	Single finds area 2	Single finds area 3	Single finds area 4
area (ha)	34.49	29.64	7.70	37.40
number of levellings	1763	1286	847	2771
maximal height difference (m)	6.5	3.07	2.23	7.40
average difference DGM5 and single find levelling (m)	0.09	-0.44	1.08	-0.92
corrected max. deviation (m)	1.06	0.43	0.82	2.25
corrected min. deviation (m)	-0.78	-0.72	-0.58	-0.75
% of values between 0.1m and 0.1m difference	40.34	85.88	76.32	53.21

Table 3. *Height differences between single find levelling and the DGM5.*

models, which are remarkable in some areas, though extreme values are restricted to single or few points. For the most part, anthropogenic impacts account for these extrema, like gravel-pits or bridges. But not all extreme values can be explained by scrutinizing the map.

The map of elevation differences of the area Siebengebirge **[Plate 2]** shows for example that the heights are in general higher today then they were hundred years ago and the low lying areas are lowered in comparison to the historical map. The same phenomenon can be observed in all other analyzed areas, though in different extend. This is of course contradictory to all geomorphological observation.

Furthermore PN and TK25 show roughly the same differences from the DGM5 **[Plate 2]**. Smaller differences between the two topographic maps may be explained by a slight offset between these. A profile of the northwestern slope of the Großer Ölberg **[Fig. 3**, Profile A-B] shows that the elevation models of PN and TK25 are for the most part congruent, whereas the DGM5 differs considerably.

Though the PN was actualized and modernized continuously, this is only true for roads, buildings and other anthropogenic construction: the elevation model was just copied from the old version to the new. It was not systematically actualized or corrected. This can be shown by comparison between TK25 and PN in different map issues. For the area Siebengebirge the elevation models of the 1910 and 1926 issues were compared with the PN and the TK25, for the areas Genhülsen and Bell the issue of 1953 was available. All compared elevation models agree. Only in one of the areas analyzed the contour line of the PN and the TK25 differed. Apparently, the contour lines were remeasured and redrawn. This is the area of Kleve, where the conversion of forest into arable land made a new survey necessary.

The transfer of the elevation model from map issue to map issue however does not explain the phenomenon of heightened heights and lowered low lying parts. To trace this further, the accurateness of the DGM5 elevation model was tested. For this test (analogue to Herzog 2001) four areas in the Rhineland **[Table 3]** were chosen where levelling of single finds exist.

From the differences between the DGM5-model and the levelling of the finds the average deviation was subtracted, as only the relative differences in height were of interest. On the whole the heights of the DGM5 are in good agreement with the heights of the single find levelling. The accurateness of the DGM5 was thus determined sufficiently. As a next step, contour lines were constructed from the points of the DGM5. These contour lines show great aberrations compared with the PN or the TK25 in some parts. This is shown by the example of the area Siebengebirge. **Plate 2** shows a

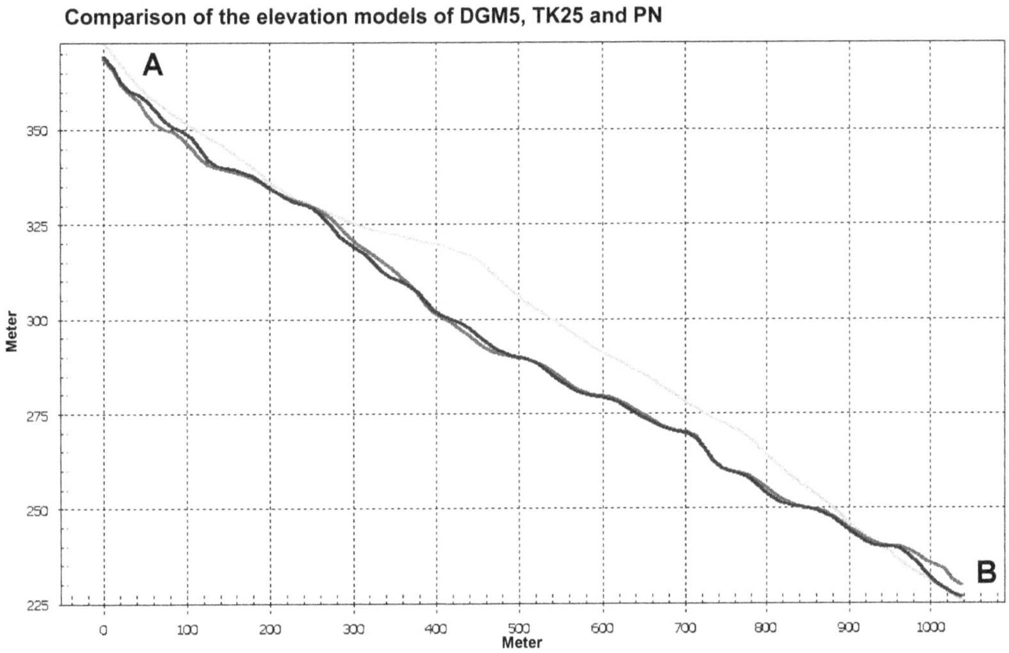

Figure 3: Comparison of the elevation models of DGM5 (green), PN (red) and TK25 (blue).

considerable heightening at the northwestern slope of the Großer Ölberg. If the contour lines of the DGM5 and the topographic map (here the TK25 **[Fig. 4]**) are superimposed, lines of similar height run in a distance of more than 100 m in some parts. This corresponds to a height difference of over 13 m. In other parts of the map however, the elevation models are congruent. Particularly great differences between the digital elevation model and the PN lie in forested areas, as further comparisons between the DGM5 and the PN show, here once more for a section of the sheet 5505 Blankenheim **[Fig. 5]**. The reason for this is that all measurements for the heights had to be carried out in the field and depended on visible points in the landscape. In the forested areas, however, the visibility was strongly restricted. Therefore the contour lines had to be interpolated in these areas. Regulations concerning the error range did not exist for the PN and do not exist until today for the scale 1 : 25,000 (personal communication M.Oster, Landesvermessungsamt Nordrhein-Westfalen).

On the whole this little project could show, that the contour lines of the PN historical map are unsuitable to visualize and quantify mass movements and slope processes of the last 100 years. The aberrations of the PN are far too great and too unsystematic to carry out detailed analyses on the basis of this map. However, this paper is the first attempt to evaluate the accurateness of the *Preussische Neuaufnahme* and is thus a contribution to source critique.

Bibliography

Ducke, B. 2004. "A Geo-Archaeological Model of Holocene Landscape Development and its implications for the Preservation of Archaeological Sites," in *Magistrat der Stadt Wien, Abteilung Kulturelles Erbe, Enter the Past–The e-way into the four Dimensions of Cultural Heritage, CAA 2003, April 8-12, Wien*, B.A.R. International Series 1127, Oxford: BAR Publishing.

Herzog, I. 2001. "Ehemalige Materialentnahmegruben erkennen–Auswertung von Höhendaten," in *Archäologische Informationen* 24/1: 39-43.

Landesvermessungsamt NRW, http://www.lverma.nrw.de/produkte/landschaftsinformation/hoehenmodelle/ (seen August, 2004).

Chapter 8
LIDAR-based surface height measurements: applications in archaeology

Height measurements based on laser technology (LIDAR) result in high-accuracy and high-density information. Based on an overview of the technical background and visualization techniques of LIDAR data, this study describes archaeological applications roughly grouped into two areas, landscape reconstruction and site-tracing. A host of research opportunities and approaches arise through such applications, for instance the reconstruction of historical geographical elements and paleogeographical analysis, the tracing of individual monuments with pattern-recognition techniques, the identification of sub-recent disturbances, and predictive modelling. It is concluded that the utilization of LIDAR data can contribute substantially to archaeology, in terms of efficiency and quality of research.

Arjan G. de Boer[†], Walter N. H. Laan[•], Wouter Waldus[†] & Wilko K. van Zijverden[†]
[†] ADC-Archeoprojecten B.V., The Netherlands
[•] ARCHOL B.V., The Netherlands

Light detection and ranging (LIDAR) is an airborne remote-sensing technique that can measure terrain elevation. The first LIDAR surface height measurements for parts of the Netherlands became available in 2001. By 2004, the database covered the entire country. The first digital elevation models (DEM) based on these data showed more landscape detail than ever achieved before. Studies of applications in geomorphological mapping were quickly published after the release of the first databases (Brus & Kiestra 2002). The first application to archaeological research was a paleogeographical reconstruction of an area where 49 fish traps and 11 fish weirs were found during an excavation in a residual gully (van Zijverden 2002). It proved impossible to make a paleogeographical reconstruction of this landscape using conventional hand auger equipment (e.g. Palarczyk 1986; Gehasse 1990), but a combination of archived core descriptions and a DEM allowed for a surface reconstruction within an hour. Based on this experience, a research proposal to investigate the possibilities of this new technology for archaeological research was put together. In 2003, the project was funded by SENTER, an agency of the Dutch Ministry of Economic Affairs that coordinates projects to stimulate the application of new technologies by companies and research institutions.

This article presents a brief overview of recent applications of LIDAR-based DEMs in archaeological research (for a full publication of the study results, see Waldus & van der Velde in press). First, we outline the technical background of LIDAR surface height measurement and databases. Then, we describe applied visualization techniques, followed by an overview of applications in archaeology. Other remote-sensing techniques (aerial photography, infrared and multispectral analysis) are compared to laser altimetry to assess their value for archaeological research.

Technical background

Laser altimetry techniques

LIDAR systems transmit laser pulses from an airplane to the ground and sense the 'echo' pulses when they return. The time that it takes for a pulse to return to the sensor is a measure for the distance between the laser head and the ground. Early airborne LIDAR systems had problems georeferencing the laser measurements, but modern accurate differential global positioning systems (dGPS) and inertial measurement units (IMU) that record the angle orientation of the sensor to the ground fixed the problems. It is now possible to measure surface elevations with an accuracy of ca. 15 cm. Modern LIDAR systems can sense several returns per pulse, making it possible to discriminate between forest canopy and bare ground (Lillesand & Kiefer 2004). There are also sensors that can measure the intensity of the return signal and provide additional information about the nature of the surface.

Between 1996 and 2004, Dutch governmental institutions measured the entire country's surface elevations with LIDAR, at a minimum density of one measurement per 16 m^2 (except in areas with large water surfaces or forests, where the density was one measurement per 36 m^2). The surveying flights were carried out during the winter, with an overlap between strips to cover the entire country's surface. The data were then compared with conventional measurements to get an impression of the accuracy of the results. If multiple pulses return to the sensor, it can be assumed that only the final pulse is reflected from the surface and the rest are from other sources, such as vegetation. This principle was used to filter out vegetation from the landscape measurements. Buildings were filtered out with other topographical data and visual inspections.

The accuracy of the measurements is calculated as the sum of the random error and the systematic error. The random error is particular to the laser scan equipment and varies with every measurement. It has a standard deviation of 15 cm (68% of the measurements show an error less than this). The systematic error is the same for groups of measurements per recorded strip. It is related to the IMU and GPS and is considered to be less than 5 cm. A complicating factor is the presence of vegetation. Logically, the higher and denser the vegetation, the more it influences the measurement, but it is not easy to quantify this error.

Interpolation and visualization techniques

Parallel to the development of LIDAR, software and personal computers have improved to the degree that it is both affordable and feasible to work with the huge amount of data that LIDAR creates and to generate digital elevation models (DEM) from the LIDAR databases. The DEMs represent the surface topography in digital format. A major concern in creating a DEM is the choice of an interpolation method for the irregular-spaced measuring points that LIDAR produces.

A method often used for altitude data is inverse distance weighting (IDW: for this and other interpolation techniques, see Burrough 1994). In this method, the estimated value of a grid cell depends on its distance to neighboring data points. In general, the greater the distance, the smaller the data point's influence on this value. This relation depends on an exponent that is defined by the user. In addition, the user determines the radius within which data points are used to calculate a grid cell value. The radius and exponent are determined on the basis of expert judgment. The disadvantages of this method are its tendency to smooth out small-scale relief and the clustering effect around data points.

Another widely used interpolation method is a triangulated irregular network (TIN). This method produces a network of triangles that connect all data points. The values of the grid cells are calculated using the slope and shape of the triangles. The user determines (based on expert judgment) the maximum length of the triangle sides and an exponent. A disadvantage of using a TIN for calculating a DEM is that it can produce unnatural visual effects which are related to the shape of the triangles.

The final interpolation method considered here is kriging. Kriging has the reputation that it is based on the most solid theoretical principles. This method assumes that, factoring in local trends and random noise, a variable's value can be estimated through the data's spatial characteristics. The spatial characteristics are modelled in a variogram, where the squared difference of pairs of data points is plotted as a function of their spacing. Based on the position of these points in the variogram, a mathematical function is generated and then used for the interpolation. The way the researcher interprets the spatial relationship is explicitly expressed via the type of function chosen and the method to obtain the best fit. Thus, choice of the interpolation parameters is (to a certain degree) objective, since it is based on the variogram. The disadvantages of kriging are the complexity of the method and the difficulties of filtering out the natural trends in larger study areas.

Plate 1 shows a cross section through a ridge of a Celtic field on a DEM generated with IDW, TIN, and kriging and a comparison between the different interpolation methods. It is clear that the shape of the ridge differs in each DEM. The TIN DEM has the least smoothing effect on the data. When looking at detailed features this smoothing effect is undesired. Therefore, most DEMs shown in this article are created with TIN interpolation.

By making a visual representation of the DEM, printed or on screen, researchers can study relevant patterns of the terrain surface in detail. Such maps are often used in forestry assessments, infrastructure plans, water management, and feature recognition. Visualization is usually enhanced with a combination of colour shades and artificial shadows. Shades of gray or a limited colour spectrum have long been used to represent a variable's spatial variations. Because the human eye is able to distinguish colour shades more easily than gray shades, the former is often preferred. To represent a gradual change of altitude, it is better to use gradually changing colour shades rather than fixed-altitude classes with the same colour, because otherwise interclass altitude variations may become invisible. Since human eye can only distinguish seven or eight separate colours within one image (Ormeling & Kraak 1987), when a DEM utilizes gradual colour changes over a wide palette covering a large surface, small-scale altitude variations (of great interest to archaeologists) may be difficult to distinguish. In such cases, an artificial shadow is helpful for tracing small details. The shadow is created by adding a skimming light coming from a northerly direction. Shadows created by light coming from other, more realistic, directions are more difficult for the human brain to interpret (highs become lows, and vice versa).

Applications in archaeology

Landscape reconstruction

In Dutch archaeology the physical landscape traditionally plays a major role in the study of settlement patterns and is often used as the determining factor in questions of when, where, and why people have settled or abandoned a certain area. Policy documents, such as the Indicative Map of Archaeological Values (IKAW), that indicate areas with a high, medium or low expectation for archaeological sites, are based solely on the correlation between soil, geomorphological, and hydrological characteristics, and site locations (Deeben *et al.* 2002).

Therefore, most surveys in the Netherlands start with an exploration of the geological, geomorphological, and soil characteristics of a study area, and use high quality maps (scale 1: 50,000), as well as, in some cases, additional coring. An assessment is then made of an area's potential for archaeological sites, based on known landscape characteristics. It is common practice for archaeological surveys to focus on high- and medium-expectation areas. For example, in the Dutch river area floodplains are regularly inundated and are therefore considered unsuitable for habitation and have a low archaeological expectation. The so-called 'dry feet criterion' is decisive in prospective research. However, several excavations carried out during construction of a freight railway from Rotterdam to the German border proved that local elevations in the floodplains are due to natural levee breakthroughs (crevasse splays) and had been inhabited in the past (van Dinter & van Zijverden 2002). These local elevations are not represented on the current maps due to their irregular morphology and lithology. But LIDAR-based DEMs and digital coring databases, as demonstrated by van Zijverden (2002) and Laan and van Zijverden (2004), make it possible to map these local elevations to a certain extent.

In general, the assumption that geomorphology is a primary factor in settlement patterning is also applicable to the Pleistocene wind-borne sand deposits. In these areas, expectations for archaeological remains are high in environmental gradients towards stream valleys and sand deposits, and low in areas with podzols with hydromorphic properties. Areas with drift sand also have low expectations for archaeological sites. LIDAR-based DEMs show a much greater detail of the natural landscape in this area than the high-quality maps. In the terraced river landscape of the Meuse valley, former river gullies, river dunes, and small sand complexes can easily be identified on these images.

Rijnenburg in the Dutch river area is a good example of how a DEM can be used for predictive modelling. In this area, a survey was carried out using the most detailed map available, a geomorphogenetic map on a 1: 25,000 scale (Berendsen 1982). During the survey, several sites dating to the Late Iron Age and the Roman period were discovered. But, compared to the geomorphogenetic map, the DEM shows much greater geomorphological detail **[Plate 2]**.

The combination of survey results with the DEM shows that all sites occur on scrollbars close to the residual gully. However, on several scrollbars sites seem to be absent. Based on this obvious correlation, a second limited survey has been carried out in two of the three 'empty' areas. Surprisingly, in both selected areas pottery and other remains were found indicating the presence of an archaeological site. Apart from better indicating high- and medium-expectation areas, the DEM in the Rijnenburg case provided more information on the area's prehistoric habitation pattern.

Tracing archaeological sites

A) Expert scanning

To detect archaeological sites on a DEM, the DEM is generally displayed on a screen and scanned for irregularities and patterns. The success of this method is determined to a large degree by the researcher's ability to evaluate and recognize certain types of archaeological sites. In addition, it is vital that the researcher knows how to manipulate visualizations and to optimize colours and shadows in order to reveal potential sites. During recent archaeological research, LIDAR data proved useful in tracing the location of medieval moats, Roman roads, burial mounds, and Celtic fields **[Plate 3]**. The spectacular results of this research made it a standard request to include LIDAR data in Dutch archaeological research.

A wide range of processes is responsible for the degradation of archaeological sites in the Netherlands. One of the major problems has been (and still is) the levelling of land for agricultural purposes. Since the introduction of large-scale mechanization in agriculture after World War II, almost the entire agricultural area in the Netherlands has been affected to some degree by this practice. Another major problem is sub-recent mining of raw materials, e.g. clay for the brick industry and peat for fuel. Both practices have affected extensive areas and have been mapped in a very limited way. In the Netherlands, a detailed topographical/elevation map (scale 1: 10,000) exists, which is based on measurements recorded between the late 1940s and early 1980s. These measurements are also available in digital form. Because the first large-scale levelling of the Dutch landscape took place in the late 1940s and continued until the early 1990s, these databases are often a reliable source for the original surface height. The new LIDAR-based height measurements can now be used to model the effect of the levelling, by correlating the old recordings to the LIDAR databases. A first attempt was made for the municipality of Deurne. A 1954 map of the area was used for this purpose (scale 1: 5,000). When compared to the LIDAR data, a complete stream valley appeared to have been relocated **[Plate 4]** (Oudhof 2003). These results indicate that some areas can be neglected in future archaeological surveys in this area, because the original surface has been artificially lowered by more than 1 m since 1954.

Herzog (2002) and Gerlach *et al.* (this volume) have presented a study of clay pits in Nord-Rhein Westfalen (Germany) which had been dug in the context of the brick industry. They suggest that that in the process of pit-digging, the topsoil was removed and replaced, which has not only disturbed archaeological sites, but has also led to the misidentification of sites based on non-original surface material. A combination of a LIDAR-based DEM and historical maps indicates the need for a reclassification of such 'pseudo-sites'. Field surveys in agricultural parcels in the Dutch river area, where soil disturbance has also occurred, present similar results and 'pseudo-sites'. However, in the Netherlands, the topsoil was removed from entire parcels and replaced, and the clay subsoil was also removed. Therefore, surveys with hand-auger equipment resulted in a less dense site pattern compared to intact areas. Trenches were dug in a large test area encompassing both stripped and intact areas. The result was a much denser site pattern in the stripped areas than had been expected from the survey. The LIDAR-based DEMs proved vital in identifying which parcels were stripped **[Plate 5]**. Moreover, they can be used to estimate the quantity of soil removed from a parcel. A LIDAR-based DEM is an essential element when making an informed decision as to which survey technique to use, especially in areas affected by levelling.

B) Pattern-recognition techniques

Computer science uses pattern recognition to study the design and operation of systems (Theodoridis & Koutroumbas 1999). Applications can be found in biometrics research (e.g. face recognition, finger-print matching, see Jain & Ratha 2004), text-processing (Rice *et al.* 1999), speech-processing (Rabiner & Juang 1993) and industrial inspection (Casasent 1983). Thus far, applications for archaeology are virtually non-existent. However, pattern-recognition algorithms offer a promising opportunity to explore large amounts of data in a structured and cost-effective way. The introduction of large amounts of high-quality LIDAR data has strengthened the need to apply these techniques towards archaeological purposes.

Pattern recognition uses techniques such as feature extraction, discriminant analysis, principal component analysis, cluster analysis, neural networks and image-processing to search for data with a set of predefined characteristics. Algorithms can be categorized into two

Fig. 6. *Burial mound.*

classes: template-based and feature-based (Brunelli & Poggio 1993). Template-based algorithms calculate the correlation between one or more templates and selected data. This method isolates a small part of the data that represent the phenomenon in question. Next, using a correlation technique, the whole dataset is analyzed for similar patterns, which will yield a high correlation factor. Feature-based algorithms analyze local features in the data and their spatial relationships. Features that might be extracted from surface altitude data include absolute and relative altitude, slope, change of slope, roughness and smoothness of the surface, and exposition. Next, using a known relationship between the occurrence of these features and the occurrence of the phenomenon in question, the latter can be traced.

A pilot study described by Laan and De Boer (in press) has explored the use of a template-based algorithm to search LIDAR data for burial mounds in the central part of the Netherlands. The hemispherical burial mounds mostly date from the Neolithic to the Iron Age and typically have a diameter of 10 m and a height of 1 m **[Fig. 6]**, though their size may vary considerably (e.g. Theunissen 1999). As a result of the reclamation of previously uncultivated land, especially in the beginning of the 19th century, many burial mounds were destroyed. Today, the best preserved mounds are in forested areas that were considered unsuitable for cultivation. It is likely that many more burial mounds exist in these areas but they are relatively difficult to detect in the forest using field surveys. In the pilot study, the correlation (r) between the template (T) and a sample of the image (S) was calculated using the following formula, where i and j are the index numbers of the rows and columns of the data, d is the size of T and S, and σ is the standard deviation:

$$r = \frac{\sum_{j=1}^{d}\sum_{i=1}^{d}(T_{i,j} - \overline{T})(S_{i,j} - \overline{S})}{\sigma_T \sigma_S d^2}$$

Using a template of an idealized DEM of a burial mound **[Fig. 7]** and the above formula, a map with correlation values was constructed **[Plate 8]**. This proved that many locations were present with a high correlation, their surface resembling a burial mound. These positions of these potential burial mounds were compared to those of known mounds using a database from the National Service for Archaeological Heritage. Almost all known burial mounds were trace. An interesting detail is that the coordinates in this database often proved to be inaccurate; thus, the techniques discussed above can also be used to verify coordinates.

Morphologically similar archaeological sites—e.g. deposited house remains, village mounds and aeolian dunes covered by Holocene deposits—can be traced using the same techniques. In general, all archaeological sites that are visible in the local surface morphology can potentially be traced via pattern recognition techniques in combination with LIDAR data. This includes a wide range of archaeological features and landscape types, e.g. historical routes, Celtic fields, sand pits, medieval parcel structures, meander belts, and crevasse splays.

Fig. 7. *3D template of a burial mound.*

Traditional remote-sensing techniques versus laser altimetry

Various remote-sensing techniques, such as orthogonal and oblique aerial photography, are commonly used in archaeological research. Apart from black-and-white photography, false and true colours, infrared, and thermic infrared techniques can be used. All these techniques have one thing in common: they trace soil marks and crop marks. Both soil and crop marks are strongly influenced by vegetation type and climate. Images of the same location taken at different times may give different results. Multispectral analyses are very rare in archaeological research. Their applications are currently limited due to the relatively large pixels available from satellites. However, a good example of such an application is the research of Fletcher *et al.* (2002) at Angkor, Cambodia.

Apart from densely forested areas with pine and areas vegetated with reed swamps, the quality of a LIDAR-based DEM is independent of vegetation and climate. Where the other techniques reflect height, moisture, and nutrient supply, LIDAR-based DEMs reveals only height differences. It is known, for example, that compaction affects infill of ditches more than the undisturbed surrounding surface. Therefore, ditches are generally represented on both LIDAR-based DEMs and on the other remote-sensing images. Discolorations in the soil are not registered by LIDAR, so aerial photography might in some circumstances be complementary to LIDAR-based DEMs.

A good example of the combined use of these different techniques is the research on Zijderveld, a large settlement site in the Dutch river area with house remains dating to the mid-Bronze Age and early Iron Age. Almost 2 ha of the overall site were excavated in 1967-1971 by the National Service for Archaeological

Heritage (Theunissen 1999). Recently, the University of Leiden excavated another 1.2 ha (Arnoldussen 2003; Knippenberg & Jongste 2005). During the last excavation, infrared photography was used to identify archaeological remains in the area surrounding the first excavation (Du Fijn *et al.* 2003). A very good orthogonal black-and-white image, taken during World War II by the Royal Air Force, was used, together with a LIDAR-based DEM that became available during the last field campaign. Comparing these three images, the LIDAR-based DEM clearly provides the most detailed information on parcel structures and landscape **[Plate 9]**. Archaeological remains are invisible in all three images, but site-related geological features could be clearly distinguished.

Conclusion

LIDAR-based DEMs are of great potential for archaeological research. The quality and amount of data provided by these images are better than any other remote-sensing technique. The research presented here demonstrates this instrument to be invaluable. For the construction of LIDAR-based DEMs, knowledge of interpolation techniques is crucial. Interpretation depends strongly on the visualization technique used and the quality of the image. DEMs are far from static; small adjustments in colours and shadows have a significant influence on the way small details are presented. LIDAR-based DEMs should be used alongside other sources of information, such as historical and geological maps, digital coring databases, and aerial photography. The images themselves should be analyzed by a multidisciplinary team. We have found that close collaboration of a physical geographer, an archaeologist, and a historical geographer is most effective and leads to the best results.

Our research has been a first exploration of this technique for archaeological research. It is anticipated that, in the near future, LIDAR-based DEMs will be part of more archaeological projects carried out in the Netherlands and elsewhere. LIDAR-based surface height measurements are becoming available at a rapid pace in other countries, including Great Britain, Belgium, France, Germany and Australia. Companies like Geocom can deliver LIDAR databases for any geographical area on demand, for prices which are only slightly higher than professional aerial photography. It is likely that within the next decade, LIDAR-based surface height measurements will be used in most European countries, since the technique has already proven to be an important tool for water management and infrastructure planning. One would hope that archaeological research benefits from such developments.

Bibliography

Arnoldussen, S. 2003. *Archeologisch onderzoek van de randzone van een nederzetting uit de Midden-Bronstijd te Zijderveld*, ARCHOL-Rapport 23, Leiden: ARCHOL.

Berendsen, H. J. A. 1982. "De genese van het landschap in het zuiden van de Provincie Utrecht", unpublished Ph.D. dissertation, University of Utrecht.

Brunelli, R. & Poggio, T. 1993. "Face recognition: features versus templates", *Institute of Electrical and Electronics Engineers, Transactions on Pattern Analysis and Machine Intelligence* 15/10: 1042-1052.

Brus, D. J. & Kiestra, E. 2002. *Kan de efficiëntie van bodemkarteringen op schaal 1 : 10,000 worden vergroot met het Actuele Hoogtebestand Nederland?*, Alterra-Rapport 498, Wageningen: Alterra.

Burrough, P. A. 1994. *Principles of Geographical Information Systems for Land Resources Assessment*, Monographs on Soil and Resources Survey 12, Oxford: Clarendon Press.

Casasent, D. P. 1983 (ed.). *Robotics and Industrial Inspection, 26th Technical Symposium and Exhibition of the International Society for Optical Engineering (San Diego, August 24-27, 1982)*, SPIE Proceedings 360, Bellingham, Washington: International Society for Optical Engineering.

Deeben, J., Hallewas, D. P. & Maarleveld, T. J. 2002. "Predictive modeling in archaeological heritage management of the Netherlands: the Indicative Map of Archaeological Values (2nd generation)", *Berichten van de Rijksdienst voor Oudheidkundig Bodemonderzoek* 45: 9-57.

Du Fijn, H. G., Voss, F., Welzer, W. & Schultz, C. 2003. "Historisch onderzoek en multitemporele luchtfoto-uitwerking van het project Rijksweg A2, aansluiting Culemborg", report of the Risk Management Group BV, Institut für Geographie Berlin and Ministerie van Verkeer en Waterstaat. Berlin: Institut für Geographie Berlin.

Fletcher, R., Evans, D. H. & Tapley, I. J. 2002. "AIRSAR's contribution to understanding the Angkor World Heritage Site, Cambodia—objectives and preliminary findings from an examination of PACRIM2 datasets", *Proceedings of the 2002 AIRSAR Science and Application Workshop, NASA-JPL,* http://airsar.jpl.nasa.gov/documents/workshop2002/papers/P1.pdf

Gehasse, E. F. 1995. "Ecologisch-archeologisch onderzoek van het Neolithicum en de Vroege-Bronstijd in de Noordoostpolder met de nadruk op P14", unpublished Ph.D. dissertation, University of Amsterdam.

Herzog, I. 2002. "Ehemalige Materialen entnahmegruben erkennen—Auswertung von Höhendaten", *Archäologische Informationen* 24/1: 39-43.

Jain, A. K. & Ratha, N. K. 2004 (eds.). *Biometric Technology for Human Identification,* SPIE Proceedings 5404, Bellingham, Washington: International Society for Optical Engineering.

Knippenberg, S. & Jongste, P. F. B. 2005. *Terug naar Zijderveld, archeologische opgravingen langs de A2,* ARCHOL-Rapport 36, Leiden: ARCHOL.

Laan, W. N. H. & de Boer, A. G. 2005. *AHN onderzoek West-Veluwe,* ADC-Rapport, 447, Amersfoort: ADC-Archeoprojecten.

Laan, W. N. H. & van Zijverden, W. K. 2004. "Landscape reconstructions and prospective modeling in archaeological research-using a laser altimetry based DEM and digital boring database", unpublished paper, *Workshop 9 Archäologie und Computer (Vienna, November 3-5).*

Lillesand, T. M. & Kiefer, R. W. 2004. *Remote Sensing and Image Interpretation,* New York: John Wiley and Sons.

Ormeling, F. & Kraak, M. J. 1987. *Kartografie, ontwerp, produktie en gebruik van kaarten,* Delft: Delftse Uitgeversmaatschappij.

Oudhof, J.-W. M. 2003. *Archeologische effectrapportage Vlierdenseweg Deurne,* Vestigia-Rapport 43, Bunschoten: Vestigia.

Palarczyk, M. J. 1986. "Slootkantverkenning in de Noordoostpolder", unpublished M.A. dissertation, University of Amsterdam.

Rabiner, L. & Bing-Hwang, J. 1993. *Fundamentals of Speech Recognition,* Englewood Cliffs: Prentice-Hall.

Rice, S., Nagy, G. & Nartker, T. A. 1999. *Optical Character Recognition: an Illustrated Guide to the Frontier,* Kluwer International Series in Engineering and Computer Science 502, New York: Kluwer.

Theodoridis, S. & Koutroumbas, K. 1999. *Pattern Recognition,* New York: Academic Press.

Theunissen, L. M. 1999. "Midden-bronstijdsamenlevingen in het zuiden van de Lage Landen", unpublished Ph.D. dissertation, University of Leiden.

van Dinter, M. & van Zijverden, W. K. 2002. "Crevasses een ondergewaardeerd landschapstype", *ADC-Info* 2002/1: 4-19.

van Zijverden, W. K. 2002. "Landschappelijke context", in E. B. Everhard, F. Bulten, J. G. van der Heijden & T. Hamburg, *Emmeloord: prehistorische visweren en visfuiken*, ADC-Rapport 140, Bunschoten: Archeologisch Diensten Centrum: 17-30.

van Zijverden, W. K. & Laan, W.N.H. 2005. Landscape reconstructions and predictive modelling in archaeological research, using a LIDAR based DEM and digital boring databases, *Archäologie und computer* 2004. Workshop 9, Wien.

Waldus, W. & van der Velde, H. 2006 (eds.). *Archeologie in vogelvlucht: een onderzoek naar de toepassingsmogelijkheden van het AHN voor de archeologie, Geoarchaeological and Bioarchaeological Studies, 6*, Amsterdam: Vrije Universiteit Amsterdam.

Chapter 9

Voxel-based 3D GIS: modelling and analysis of archaeological stratigraphy

The 3D representation of archaeological stratigraphy and interrelationships of stratified features was described until recently as an illusive goal (e.g. Harris & Lock 1996: 307). This paper takes up this statement as a challenge. The creation of a new module generating voxel-based reconstructions of archaeological stratigraphy paves the way to a new approach in dealing with archaeological data and their spatial analysis. In this paper, a voxel-based structure for obtaining georeferenced, 3D models of archaeological stratigraphy is used at the site of Akroterion at Kastri in Kythera (Greece). The results of this 3D GIS are compared to inferences drawn by the excavators concerning the stratigraphy of the site (Coldstream & Huxley 1972), while a prototype of an Open Source Software (OSS) GIS, which attempts to overcome known limitations of extant OSS, is introduced.

Undine Lieberwirth
Institut für Ur- und Frühgeschichte, Humboldt-Universität zu Berlin, Germany

Model-building in archaeology

The *raison d'être* of archaeology is the interpretation of past human cultural remains, and the reconstruction of 3D objects is frequently part and parcel of archaeological interpretation. The notion of 3D modelling as a means to represent the real world is not new; physical models or maquettes have been the traditional means of gaining a better understanding of the interrelationship of objects in their 3D environment. Geographic Information Systems (GIS), however, offer a more advantageous approach to archaeological modelling. A GIS can handle and access a vast amount of data, but also analyze them in their spatial context on any scale. The broad recognition of GIS as a science, not a mere tool, has created a potential far beyond its originally designated purpose as a cartographic instrument. GIS can be a platform for data retrieval, spatial analysis, the creation of new data through calculation, theory development and hypothesis-testing. Moreover, model-building technology through GIS is advanced enough to enable the reconstruction of excavation data with x, y, z coordinates, as recorded in the field, and the creation of more accurate 3D solid models approximating the real world[1] and suitable for post-excavation spatial analysis. Not only can GIS modelling enable the understanding of the comprehensive structure of archaeological

1. Any model is an imperfect representation of the real world. Abstraction and distortion are intrinsic in the modelling process and derive from many parameters, such as legacy data, technology and software applied, scale and purpose of the model. Choosing the right model for a certain purpose is a vital part of the overall modelling process (Ervin & Hasbrouck 2001: 4).

I wish to thank Dr. A. Bevan (Institute of Archaeology, University College, London) for encouraging me in this approach and offering the case-study data. Furthermore, I would like to thank A. Kakissis (British School at Athens), Dr. C. Broodbank (Institute of Archaeology, University College, London) and my supervisor in Germany, Dr. M. Meyer (Brandenburgisches Landesamt für Denkmalpflege und Archäologisches Landesmuseum). Thanks also go to B. Ducke (Institut für Ur- und Frühgeschichte, Christian-Albrechts-Universität, Kiel), for providing the new GRASS GIS module r.vol.dem.

stratigraphy; it is also a means for intellectual reflection upon the data (Johnson 2004: 17).

3D model-building in archaeology

A 3D GIS solid model of archaeological stratigraphy is not aimed at reconstructing the past, but rather building a copy of the archaeological site as it was progressively brought to light through excavation. It allows interactive representation of particular areas, including features, artefacts and layer properties, whilst it allows the exploration of complex information relating to the site's environment. Such geoscientific visualization should not be conflated with the 3D VR approach (Lock 2003: 152-163), which creates hollow 3D polygon (vector) objects; and hence does not provide inside object information for further analysis in a georeferenced space and contains no quantified background information for statistical analysis.

Solid models

In order to use 2D GIS for the third dimension, it is necessary to create a solid model of the world with inside as well as outside information. These models need to be placed within a real-world 3D space. Therefore, the Cartesian space in GIS has to be extended because

> ...the limitations of conventional GIS software yield erroneous results. These limitations are based on the fact that conventional GIS packages interpret z values as attributes rather than as true spatial coordinates. (Nigro *et al.* 2003: 317)

Hence, in a 3D GIS it is essential to handle three coordinate axes independently. For this reason, the third axis needs to be added perpendicularly. Each vector point is then expressed as a triple (x, y, z). This process creates the geometrical background of a volumetric model. Like in an advanced 2D GIS, where vector and raster data can be depicted simultaneously, there are two technical possibilities to create a volumetric model. First, vectors (polygons) can be extended into the third dimension in the Cartesian space to a 3D polygon or polyhedron. The second option is the extension of raster pixel into the third dimension. 3D polygons are the building blocks of VR models. Due to their structure, they do not consist of any inside information and can therefore act only as a 3D masks or hulls, which in turn requires the use of 3D pixels.

3D visualization of archaeological stratigraphy using GIS: a research history

Some pioneering work has already been done in this area by using voxel (3D pixel) technology. Based on the software used, such work can be classified as follows. The first group used commercial software, developed for geological research; the second group developed their own software specifically for archaeological use.

In terms of the first approach, mostly dating to the early 1990s, research has relied heavily on software able to store and analyze 3D volumetric forms (Harris & Lock 1996: 307). At that time, software with the capability of handling graphical databases in combination with relational databases were available mainly for subjects like geology or medicine. The first successful 3D visualization of archaeological stratigraphy employed geological software (Reilly 1992). In another project (Harris & Lock 1996) the utilization of Dynamic Graphic's Earthvision software enabled the successful visualization of stratigraphical units, their display in categories, the 'slicing' of deposits in horizontal and vertical directions, and the calculation of deposit volumes. Later on, in 1999, the Swartkrans pilot project successfully integrated old and new excavation data loaded and analyzed in a GIS. This GIS was furthermore able to discover patterns by using the SPLUS extension. The extension module also applied descriptive statistics for exploiting minimum numbers of individuals or minimum numbers of elements (Nigro *et al.* 2003: 323). It also became possible to define stratigraphical units using ArcView's 3D Analyst, 'slice' them, calculate their volumes and surfaces; as well as study finds in their corresponding context. The complete site's interior was reconstructed by means of a voxel-based model.

A growing familiarity with GIS applications and the development of faster and all-inclusive technologies eventually gave rise to archaeology-oriented software; the remaining five case-studies (four of which presented at the CAA 2003 conference) exemplify the latter approach. The first among these projects was based on a 3D GIS program designed to meet the needs of archaeological stratigraphy, and combined visualization and hypothesis-testing capabilities with a query tool (Green 2003). Another study (Cattani *et al.* 2004) explored the differences between two software types in managing 3D data, which were surveyed using a total station; the first produced a voxel model (RochWorks2002, designed for use in geology), the second a vector model (SDRC Surfer). The density distribution of metallurgical slag was visualized; 3D vectors and voxel objects could be visualized simultaneously. In attempting to create a 'system for 3D capture of a large scale archaeological excavation' through an architectural case-study, Zabulis *et al.* (2005) made use of photogrammetry in combination with a total station for georeferencing. The special software designed for this purpose calculated solid voxel models out of the image tuples, thereby maintaining image colours. In a similar vein, Barceló and Vicente (2004) employed a photogrammetric technique for obtaining a georeferenced 3D model of archaeological stratigraphy. Image modification allowed the creation of a 3D geometric model as an adequate representation of archaeological records and, hence, the analysis of taphonomic and site formation processes. Kochnev *et al.* (2004), on the other hand, modelled archaeological units using geophysical data. They were able to describe the correct location of geophysical anomalies, as well as their depth and distribution; their results were subsequently combined with general archaeological information.

The latest study in the field by Arc-Team (Bezzi *et al.* 2006) relates to the creation of a voxel model of archaeological stratigraphy using the OSS programs GRASS GIS, Blender and ParaView. They used the GRASS GIS module r.to.rast3 to create voxels, yet they describe their model as 'hollow' rather than a 'real voxel'.[2]

It is evident that the commercial software are the most powerful ones (e.g. Cattani *et al.* 2004). However, specialized software compare favourably with the former in terms of the advanced results achieved. In one case (Kochnev *et al.* 2004), such specialized software even enabled a depiction of interpolated voxel values. In general, the above case-studies show the usefulness and great potential of a 3D GIS approach to archaeological data. Remarkably, none of these packages were used in follow-up projects. The user-unfriendly interfaces of 3D GIS software in general and a focus on analysis rather than visualization (Lock 2003: 152) might have something to do with this. But since the source codes of the above specialized software were not revealed, as with their commercial counterparts, it is likely that the lack of continuity also has to do with the fact that they did not run under the OSS licence and therefore were not easily available for further projects. Needless to say, complete insight into the underlying processes of such software is vital for scientific applications. The study of these previous steps towards 3D GIS helped articulate my principle research aim, which is to overcome the shortcomings of hitherto applied software in the field.

Voxel structure and creation

The term 'voxel' is a combination of the words 'volume' and 'pixel.' A voxel, in essence a 3D pixel, is a volume element which can be sliced or exploited for the creation of iso-surfaces. Like a pixel, a voxel can contain one scalar numeric (w-) value, like colour, category, density, or geostatistical values like mineral values, precipitation, air pressure etc. Voxels are able to represent an inside and outside world, as well as build the quantified basis

2. The raster maps were stretched perpendicularly up to a defined boundary, e.g. a second raster map. The voxel created this way does not contain any new information, i.e. a fourth value (w-value, see section 'Voxel structure and creation–Interpolation') for further analysis. Hence this extension is graphical rather than quantified.

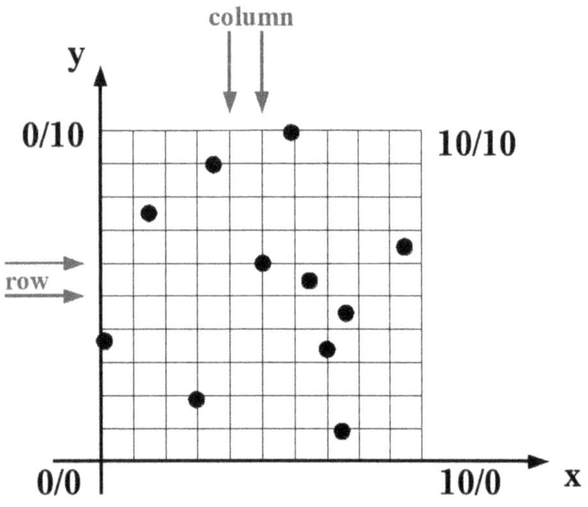

Fig. 1. *2D Cartesian coordinate system with points for interpolation.*

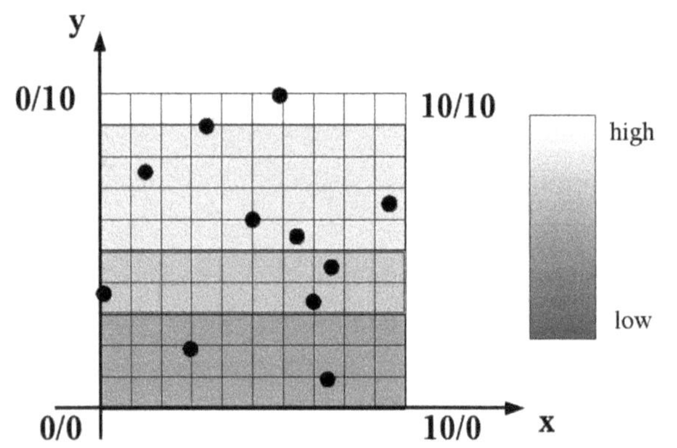

Fig. 2. *2D Cartesian coordinate with points and interpolated raster.*

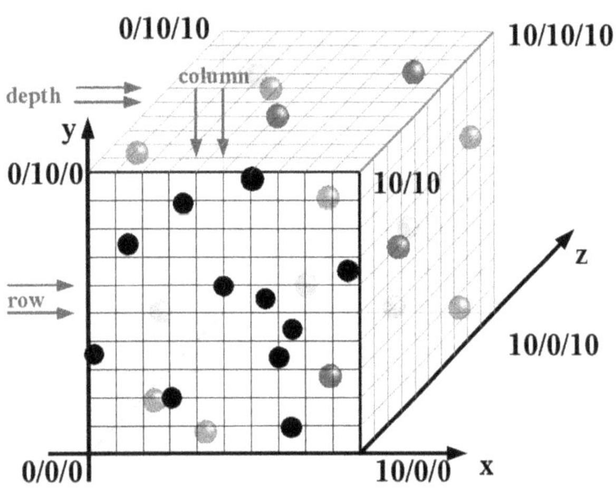

Fig. 3. *3D Cartesian coordinate system with points for interpolation.*

for numerical analysis and statistics. They are therefore indispensable to 3D GIS modelling. At present, there are two ways to create a voxel, interpolation and 'flood-filling'.

Interpolation

As with interpolation algorithms in 2D **[Figs. 1-2]**, it is possible to interpolate vector points in a 3D space. The 3D algorithm works in the same way, but with the addition of the third dimension **[Fig. 3]**. The 3D interpolation algorithm, for example Nearest Neighbor, Spline etc., interpolates between the 3D vector points. Unlike 2D interpolation, however, the value which is interpolated is not the z-value (normally elevation) but the w-value. The w-value, like the z-value in 2D, is defined as an attribute. These attribute values have to be expressed as floating-point numbers which are normally provided by measurements. The 3D interpolation creates fuzzy transitions **[Fig. 4]** and is therefore suitable for vague strata boundaries.

Flood-filling

Unlike interpolation estimating the value within two known values by using a mathematical function, the algorithm of the flood-filling process fills the 3D space between defined boundaries with voxels **[Figs. 5-7]**. Using this method, we can create categorical volume grids with clear boundaries. This approach is best suited to clearly defined stratigraphical units. Since 'for the stratigraphic record the deposit is reduced to a unique number in the stratigraphic sequence' (Doneus & Neubauer 2004: 113), this method is suitable for creating archaeological units with arbitrarily allocated context numbers and for modelling strata with numerical labels.

An OSS 3D GIS

Since a suitable OSS GIS module for creating real voxel-based models of archaeological stratigraphy does not yet exist, I utilize the new GRASS GIS module r.vol.dem (courtesy of B. Ducke), which takes advantage of the flood-filling process. In combination

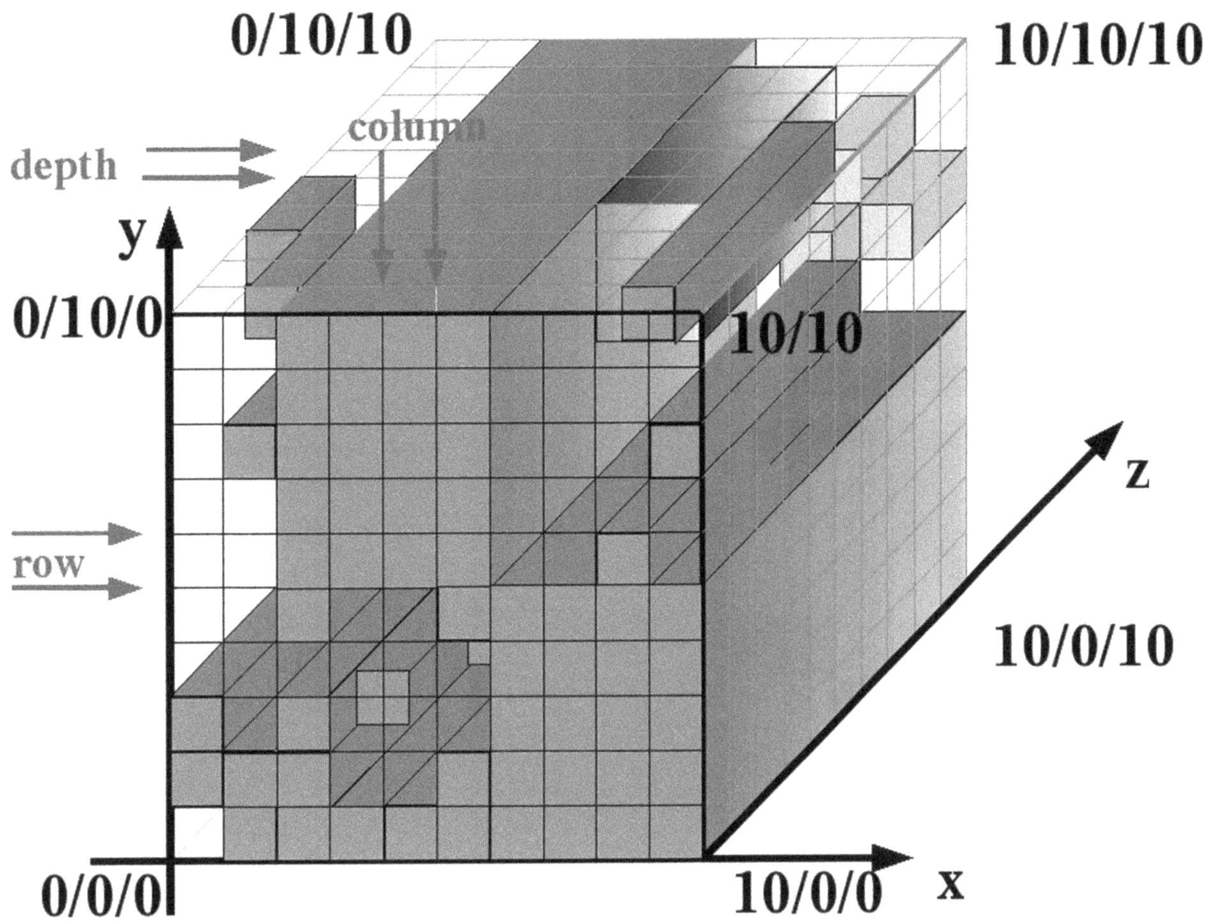

Fig 4. *3D Cartesian coordinate system with points and interpolated voxel.*

with the visualization software ParaView, this software can certainly compete with other software packages mentioned earlier. The module's objective is to handle ordinal numerical expressions of archaeological units in order to create 3D volume grids of archaeological stratigraphy. This new module is able to calculate voxel maps between at least two digital elevation models (DEMs). The flood-filling algorithm adjusts the same label value (w-value) to each voxel per 3D unit.

The Akroterion case-study

Legacy data

Trench IX of the Akroterion excavation (Coldstream & Huxley 1972) was chosen because it provided the greatest amount of input data with two cross-sections (unlike other trenches) and one plan drawing **[Figs. 8-10]**. Trench IX features a complex stratigraphy of 12 units dating from the Middle Minoan IB period to Byzantine times, as well as architecture from different periods. Wall α **[Figs. 8-9]** forms the outer wall of the 'West House',[3] which borders three superimposed walking surfaces: Unit Surface 3 (Late Minoan IB), Unit Surface 11 (Late Minoan IB) and Unit Surface 12 (Middle Minoan III). The 'West House' and therefore wall α was dated to the Late Minoan IB period. The surfaces in question were destroyed to the west by the Byzantine wall β,[4] which had roughly the same orientation as wall ε beneath it **[Fig. 10, Plate 13]**.

3. This is one of the three Late Minoan IB houses on the site (North, South and West House).

4. This feature does not show in the paper drawings (Simpson & Lazenby 1972: 57).

Figs. 5-7. *Flood-filling process.*

Period	Stratigraphic units	Volume (m^3)
MM	8, 10, 12	12.57
LM	3, 7, 11, 15	7.6
Byzantine	4	6.83
Modern	2	17.54

Table 1. *Volume calculation of deposits within Trench IX*

Byzantine occupation destroyed a great part of Unit 7 (Simpson & Lazenby 1972: 57-58).

The voxel-based model

All stratigraphic elements within Trench IX were transformed into 3D voxel-based objects through the GRASS GIS module r.vol.dem mentioned earlier; the result was visualized through the software ParaView **[Plate 11-16]**. Not only did it become possible to confirm the excavators' interpretations in this way (Simpson & Lazenby 1972); additional information about the trench was furnished. For example, the orientation of the unit surfaces **[Plates 14-15]** and the walls inside the trench became more easily perceptible, while the various architectural fragments could be measured precisely at any point in 3D space. The latter task was quite difficult for the excavators, since wall width varied considerably between the two documented cross-sections.

Occupation phases

The stratigraphy was not described in adequate detail by the excavators, so that a comprehensive comparison with the results of this paper is not possible. However, some new inferences can be drawn on the basis of the following actions: a) the exact volume of each stratigraphical unit was calculated according to the cell counts of the voxel-based stratigraphical models **[Table 1]**, then compared with each other; b) the process of construction of the architectural features within Trench IX, as well as the occupation phases in a relative chronological order, were clarified.

The 3D GIS model of the Trench IX features suggests that the first occupation took place with the construction of walls γ, δ and ε, which are part of Unit 10 (Middle Minoan IB–IIIA periods) **[Figs. 8–10** and **Plate 11**, light green colour]. This first occupation postdates Units 13-14 **[Plate 11**, dark brown and dark green colours], which are not dateable and might not even have resulted from human activity. Walls γ, δ and ε, of Unit 10 are superimposed by Unit 8 **[Plate11**, brown colour], which roughly dates to the same

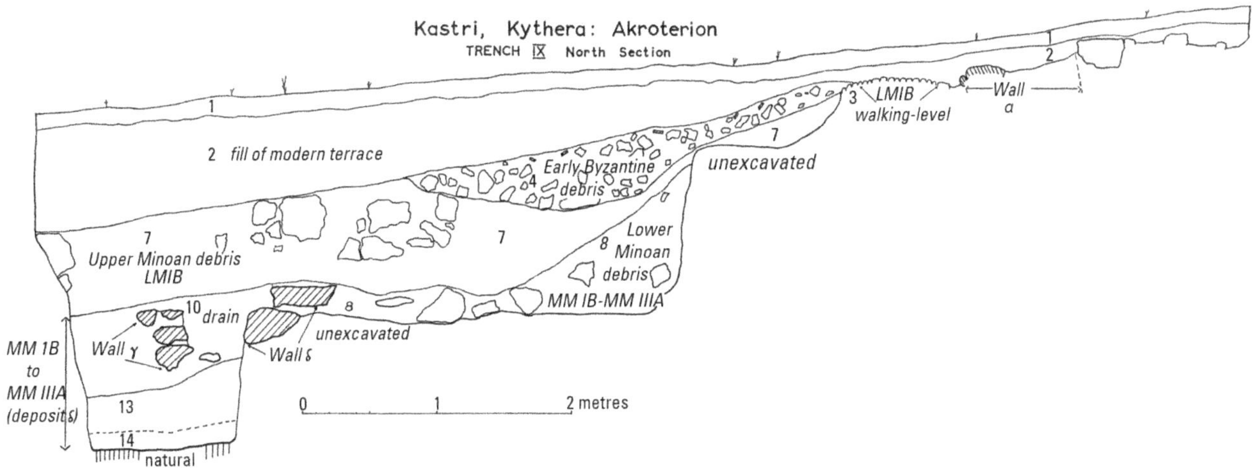

Fig. 8. *Kythera, Kastri, Akroterion Trench IX, north section (after Simpson & Lazenby 1972, fig. 20).*

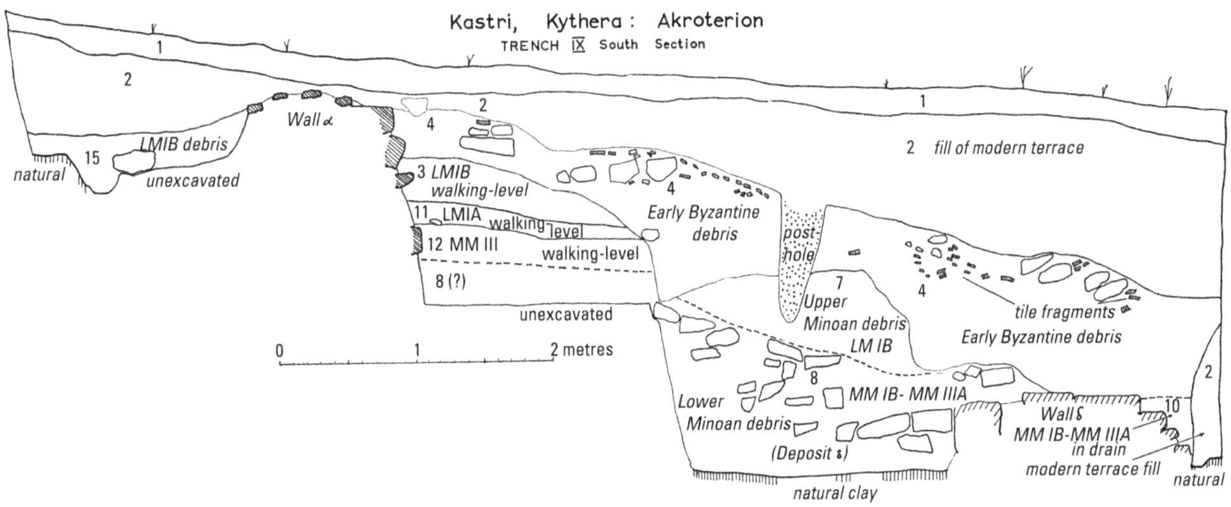

Fig. 9. *Kythera, Kastri, Akroterion Trench IX, south section (after Simpson & Lazenby 1972, fig. 21).*

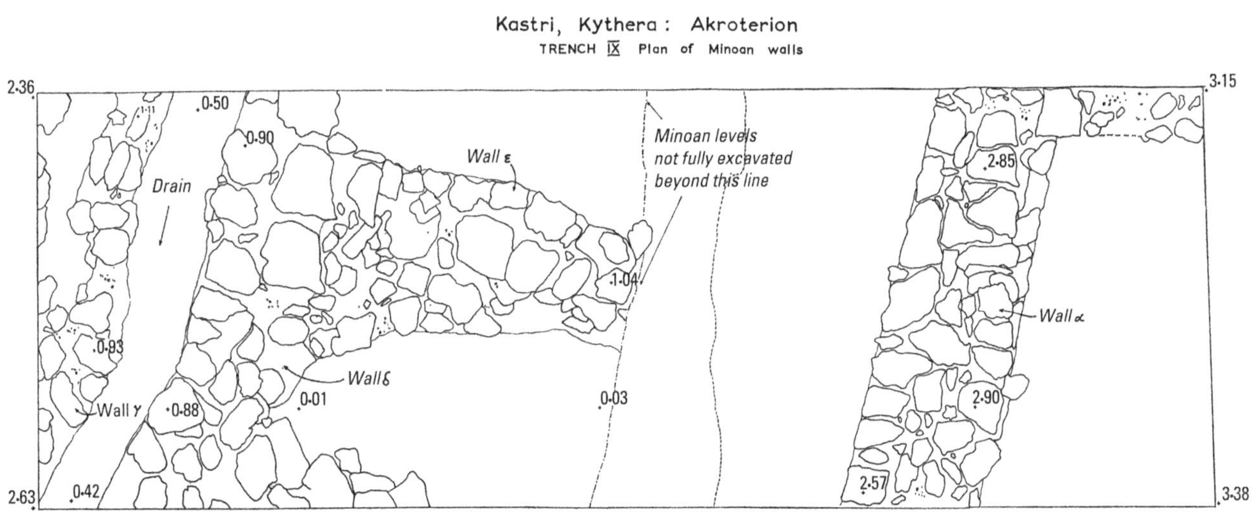

Fig. 10. *Kythera, Kastri, Akroterion Trench IX, plan of Minoan walls (after Simpson & Lazenby 1972, fig. 22).*

period. Thus, they belong to structures that were in use for only a short period of time. Unit 8, on the other hand, consists of remains from several periods without stratigraphic interruption, which suggests a continuous occupation at the site after the first habitation phase. The site remained in use following the long Middle Minoan period (ca. 200 years, represented by Units 8, 10 and 12). This is demonstrated by the paved area belonging to Unit 11 (Late Minoan IA period, refurbished in Late Minoan IB). Unit 7 lies atop the Middle Minoan Unit 8 **[Plate 11**, light orange colour**]**. Since Unit 7 dates to the Late Minoan IB period, we can conclude that Unit 8 was not covered up in the Late Minoan IA period. Units 3, 7 and 15, also dating to the Late Minoan IB period, are associated with the 'West House' (represented by walls α and α1). Based on the publication, there is no evidence for post-Minoan habitation other than the much later reoccupation of the site during the early Byzantine era. The destruction of Minoan strata by the later occupation is evident in the 'negative', lower part of Unit 4 **[Fig. 14]**, which can be only the result of human activity. The upper part of Unit 4 **[Fig. 15]**, however, could be due to erosion.

Volumetrics

The deposit volume of the Middle and Late Minoan periods together was three times greater than that of Byzantine period[5] **[Table 1]**. Since the parts of the Minoan and Byzantine periods at issue are of the same duration approximately (ca. 200 years), it would appear that that there was a much greater activity during the Middle Minoan period, at least at this site, than in Byzantine times.[6] It is also evident that the Late Minoan occupation left fewer traces than the Middle Minoan ones, arguably due to its shorter time interval. Finally, the deposit volume calculation clearly shows that the modern stratum (Unit 2)[7] represents the largest volume **[Plate 11**, orange colour**]**.

5. In this calculation I do not take into account destroyed volume, which could be estimated and added in a future project (see below).

6. In order to be reliable, such volumetric comparisons generally ought to take into account factors such as erosion, the nature of the deposits in question, building materials used for structures etc.

Conclusion and future work

Every excavation fills gaps in the puzzle of the past. The same is true for post-excavation analysis. Reconstructions and models of a site are not just a means to store, combine and present recorded information, but they can also help articulate and convey additional information implicit in the data. Such models allow a better understanding of the interrelationship of strata in its 3D environment and more comprehensive investigation of the site. As with a simulation, a geometric and dynamic model permits better control of variables and parameters (Blankholm 1991: 55). Thus, I would agree that "for the real 3D documentation and analysis of future archaeological excavations, the use of Voxel will become indispensable!" (Bezzi *et al.* 2006: 29).

This paper shows how archaeological information can be retrieved, for instance in terms of volumetric and spatial analysis, while it also demonstrates the advantages of the 3D approach in tackling spatial problems in archaeological stratigraphy. The utilization of GRASS GIS and ParaView in combination presents the following principal advantages, in particular:

- Each stratigraphical unit can be depicted separately, which in turn allows the reconstruction of taphonomic, accumulation and erosion processes in 3D **[Plates 13, 15]**. Deposits can be visualized by category (e.g. period, soil type, colour etc.) **[Plates 11-12]**. Implicit spatial patterns can emerge in this fashion.

- The complete stratigraphy over the entire trench width can be displayed, which may reveal ancient surfaces not hitherto perceptible **[Plates 14-15]**.

7. Unit 2 was not investigated in detail.

- Stratigraphic sequences can be visualized in relative and absolute chronological order; by creating a time series, the 3D GIS therefore converts into a 4D GIS.

- The excavation can be recreated virtually, step-by-step, through horizontal 'slicing' at any level. Horizontal, vertical and diagonal slices are possible, offering insight into deposit structure **[Plate 12]**; such slices make it possible to disregard the original, conventional excavation layers and to follow the strata in their natural form and thickness.

- 3D data (architecture, pits, postholes, and artefacts) can be mapped in 3D georeferenced space and retrieved according to their numeric label **[Plate 16]**. Deposits can be compared **[Table 1]** and analyzed for volume, extent, shape and size. This makes the 3D GIS approach ideal for heritage management.

- Measurements, such as stratigraphic depth (even within a single layer) and distance between two points, can be taken in Euclidean space.

The outcome can be described as a '3D interactive geographic map' of archaeological stratigraphy. Notably, the above list is far from exhaustive; further advantages may arise through the application of this method on a different set of data. The implementation of 3D statistics, query functionality, the ability for multitrench visualization and analysis (including analysis of erosion and accummulation processes), the inclusion of predictive modelling features and a complete shift to OSS software are areas worthy of future work and development.

Bibliography

Barceló, J. A. & Vicente, O. 2004. "Some problems in archaeological excavation 3D modelling", in K. F. Ausserer, W. Börner, M. Goriany & L. Karlhuber-Vöckl (eds.), *Enter the Past: the E-way into Four Dimensions of Cultural Heritage (CAA 2003, Proceedings of the 30th Conference, Vienna, Austria, 8-12 April, 2003)*, B.A.R. International Series 1227, Oxford: BAR Publishing: 427-431.

Bezzi, A., Bezzi, L., Francisci, D. & Gietl, R. 2006. "The application of voxel in archaeology", in *Settimo meeting degli utenti italiani di GRASS (Genova, 23-24 febraio 2006)*, http://www.arc-team.com (accessed 10.06.06).

Blankholm, H. P. 1991. *Intrasite Spatial Analysis in Theory and Practice*, Aarhus: Aarhus University Press.

Cattani, M., Fiorini, A. & Rondelli, B. 2004. "Computer applications for a reconstruction of archaeological stratigraphy as a predictive model in urban and territorial contexts", K. F. Ausserer, W. Börner, M. Goriany & L. Karlhuber-Vöckl (eds.), *Enter the Past: the E-way into Four Dimensions of Cultural Heritage (CAA 2003, Proceedings of the 30th Conference, Vienna, Austria, 8-12 April, 2003)*, B.A.R. International Series 1227, Oxford: BAR Publishing: 299-303.

Coldstream, J. N. & Huxley, G. L. 1972 (eds.). *Kythera: Excavations and Studies*, London: Faber and Faber.

Doneus, M. & Neubauer, W. 2004. "Digital recording of stratigraphic excavations", in K. F. Ausserer, W. Börner, M. Goriany & L. Karlhuber-Vöckl (eds.), *Enter the Past: the E-way into Four Dimensions of Cultural Heritage (CAA 2003, Proceedings of the 30th Conference, Vienna, Austria, 8-12 April, 2003)*, B.A.R. International Series 1227, Oxford: BAR Publishing: 113-116.

Ervin, S. M. & Hasbrouck, H. H. 2001. *Landscape Modelling: Digital Techniques for Landscape Visualization*, New York: McGraw-Hill.

Green, D. A. 2003. "Stratigraphic visualisation for archaeological investigation", unpublished Ph.D. dissertation, Brunel University, London.

Harris, T. M. & Lock, G. R. 1996. "Multidimensional GIS: exploratory approaches to spatial and temporal relationships within archaeological stratigraphy", *Analecta Praehistorica Leidensia* 28: 307-316.

Johnson, A. L. 2004 (ed.). *Processual Archaeology: Exploring Analytical Strategies, Frames of Reference, and Culture Process*, Westport: Praeger.

Kochnev, V., Zdanovich, G. & Punegov, B. 2004. "The experiment in applying 3D technology of magnetic fields interpretation at the archaeological site 'Arkaim'", in K. F. Ausserer, W. Börner, M. Goriany & L. Karlhuber-Vöckl (eds.), *Enter the Past: the E-way into Four Dimensions of Cultural Heritage (CAA 2003, Proceedings of the 30th Conference, Vienna, Austria, 8-12 April, 2003)*, B.A.R. International Series 1227, Oxford: BAR Publishing: 64-67.

Lock, G. 2003. *Using Computers in Archaeology Towards Virtual Pasts*, London: Taylor and Francis.

Nigro, J. D., Ungar, P. S., de Ruiter, D. J. & Berger, L. R. 2003. "Developing a Geographic Information System (GIS) for mapping and analysing fossil deposits at Swartkrans, Gauteng Province, South Africa", *Journal of Archaeological Science* 30: 317-324.

Reilly, P. 1992. "Three-dimensional modelling and primary archaeological data", in P. Reilly & S. Rahtz (eds.), *Archaeology and the Information Age: a Global Perspective*, London: Routledge: 147-173.

Simpson, R. H. & Lazenby, J. F. 1972. "The Akroterion excavations", in J. N. Coldstream & G. L. Huxley (eds.), *Kythera: Excavations and Studies*, London: Faber and Faber: 52-66.

Zabulis, X., Patterson, A. & Daniilidis, K. 2005. "Digitizing archaeological excavations from multiple views", in *Proceedings of the 5th International Conference on 3-D Digital Imaging and Modelling, (3DIM 2005)*: 81-88.

Chapter 10

A software system to work with 3D models in cultural heritage research

The availability of intuitive, user-friendly, and specialized software to work with 3D models of cultural heritage artefacts is as important as the availability of low-cost and robust data acquisition techniques for the adoption of digitized 3D models in cultural heritage research. The number of available high-quality digitized artefacts increases rapidly with the advent of low-cost 3D scanning technologies. Consequently the need for specialized software for cultural heritage research and practice on 3D models becomes more apparent. The lack of spatial measurement tools familiar to cultural heritage experts in traditional 3D modelling packages motivated us to create a simple, freely available, and extensible measurement tools system, CH Toolbox, that was designed exclusively for cultural heritage research. Here we discuss our design decisions regarding the interaction scheme of the software system and introduce three virtual counterparts of real-world spatial measurement tools, more specifically the tape measure, the caliper, and the rim-chart.

Can Ozmen & Selim Balcisoy
Computer Graphics Laboratory, Sabanci University, Turkey

Introduction

With the emergence of accessible high-computing power and advanced interactive technologies it is now possible to develop digital tools for archaeology. There are a number of advantages of using digitized 3D models in cultural heritage research. Once an artefact has been digitized with the use of 3D scanner technology and modelling software, it is converted to a 3D model consisting of geometric and photometric information which can then be used in computer graphics, Virtual Reality or computational analysis. Computer graphics techniques make it possible to display cultural heritage assets in a cheaper, safer, and more secure way compared to traditional displays. Especially in the case of artefacts prone to decay and harm caused by environmental factors such as lighting, noise, temperature, humidity and pollution, a virtual display might be the only way to preserve and share these assets at the same time. Another factor in favour of digital replicas is their ease of storage, transportation, and duplication over the Internet and other computer networks. Combined with advances in network security, both cultural heritage researchers and the public can have different levels of access to these valuable assets without compromising the original artefacts. Such secure worldwide access, in turn, would allow greater options for collaboration between experts.

Computer-aided cultural heritage research makes new techniques available that were not possible before. For example, irreversible processes such as reconstruction and restoration can be planned, simulated and evaluated on 3D models without harming the originals. Furthermore, the effects of ageing, oxidization, and pollution can be simulated and visualized in order to

This research was partially supported by TUBITAK EEAG 104E155. We would also like to thank the Digital Michelangelo project for giving us access to the David model.

gain insight as to how the artefacts looked in the past and how will they look in the future. Digitization is also beneficial for research tasks that require computational analysis, such as the derivation and verification of statistical models, obtaining spatial measurements and estimations, as it makes it easier to compute and verify results by different experts.

Creation of 3D models

A detailed digital 3D model is obtained either through 3D optical scanning; or by means of 3D modelling software, such as Maya and 3Ds Max, with the help of photographs, drawings and measurements of an artefact. The quality of a manually created 3D model depends on the accuracy of the measurements taken with optical theodolites, tapes and calipers (Levy & Dawson 2006). A major drawback of manual modelling is the long amount of time it takes to collect the data and then model the artefact. The modelling skills of the researcher and her familiarity with the software are important factors determining both the cost and quality of the digital reproduction. By comparison, automated or semi-automated 3D modelling produces more accurate 3D models, and is faster. Automated modelling is achieved by first generating numerous partial range images of the artefact from all sides, then aligning these images, and finally merging them to create the 3D geometric mesh of the object (Kawasaki & Furukawa 2004). Range images, or maps, can be obtained with two different techniques, triangulation or time-of-flight (TOF)-based scanning. See **Plate 2** for two example system setups using triangulation and TOF-based scanning.

A) Triangulation-based scanning

Triangulation-based techniques work by capturing a photograph or video frame of the object to be scanned that has been illuminated using a striped laser or light pattern. Afterwards, the projection of the predetermined pattern on the surface of the object is used to generate a cloud of points with the help of image-processing algorithms. This range image consists of the set of distances between the sampled points on the surface and the camera. As this range image is derived from a 2D photograph, a single image is not sufficient to generate a point cloud that completely describes the object. A number of such partial images taken from different sides of the object, combined with the knowledge of the position and orientation of the camera, if the object is stationary and the camera is moved, or the knowledge of the axis and angle of rotation of the object, if the camera is kept stationary and the object revolved on a turntable, are aligned using complex algorithms to produce complete point clouds. The accuracy of a range map produced with triangulation depends on the distance between the camera and the object, thus the striped area photographed must be kept small for accurate results. This in turn increases the number of range images that must be taken to cover the object and results in an increase in the time needed to scan the object and align the range images. Depending on the size of the object, hundreds of scans might be needed to keep the error in the range of 0.1 mm (Guidi *et al.* 2002).

B) TOF-based scanning

The main difference between TOF- and triangulation-based scanning is the technique used to generate the point cloud describing the scanned object. The time of flight of laser pulses sent to the surface of the object is used to determine the distance between the light source and a point on the surface. This distance, combined with the vertical and horizontal angles between the point and the light source, is used to create the partial range image. Similar to triangulation-based scanning, these partial maps then must be aligned to produce the cloud of points that completely describe the scanned object. The error of TOF-based scans is usually measured in centimeters, which is much worse than triangulation-based scans. The strong point of this technique is that it allows long-range scans and it is a faster process. Consequently, it is used in situations where close scanning and lengthy scan times would be harmful to the scanned artefact and the site it belongs to, or when the error rate is found to be acceptable for the intented use of the 3D model.

Trends in 3D scanning technologies

The use of 3D scanning in cultural heritage research has been successfully demonstrated in a number of projects involving very detailed 3D models of sculptures, building, structures, and archaeological finds (Levoy *et al.* 2000; Miyazaki *et al.* 2001; Bernardini *et al.* 2002). As with any emerging technology, these initial systems are hard to operate, fragile, and are prohibitively expensive. Recent work in the area is in the direction of producing low-cost, robust, accurate, and automatic 3D scanning systems. Kawasaki and Furukawa (2004) present their model acquisition system and handheld 3D digitizer with claims to improved user convenience. Their proposed system consists of a laser projector and a turntable; both tracked using computer vision techniques, and a video camera to track them. Another low-cost 3D scanning setup is presented by Pheatt *et al.* (2005) which consists of digital camera, a motor-controlled turntable, laser diodes, and a simple micro-controller. They claim a cost of $250, excluding the camera and the PC, for the whole system. Callieri *et al.* (2004) also state that 3D scanning remains an expensive process and underutilized technology and they tackle the problem by presenting a robot-controlled and unattended 3D scanning system called RoboScan. Their contribution is the development of a new software system to control a commercially available 3D scanner moved by a robotic arm and a turntable that rotates the scanned object. The system is self-planning and can finish a complete scan unsupervised.

Motivation

Although the use of digitized models in cultural heritage research is beneficial, the adoption of such techniques is problematic because nearly all experts are trained for using traditional tools on physical artefacts. Both 3D scanning and 3D modelling requires familiarity with the hardware and software in order to produce digital models of required accuracy and detail for analysis and visualization tasks. As recent developments in 3D scanning technologies have made the digitization of artefacts affordable, the amount of digitized models available for research increases rapidly. Consequently, the need for specialized software for cultural heritage research and practice on 3D models becomes more apparent. The problem with using existing 3D modelling software for cultural heritage research on digitized artefacts is that using these programs effectively requires additional experience with the software and user interface which the researcher may lack. Such software are usually general purpose modelling tools or designed for digital content creation, architecture or manufacturing, and thus do not match the *modus operandi* of cultural heritage scholarship. Therefore, practitioners of the field cannot easily transfer their expertise in the domain to new software tools without further education or specific guidelines (Eiteljorg 1988). Applications targeting specific tasks such as archaeological pottery reconstruction exist, but they are limited by their tight focus and cannot be easily extended to other domains in analytical cultural heritage research (Melero *et al.* 2003; Sagiroglu & Ercil 2005). Similar problems arise in the medical field as well, where the disparency between computer tools and formal education methods is acknowledged. In the medical domain, the generally preferred solution to this problem is to present tools with a familiar interface based on their real world counterparts (Preim *et al.* 2002).

Design decisions

CH Toolbox is a 3D application framework for analytical cultural heritage research. It visualizes digitized models of artefacts in 3D and allows the user to analyze the pieces using a spaceball and mouse-driven interface **[Plate 1]**. Several designs were considered for the user interaction scheme of CH Toolbox. One important consideration was the amount of functionality, meaning both the number of distinct tools and the way these are presented to the user, which was suitable for CH Toolbox in order to make it as accessible as possible for cultural heritage researchers with differing backgrounds and computer skills. Grossman *et al.* (2002) consider the same issue in their digital tape drawing application, a computerized version of the technique commonly used by artists in car design, and say that although additional functionality similar to 3D modelling programs would be beneficial, the amount of functionality that can be introduced before tape artists reject it because of the perceived similarity with complicated 3D modelling software is an important question. The question is of similar importance in the design of CH Toolbox, and in the end we chose to present only a small subset of the possible functionality in order to keep our tools as simple and as close as possible to their real-life counterparts.

Interaction methodology

The three main operations in CH Toolbox are camera control, model selection and manipulation, and tool utilization. Typically, the user moves the camera to get an understanding about the object loaded into the environment and to find a suitable view for using the tool that is to be utilized next. Object selection and manipulation is useful in situations where more than one 3D model is visualized and the user finds it beneficial to move and orient the object instead of controlling the camera. Tool selection and utilization commonly comes only after the user is satisfied with the position and orientation of the camera and the 3D model. According to Balakrishnan & Kurtenbach (1999), these actions can be categorized as either pragmatic or epistemic actions. All of camera control and some object manipulation are considered epistemic actions if they are done with the intention of increasing perception and cognition. All other actions, such as tool selection and utilization, done with the intent of getting closer to accomplishing certain goals of a task are considered pragmatic actions. Epistemic and pragmatic actions complement each other, thus they do not necessarily have to be in sequential order and can be conducted in parallel. Asymmetric bimanual interaction is a familiar human trait that lends itself well to such parallelized actions. Guiard (1987) lay the theoretical foundations of skilled bimanual action with his Kinematic Chain model. According to his model, humans accomplish many tasks with two hands complementing each other. He states three principles that govern the asymmetry of human bimanual gestures:

- Right-to-left spatial reference in manual motion.
- Left-right contrast in the spatial-temporal scale of motion.
- Left-hand precedence in action.

Guiard's terms refer to a right-handed person, thus the dominant hand is the right one and the non-dominant hand is the left one. The following subsections explain these principles and their impact on our user interaction design.

A) Right-to-left spatial reference

Guiard's first principle is that in bimanual motions of the right hand finds its frame of reference from the motions of the left hand. He gives the examples of handwriting and sewing for actions where the left hand orients and stabilizes the subject of the motion so that the right hand can perform its manipulating motion easier. This principle can also be observed with the spatial measurement tools that we adopted for use with digital models. A tape measure is used by unrolling the tape with the right hand while the left hand stabilizes the starting end of the tape. A caliper is used by holding the object to be measured with the left hand while the right thumb carefully adjusts the jaws of the caliper to fit the object. The usage of a bordimeter is similar to handwriting, because the left hand stabilizes the paper in both cases.

B) Asymmetric motion scale

The second principle states that the two hands operate in different scales during bimanual action, both temporally and spatially. The left hand moves less frequently and makes comparatively larger movements than the right hand. We can again confirm this principle in the utilization of the spatial measurement tools selected for CH Toolbox. The right hand performs the fine adjustment of either the tool, by moving the measuring end of the tape, altering the jaw opening of the caliper, or the object, by positioning the rim sherd to fit the circle drawn on the bordimeter.

C) Left-hand precedence

The last principle follows the first principle, and it states that in a human skilled bimanual task, the left hand starts its action before the right hand. This principle is observed especially in tasks where the postural and manipulative roles of the hand are clearly separated, e.g. handwriting, sewing, driving a screw. Such a distinction between roles is also apparent in the usage of tapes and calipers, and consequently the principle of left-hand precedence can be observed in these actions. In the case of the tape measure, the left hand must place and hold the end of the tape before the right hand can unroll it. Similarly, in the case of caliper use, the left hand must position and hold the object to be measured before the right hand can position the caliper and adjust its dial to obtain a precise measurement. In the final case of bordimeter use, the left hand must hold the paper steady while the right hand moves the sherd to be fitted, and thus its actions must precede the actions of the right hand.

Input device and interaction scheme

Based on the initial analysis of the real world counterparts of the spatial measurement tools and their usage, we chose a bimanual interaction scheme for CH Toolbox, where the mouse is used to switch between tools, toggle visualization modes, select the artefacts to be manipulated, and precise utilization of the measurement tool and the spaceball is used to translate and rotate the selected artefacts or the 3D widget that represents the tool, and to control the camera **[Plate 3]**. As stated earlier, bimanual interaction is a familiar human trait and increases productivity in 3D camera and object manipulation tasks by enhancing depth perception through motion (Hinckley *et al.* 1998; Balakrishnan & Kurtenbach 1999). Considering the additional benefits gained by parallelization of pragmatic and epistemic actions, such an interaction scheme is a good candidate for tasks that follow Guiard's theory of skilled bimanual interaction.

Tools

Spatial measurements and estimations based on these play an important part in the analysis of cultural heritage artefacts. In the next subsections, we consider the case of archaeological pottery reconstruction and three tools that are commonly used. These are the tape measure, caliper, and the rim chart. A discussion of the real tool along with its virtual counterpart is given.

Tape measure

The tape measure is used for determining the dimensions of a sherd and the surface distance between any two points on the sherd. These measurements are used for classifying a piece, along with its weight and thickness. It is also used for measuring fracture lengths to aid in reconstruction. The main purpose of the tape measure is to find geodesic distances either on the surface, along the rim, if the sherd is part of the rim, or along the fractured edges. The tool is used with two hands. The protrusion on the edge of the tape is fastened to one of the end-points of the distance to be measured, then it is held in place using one hand while the other hand pulls the measure and extends the tape to the other end-point. The measurement can be more easily read by locking the tape at the desired length. The tape measure is, in essence, an easier to use metered rope.

We use the notion of a geodesic curve to implement a virtual tape measure that works on 3D digitized models. A geodesic curve is the shortest path between two points on a surface. Common areas of use include navigation, path-finding, motion planning and network optimization. It is also an important step in many computer graphics algorithms such as mesh parametrization, mesh segmentation and mesh editing (Krishnamurthy & Levoy 1996; Floater & Hormann 2002; Funkhouser *et al.* 2004). Current graphics hardware all use a triangular mesh format to process and visualize 3D geometries, thus most geodesics research is done for the discrete case (Mitchell *et al.* 1987). The

Djikstra shortest-path algorithm is not sufficient to solve the discrete geodesic problem because the shortest path on a surface does not always follow along the edges of the mesh. The simplest solution is to augment the original mesh with extra points before running Djikstra. Lanthier *et al.* (1997) compare different ways of populating a mesh with additional vertices on existing edges, called Steiner points, and show that a bounded approximation to the geodesic can be obtained with this method. The error bound and complexity of the algorithm depends on the number and distribution of these Steiner points. A description of the algorithm using a fixed-point distribution scheme, which we used, will be presented in the next section. A survey of approximate algorithms can be found in Mitchell (2000). Several algorithms giving an exact solution to the discrete geodesic problem have been proposed. The 'single source—all destinations' algorithm described by Mitchell *et al.* (1987)—henceforth MMP algorithm—uses the continuous Djikstra method and has a worst case running time of $O(n^2 \log n)$, where n is the number of vertices. The MMP algorithm was recently implemented by Surazhky *et al.* (2005), who conclude that it performs much better than the worst case analysis suggests. An exact algorithm with $O(n^2)$ running time based on surface unfoldings was proposed by Chen & Han (1990).

The virtual tape measure is used for measuring the surface distance between two points on a model. The user fixes a point, then moves the mouse to interactively visualize and measure geodesics originating from the start point as seen in **Plate 4**. We solve the geodesic problem in the pre-processing stage before the artefact model is visualized inside the CH Toolbox environment. The approximate geodesic solution proposed by Lanthier *et al.* (1997) is used. The algorithm is as follows:

- The original mesh is loaded and converted to a triangle mesh.
- Original edges are subdivided to create extra vertices, called Steiner points.
- New edges are created between two Steiner points if they are adjacent on the same triangle edge or they lie on different edges of the same triangle.
- The single-source all-destinations Djikstra is run for each vertex.

We used a fixed scheme to evenly add two Steiner points per edge, therefore six vertices and 27 edges are added to a triangle in the pre-processing stage **[Fig. 7]**. Lanthier *et al.* (1997) proved that the algorithm runs in $O(n^5)$ for the single-source all-destinations problem, where n is the number of triangles in the original mesh. The geodesic is visualized by traversing vertices on the shortest path between the two end points of the tape measure. We choose to visualize the extra edges only if they lie on the shortest path solution, thus the tool has negligible impact on the interactivity of CH Toolbox.

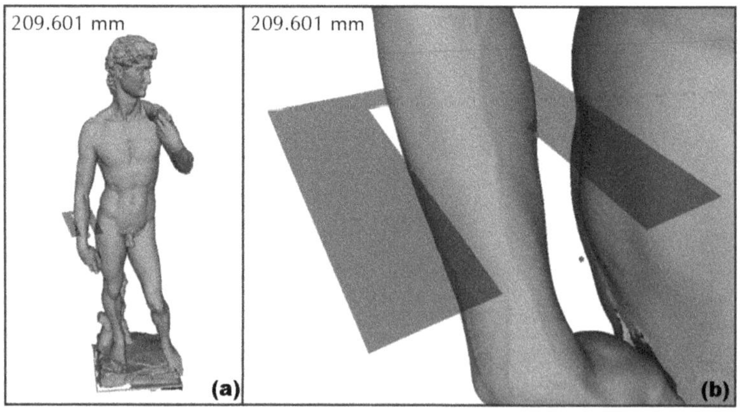

Fig. 5. *Screenshot of the caliper in action.*

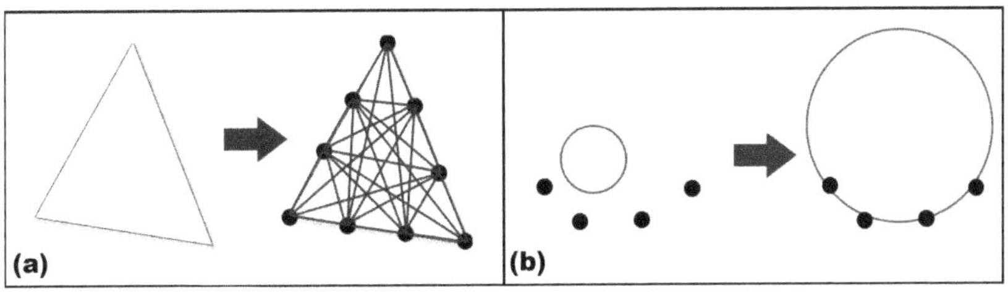

Fig. 7. A. Additional vertices, called Steiner points, and edges are added to the original triangle for better accuracy; B. a circle is iteratively fit to a set of points.

The bimanual interaction scheme of the framework is also conserved while using the virtual tape measure.

Caliper

The caliper is used for measuring the linear distance between an object's two opposite sides. The thickness of a sherd is useful in pottery analysis as it might give insights about the material and techniques used in making the pot as well as the intended usage of the vessel. Furthermore, precise drawings and reconstructions of any artefact depend on precise measurements taken with a caliper. The tool is held with one hand, while the other hand manipulates the object to be measured. The tips of the caliper are then adjusted to get a firm touch on the surface of the object, after which a reading can be made. A too-tight clamping action can deform both the caliper and the object depending on their material properties, which can yield an inaccurate measurement. We developed a virtual caliper based on the same idea of clamping the tips to the point of touching the measured object. The caliper is visualized as a semi-transparent plane that can be manipulated with the spaceball [**Fig. 5**]. The plane has four cubes on the midpoints of each side, the top and bottom ones being fixed. The left and the right cubes are movable using the mouse wheel or the keyboard left and right arrows. These moveable cubes represent the tips of the caliper, which upon clicking get stuck in their relative positions. In a regular caliper only one tip is moveable, but in our virtual caliper implementation either the left, right or both tips can be adjusted. In our caliper implementation we used a very simple collision detection technique to determine if a tip touches the 3D model, and thus is unable to move into the object. The closest face of the cube is checked for intersections with the model, with only one point of intersection meaning that the tip has just touched the surface of the object.

Radius estimation

A bordimeter, also called a rim chart, is a set of concentric circles drawn on a piece of paper or cardboard. It is used for estimating the rim radius of a vessel given a sherd belonging to the vessel's rim. The rim radius is used in calculating the rim size, which in turn helps archaeologists to assess a pot's function (relating to open versus closed shapes etc.). Radius estimation is also used in volume, and consequently, capacity estimation. Both assessments help in the classification of the vessel. The tool is placed on a flat surface, then a rim sherd is put rim-side down to find the best fitting circle, which is then used to estimate the radius. Because the bordimeter is a solid piece of paper, radius estimation cannot be done with pieces other than rim sherds.

The problem of fitting a circle to a given set of co-planar points is called 2D circle fitting. It is a non-linear least squares problem, which can be solved iteratively by reducing it to a set of linear least squares problems (Gander *et al.* 1996). A best fit circle is computed and displayed interactively as the user moves the mouse over visualization of the artefact model as seen in **Plate 6**. The tool works as follows:

Model	Faces	Stn. points	time1 (s)	time² (s)
Sherd	17696	89859	0.03500	1.86438
Sphere	50986	255002	0.10150	6.77794
Sphere	204552	1023002	0.40625	28.22556
David	483498	2526815	1.02325	62.44571

Table 1. *Performance of approximate geodesic algorithm.*

Tool	Real (cm)	Virtual (cm)	Rel. error
Tape	15.35	15.44	0.6%
Caliper	1.92	2.01	4.7%
Bordimeter	12.74	12.17	4.5%

Table 2. *Error rate of virtual tools.*

- The plane defined by moving the mouse is intersected with the model to obtain a set of points on the plane.
- The average of the points is taken as the initial estimate for the circle.
- The circle is fit iteratively using least squares fitting to these selected points [**Fig.** 7].
- The centre and the radius of the circle is computed.

Even if the least squares solution does not converge, the iteration for fitting the circle is stopped after a certain number of steps to maintain interactivity. We found that the solution converges in sufficient time if the points are not nearly linear. Otherwise, a warning message is displayed. This is not a problem with our test case since archaeological pottery has a curved surface. The circle and its centre is visualized in addition to the text display of the location of the centre and its radius because it helps the expert to visually verify the suitability of the numeric solution as the rotational axis of the artefact. During the measurement process the expert can use the spaceball to move and orient the model. She can also change the transparency of the circle visualization to prevent it from obscuring the artefact.

Results

CH Toolbox is developed in C++, using the open-source scenegraph library OpenSceneGraph[1] that helps visualizations in OpenGL by providing an organizational hierarchy. The CH Toolkit and the interactive spatial measurement tools developed for it are available for all the operating systems that OpenSceneGraph supports. Our application runs in real-time on desktop PCs. We tested the surface distance algorithm on an AMD Opteron 2.6GHz PC with 8GB RAM. For a sherd mesh with 17K triangles, our algorithm takes 0.035 seconds for the pre-processing stage as seen in **Table 1**. The number of extra vertices and edges, and its impact on performance is also reported. Although the perfomance is not adequate for real-time interaction, our interviews with cultural heritage experts show that the time needed for the pre-processing step is acceptable for real world use cases.

1. See http://openscenegraph.org.

We also compared rim estimations and surface distances measured on a real pot with the approximate results we got using our virtual tools on a sherd mesh **[Table 2]**. The error rate of the caliper and the bordimeter is rather high, but is still consistent with the bound proven by Lanthier *et al.* (1997). Since these measurements were taken on the rim of the sherd mesh and are almost twice as great as the errors we encountered on generated meshes such our sphere model, we suspect that the difference is due to the accumulation of the error from the 3D scanning step.

Conclusion and future work

Our main contribution is the development of a platform for interactive computer-aided cultural heritage tasks. We implemented measurement tools that archaeologists use daily in real life by adapting algorithms developed for other computational geometry tasks. The algorithms we chose are suitable for use in a real-time interactive environment. Another contribution is the introduction of bimanual interaction to the cultural heritage domain, though possible benefits need to be further investigated with usability studies conducted with cultural heritage experts. The next step would be improving the accuracy of our tools, especially the radius estimation tool. We suspect that the relatively high error rate is due to errors in the 3D scanning technology we used. Our tools should be tested with models obtained from other scanning technologies. We feel that the establishment of databases of peer-reviewed 3D models of cultural heritage artefacts will provide us with the opportunity to test our tools more thoroughly. Finally, CH Toolbox is released as an open-source application to aid researchers in the cultural heritage domain and is available online.[2]

Bibliography

Balakrishnan, R. & Kurtenbach, G. 1999. "Exploring bimanual camera control and object manipulation in 3D graphics interfaces", in M. W. Altom & M. G. Williams (eds.), *CHI '99: Proceedings of the SIGCHI Conference on Human Factors in Computing Systems*, New York: ACM Press: 56–62.

Bernardini, F., Rushmeier, H., Martin, I. M., Mittleman, J. & Taubin, G. 2002. "Building a digital model of Michelangelo's Florentine Pietà", *Institute of Electrical and Electronics Engineers, Computer Graphics and Applications* 22/1: 59–67.

Callieri, M., Fasano, A., Impoco, G., Cignoni, P., Scopigno, R., Parrini, G. & Biagini, G. 2004. "Roboscan: an automatic system for accurate and unattended 3D scanning", in Y. Aloimonos & G. Taubin (eds.), *3DPVT '04: Proceedings of the 2nd International Symposium on 3D Data Processing, Visualization, and Transmission*, Washington: Institute of Electrical and Electronics Engineers Computer Society: 805–812.

Chen, J. & Han, Y. 1990. "Shortest paths on a polyhedron", in R. Seidel (ed.), *SCG '90: Proceedings of the 6th Annual Symposium on Computational Geometry*, New York: ACM Press: 360–369.

Floater, M. & Hormann, K. 2002. "Parameterization of triangulations and unorganized points", in A. Alske, E. Quak, & M.S. Floater (eds.), *Tutorials on Multiresolution in Geometric Modelling*, Berlin: Springer: 287–315.

Funkhouser, T., Kazhdan, M., Shilane, P., Min, P., Kiefer, W., Tal, A., Rusinkiewicz, S. & Dobkin, D. 2004. "Modelling by example", *Association for Computing Machinery Transactions on Graphics* 23/3: 652–663.

Gander, W., Golub, G. H. & Strebel, R. 1994. "Least-squares fitting of circles and ellipses", *BIT Numerical Mathematics* 34/4: 558–578.

Grossman, T., Balakrishnan, R., Kurtenbach, G., Fitzmaurice, G., Khan, A. & Buxton, B. 2002. "Creating principal 3D curves with digital tape drawing", in E. Dykstra-Erikson & M. Tscheligi (eds.), *CHI '02: Proceedings of the SIGCHI Conference on*

2. http://graphics.sabanciuniv.edu/chtoolbox.

Human Factors in Computing Systems, New York: ACM Press: 121–128.

Guiard, Y. 1987. "Asymmetric division of labor in human skilled bimanual action: the kinematic chain as a model", *Journal of Motor Behavior* 19/4: 486–517.

Guidi, G., Tucci, G., Beraldin, J.-A., Ciofi, S., Ostuni, D., Constantini, F. & El-Hakim, S. 2002. "Multiscale archaeological survey based on the integration of 3D scanning and photogrammetry", in W. Boehler (ed.), *Proceedings of the International Workshop on Scanning for Cultural Heritage Recording: Complementing or Replacing Photogrammetry (Corfu, 1-2 September, Greece)*: 58–64.

Hinckley, K., Pausch, R., Proffitt, D. & Kassell, N. F. 1998. "Two-handed virtual manipulation", *Association for Computing Machinery Transactions on Computer-Human Interaction* 5/3: 260–302.

Eiteljorg II, H. 1988. "Computer-assisted drafting and design: new technologies for old problems", http://www.csanet.org/inftech/cadbklt.html (seen March 10, 2007).

Kawasaki, H. & Furukawa, R. 2004. "Entire model acquisition system using handheld 3D digitiser", in Y. Aloimonos & G. Taubin (eds.), *3DPVT '04: Proceedings of the 2nd International Symposium on 3D Data Processing, Visualization, and Transmission*, Washington: Institute of Electrical and Electronics Engineers Computer Society: 478–485.

Krishnamurthy, V. & Levoy, M. 1996. "Fitting smooth surfaces to dense polygon meshes", in H. Rushmeir (ed.), *SIGGRAPH '96: Proceedings of the 23rd Annual Conference on Computer Graphics and Interactive Techniques*, New York: ACM Press: 313–324.

Lanthier, M., Maheshwari, A. & Sack, J.-R. 1997. "Approximating weighted shortest paths on polyhedral surfaces", in J.-D. Boissonnat (ed.), *SCG '97: Proceedings of the 13th Annual Symposium on Computational Geometry*, New York: ACM Press: 274–283.

Levoy, M., Pulli, K., Curless, B., Rusinkiewicz, S., Koller, D., Pereira, L., Ginzton, M., Anderson, S., Davis, J., Ginsberg, J., Shade, J. & Fulk, D. 2000. "The digital Michelangelo project: 3D scanning of large statues", in J.R. Brown & K. Akeley (eds.), *SIGGRAPH '00: Proceedings of the 27th Annual Conference on Computer Graphics and Interactive Techniques*, New York: ACM Press/Addison-Wesley: 131–144.

Levy, R. & Dawson, P. 2006. "Reconstructing a Thule whalebone house using 3D imaging", *Institute of Electrical and Electronics Engineers, Multimedia* 13/2: 78–83.

Melero, F. J., Torres, J. C. & Leon, A. 2003. "On the interactive 3D reconstruction of Iberian vessels", in Arnold, D., Chalmers, A. & Niccolucci, F. (eds.), *Proceedings of the 4th International Symposium on Virtual Reality, Archaeology and Intelligent Cultural Heritage (VAST 2003, Brighton, November 5–7, 2003)*, Aire-la-ville: Eurographics Association: 71–78.

Mitchell, J. S. B. 2000. "Geometric shortest paths and network optimization", in J.-R. Sack & J. Urrutia (eds.), *Handbook of Computational Geometry*, Amsterdam: Elsevier Science: 633–701.

Mitchell, J. S. B., Mount, D. M. & Papadimitriou, C. H. 1987. "The discrete geodesic problem", *Society for Industrial and Applied Mathematics Journal on Computing* 16/4: 647–668.

Miyazaki, D., Oishi, T., Nishikawa, T., Sagawa, R., Nishino, K., Tomomatsu, T., Takase, Y. & Ikeuchi, K. 2001. "The great Buddha project: modelling cultural heritage through observation", in K. Ikeuchi & Y. Sato (eds.), *Modeling from Reality*, Boston: Kluwer: 181–193.

Pheatt, C., Ballester, J. & Wilhelmi, D. 2005. "Low-cost three-dimensional scanning using range imaging", *Journal of Computing Sciences in Colleges* 20/4: 13–19.

Preim, B., Tietjen, C., Spindler, W. & Peitgen, H.-O. 2002. "Integration of measurement tools in medical 3d visualizations", in H. Pfister, M. Bailey, & J.E. Swan

II (eds.), *VIS 2002: Proceedings of the Conference on Visualization*, Washington: Institute of Electrical and Electronics Engineers Computer Society: 21–28.

Sagiroglu, M. S. & Ercil, A. 2005. "A texture based approach to reconstruction of archaeological finds", in M. Mudge, N. Ryan, & R. Scopigno (eds.), *Proceedings of the 6th International Symposium on Virtual Reality, Archaeology and Intelligent Cultural Heritage (VAST05, Pisa, November 8-11 2005)*, Aire-la-ville: Eurographics Association: 137-142.

Surazhsky, V., Surazhsky, T., Kirsanov, D., Gortler, S. J. & Hoppe, H. 2005. "Fast exact and approximate geodesics on meshes", *Association for Computing Machinery Transactions on Graphics* 24/3: 553–560.

CHAPTER 11
A DIGITAL MODEL OF THE INCA SANCTUARY OF THE SUN

This paper is a 'virtual-empirical' test of a hypothesis put forth by Dearborn *et al.* 1998, concerning the alignment of two Inca towers at the north end of the Sanctuary of the Sun (Island of the Sun, Lake Titicaca, Bolivia), namely that the towers marked the position of the sun at sunset on the winter solstice, in the context of solstitial ritual. Our virtual-empirical test validates the Dearborn-Seddon-Bauer hypothesis, while it shows the potential of 3D modelling as a heuristic and communicative tool. The paper also presents a scaleable tool allowing researchers to explore work performed at the Cultural Virtual Reality Laboratory (CVR Lab) for future research.

Chris Johanson[†] & Bernard Frischer[•]

[†] Cultural Virtual Reality Laboratory, University of California at Los Angeles, USA

[•] Institute for Advanced Technology in the Humanities, University of Virginia, USA

Background: the Island of the Sun, and the project

The Island of the Sun **[Plate 1]**, located in Lake Titicaca, Bolivia, served as a state-sponsored pilgrimage centre for the Tiwanaku and later Inca civilizations (Stanish 2003: 200-201; Stanish & Bauer 2004: 1-20). The island was thought to have housed the birthplace of the Sun, as Bernabé Cobo, an early 17th century Spanish chronicler, relates:

> [...] the people of ancient times tell of being without light from the heavens for many days, and all of the local inhabitants were astonished, confused, and frightened to have total darkness for such a long time. Finally, the people of the Island of Titicaca saw the Sun come up one morning out of that crag with extraordinary radiance. For this reason they believed that the true dwelling place of the Sun was that crag [...] (Cobo 1990: 91-92).

The Inca elite appropriated this belief and incorporated it into their own origin myth, which claims that the Sun enjoined the Inca people to take the Sun as their father (Dearborn *et al.* 1998: 244-246). The Sacred Rock and its surrounding precinct was the culminating point of the pilgrimage. On the June solstice, the elite were able to view the sun as it rose above the Sacred Rock and possibly reenacted the origin myth on that occasion.

This paper is a 'virtual-empirical' test of a hypothesis put forth by Dearborn *et al.* in 1998 (henceforth Dearborn-Seddon-Bauer hypothesis), concerning the alignment of two Inca towers at the north end of the Sanctuary of the Sun. According to this hypothesis, the towers were not tombs (as has been asserted by other scholars), but markers of the position of the sun at sunset on the winter solstice, enabling large-scale audience participation in solstitial ritual. Dearborn *et al.* reached this conclusion through 2D analysis; they employed a limited subset of data due to the fact that a) *in situ* empirical testing could only be performed at certain time during the year (sunset on or near the June solstice) and b) critical architectural elements are only partially preserved. Our project circumvents such constraints of time and space; it utilizes a 3D model of the island's topography and the sanctuary, and ephemeris data supplied by NASA's Jet Propulsion

Laboratory (JPL), which enabled the reconstruction of the apparent course of the sun through the sky at sunset on dates surrounding the winter solstice in the year 1500 CE (the approximate date for ceremonies attested by the Spanish chroniclers).

The creation of a generalized tool-methodology

At all times during the project, an emphasis was a placed on maximizing technology while minimizing costs. To this end, publicly available data or data acquired through an educational license were employed. The goal of the project was both to test the Dearborn-Seddon-Bauer hypothesis and to create a generalized tool that could scale to applications at other archaeological sites. It is acknowledged that the integration between GIS packages and real-time visualization is still not robust. Thus, the following methodology is presented both to provide verification and validation of the underlying data used, and to lay bare areas which an observant scholar (or further advances in technology) might improve.

The model

The mission of the CVR Lab is to create scientifically authenticated and validated historic reconstructions and restorations of ancient monuments. The CVR Lab attempts to create models that correspond in some measurable way to the physical world. Be it archaeological remains that connect to the real world through the use of geographic coordinate systems, or the physical landscapes themselves, every element modelled in the application has a scientifically validated reason for being in the very place where it (virtually) is. Hence, the desired goal of the CVR Lab was to recreate, as accurately as possible, a 3D model of the Island of the Sun, its surrounding islands, and the corresponding surrounding topography. It was deemed equally important that all the geographic elements conform relatively precisely (ca. 1 m) to real-world elements. The sun's location in the sky as seen from the Island of the Sun also needed to accurately and verifiably reflect the approximate path of the sun in the sky 500 years ago.

The initial model of the island itself was derived from a digitized contour map. The map and contour lines served as a simplified test-case for a study of the area. The archaeological remains of the Sacred Rock and the separate precincts were then built on this monument. Since the CVR Lab did not have access to high-resolution survey information, a digitized paper map (5 m contours) was used to create a 3D representation of the island. This contour map was then draped over the resulting model to better illustrate the changing elevation. To build the surrounding shoreline and topography, the CVR Lab team used publicly available digital information to create the real-time model. Source data for the digital elevation model (DEM) came from the Shuttle Radar Topography Mission (SRTM), acquired from JPL. Low-resolution (90 m) satellite imagery was obtained from Earth Science Data Interface (ESDI) in geotiff format. The coverage area spanned two separate satellite images, so the two were merged together using ESRI's suite of GIS software (ArcMap, ArcToolbox versions 8 and 9).

The creation of a useful, real-time model demanded the use of third-party commercial software. Many software packages can output various 3D model formats, but the CVR Lab required a solution that was scaleable and contained a means of producing level of detail tiles. The software used for this purpose was Creator Terrain Studio from Multigen-Paradigm. The product allows the user to create a work-flow built upon DEM and satellite imagery **[Plate 9]**. Once the work-flow is created, the user can build and rebuild the terrain according to differing specifications. Hence, a particular tile and level of detail model can be built that takes into account present-day technological limitations, and when graphics technology improves (as it always does), a new, more detailed, higher-resolution model can be generated using the same underlying data and workflow. The final topographical context model **[Plate 10]** included all of Lake Titicaca as well as the Bolivian mountains to the east. Thus when the CVR Lab works with or presents the model, the highest level of detail can be manual set to display, or one can use an automatic process which displays higher resolution, based on one's proximity to an object (which allows for better performance).

The creation of the sun

There are various different ways to create a digital representation of the sun. Accuracy, portability, scaleability, and real-time capability were the most important factors to be considered. Rather than create a simulated ball of fire one astronomical unit away from a simulated earth, the CVR Lab team followed an ancient model of the universe, the celestial dome. The sun resides on the interior concave of a dome of an arbitrarily small radius (e.g. in the accompanying figures the sun is 1 (virtual) km away from the viewer. The depiction of the sun is a 2D texture mapped to a unit rectangle **[Plate 11]**. The unit rectangle is a point-axis billboard, i.e. the sun always faces the viewer by rotating around its own centre-point axis. Since the actual sun is quite a lot more than 1 km away from an earthbound viewer, it appears, for all intents and purposes, to act like an object that is at infinite distance from the viewer. Hence, when one walks along the earth, or drives a car, the sun appears to be moving with the observer, in reference to distant buildings, mountains, etc. Therefore, this virtual sun, is attached to the viewer's head. It rotates with the scene, but transforms with the viewer. In scenegraphic terms, the sun is hung on the scenegraph above the navigation node, which is transformable, but applies the same rotation matrix as that of the navigation node.

Highly accurate ephemeris data came from JPL's Horizon software, an online ephemeris generator, which can generate data for many natural and man-made celestial bodies and calculate what that body would look like when viewed from another. Therefore, one can obtain the right ascension, declination, and angular radius of the sun at any specific time within the limits of the underlying data. The initial study was performed using time-step data of the sun, on both the summer and winter solstices to study the viewsheds from the precinct areas.

The CVR Lab team in conjunction with UCLA's Academic Technology Services (led by J. Slottow) combined Fortran code provided by D. Dearborn with algorithms described by Montenbruck and Pfleger (2000) to create a more robust and interactive mechanism to interact with the sun data. Using the open source real-time application, vrNav, and its java-based GUI, the user can now choose any date and time to view the sun's location in the sky at a given latitude **[Plate 12]**. For each solar experiment, this real-time generated data is cross-checked with the results from JPL, and where necessary, the more accurate JPL data is used instead.

Geographic space and scientific accuracy

An underlying geographic coordinate system tied together the three disparate pieces, and an additional combination of georeferenced satellite imagery provided the acceptable level of accuracy demanded by the archaeo-astronomical problem. The CVR Lab used high-resolution satellite imagery acquired via educational license from DigitalGlobe (2.4 m multispectral and 60 cm panchromatic imagery) both to geolocate and geocalibrate the original model. That is to say, the original model was modified by correcting any anomalies in the original paper map (geocalibration) and it was then planted into the surrounding terrain (geolocation), which was already georeferenced through the Creator Terrain Studio process. Now that the underlying geometry contained a unified geographic coordinate system (UTM), the coordinates for the location of the user were extracted at run-time and fed into the real-time ephemeris generator. The same data are also displayed by a virtual GPS readout on the vrNav GUI. The GUI is a separate appplication from vrNav, and connects to the application via TCP. Therefore, it can run simultaneously on the display computer, a separate computer, or even a wirelessly networked palm device. A user in the field can carry the GUI, control the display on the vrNav graphic display, and interpret the virtual GPS readout displayed on the palm device without being tied to a larger form factor computer.

The pilgrimage: a visual narrative

Chroniclers describe the official pilgrimage route. It began at Yunguyu (Stanish 2003: 246), whence the pilgrims would walk north through modern Copa Cabana, and travel by reed boat to the southern end of the island **[Plate 2]**. From there, they would walk north, along the spine of the island until they reached some sort of structure that restricted access for the bulk of the pilgrims to the Sacred Rock sanctuary **[Plate 3]**. The VR model depicts the outline of the walls delineating what appears to be the remains of this sanctuary **[Plate 4]**. Further to the north, at the site of the Sacred Rock, the elite and high priesthood performed the ritual, which involved offerings and chicha libations into a round stone altar. Around the time of the June (winter) solstice, the elite could view the sun rise above the Sacred Rock, as it did in the origin myth **[Plate 5]**. Dearborn *et al.* (1998: 250) observed that two pillars, located on a slight rise to the northwest of the sanctuary played a role in the ritual as well. The pillars appeared to have been aligned with the setting sun of the June solstice, when viewed from the sanctuary adjacent to the Sacred Rock. Furthermore, these two structures contained no fragments of occupation; they were rectangular and made of stone, all features consistent with other Inca towers used to mark solar positions (Seddon & Bauer 2004).

The VR model clearly illustrates the path of the June solstice as it would have appeared in 1500 CE and confirms the Dearborn-Seddon-Bauer hypothesis **[Plate 6]**. The solar pillars would have been visible to the masses of devotees standing to the south. Dearborn *et al.* (1998: 255-257) propose that these pillars permitted some non-elite participation. The VR model illustrates the viewshed available to that audience **[Plate 7]** and is a good example of the strengths of VR modelling. Given that the area in question is further away from the pillars than that reserved for the elite, the spatial and temporal 'window' through which non-elite viewers could have stood to watch the sun set between the pillars is very small. The model reveals that, while the area demarcated for a wider audience enabled some non-elite participation, it limited the scope of such participation; furthermore, the preferential access to ritual performance and experience by the elite seems to have underscored the inability of the wider audience to participate fully in the ritual. In other words, the computer model takes into account real-world perspective, which cannot be adequately illustrated in 2D diagrams.

Additional observations

The model gave rise to additional lines of enquiry. A number of sanctuaries on the island located along the pilgrimage route to the Sacred Rock require alignment testing. Equally interesting, though yet to be investigated thoroughly, is a Tiwanaku structure on the western slope of the island. When standing further down the western slope near the Tiwanaku structure, one can see the winter solstice sun setting between two noticeable natural peaks on the small island just to the west of the island of the sun **[Plate 8]**. These peaks may have functioned as a possible source of inspiration or at least a natural analog to the man-made pillars. Looking further afield, the underlying geographic coordinate system can allow users of the digital application to extract the location of the viewer and shoot a vector from their location to an area in the distance that appears to represent a particular alignment. The initial hypothesis was advanced through the combined use of various 2D resources. Dearborn *et al.* (1998: figs 11-16) produced a series of diagrams illustrating the spatial relationships between the sacred ritual site, the outlying platform for the non-elite, and the solar markers. Such a methodology is effective for illustrating an initial hypothesis tied to a few locations, but becomes extraordinarily time-consuming and laborious when the viewsheds of a range of locations are to be studied effectively and efficiently. The use of a 3D real-time computer graphics application is much better suited to such a task. Moreover, 2D analysis does not scale effectively to archaeological sites in other geographic locations, whereas the generalized computer application can enhance the accuracy of the investigation and can easily be applied to any archaeological site.

Conclusions and future directions

The initial investigation and validation of a hypothesis quickly expanded into a scaleable tool applicable to analogous, viewshed-related problems. The real-time archaeo-astronomical application offered a new, digital laboratory within which the previous hypothesis was verified and some of its claims were more completely examined. The degree of accuracy and the real-time ability to check the results, specifically regarding audience-scale participation, could only be done through the use of the computer. The addition of JPL data and high-resolution satellite imagery advanced the level of accuracy in the underlying study as well. Thus, this new tool further rooted the study in empiricism and at the same time lay bare the research methods employed so that others can critique the methodology and understand the validity of the spatial relationships. Notably, conventional 2D studies and accompanying sketches force the reader to trust the author's observation; whereas accurately modelled 3D studies, coupled with high-resolution satellite imagery, force the author to conform to real-world spatial constraints. The underlying GIS core allows the researcher to cross-reference the virtual world with the real world and perform an enormous amount of accurate investigation *in* (virtual) *situ* before travelling to the field. As a case-study, the calculations performed for the original hypothesis could all have been studied within the virtual application and further work, which would normally require repeated trips to the field, can be tested and validated during the research process. In the case of viewshed problems, the field need not be the final empirical test for a hypothesis, rather, the VR simulation functions as proof enough.

Armed with this tool, researchers can pursue numerous avenues of future enquiry. Not only can they test viewsheds at numerous and disparate sites (separated by various forms of geographic impediments) in a few hours, though the real-world equivalents might take months or years to verify, but they can also look beyond currently mapped sites. By directing an enquiry vector towards distant natural features that align with celestial phenomena, they can extract the coordinates where the vector intersects with the feature and then target future areas of enquiry, thus serving both the adventurer and the scholar.

Bibliography

Cobo, B. Fr. 1990. *History of the Inca Empire: an Account of the Indians' Customs and their Origin, together with a Treatise on Inca Legends, History, and Social Institutions (Translated and Edited by R. Hamilton)*, Austin: University of Texas Press.

Dearborn, D. S. P., Seddon, M. T. & Bauer, B. S. 1998. "The sanctuary of Titicaca: where the sun returns to earth", *Latin American Antiquity* 9/3: 240-258.

Montenbruck, O. & Pfleger, T. 2000. *Astronomy on the Personal Computer*, New York: Springer.

Seddon, M. T. & Bauer, B. S. 2004. "Excavations at Tikani", in C. Stanish & B. S. Bauer (eds.), *Archaeological Research on the Islands of the Sun and Moon, Lake Titicaca, Bolivia: Final Results of the Proyecto Tiksi Kjarka*, Los Angeles: Cotsen Institute of Archaeology.

Stanish, C. 2003. *Ancient Titicaca: the Evolution of Complex Society in Southern Peru and Northern Bolivia*, Berkeley: University of California Press.

Chapter 12

Applications of 3D technology as a research tool in archaeological ceramic analysis

This paper describes the stages of integrating 3D technology in archaeological pottery analysis, from general visualization instruments, more than a decade ago, to high-resolution systems used today for accurate data acquisition. As an example of the great potential of this technology, two new quantitative measurements are defined: the uniformity of a vessel and the degree of its deformation. The uniformity is defined based on correlations between many profiles of the same vessel, and the deformation value is defined from the roundness of its horizontal sections. Both quantities, which could not be traced using traditional methods, are highly relevant in finding solutions to real archaeological problems.

Avshalom Karasik
Weizmann Institute of Science, and Archaeological Institute, Hebrew University, Israel

Introduction

The potential of 3D scanning for pottery analysis was recognized more than a decade ago. 3D modelling is increasingly used in archaeology in general and for pottery in particular. Most of the 3D applications in the past have concentrated on visualization—either for teaching or for publication—and on fast and accurate data acquisition. The advantages of 3D technology in these topics over the traditional methods are self-evident. However, there have been few efforts to harness this new technology for the development of new research tools. In the last four years, a joint Israeli research group at the Institutes of Archaeology at Hebrew University and Haifa University, in collaboration with the Weizmann Institute of Science, has developed new methodological tools for pottery analysis in archaeology (Gilboa *et al.* 2004; Saragusti *et al.* 2005). We started our project by developing computerized tools for classification and typological analysis of 2D profile drawings, of the type found in every archaeological report. Experience with these drawings convinced us that the future is in 3D technology. The biggest obstacles to pottery analysis are the huge amount of data and the expense, as well as the lack of accuracy of manual drawings. Experimentation has shown that 3D scanning is not only more accurate than manual drawing of profiles, and provides much more information on the potsherd, but is actually much faster. An added bonus is that 2D scanners generate raster images, but 3D scanners typically produce output in vector format, which is more amenable to mathematical manipulation. As will be demonstrated in the text, the tools which we have developed for 2D analysis are the basis of 3D investigation as well. This paper describes the main contributions and applications of 3D scanners used so far in pottery analysis. It also provides a short description of the tools developed by our group and

This research was supported by a BIKURA grant from the Israel Science Foundation and by the Kimmel Center for Archaeological Sciences in the Weizmann Institute of Science. I wish to thank my supervisors Dr. Ilan Sharon and Prof. Uzy Smilansky for their guidance and comments. The results discussed in this paper have been presented on several occasions (Gilboa et al. *2004; Mara* et al. *2004; Saragusti* et al. *2005; Karasik* et al. *in press 1; in press 2). I wish to thank my coauthors in the above contributions: Uzy Smilansky and Ilan Sharon, as well as Ayelet Gilboa, Liora Bitton, Hubert Mara and Robert Sablatnig.*

some results (Karasik *et al.* in press; 2007; Mara *et al.* 2004). These tools offer new quantitative measures for attribute analysis, dependent on 3D techniques. Finally, I discuss possible future directions for research.

The history of pottery visualization and data acquisition using 3D scanners

Manual drawings remain the standard means of presenting and publishing pottery. Most post-excavation research is based on such drawings. The justification for using a 2D abstraction of 3D pots and potsherds is that most ceramic vessels are axially symmetric, especially wheel-thrown ones. Where a vessel is axially symmetric around its centre (henceforth 'axis of rotation'), a single profile is thought to reveal all morphological information. However, this is only true in a perfect world. Deformation can occur throughout the production process, e.g. when a vessel is removed from the wheel to dry elsewhere, when several (wheel-thrown or handmade) parts are assembled to make a composite pot, during the finishing and/or decoration process (necessitating remounting on the wheel or not), or during firing. Therefore, 3D modelling can improve our understanding of pottery production and add a new dimension in the representation and publication of pottery.

Researchers wishing to improve the process of pottery data acquisition for applications such as visualization, VR presentations, computerized restoration, and so forth were first drawn to 3D scanning because of its speed and accuracy, as well as the ease and accuracy of manipulating vector models in operations such as rotation, zooming, etc. Several groups around the world are researching pottery using 3D technology. They use different devices and software but their goal is the same: to acquire accurate reconstructions of artefacts. Here, a distinction ought to be made between two orientations or interests. One is the technological development of ever more sophisticated and precise 3D devices and accompanying software. The leaders in this field are large companies developing products for industrial purposes. A quick search on the internet reveals several websites that sell 3D technology.[1] Despite the fact that some refer to archaeological finds, the companies in question are sometimes unfamiliar with the specific needs of archaeologists. The second (and for our purposes, more important) direction is dependent upon technology developed by the latter group, but aims at 3D applications designed specifically for archaeological research. Groups engaged in the latter kind of research are few (even fewer focus on ceramics) and are to be found, for obvious reasons, in the academic and non-profit sector.

One of the earliest research centres to have published on the subject is the PRIP group[2] at the Technical University of Vienna. Menard and Sablatnig (1992) described two methods for 3D data acquisition of pottery. Later on, they suggested that the 3D technology used for automatic pottery data acquisition may serve in the future for classification and deeper analysis (Menard & Sablatnig 1996). However, since archaeologists were accustomed to work with 2D profiles, they concentrated on extracting the same kind of profiles more accurately from the 3D models. Nevertheless, in the last few years, the Vienna group offered new tools that utilize data which can only be given by 3D reconstructions. For instance, they studied the colours of the ceramic surface in order to detect lines of decorations (Kammerer *et al.* 2005). They also tried to reconstruct sherds into a complete vessel based on its geometry (Kampel & Sablatnig 2004).

Another group that invested considerable effort in harnessing 3D technology for pottery analysis is located at Brown University.[3] Their publications on the subject go back to late 1980s. They, too, started with the analysis

1. E.g. Arctron (http://www.arctron.com/Archaeology/), Cyberware (http://www.cyberware.com/ index.html), Fastscan (http://www.fastscan3d.com/), Scantech (http://scantech.dk/) and Polygon Technology (http://www.polygon-technology.com/). Of these, only Arctron is a company dedicated specifically to archaeological applications.

2. http://www.prip.tuwien.ac.at/Research/ArcheologicalSherds/index.html.

3. http://www.lems.brown.edu/~leymarie/.

of 2D contour profiles (Leymarie & Levine 1988), but they have recently used 3D technology for pottery analysis as a part of larger project for computerized archaeology, SHAPE (Leymarie *et al.* 2001). They focus on visualization but also deal with tasks like pottery classification and reconstruction from sherds using 3D representations (Willis & Cooper 2004). A third project, PRISM-3D Knowledge, is based at Arizona State University. This project concentrated on acquisition, representation and analysis of all kinds of archaeological finds, including pottery.[4] In their publications one can find general papers that describe the project (Razdan *et al.* 2001) and specific papers dealing with the details of the research. With regard to pottery analysis, their efforts were towards fast and accurate data acquisition and the utilization of such data for 2D-profiling, height, maximum diameter measurement, as well as the calculation of attributes that are harder to measure by traditional means, e.g. volume, surface area, volume of vessel wall and symmetry (Henderson *et al.* 1993).

Most researchers in the field of computers and archaeology have presented and published their work in the annual CAA conferences. In the 1990s, the occasional paper dealing with 3D applications could be found. Only as late as 2002 was there a full session (*Visualization Techniques and Photogrammetry*) on such applications. Even then, the only paper on ceramic vessels dealt with 3D modelling merely as a means to extract accurate profiles, analyzed using statistics—and was therefore presented in the statistics session (Kampel *et al.* 2002). In the 2005 conference, on the other hand, four sessions were dedicated to these applications. Such a dramatic growth reflects not only the excitement of the archaeological community with these innovative 'toys', but also the maturation of 3D technology in recent years. Considerable technological improvements now make high-resolution reconstruction potentially available to any archaeologist. Granted, 3D models which can be zoomed and rotated on the screen are cool, but the $64,000 question is what do we do with them? We chose to concentrate on the extra information available in the 3D model in order to investigate issues that were rarely studied before.

4. http://3dk.asu.edu/home.html.

Uniformity and deformations: new quantitative definitions for pottery analysis

As mentioned above, potsherds should have axial symmetry. But no vessel is perfectly symmetric, hence a single section as supplied in a conventional drawing is not an accurate representation of the entire vessel. Hand-drawn profiles provide, at best, an average section of a pot. This would be good enough for most archaeologists. But, one wonders, what is the effect of real-world variability on profile-based typologies? Or, can deviations from uniformity be archaeologically interesting as well? The study of such deviations and deformations can supply invaluable information regarding the *chaînes opératoires* that characterize specific production processes, workshops, or even craftsmen/-women. What is aimed at here is the extraction and comparison of many vertical and horizontal sections of a single vessel. Summarizing these comparisons enables the evaluation of a pot's *uniformity* as well as its *variability*, construed as the correlations between these sections. To my knowledge, this has not been attempted to date.

Uniformity

The comparison and correlation of different profiles of the same sherd is utilizing the same method adopted for the comparison of profiles of different vessels (Gilboa *et al.* 2004). It is based on the idea that one can represent the profiles by *planar curve* functions (Saragusti *et al.* 2005). The curvature function $k(s)$ is used as the curve representation. In the past we have shown that the curvature function is very sensitive and useful in the analysis of ceramic profiles (Gilboa *et al.* 2004; Saragusti *et al.* 2005). Its main advantage is that it is a function of one parameter that completely characterizes the 2D profile. Moreover, it emphasizes naturally curved sections usually more important in archaeological studies, such as rims, carination points

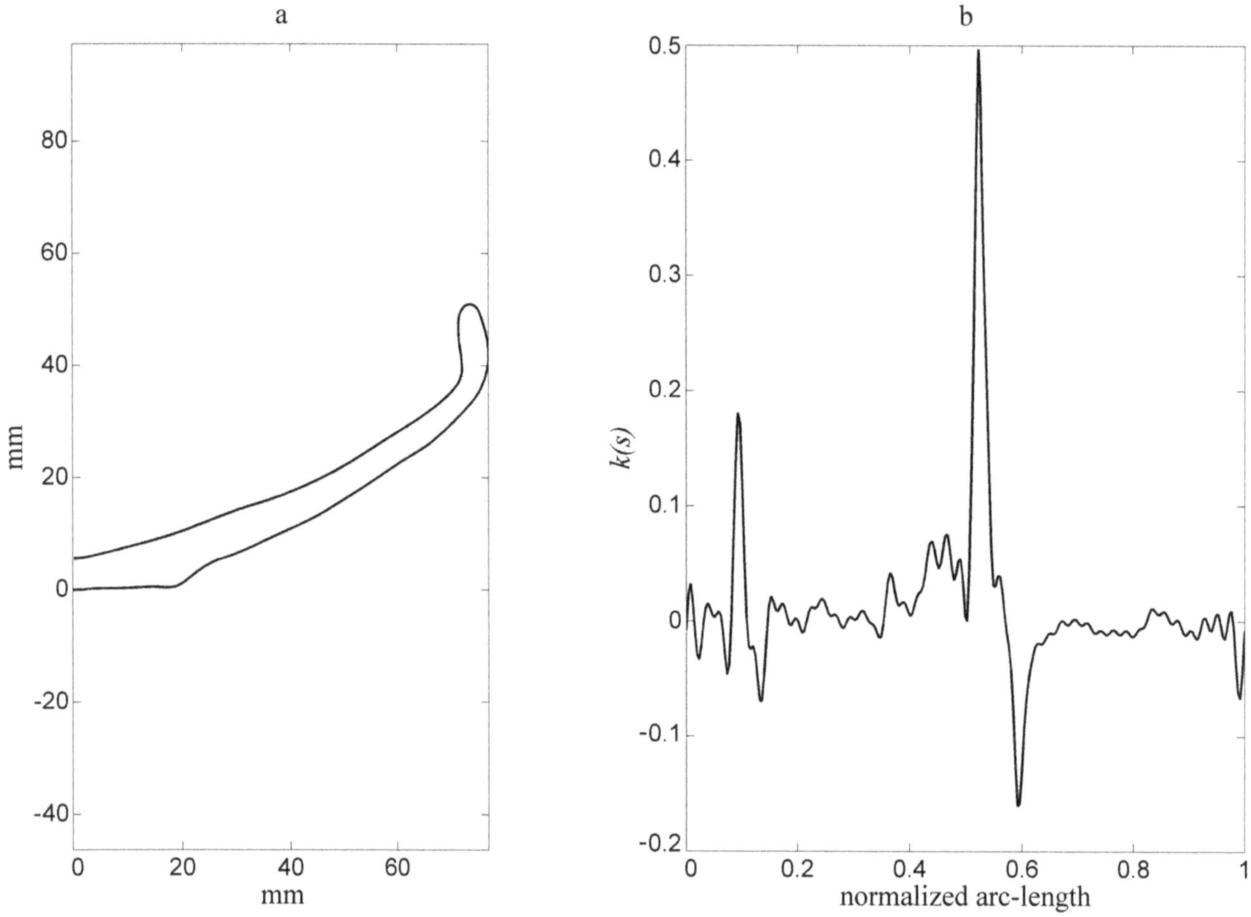

Fig. 1. *A. A profile of a bowl; B. its corresponding curvature as a function of the normalized arc-length.*

etc. **Fig. 1A** shows a bowl profile while **Fig. 1B** shows its corresponding curvature function. The correlation between two profiles is defined in terms of the scalar product of their corresponding curvature functions $\boldsymbol{k_1(s), k_2(s)}$ (after the profiles are scaled to a constant length). The correlation is given as:

$$C(k_1, k_2) = \frac{\int k_1(s) \cdot k_2(s)ds}{\sqrt{\int k_1(s)ds}\,\sqrt{\int k_2(s)ds}} \ .$$

Equation 1

Notice that $\boldsymbol{-1 \leq C(k_1, k_2) \leq 1}$ and that it assumes the highest value if and only if $k_1=k_2$. The smaller the correlation, the less similar are the compared profiles. A correlation value smaller then 0.5 usually indicates a significant difference between the compared profiles.

Let $k_n(s)$ with $1 \leq n \leq N$ be the curvature functions of N profiles of *different* sections of the same vessel. Using **Equation 1** we compute the correlations matrix $\boldsymbol{C_{i,j} = C(k_i, k_j) = C_{j,i}}$ for the profiles under study. The *uniformity* of the vessel is defined as:

$$uniformity = \frac{\sum_{i,j}^{N} (C_{i,j})^2}{N^2}$$

Equation 2

Notice that $\boldsymbol{1/N \leq uniformity \leq 1}$. The uniformity reaches its maximum value when all the entries in the correlation matrix have the value 1. That is to say, when all the profiles are identical. The minimum value is

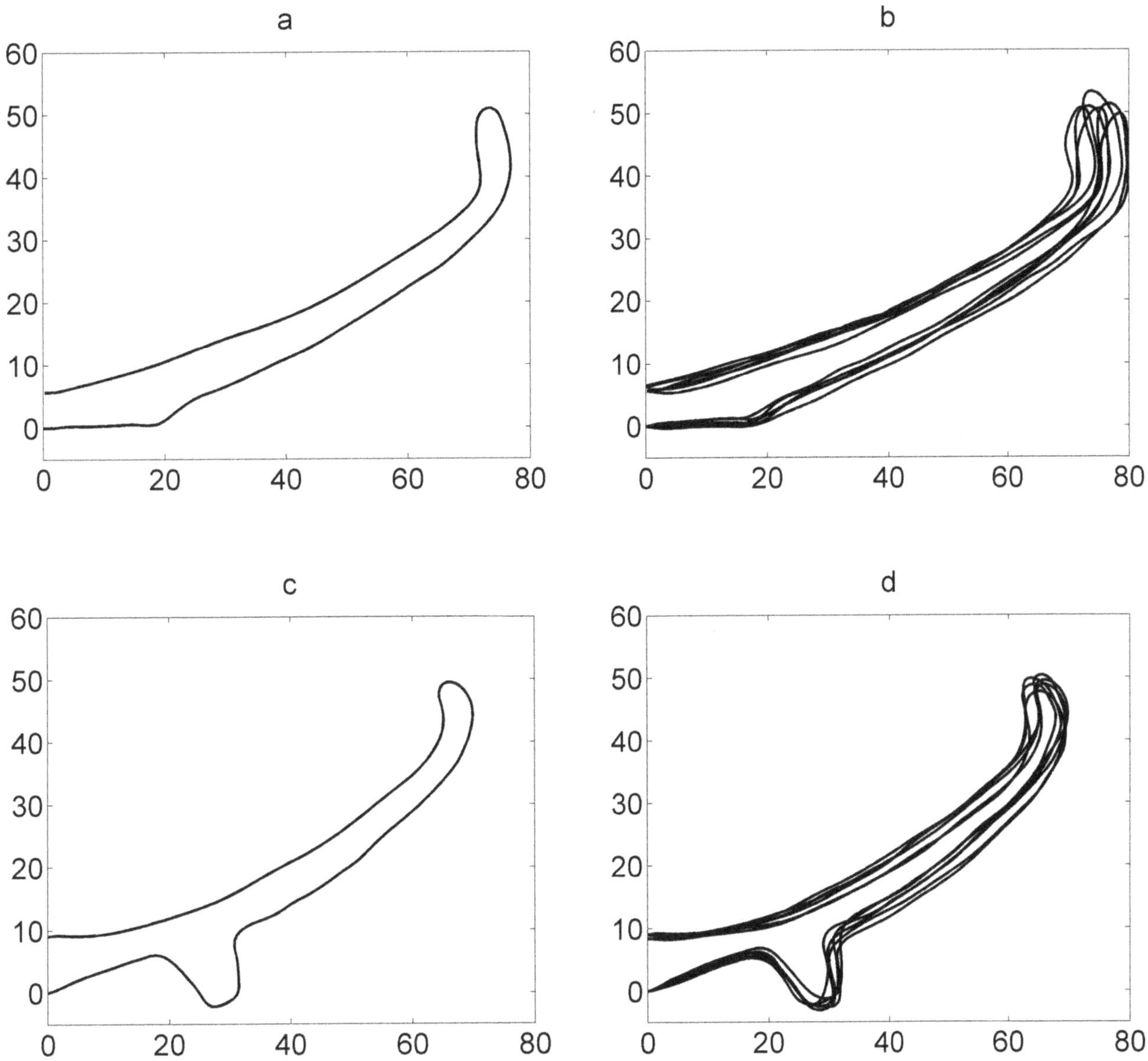

Fig. 2. *A, C. Single profiles of two different bowls from Tell Dor, Israel; B, D. the overlap of six profiles of the same bowls, respectively.*

obtained when the only non-vanishing entries are on the diagonal, i.e. every profile is similar only to itself and is very different from all the others. Obviously this definition of uniformity makes better sense when a larger number of sections are measured, and $1/N$ asymptotically approaches 0. In the same way, we can also measure the correlation as prescribed by **Equation 1** between profiles of different vessels, as we have done elsewhere (Gilboa *et al.* 2004). Thus, the variability of an entire assemblage of vessels (e.g. a 'type') can be quantified in terms of the *uniformity* defined in **Equation 2**. We can thus compare two measures of uniformity, the *intra-vessel* and the *inter-vessel* uniformities, the former representing the quality of the production of single vessel, and the latter measuring the reproducibility of the manufacturing process.

To test this measure, two different assemblages of complete vessels were analyzed. The first is a collection of 16 bowls, which were picked randomly from the Tell Dor collection. Their dates span the period between the Early Iron Age and the Hellenistic period and therefore do not represent a homogeneous assemblage or a single morphological type. The second assemblage

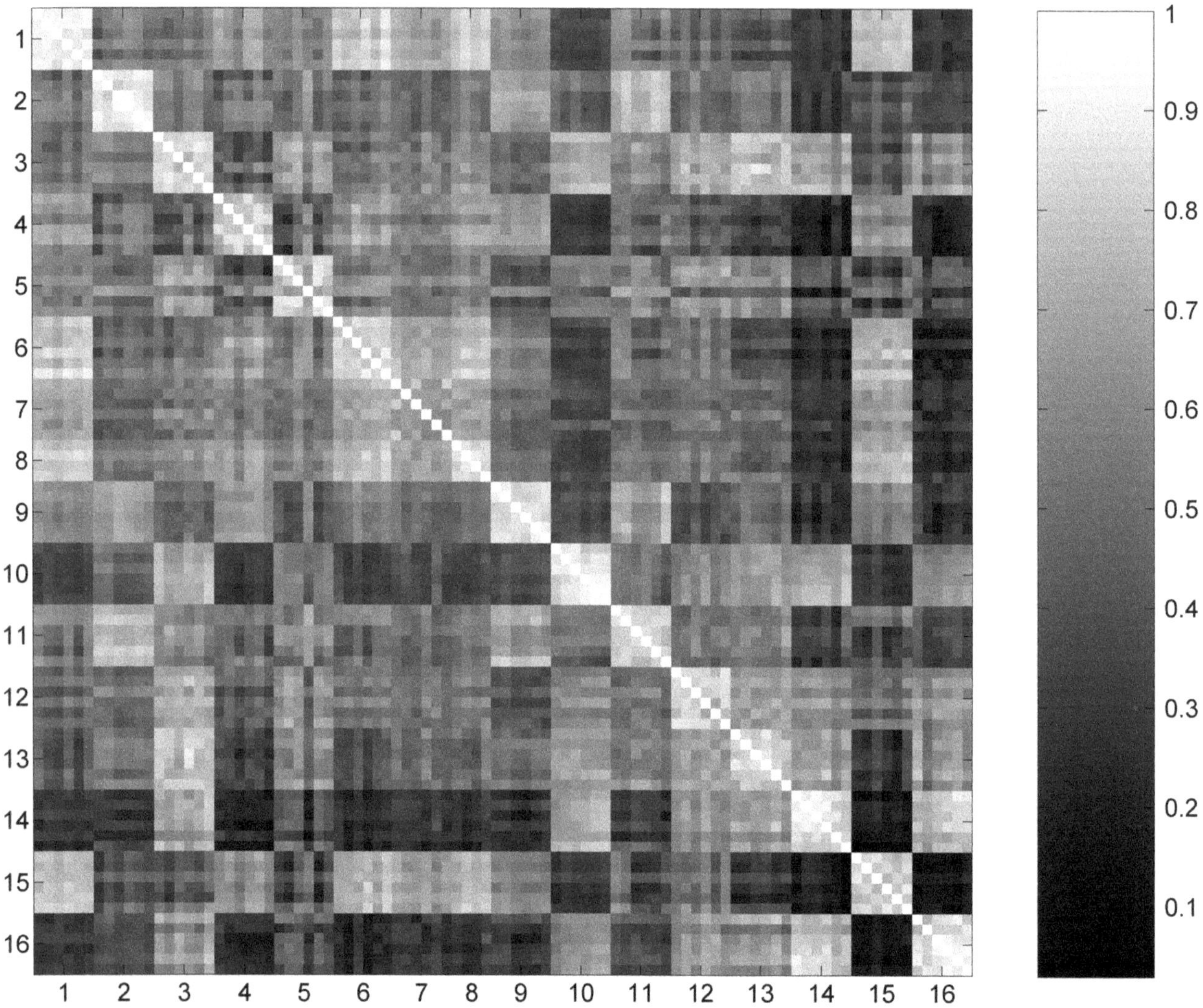

***Fig. 3**. The correlations matrix of Tell Dor bowls. The index of the bowls is given along the axes.*

is composed of 11 flower pots, which were produced by a contemporary potter who uses the traditional kick wheel. This was used as a control group to represent an assemblage which is as homogeneous as wheel-made pottery can be. For each vessel, six section profiles were measured with an accuracy margin of 0.2 mm using a profilograph. Typical sections which illustrate the deviations from perfect cylindrical symmetry are shown in **Fig. 2**. These deviations were observed to be as large as several mm. While the profilograph is not a 3D scanner, it enables the extraction of several profiles from the same vessel. These profiles were judged to be good enough to test the method and the mathematical definitions which we have developed here. When a 3D scanner is used instead of the profilograph, more sections can be drawn and the accuracy of the method will be higher.

The correlations matrix of the bowls from Tell Dor is shown in **Fig. 3**. The columns and rows are arranged such that sections of each bowl appear consecutively (six per vessel, except Bowl 8 which is represented by only four sections). The value of the correlation of any two profiles is given by the gray level of the pixel at the intersection of the corresponding column and row. The numerical equivalents of the gray levels are provided by the bar at the right of the figure. The intra-vessel correlations are represented by the 16, 6 x 6 square matrices on the diagonal. The values of these correlations are usually higher than the inter-vessel

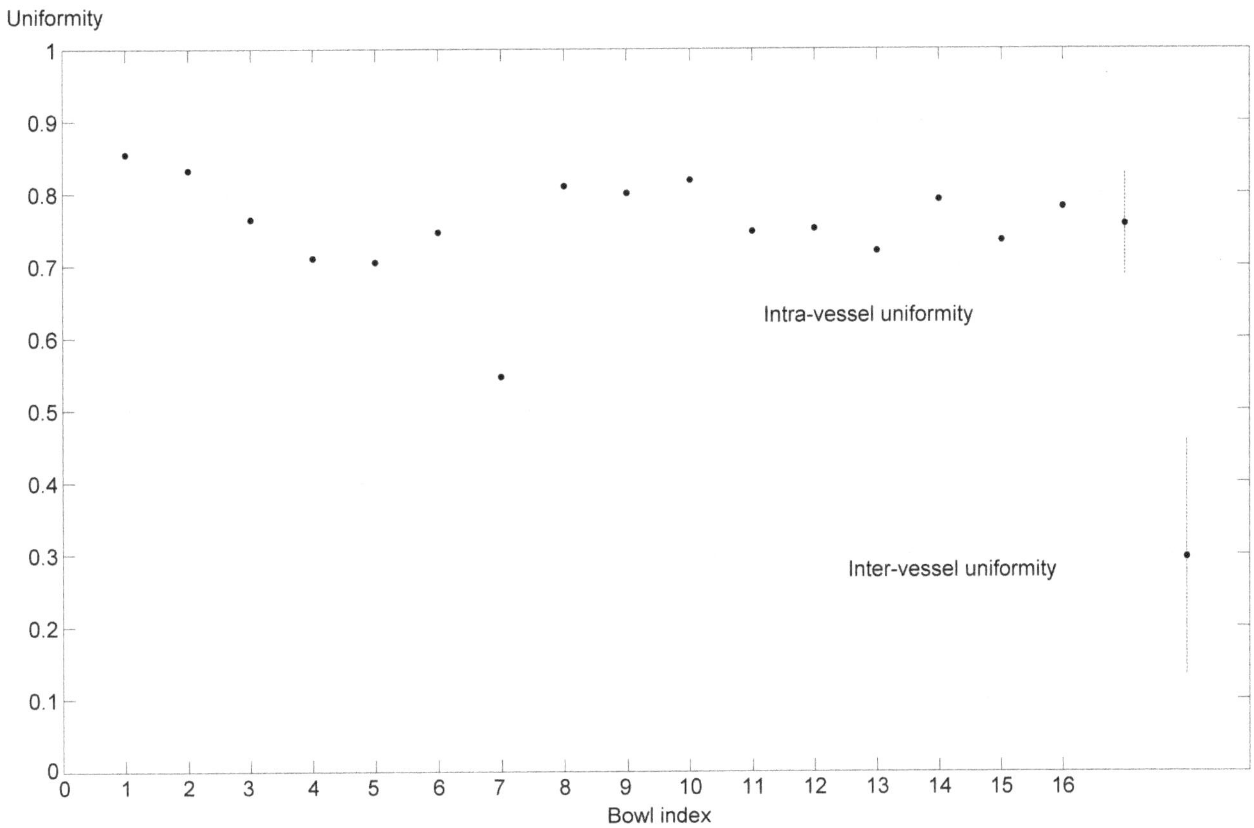

Fig. 4. *Summary of the inter/intra-vessel uniformity values for the Tell Dor bowls.*

correlations, as can be seen by the lighter gray squares along the diagonal. Some high inter-vessel correlations do exist, for instance between the profiles of Bowls 1 and 15. On the other hand, the intra-vessel correlations are not uniform and darker pixels can be seen, for example in the intra-vessel matrix of Bowl 7.

We used the formulae of the previous section to compute the inter- and intra-vessel uniformity for the Tell Dor assemblage. The results are summarized in **Fig. 4**. The mean intra-vessel uniformity is about .75, with Bowl 7 being exceptionally non-uniform. The mean of the inter-vessel uniformity is approximately 0.3, i.e. much lower than the typical individual uniformities. This difference is consistent with the fact that the bowls were chosen randomly and do not represent a typologically homogeneous assemblage. Different results are expected in the analysis of a uniform assemblage, such as the flower pots. A preliminary inspection of those immediately reveals that most are deformed: their base and rim planes are not parallel and opposite profiles have different lengths, which might have been caused by the removal of the wet pots from the wheel using string. Nevertheless, the pots look very similar by eye. To give a quantitative description of the above observation we compared the pot sections, which were truncated at five levels shown in **Fig. 5**. The first level corresponds to the upper part of the pot, and the fifth level is the entire profile including the base. The truncated sections can be considered as representing rim sherds, and their correlations can be obtained by using the formulae of the previous section with minor modifications. The results of the inter/intra-vessel uniformity as a function of the truncation level are shown in **Fig. 6**. The most prominent trend in this illustration is that the inter/intra-vessel uniformities are rather high so long as the base is not included in the analysis. The numerical values of the inter-vessel uniformity are almost as high as the intra-vessel uniformity. The difference becomes larger when the complete profiles are considered. Thus quantitative analysis confirms the intuitive expectations

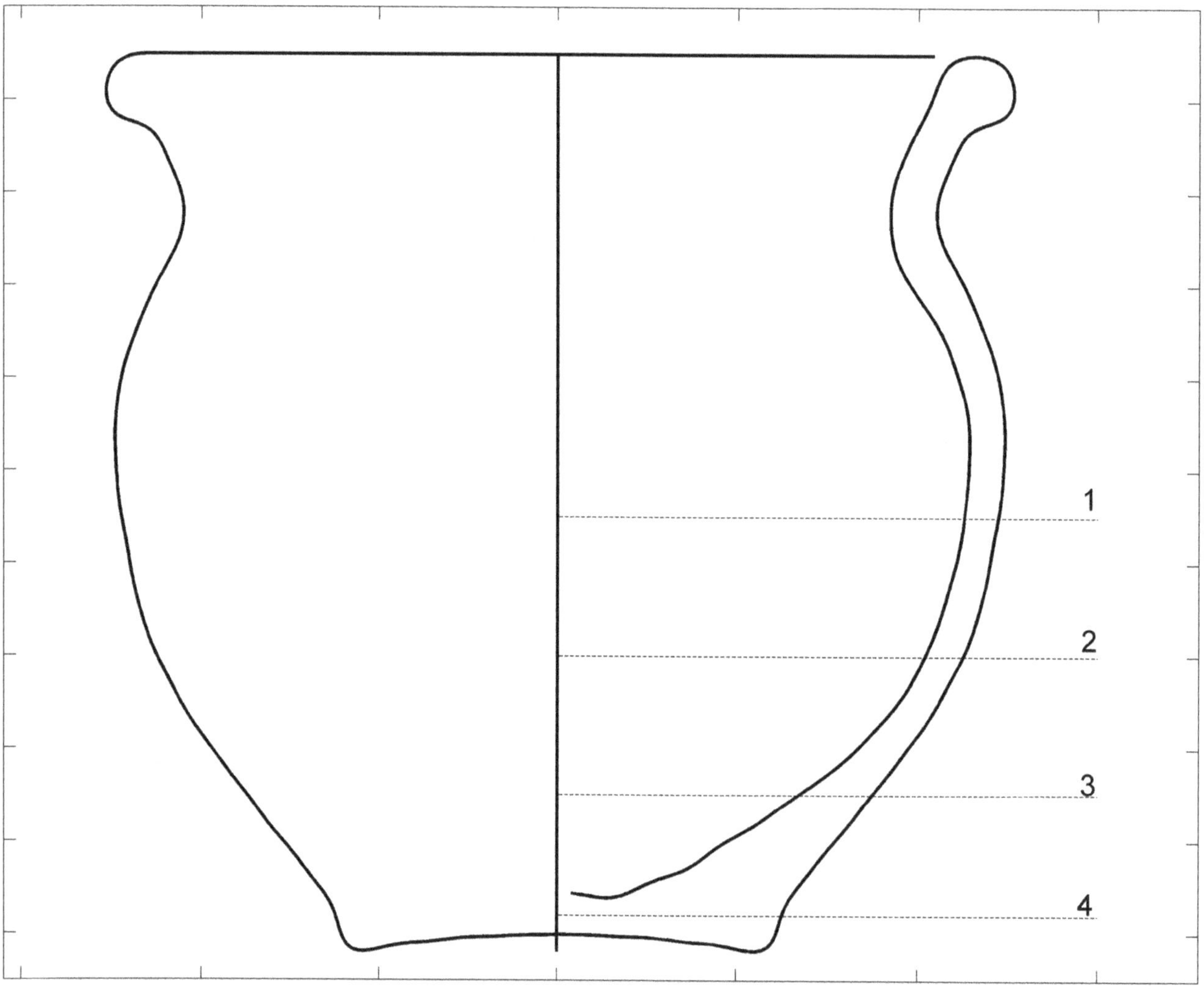

Fig. 5. Four truncation levels of a profile. The corresponding 'fragments' were analyzed separately.

Fig. 6 (right, top). *The mean and the standard deviation of the inter/intra-vessel uniformities for each section size of the flower pots assemblage. The smaller the section the higher the correlations.*

Fig. 7 (right, bottom). *A. Two horizontal sections of the jug shown on the left in Fig. 8; B. the leading ten Fourier coefficients (scaled by* r_0*) of the sections shown in 7A.*

concerning this assemblage. In contrast with the previous assemblage, the similar values of the inter/intra vessel uniformities show that we are dealing with a typologically homogeneous assemblage.

Uniformity analysis can be very useful for the analysis of ceramic assemblages. For instance, two rim sherds found at a small distance from each other, but whose fracture lines do not match, may or may not belong to the same vessel. If two such sherds covering approximately the same fraction as 'section 1' of **Fig. 5** have a correlation of approximately 0.9, they might belong to the same vessel; whereas a correlation around 0.7 or less may suggest that the two sherds belong to different pots.

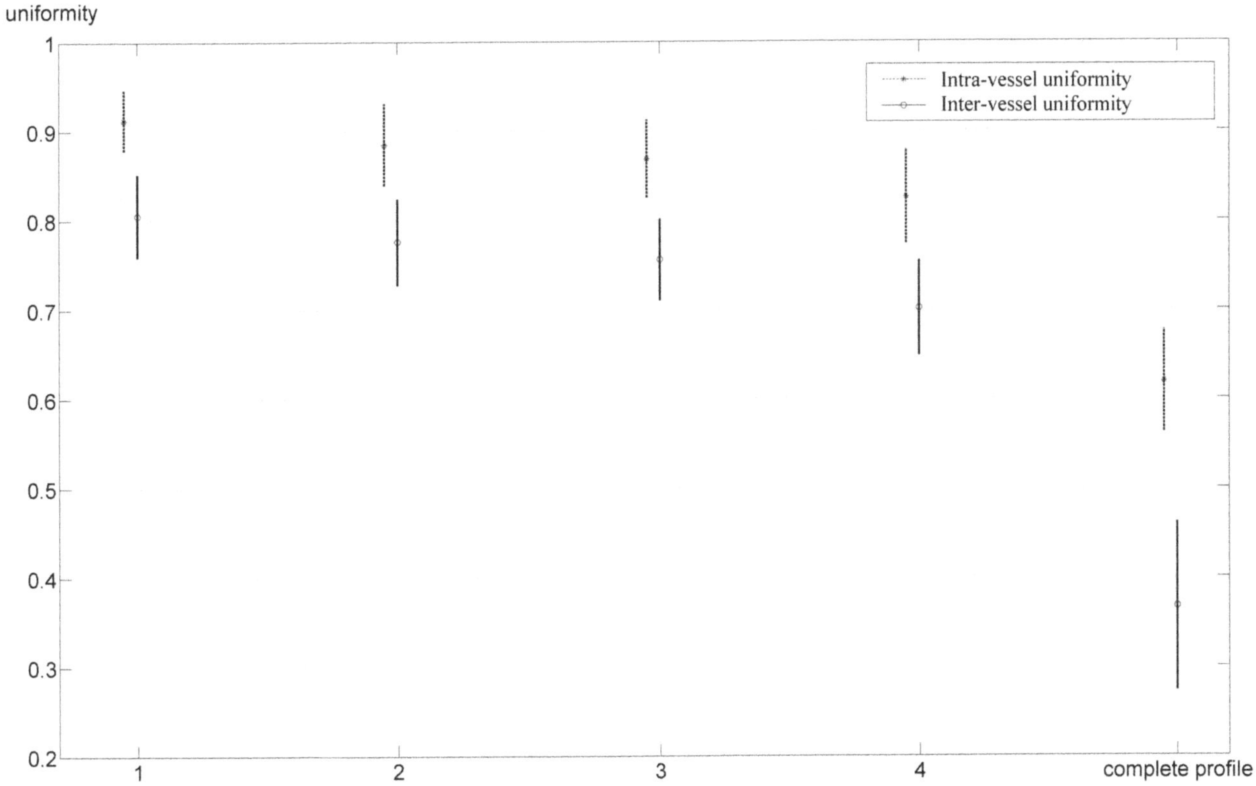
uniformity
1
0.9
0.8
0.7
0.6
0.5
0.4
0.3
0.2
1
2
3
4
complete profile
Intra-vessel uniformity
Inter-vessel uniformity

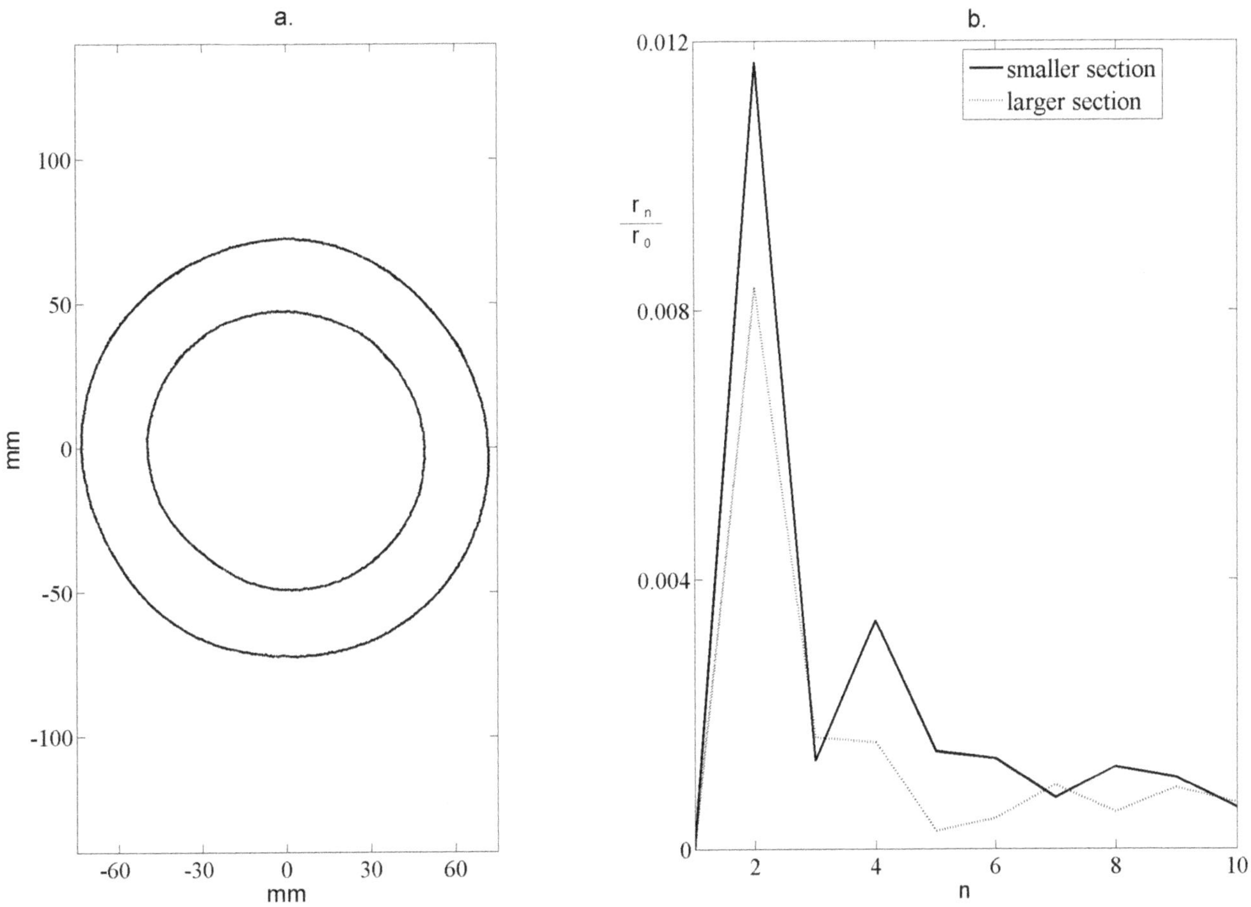
a.
100
50
0
-50
-100
mm
-60
-30
0
30
60
mm
b.
0.012
0.008
0.004
0
smaller section
larger section
r n
r 0
2
4
6
8
10
n

Deformation

A horizontal section through a pot with perfect axial symmetry should look like two concentric circles, representing the inner and outer surface of the vessel. Any deviation from this is a deformation. A quantitative measure of the deformations can be obtained by using the polar representation of the curves of the horizontal sections. **Fig. 7A** shows the curves obtained by measuring two horizontal sections of a jug using a 3D camera. The jug in question is a closed and complete vessel and therefore the 3D camera provided only the horizontal section of its exterior surface. As can be seen in **Fig. 7B**, the curves are certainly not the ideally expected concentric circles, to be explained below. The points on this curve can be specified by their polar coordinates ***(r(s), φ(s))*** relative to an arbitrary origin in the interior. For convex curves ***φ(s)*** is a monotonic function of the arc length ***s***, and one can describe the curve by the function ***r(φ)*** (Gero & Mazzullo 1984; Liming *et al.* 1989). If the point of origin is taken as the best estimate of the centre of revolution then for each angle ***φ*** (relative to some arbitrary line) ***r(φ)*** gives the radius of the section of the vessel at that angle. For an axially symmetric vessel ***r(φ)*** would be constant. A deformed vessel would represent some sort of a wave function as ***φ*** revolves around the section. Thus we can use the Fourier coefficients of ***r(φ)***

$$\hat{x}_n = \frac{1}{2\pi}\int_0^{2\pi} d\varphi \cos n\varphi \; r(\varphi) \quad ;$$

$$\hat{y}_n = \frac{1}{2\pi}\int_0^{2\pi} d\varphi \sin n\varphi \; r(\varphi)$$

to define the nth deformation parameter and associated phase by:

$$r_n = \sqrt{\hat{x}_n^2 + \hat{y}_n^2} \quad ; \quad \alpha_n = \arcsin\left(\frac{\hat{x}_n}{r_n}\right).$$

The deformation parameters are determined in an unambiguous way when the origin is chosen such that the coefficients $\hat{x}_1$ and $\hat{y}_1$ are zero. For simple shapes, this choice is equivalent to setting the origin at the centre of gravity of the curve. For an axially symmetric vessel, the centre of gravity is the axis of revolution and all the coefficients would be zero. The parameter r_0 is the mean radius, and it serves to set the scale (size) of the section. The first non trivial coefficients $(\hat{x}_2, \hat{y}_2)$ or equivalently (r_2, α_2) determine the parameters of the ellipse which fits the curve best: $\frac{r_2}{r_0}$ is proportional to the eccentricity and α_2 is the tilt angle of the main axes of the ellipsoid relative to the coordinate axes. The higher order parameters provide information on deformations on smaller scales.

Fig. 7B shows the values of ten scaled Fourier $\frac{r_n}{r_0}$ coefficients for the sections shown in **Fig. 7A**. To demonstrate the potential value of the study of deformations in the archaeological context, a case study is discussed below, in which the deformation of the horizontal sections can yield information about manufacturing processes. Two contemporary but traditionally produced wheel-thrown jugs were scanned by a 3D scanner **[Fig. 8**, left]. This scanner provides a complete 3D digital representation of the studied object, from which the horizontal sections at various heights were computed (Sablatnig & Menard 1996; Adler *et al.* 2001). This detailed information was used to determine various quantities that are relevant to the shape of the objects and their deviations from cylindrical symmetry (Mara *et al.* 2004). Here I will only discuss the information provided by the ten leading Fourier coefficients computed for 45 different horizontal sections for each of the jugs.

Even though the two jugs look rather similar, their averaged scaled Fourier coefficients $\frac{r_n}{r_0}$ are quite different, as can be seen in **Fig. 9**; the right-hand jug is more deformed than the one on the left. A detailed investigation (below) reveals that the deformation is not uniform along the jar, which indicates that different parts underwent different types of stress and pressure before the final shape was set. To reach this conclusion, deformations were analyzed by dividing the 45 horizontal sections into four groups **[Fig. 8**, right]:

- The neck (upper eight horizontal sections).

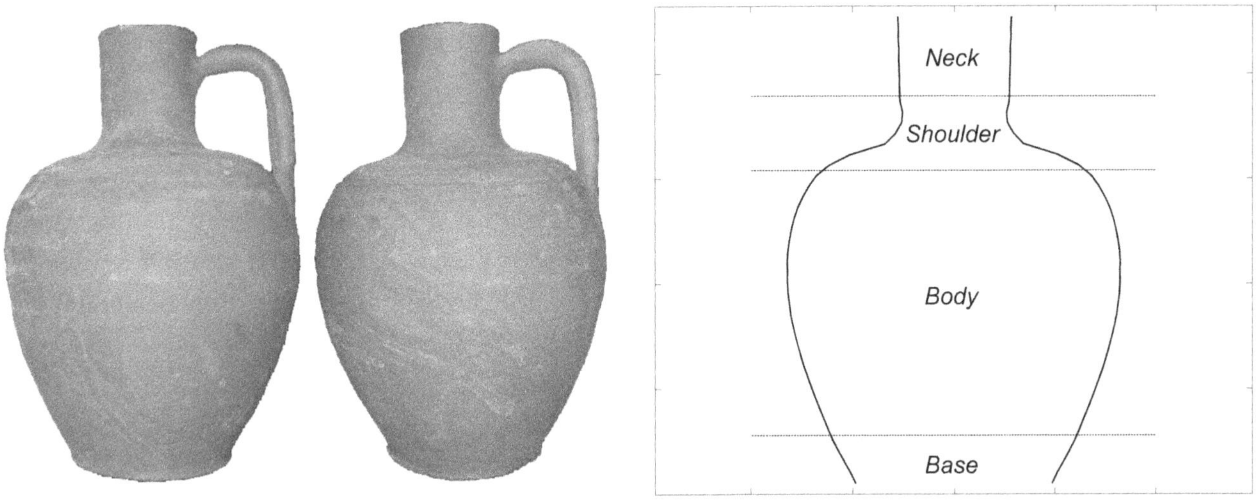

Fig. 8. *Two similar wheel-made jugs from the market of Vienna, left; a plan view of a jar where the four regions used in the current study are indicated, right.*

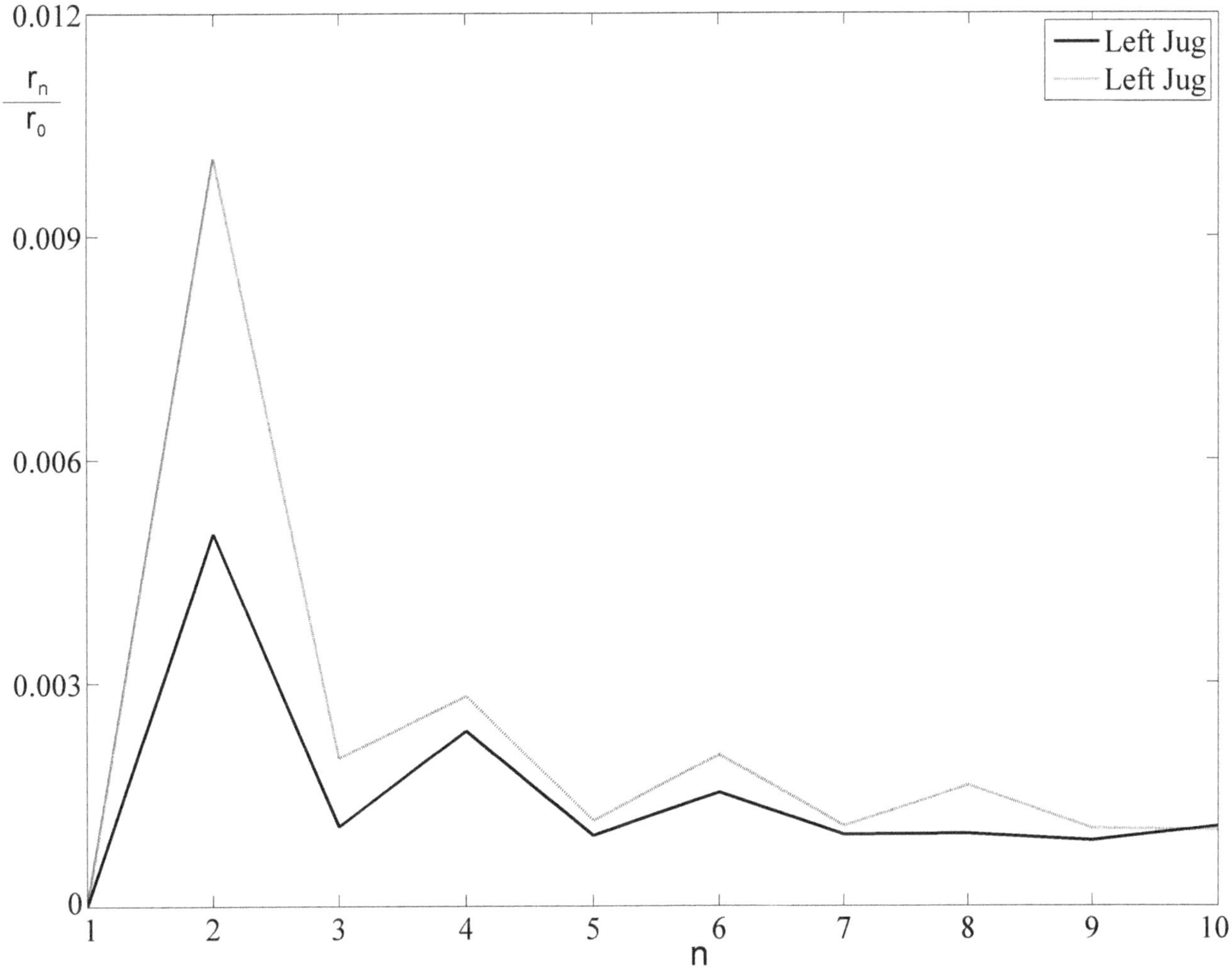

Fig. 9. *The mean scaled Fourier coefficients averaged over the entire height.*

- The shoulder (the next seven sections).
- The body (the next 25 sections).
- The base (the lowest five sections).

Since some horizontal sections include the handle, the points on the 180° arc opposite the handle were used. The mean scaled Fourier coefficients for each group were computed, and they are shown in **Fig. 10**. The lowest coefficients for both jugs are to be found on the body section. Therefore, the bodies of the two jugs are the closest to perfect circles. This implies that the deviations from perfect symmetry were not caused by external pressure caused, for instance, by placing too many vessels in the kiln. Moreover, if the potter could produce such symmetric vessels with maximum deviation of about 0.5% of the radius, he/she was probably well-trained and the wheel used was well-balanced. The right-hand jug is more deformed as far as the neck and shoulders are concerned, although its base is less deformed than the base of the other jug. On the other hand, the base of the left-hand jug is more deformed than the one on the right jug (although on a smaller scale). Previous analysis showed that the most significant deformation of the neck is probably due to the attachment of the handle, which was pressed onto the still soft neck. The difference between the two neck deformations can be explained by the application of stronger force when the potter attached the handle to the right-hand jug. Such action affected the circular symmetry of the vessel, but preserved the mirror symmetry about the line that crosses through the handle. Indeed, when the phase of the best-fitted ellipse to the neck of the deformed jug was computed, it was found out that the axis of mirror symmetry crosses exactly through the handle area, which corresponds to our assumption (Mara *et al.* 2004, for further details). The deformation on the base is probably the result of the removal of the vessel from the potter's wheel. Even if the potter produced similar vessels, as suggested by the low deformation values of

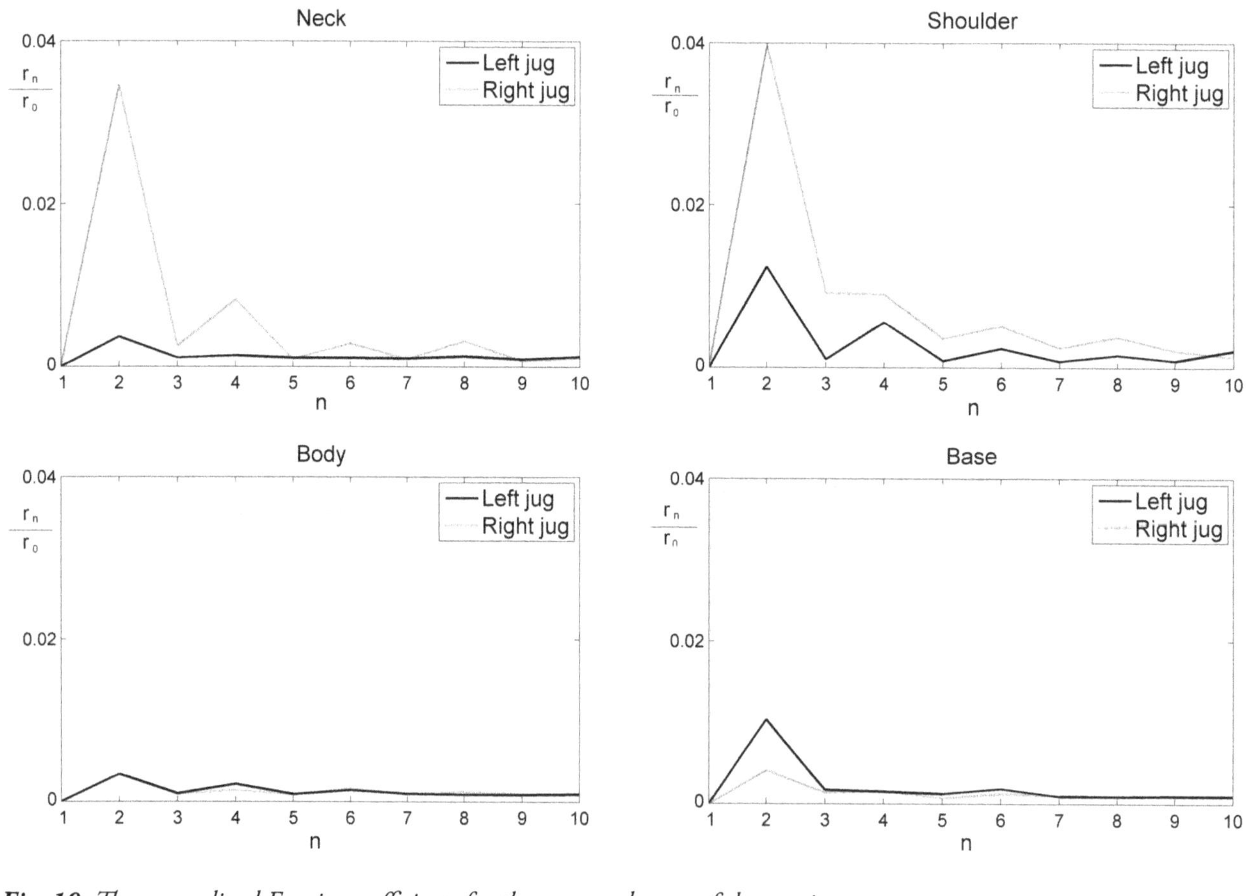

Fig. 10. *The normalized Fourier coefficients for the separated parts of the two jugs.*

the body, he/she deformed them in different ways while adding decoration, handles, or string-cutting the base to remove the pot from the wheel.

Summary and conclusion

In this paper I have traced the development of 3D analysis of pottery to date, and described two new quantitative tools. One evaluates the uniformity of a single vessel versus that of a vessel type. The other measures minute deformations—differences among vessels hardly detectable by eye. The value of such tools will only be apparent once they are applied to larger assemblages and real archaeological problems, but certain questions already spring to mind: can one assess the motor skills of individual potters using uniformity? Does uniformity improve with practice? Can a professional potter create an assemblage where inter-vessel uniformity equals intra-vessel uniformity? Can uniformity be used to differentiate between mass production and home-based industries? Can it be used to differentiate between a 'type' or 'tradition' in general and the production of a single workshop or even a single potter within a workshop? Can we use uniformity and deformation to differentiate between handmade and wheel-thrown vessels? Or distinguish between a fast wheel and a tournette? Further, can we identify preformed sections of composite pots?

The analyses proposed here are but the tip of the iceberg. Since this is an emergent technology, and the amount of information in an accurate 3D model vastly supersedes that encoded in a 2D section drawing, it is only a matter of time until new methods to mine such additional information will emerge, to highlight more general issues such as technological and cognitive capabilities, motor skills, production centres, and perhaps even identify individual potters in the archaeological record. In the next decade the number of excavations using 3D scanning devices for pottery drawings will increase dramatically—if only because the production of 3D models is so much faster and more accurate than that of a hand-drawn profile. Right now 3D scanners are still prohibitively expensive, but this will surely change, and soon archaeological institutions and even individual archaeologists will find such a tool to be indispensable. The challenge is to be able to use the full potential of this modern technology in order to improve our understanding of the past.

Bibliography

Gilboa, A., Karasik, A., Sharon, I. & Smilansky, U. 2004. "Towards computerized typology and classification of ceramics", *Journal of Archaeological Science* 31/6: 681-694.

Henderson, M. R., Srinath, G., Stage, R., Walker, K. & Reglib, W. 1993. "Boundary representation-based feature identification", in J. Shah (ed.), *Advances in Feature Based Manufacturing*, Amsterdam: Elsevier/ North Holland Publishers: 15-38.

Kammerer, P., Mara, H., Kratzmüller, B. & Zolda, E. 2005. "Detection and analysis of lines on the surface of archaeological pottery", in V. Cappelini & J. Hemsley (eds.), *Electronic Imaging and the Visual Arts*, Florence/ Bologna: Pitagora: 154-159.

Kampel, M. & Sablatnig, R. 2004. "On 3D mosaicing of rotationally symmetric ceramic fragments", in J. Kittler, M. Petrou & M. Nixon (eds.), *Proceedings of the 17th International Conference on Pattern Recognition, Cambridge, U.K.*, vol. 2, Cambridge: Institute of Electrical and Electronics Engineers Computer Society: 265-268.

Kampel, M., Sablatnig, R. & Mara, H. 2002. "Profile segmentation scheme for automated classification of archaeological sherds", in M. Doerr & A. Sarris (eds.), *The Digital Heritage of Archaeology (CAA 2002, Proceedings of the 30th Conference, Heraklion, Crete, April 2002)*, Athens: Archive of Monuments and Publications, Hellenic Ministry of Culture: 275-280.

Karasik, A., Bitton, L., Gilboa, A., Sharon, I. & Smilansky U. in press. "Quantitative measures of the uniformity of ceramics", in F. Niccolucci & S. Hermon (eds.), *Beyond the Artifact: Digital Interpretation of the Past (CAA 2004, Proceedings of the 32nd Conference, Prato, Italy, 13-17 April 2004)*, Budapest: Archeolingua.

Karasik, A., Mara, H., Sablatnig, R., Sharon, I. & Smilansky, U. 2007. "Measuring deformations of wheel-produced ceramics using high resolution 3D reconstructions", in A. Figueiredo & V. Leite (eds.), *Proceedings of the 33rd Computer Applications and Quantitative Methods in Archaeology Conference (CAA 05, Tomar, Portugal, March 2005)*, Tomar: C.

Leymarie, F., Cooper, D., Joukowsky, M. S., Kimia, B., Laidlaw, D., Mumford, D. & Vote, E. 2001. "The SHAPE Lab—new technology and software for archaeologists", in Z. Stančič & T. Veljanovski (eds.), *Computing Archaeology for Understanding the Past (CAA 2000, Proceedings of the 28th Conference, Ljubljana, Slovenia, 18-21 April 2000)*, B.A.R.. International Series 931, Oxford: BAR Publishing: 79-89.

Leymarie, F. & Levine, M. D. 1988. "Curvature morphology", Technical Report TR-CIM-88-26, Computer Vision and Robotics Laboratory, McGill University.

Mara, H., Sablatnig, R., Karasik, A. & Smilansky, U. 2004. "The uniformity of wheel-produced pottery deduced from 3D image processing and scanning", in W. Burger & J. Scharinger (eds.), *Digital Imaging in Media and Education: Proceedings of the 28th Workshop of the Austrian Association for Pattern Recognition (June 17-18, 2004)*, Hagenberg: OAGM/AARP: 197-204.

Menard, C. & Sablatnig, R. 1992. "Two different methods for the 3D-acquisition of archaeological finds: stereo and structured light", in H. Bischof (ed.), *Pattern Recognition 1992: Proceedings of the 16th Workshop of the Austrian Association for Pattern Recognition*, Munich: Oldenbourg: 150-160.

Menard, C. & Sablatnig, R. 1996. "Pictorial, three-dimensional acquisition of archaeological finds as basis for an automatic classification", in H. Kamermans & K. Fennema (eds.), *Interfacing the Past: Computer Applications and Quantitative methods in Archaeology (CAA 1995, Proceedings of the 23rd Conference, Leiden, 1995)*, Analecta Praehistorica Leidensia 28, Leiden: University of Leiden: 139-145.

Razdan, A., Liu, D., Bae, M., Zhu, M. & Farin, G. 2001. "Using geometric modeling for archiving and searching 3D archaeological vessels", unpublished paper in *International Conference on Imaging Science, Systems, and Technology (CISST 2001, Las Vegas).*

Saragusti, I., Karasik, A., Sharon, I. & Smilansky, U. 2005. "Quantitative analysis of shape attributes based on contours and section profiles in archaeological research", *Journal of Archaeological Science* 32/6: 841-853.

Willis, A. & Cooper, D. B. 2004. "Bayesian assembly of 3D axially symmetric shapes from fragments", *Proceedings of the 2004 IEEE Computer Society Conference on Computer Vision and Pattern Recognition/CVPR 2004 (27 June-2 July, 2004)*, vol. 1, Washington: Institute of Electrical and Electronic Engineers: 82-89.

Chapter 13

Virtual archaeology and computer-aided reconstruction of the Severan Marble Plan

The Severan Marble Plan was an immense marble map of Rome constructed in the early 3rd century during the reign of Septimius Severus, and is a primary source of topographical knowledge of the ancient city. We have digitized the 3D shape, surface appearance, and incisions of the extant fragments of the Plan, and use this data as input to geometric matching algorithms to perform computer-aided reconstruction of this monumental artifact, resulting in the discovery of new joins and topographical identifications among the fragments. Additionally, we have created an online information system to make the digital versions of the fragments accessible to scholars and the public.

David R. Koller
Institute for Advanced Technology in the Humanities, University of Virginia, USA

The Severan Marble Plan

The Severan Marble Plan of Rome, or *Forma Urbis Romae*, was an enormous map of the ancient city constructed during the reign of Emperor Septimius Severus between 203-211 CE. The Plan measured approximately 18 m wide and 13 m tall, and was carved onto 150 rectangular marble slabs affixed to an interior wall of the *Templum Pacis* in central Rome. The map depicted the ground plan of every architectural feature in the ancient city at the remarkable scale of 1:240, including monumental structures and major streets, as well as tiny rooms and stairways in individual residences [**Fig. 1**].

The Plan is thus an unparalled source of information concerning the urban topography of ancient Rome. Whereas many notable Roman monuments are well known from ancient literary descriptions or modern archaeological excavations, the detailed coverage of the entire central city provided by the Plan supplies much of our knowledge of the lesser known neighbourhoods that have been destroyed in the intervening centuries or are otherwise not amenable to direct archaeological study.

Unfortunately, the Plan was itself destroyed due to neglect and scavengers, beginning in the 5th century and extending into the Middle Ages. In 1562 the Plan was rediscovered, in the form of many surviving marble fragments. Over the past 500 years, archaeologists have recovered over 1,000 fragments of the Plan, representing approximately 10% of the surface area of the original map. Reassembling these pieces like a giant jigsaw puzzle and reconstructing the Plan of the city has been a continuing challenge for Roman topography scholars.

Two primary publications in the 20th century documented the recovered fragments of the Plan and

The author acknowledges his many collaborators on the Stanford Digital Forma Urbis Romae Project, including Marc Levoy, Jennifer Trimble, Tina Najbjerg, Natasha Gelfand, and Claudia Cecamore. The project was conducted in cooperation with the Sovraintendenza Comunale of Rome; we especially thank Superintendent Prof. Eugenio La Rocca, Dr. Laura Ferrea, Dr. Susanna Le Pera, and Dr. Anna Mura Sommella. This research was sponsored in part by the United States National Science Foundation.

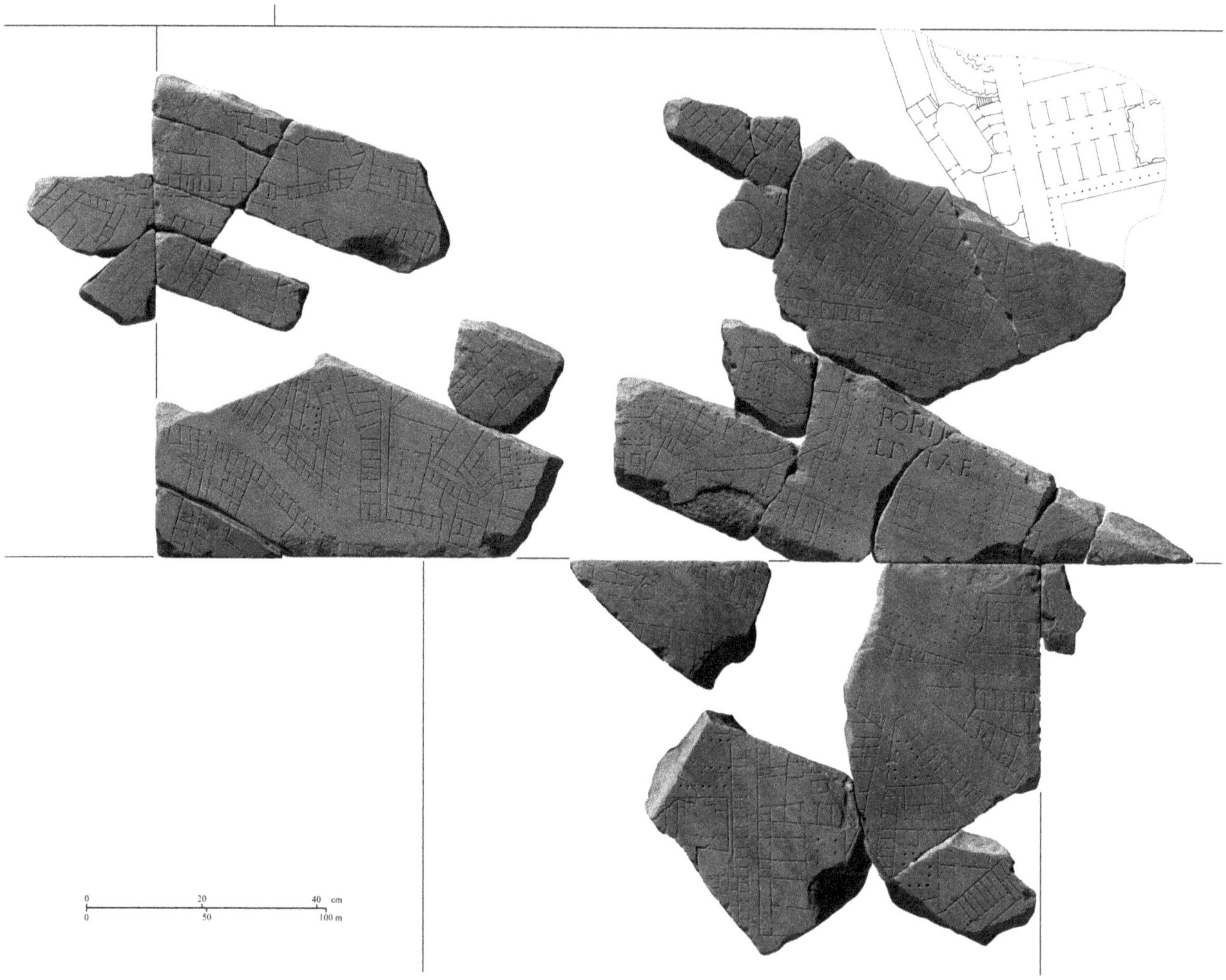

Fig 1. *Several surviving fragments of the Marble Plan that have been identified and reconstructed as depicting a portion of the Subura neighborhood and* Porticus Liviae*; straight lines indicate boundaries of the rectangular marble slabs (digital fragment photos composited after Carettoni* et al. *1960).*

the progress in their reconstruction: *La pianta marmorea di Roma antica* (Carettoni *et al.* 1960) and *Forma Urbis Marmorea* (Rodríguez-Almeida 1981). Our recently developed Digital Forma Urbis Romae Project website[1] also documents the fragments using unique digital technologies and provides updated information about scholarly research on the Plan. Readers are referred to these sources for further background information on the Plan.

1. http://formaurbis.stanford.edu

Digitizing the Plan fragments

While the Plan is an artefact of great importance in understanding the topography of ancient Rome, the previous generations of researchers working with its remnants have encountered difficulty. The surviving fragments of the Plan are numerous, and many are large and unwieldy, with the heaviest fragments weighing several hundred pounds each. Access to the fragments has been very limited; since 1998 the fragments have been stored away in crates in a basement storeroom of the Museo della Civiltà Romana. Even access to the fundamental publications about the Plan is limited, as few copies were printed and they are difficult to find outside of specialist research settings.

In an effort to increase the accessibility of the fragments and to accelerate their reconstruction, the Stanford Digital Forma Urbis Romae Project, under the aegis of the Sovraintendenza ai Beni Culturali del Comune di Roma, has digitized the shape and surface appearance of all the extant fragments (Koller *et al.* 2006). The 3D shape of each fragment was captured using a Cyberware optical triangulation 3D laser range scanner, which measured the fragment surface shapes at a resolution of 0.25 mm. These digital measurements were then input to a 3D scan data software processing pipeline to create complete 3D geometric computer models for all the fragments. Additionally, the top and bottom surfaces of each fragment were photographed with a colour digital camera at a resolution of 100 dpi. An example 3D model and photograph are shown in **Fig. 2**.

An online archaeological research tool

In order to organize and share our digitized fragment representations, and to incorporate them with related scholarly materials in order to support further study of the Plan, we have constructed an online database of the fragments. In addition to our 3D scanned models and colour photographs, the database includes up-to-date archaeological information about each fragment, as well as the Plan in general. The fragment database was developed using the MySQL database software to store the information about each fragment in a relational database, and the scripting language PHP is used to organize this information into a set of dynamic online web pages. The entire database resides on an Apache web server, and can be accessed by any user with an Internet connection. Organizing the database as a website allows for easy updating of the archive with the current state of research about the Plan, and disseminates the updated information through a familiar interface (a web browser) that can reach a wide audience.

***Fig. 2.** 3D model (top) and photograph (bottom) of fragment 10g. Fragment 10g measures 0.68 m in length and is 0.07 m thick.*

The database presents information about each of the Plan fragments via 1,200 dynamically-created web pages, one for each fragment; an example screenshot of a fragment entry webpage is shown in **Plate 3**. The 3D model of each fragment is accessed and manipulated using a custom 3D viewer that allows users to rotate the model, zoom in and out, and change the virtual lighting. Each database entry also includes our colour digital photographs of the fragment, as well as the relevant digitized photographic plates from Carettoni *et al.* (1960). An information box provides essential data including the identification numbers assigned to the fragment, which other fragments it adjoins, and general observations about its condition and archaeological features. The textual analysis section of the fragment entry includes a detailed analytical description of the fragment, a synthesis of the most relevant scholarship, and the fragment's history. Bibliographic citations specific to the fragment are linked to an annotated bibliography, and all the fragment data fields are searchable by means of a database search engine.

The online Digital Forma Urbis Romae database has been gradually deployed in phases over the last few years, as the processing of the voluminous fragment data has been slowly completed. Tens of thousands of users have accessed the database, ranging from Roman topography experts to curious laypeople. Scholarly users in particular have been empowered by the increased accessibility, searchability, and cross-referencing capabilities afforded by this new digital archaeological tool for studying the Plan. The online database eliminates many of the obstacles that had previously restrained research on the Plan, as the fragments themselves and their associated research literature were often unavailable for study. The multiple representations of each fragment presented in the database (3D model, colour photograph, scanned photographic plates, analytical drawings, textual description) have also proved valuable for users studying the Plan. These different digital representations can easily be juxtaposed and compared, allowing a more complete view and understanding of the fragments than has been possible previously, and users have a unique opportunity to conduct 'virtual archaeology' on the Plan. Measurements of fragment dimensions and observations of fractured edges can be performed simply by loading the digital 3D models into a 3D software program. We have found the 3D fragment models particularly useful for confirming several new reconstruction results proposed during our computer-aided fragment reconstruction research.

As valuable as the virtual fragment representations have proven, however, users must recognize their limits relative to working with the actual fragments themselves. The computer models and photographs of the fragments contain minor defects and distortions, and may not reflect very fine details accurately. For example, the ancient sawing marks (*scalini*) present on the backs of some fragments are too small to be adequately resolved by our 3D laser scanners, and other subtle characteristics of the marble such as texture, veining, and colour variations may be beyond the limitations of our capture devices. These details can only be accurately observed by examining the real physical fragments in person in Rome. Similarly, the valuable haptic feedback that one can feel when test fitting actual matching fragments together along their fractured edges is absent when simply manipulating virtual 3D models on a visual computer display.

Computer-aided fragment reconstruction

Beyond the archival value of digitizing the Plan, the digital representations of the map fragments enable new kinds of research and analytical study. In particular, we have investigated using computer searching and matching algorithms to aid in reconstruction of the Plan through virtual reassembly of the fragments. Traditional scholarship efforts have also focused on joining the surviving fragments and reconstructing the map, but progress has been painstaking and slow, in part due to the difficulty of accessing and working with many hundreds of unwieldy marble fragments. However, computer programs that operate on digital models of the fragments can very rapidly and systematically consider many thousands of possible fragment positions and combinations. Such computer-aided fragment reassembly procedures have been previously applied to archaeological problems (Smith & Kristof 1970; Kalvin *et al.* 1999), and are an active area of research in computer science.

The remains of the Plan include a number of properties that are potentially useful as clues for automated fragment reconstruction. The most obvious is the inscribed map topography on the marble surface, which has been the primary source of information for prior reconstruction scholarship. Another strong clue is the fracture shape along the fragment edges; adjacent fragments with edge geometry that is not substantially eroded should match together like pieces of a jigsaw puzzle. Fragments that originated from the same marble slab also typically share several common characteristics. The thickness measurements of adjacent fragments from the same slab are usually very similar, and the gradient of the thickness across a fragment can be useful for determining its placement and orientation within a slab. The marble veining direction of fragments originating from the same slab is also normally consistent. Some slabs had rough back surfaces while others had smooth sawn back surfaces, providing another property useful for the grouping and matching of fragments. The presence of straight slab edges, clamp holes, and wedge holes (*tasselli*) on the fragments can help join fragments together, as well as provide information about the orientation and position of fragments on the original map wall. All of these fragment attributes are appropriate for use in our computer algorithms due to their geometric nature. We are easily able to model the location and nature of these features in our digital representations of the fragments, and our algorithms utilize these geometric constraints to search for and find potential fragment matches. There are many other properties of the fragments that may be useful for matching that we have not yet exploited, such as geological characteristics of the marble (colour, texture, etc.), the style of incisions (*ductus*), and correlation of Latin inscriptions and the depicted topography to known excavated architecture.

We have developed and experimented with several different computer algorithms for automating reconstruction of the Plan fragments. Though the various methods employ different combinations of particular reconstruction clues as their primary inputs, all of the techniques operate by searching a large space of possible fragment correspondences and positions, and seeking the configurations which best satisfy the specified set of geometric constraints. Each automated technique outputs listings of proposed fragment matches with their specific relative positions, and assigns a score to each proposal according to its match quality. When these output lists are sorted in ranked order, archaeological experts can then review the top scoring matches proposed by the computer, and apply further human reasoning beyond the simple geometric constraints evaluated by the algorithms.

Using our computer-aided approaches, we have discovered a number of new Plan fragment joins and placements that were overlooked in the prior centuries of reconstruction scholarship. A brief overview of the various reconstruction algorithms is given below; a more detailed discussion and further new results are available in Koller (2007).

3D fracture matching

Our initial intent was to use computer algorithms to search for new matches among the fractured edge boundaries of the fragments. We experimented with adapting 3D Iterative Closest Point algorithms (Besl 1992) used for scan data registration to the fracture matching problem, and also tried converting the fragment edges to 2D contours (by extracting slices parallel to the flat fragment top surfaces) and then to 1D signals in order to apply approximate string matching algorithms. However, these initial attempts did not result in any significant new discoveries. We have attributed this failure in part to the high degree of erosion on many of the fragment edges, which can leave little salient information for matching. Additionally, some of the digital 3D models that we used as input exhibited distortions due to misregistration of the raw 3D scan data.

Boundary incision matching

The most successful fragment reassembly method that we have developed is based on boundary incision matching. We first annotated 2D images of the fragments by hand, extending all of the incised lines representing topographic features that leave the boundaries of each fragment, and indicating their relative position, direction, and architectural feature type (such as rows of columns, aqueducts, etc.). The automated computer algorithm then searches this collection of fragment boundary annotations, and returns a list of suggested pairwise fragment matches, based on a geometric scoring metric that measures the quality of the alignment of the annotated boundary features.

As an example of boundary incision matching, consider the two fragments identified as fn23 and 28a in the fragment numbering scheme. Their boundary feature annotations are depicted with varying colours in **Plate 4**. The boundary incision matching algorithm suggested a very high scoring match between these two fragments, with the five incisions at the top of fragment fn23 aligning with five similar features along the bottom edge of fragment 28a. When we checked this new suggested match between the two fragments, we were able to verify the correctness of its placement by further observing a matching correspondence between fragments fn23 and 34b. Fragment fn23 fits nicely in the corner between fragments 28a and 34b [**Fig. 5**], both of which had been identified and positioned together in earlier scholarship. The new positioning for fragment fn23 appears to depict the interior of a multi-storey warehouse that was partially visible on fragments 28a and 34b.

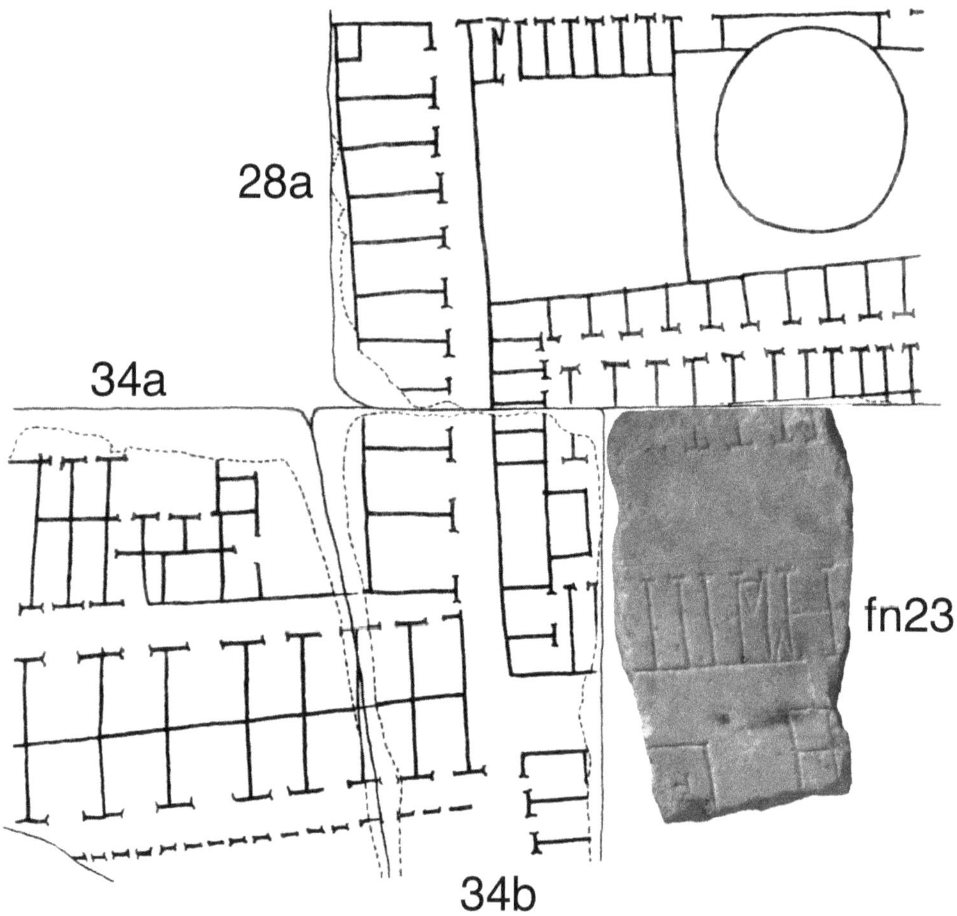

Fig. 5. *Fragment fn23 positioned in the corner between fragments 28a and 34b (after Carettoni* et al. *1960).*

Another example of a new fragment match involves fragments 330 and 354 [**Fig. 6**]. In this case, only two parallel boundary incisions delineating a road matched well between the two fragments, but the presence of distinct marble veining provided an additional geometric matching constraint, as the veining directions for fragments in the same slab must align, thus restricting the possible relative orientations of the fragments. As a result, the two fragments were scored high enough by the matching algorithm to warrant further review and examination of the 3D models. In this case, the 3D models for the two fragments both exhibited very unusual smooth, flat regions along their fractured edges [**Fig.** 7]. This suggested a fragment match directly along their boundaries, and this was confirmed by later examining the fragments in person in Rome. **Fig. 8** shows fragment 354 in its newly suggested position matching fragment 330; together the fragments seem to represent the groundplan of dense residential and commercial architecture spanning two city blocks.

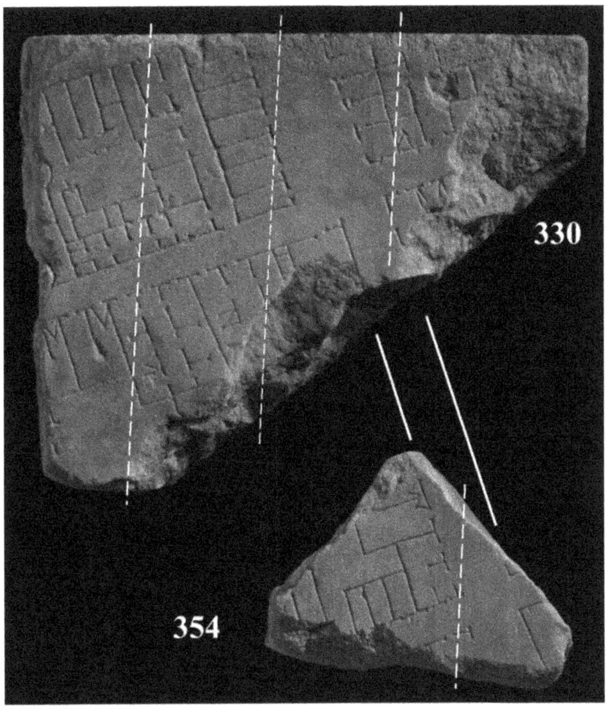

Fig. 6*. Matching incisions (solid lines) and veining direction (dashed) constraints between fragments 330 and 354.*

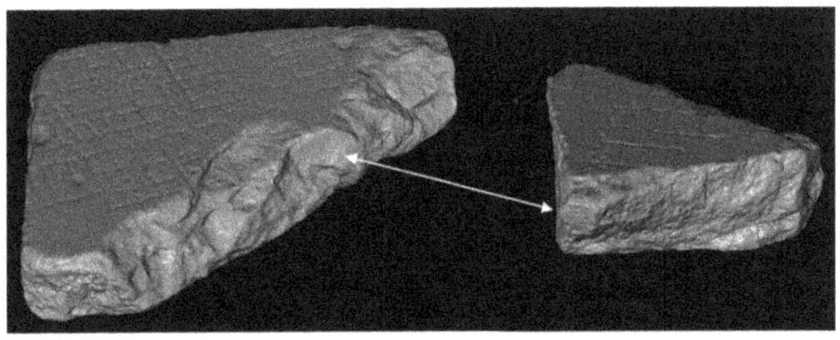

Fig. *7. 3D computer models of fragments 330 (left) and 354 (right), showing the unusual smooth, flat sections along the fractured edge surfaces near the proposed join.*

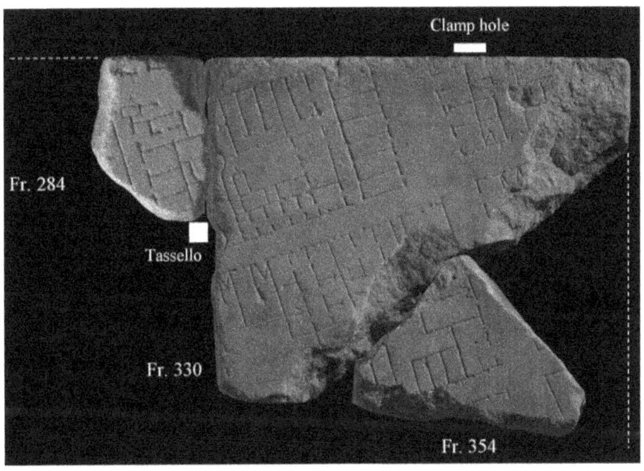

Fig. 8*. Composite image of fragments 284, 330, and 354.*

Wall feature matching

Another computer algorithm that we have used successfully to reconstruct portions of the Plan is wall feature matching. This technique employs measurements of the still extant wall on which the Plan was hung, collected by L. Cozza for the 1960 publication of the map (Carettoni *et al.* 1960: 175-195). The clamp holes and masonry patches observed on the wall by Cozza are expected to correspond directly to the clamp holes and wedge holes (*tasselli*) visible on some of the fragments (Rodríguez-Almeida 1977). The relative spacings and directions between the clamp holes, in addition to the orientation of the fragment slab edges, provide a number of geometric constraints. We have digitized Cozza's wall feature measurements, as well as the corresponding features on the fragments, and use this data as input to a computer matching process that searches all valid positions and orientations of fragments on the wall and outputs a ranked list of the strong matches [**Plate 9**].

Multivariate clustering

Whereas other matching algorithms require directly corresponding geometric features among fragments, multivariate clustering merely attempts to group fragments together based on common characteristics. We have experimented with hierarchical and partitional data clustering schemes such as the K-means algorithm to group potentially nearby fragments together, based on attributes including fragment thickness, marble veining direction, the primary axial direction of the architecture depicted on the fragment, the directions of slab edges, and the back surface condition of the fragments (i.e. whether the backs are rough or smooth).

Areal topographic matching

Because a number of Plan fragments have already been identified and located on the wall map through prior scholarship, the positions of many areal topographic features on the map (e.g. roadways and rivers) have become well-defined relative to the grid of slab boundary edges. Thus, we have attempted to develop some shape matching techniques that exploit this topographic knowledge to position unidentified fragments. The course of the Tiber River across the map, for example, can be interpolated with reasonable accuracy. We are able to identify candidate unlocated fragments that appear to depict a portion of the river, and then algorithmically search the configuration space for those fragment positions on the wall that maximize the overlap of the river region on the fragment with the hypothesized river region shape on the wall.

Conclusion

The digital capture and measurement of cultural heritage artefacts with high-resolution photography and high-precision 3D laser scanners has become increasingly realistic in the last decade, as the cost, availability, and usability of the technology continually improves. The Digital Forma Urbis Romae Project has been a pioneering effort to exploit these technologies and fully digitize, in three dimensions, a physically large and immensely valuable archaeological artefact. By creating digital representations of the Plan fragments and making them widely and freely available through an online database, we have dramatically increased the accessibility of this monument and hope to encourage a new surge in interest and scholarship concerning the Plan. Beyond simply enabling passive visualizations, we believe that the digital fragment models can enable new analyses that lead to unique archaeological discoveries. Indeed, our computer-aided fragment reconstruction algorithms are an example of one such type of digital analysis that has yielded a number of exciting new findings about the inter-relationships among the surviving fragments, with immediate applicability to better understanding the urban topography of ancient Rome.

Bibliography

Besl, P. & McKay, N. 1992. "A method for registration of 3-d shapes", *Institute of Electrical and Electronics Engineers, Transactions on Pattern Analysis and Machine Intelligence* 14/2: 239-256.

Carettoni, G., Colini, A., Cozza, L., & Gatti, G. 1960. *La pianta marmorea di Roma antica. Forma urbis Romae*, Rome: Comune di Roma.

Kalvin, A. D., Remy, A., Castillo, L. J., Morla, K., Nolasco, E., Prado, J., Fernandez, V., Franco, R. & Wiese, C. 1999. "Computer-aided reconstruction of a pre-Inca temple ceiling in Peru", in L. Dingwall, S. Exon, V. Gaffney, S. Laflin, & M. Van Leusen (eds.), *Archaeology in the Age of the Internet (CAA 1997 Proceedings, Birmingham, April 1997)*, B.A.R. International Series 750, Oxford: BAR Publishing.

Koller, D., Trimble, J., Najbjerg, T., Gelfand, N. & Levoy, M. 2006. "Fragments of the city: Stanford's Digital Forma Urbis Project", in L. Haselberger and J. H. Humphrey (eds.), *Imaging Ancient Rome: Documentation-Visualization-Imagination (Proceedings of the Third Williams Symposium on Classical Architecture,*

Rome, Italy, 20-23 May, 2004), Journal of Roman Archaeology Supplement 61: 237-252.

Koller, D. 2007. "Protected Dissemination and Computer-Aided Reconstruction of Digitized Cultural Artifacts". unpublished Ph.D. dissertation, Stanford University.

Rodríguez-Almeida, E. 1977. "Forma Urbis marmorea: Nuovi elementi di analisi e nuove ipotesi di lavoro", *Mélanges de l'Ecole Française de Rome, Antiquité* 89/1: 219-256.

Rodríguez-Almeida, E. 1981. *Forma Urbis Marmorea: Aggiornamento Generale 1980*, Rome: Edizioni Quasar.

Smith, W. S. & Kristof, E. 1970. "Computer helps scholars re-create an Egyptian temple", *National Geographic Magazine* 138/5: 634-655.

Colour Plates

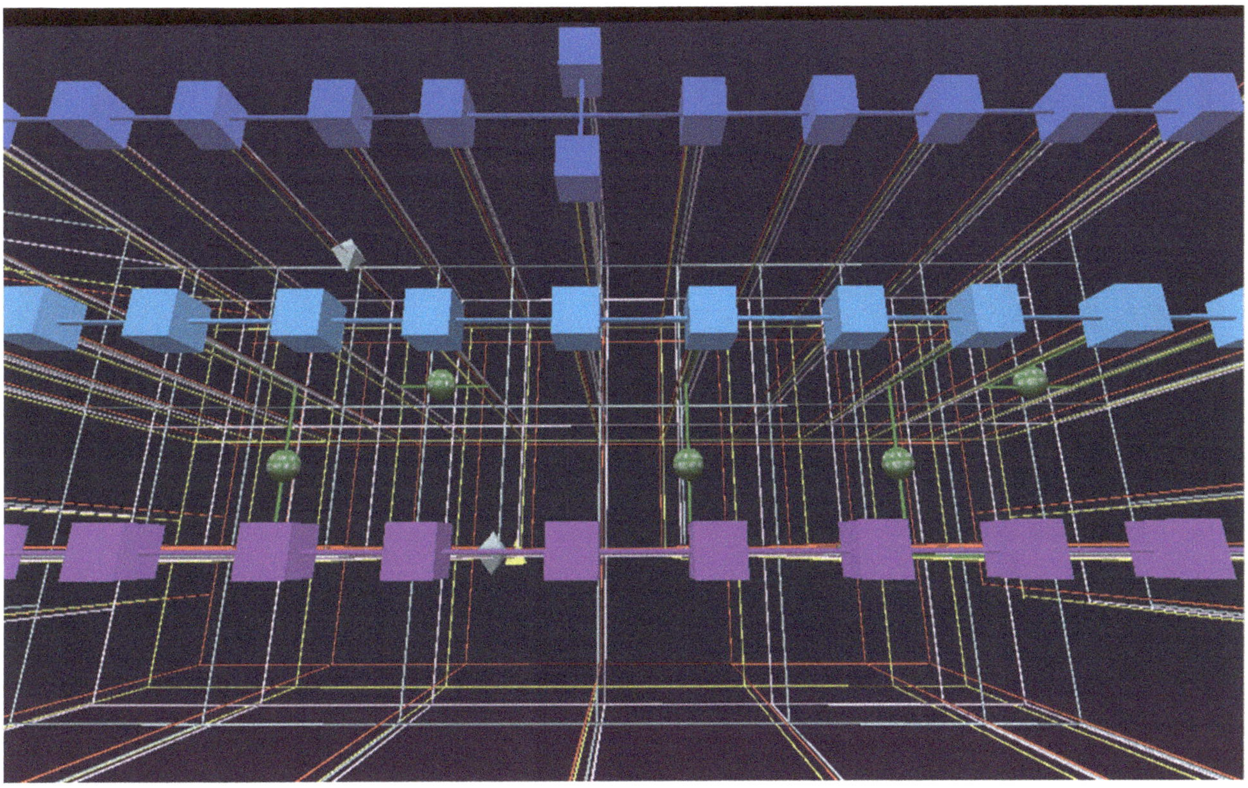

Chapter 2, Plate 1. *Cybermap of the VR system of the Scrovegni Chapel, Padua.*

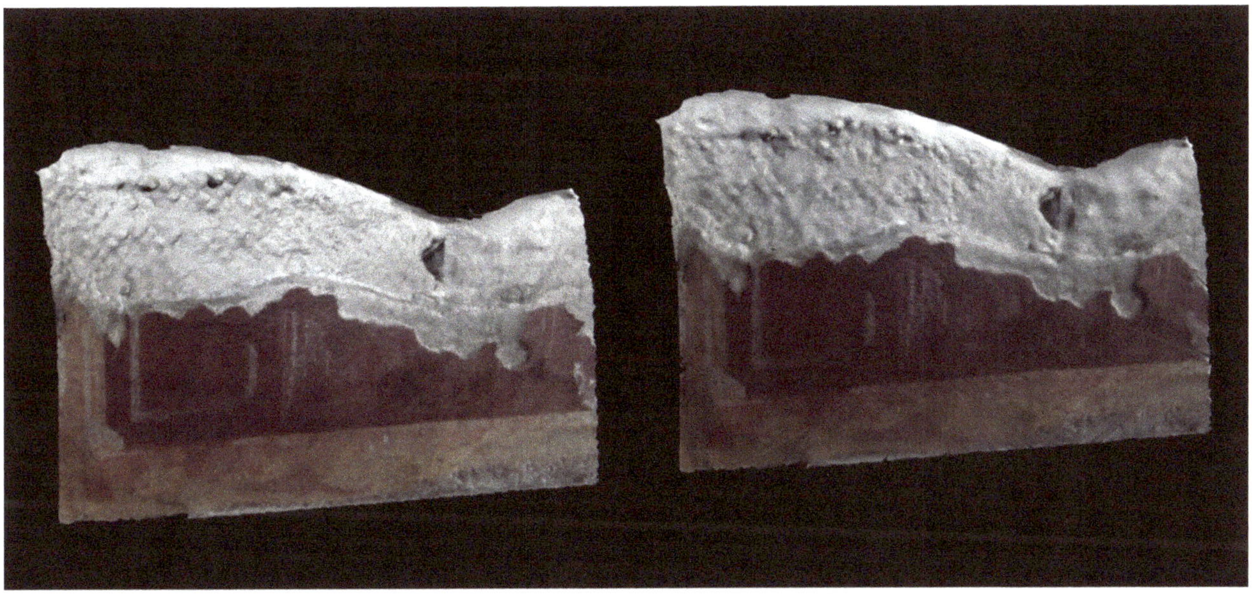

Chapter 2, Plate 4. *3D model of a Roman wall of the imperial period with a geometry of 46,145 polygons created by a point cloud made by a laser scanner (left).*

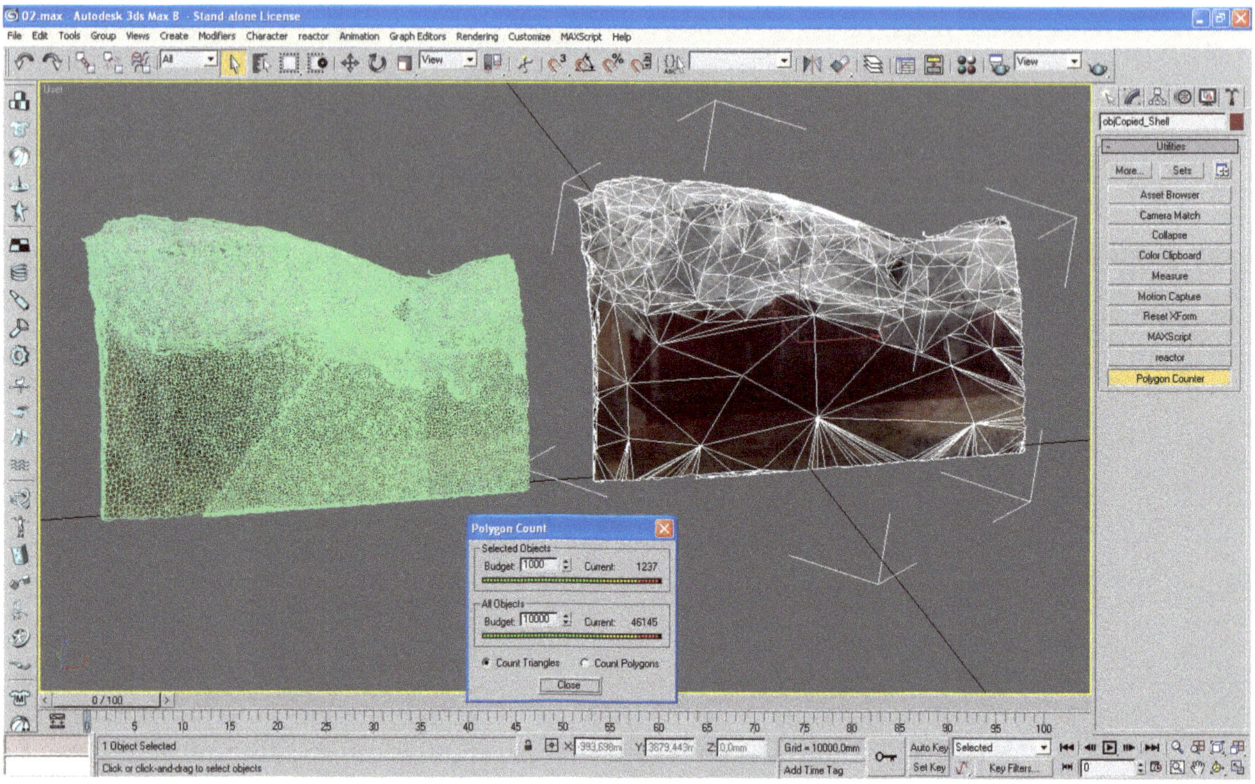

Chapter 2, Plate 5. *3D model of a Roman wall of the imperial period (same as in Fig. 4) but represented in wire frame with 1,237 polygons (right).*

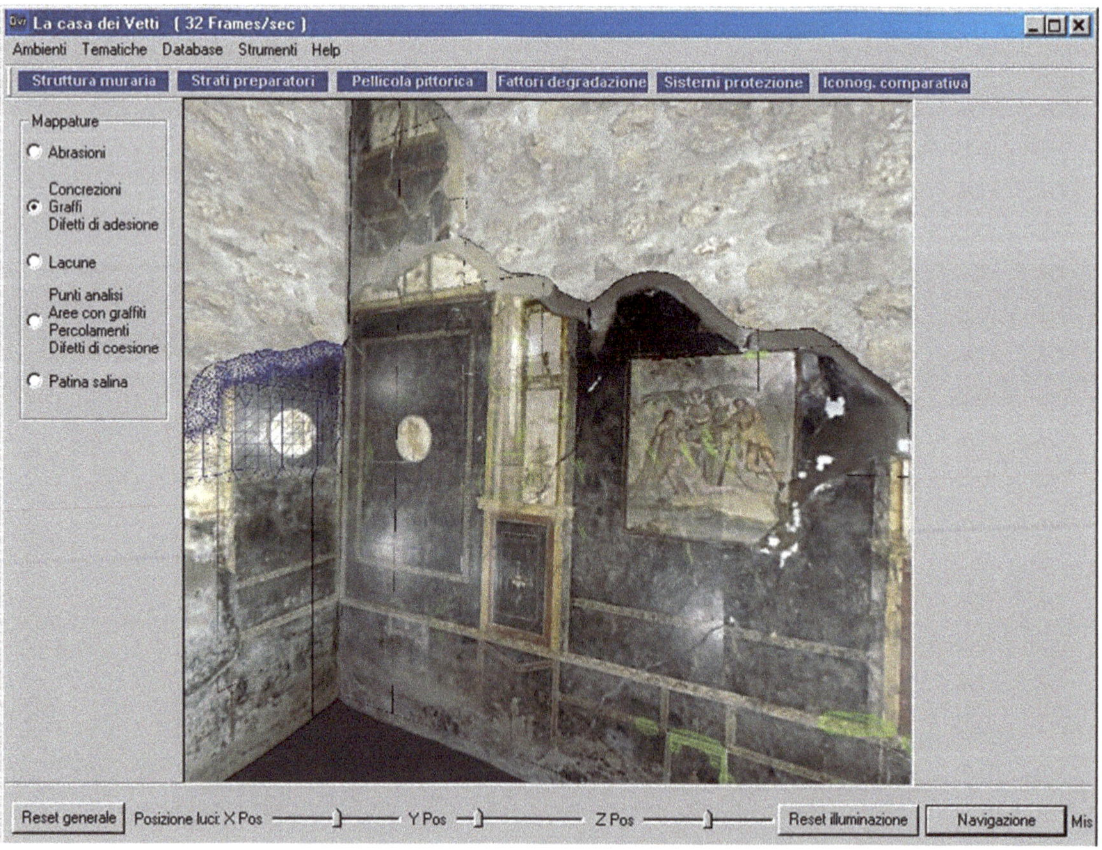

Chapter 2, Plate 6. *Prototype of the VR system created by VHLab-ITABC for the House of the Vetti, Pompeii (in partnership with the ICR).*

Chapter 2, Plate 7. *3D model with textures of the Maya Tempio de Los Mascarones (Ezdna, Mexico), created with Epoch 3D.*

Chapter 2, Plate 8. *3D model without textures of the Maya Tempio de Los Mascarones (Ezdna, Mexico), created with Epoch 3D. Note the faces of the polygons that make up the geometric model consisting of 47,484 polygons.*

Chapter 2, Plate 9. *Via Flaminia Project: Collaborative Virtual Environment reconstructed on the basis of the laser scanner data of the Villa of Livia (1st c. A.D., Rome).*

Chapter 2, Plate 10. *Via Flaminia Project: virtual reconstruction of a cubiculum of the Villa of Livia (1st c. A.D., Rome). The transparency of the model permits to contextualize the room within the landscape and to validate the reconstruction.*

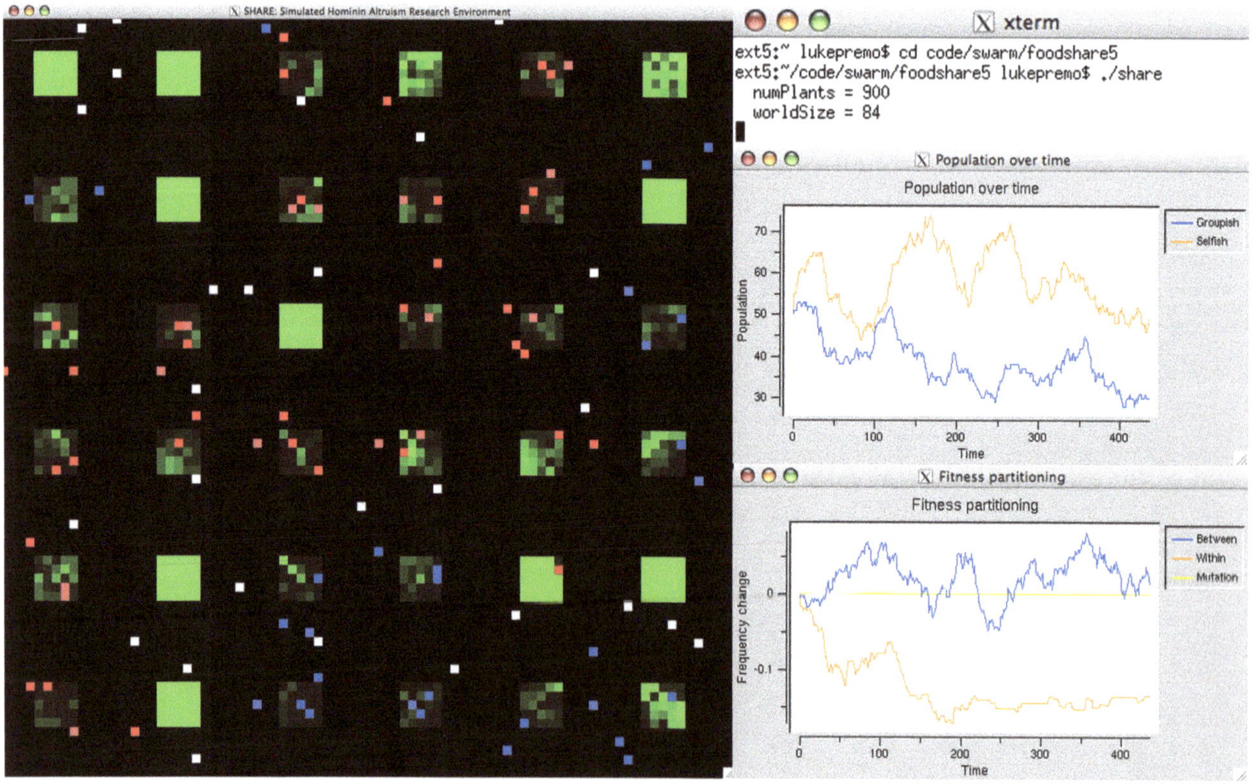

Chapter 4, Plate 1. *A glimpse of SHARE's simple visual interface. Left: altruistic foragers are blue, selfish foragers are red, plants are green, and animal carcasses are white. Each of these agents has its own set of internal variables and behaviors. Upper right: log of agent communication and agent interactions. Right: line graph of selfish (orange) and altruistic (blue) forager populations through simulated time. Lower right: line graph of within-group (orange) and between-group (blue) selection through simulated time.*

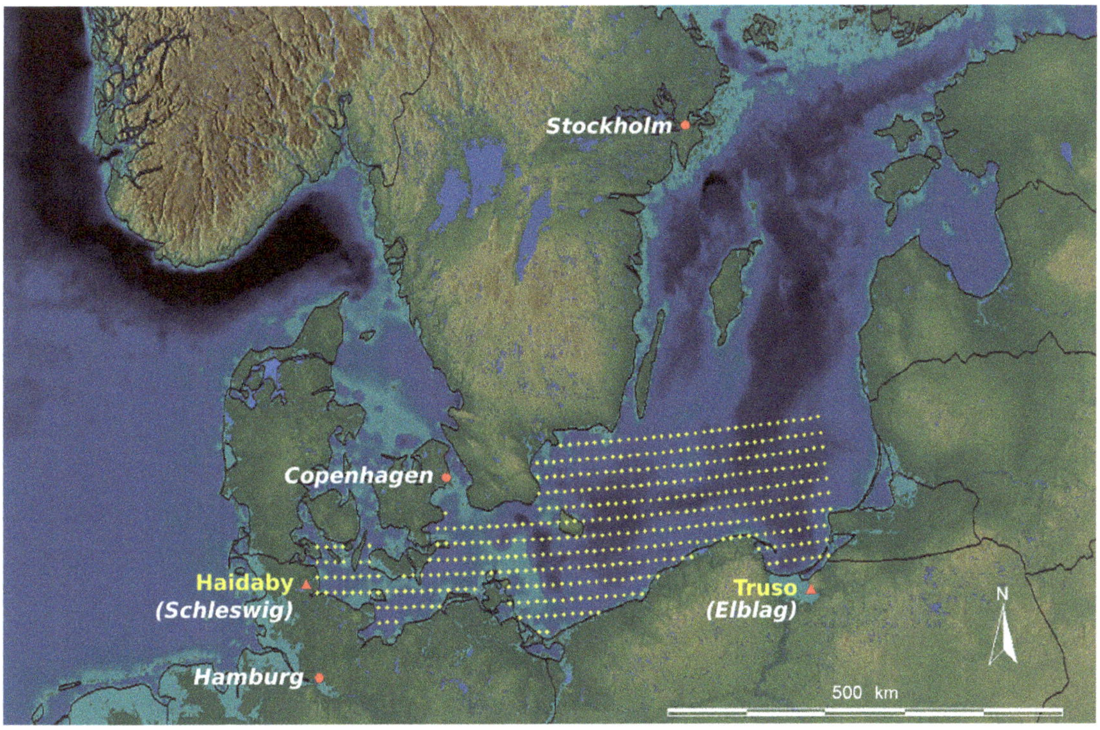

Chapter 5, Plate 1. *Study region in the Baltic, showing the area of Wulfstan's voyage (see text). Locations of wind and current data collected during the 2004 voyage of the Ottar and used in GIS modelling experiments are shown as yellow grid. The grid is used for generating a least cost path (LCP) between the beginning and endpoint. Each dot on the grid contains data on wind speed (raster) and direction (vector). The dots are 10 Nmi (18 km) apart. The grid lies between 54 and 56° north and 10 and 20° east.*

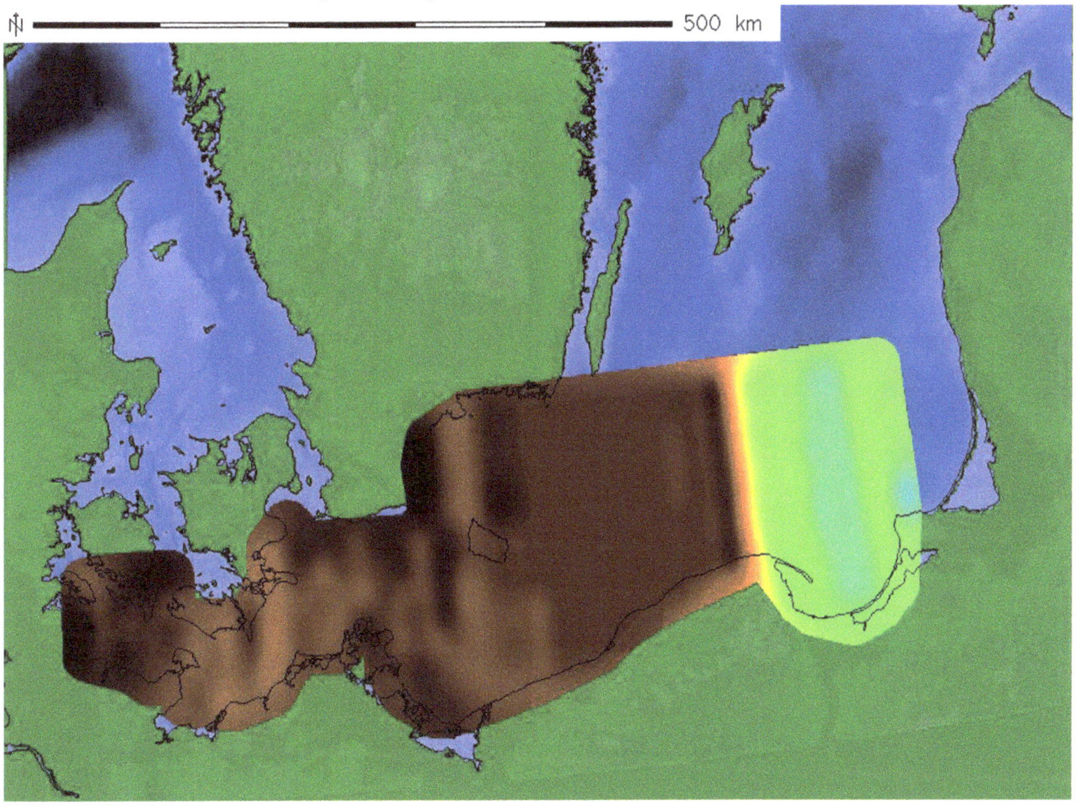

Chapter 5, Plate 2. *Wind speed raster grid map (shaded zone extending eastward from southeastern Jutland) interpolated from 10' data points in GRASS 6. Lighter is lower velocity and darker is higher velocity.*

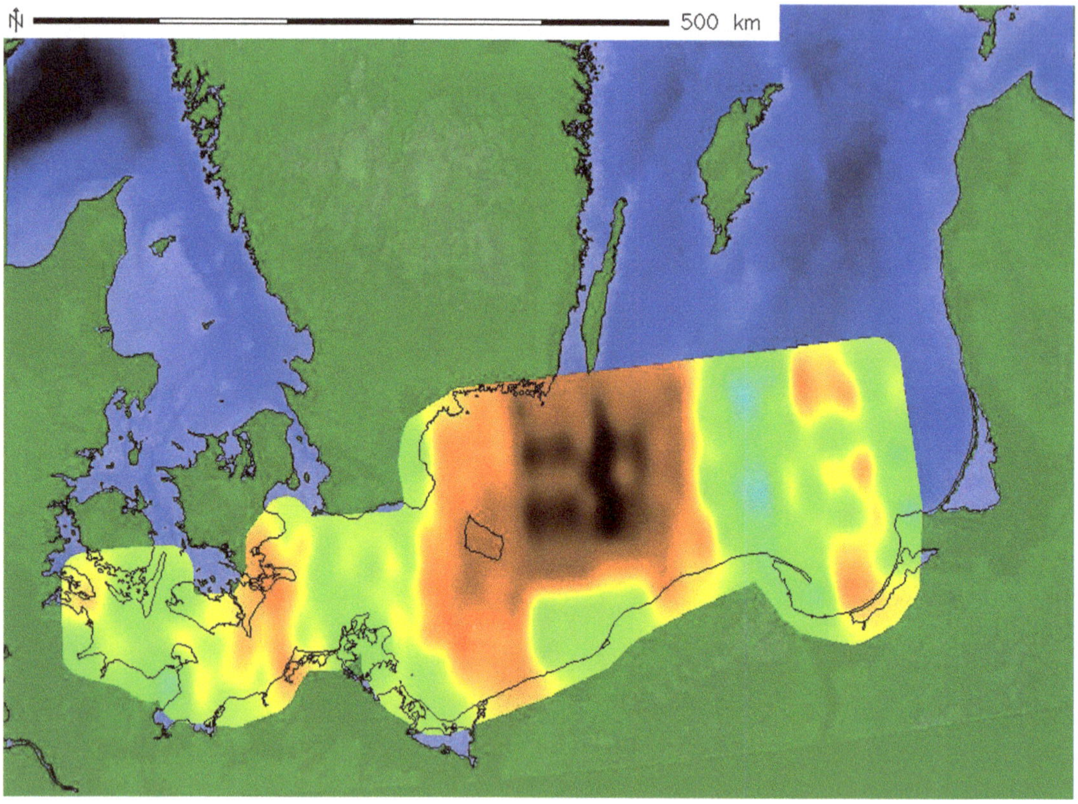

Chapter 5, Plate 3. *Wind direction raster grid map, interpolated from 10' data points in GRASS 6. Lightest is a west wind, darkest is an east wind, and medium grey is a southwest wind.*

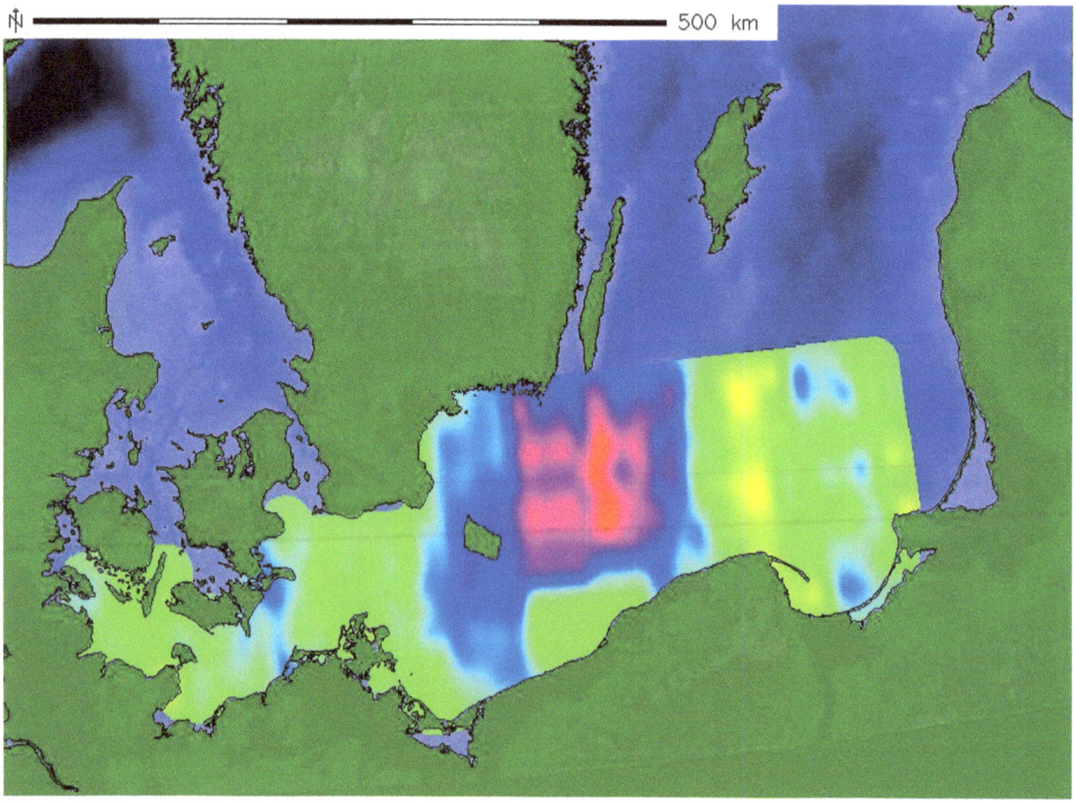

Chapter 5, Plate 4. *Maximum rate of spread (ROS) calculated in the GRASS 6 anisotropic wildfire spreading module with wind as the primary spread-generating parameter. Lightest is fastest and darkest is slowest.*

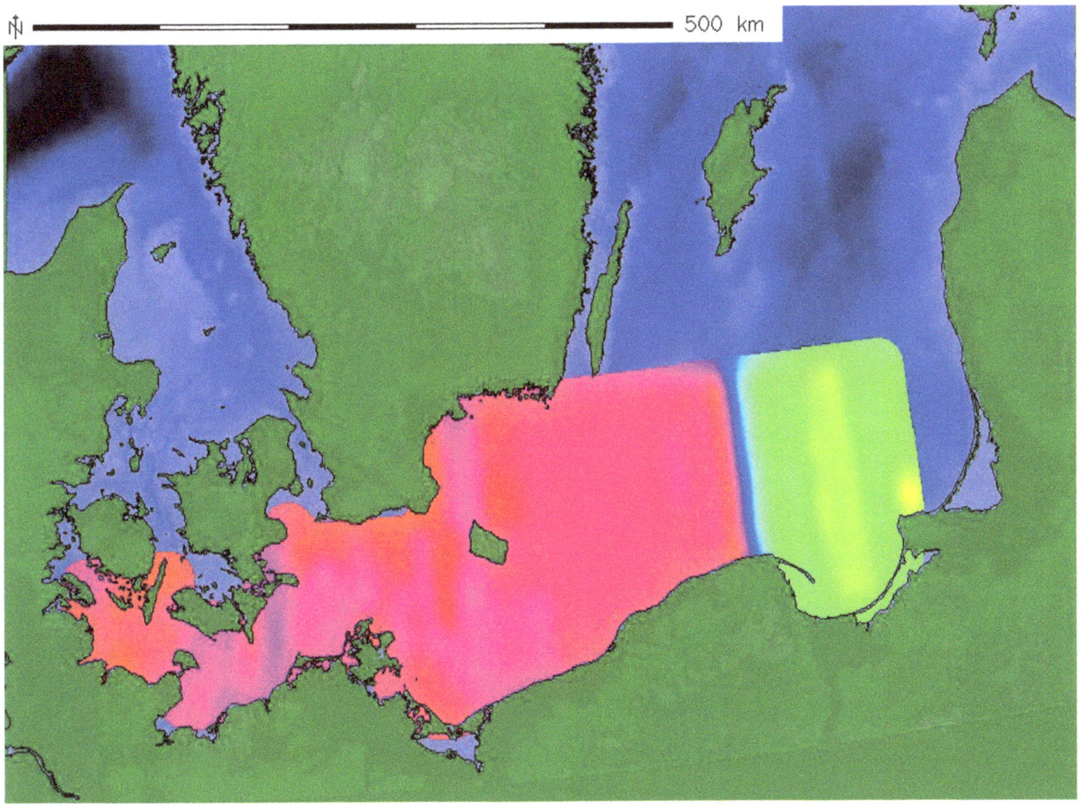

Chapter 5, Plate 5. *Direction of maximum rate of spread (ROS) calculated in the GRASS 6 anisotropic wildfire spreading module with wind as the primary spread-generating parameter. Lightest is an easterly spread, darkest is a western spread, and medium grey is a northwestern spread.*

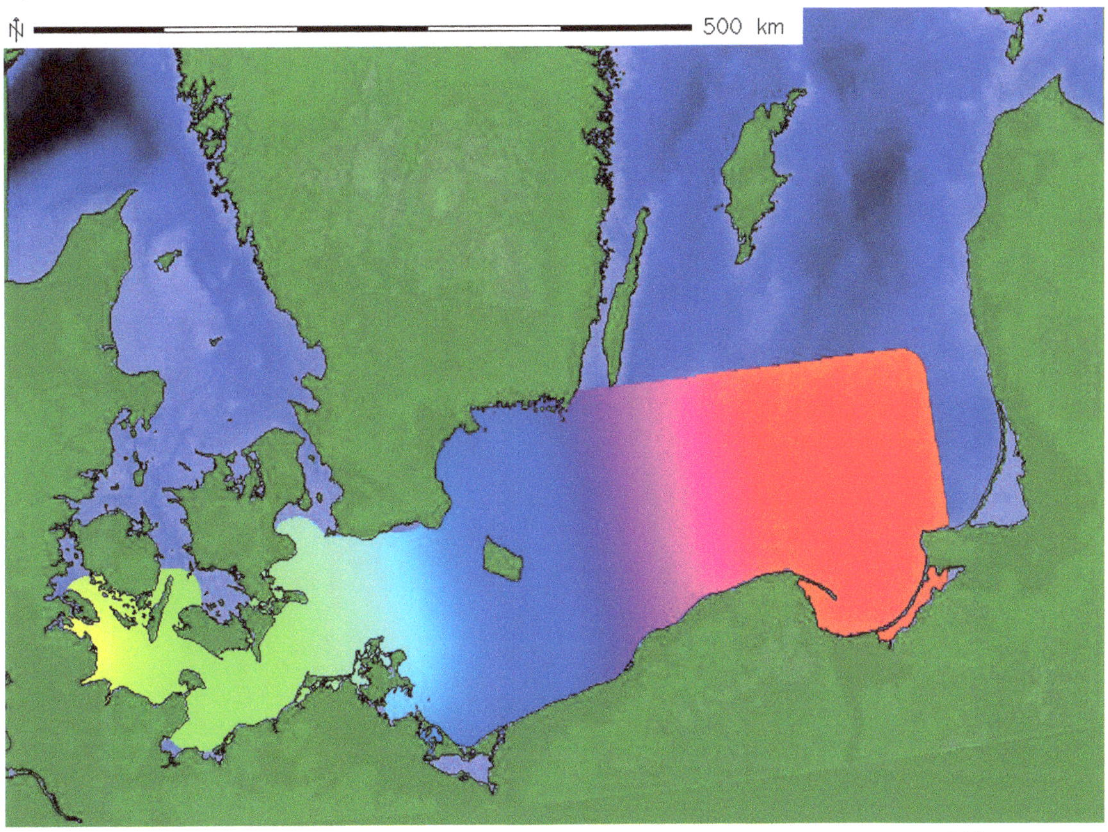

Chapter 5, Plate 6. *Cumulative spread time calculated in the GRASS 6 anisotropic wildfire spreading module. Time runs from lightest to darkest.*

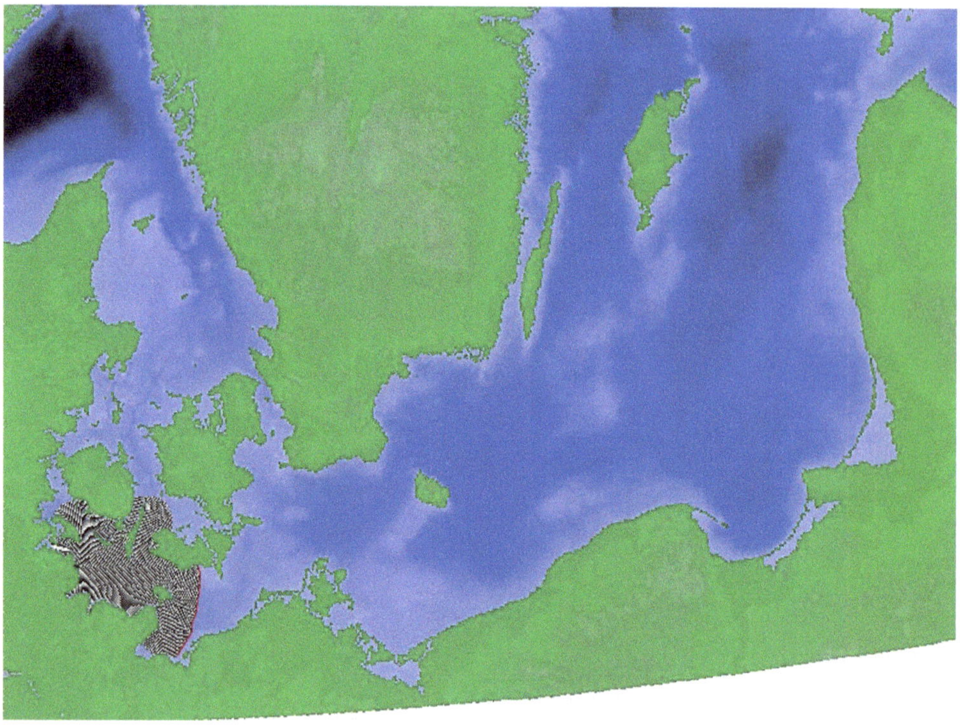

Chapter 5, Plates 7-9. *Screen shots of wind-generated spread simulation generated by the GRASS 6 anisotropic wildfire spreading module. The spread is shown as grey-patterned area beginning at the southeastern coast of the Jutland peninsula and extending progressively eastward.*

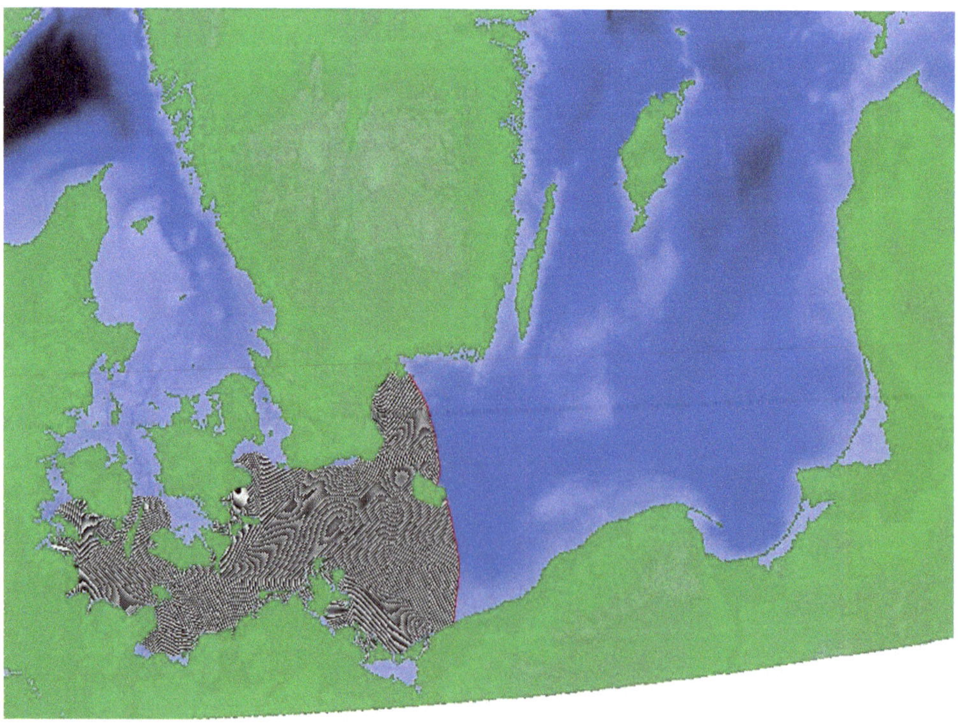

Chapter 5, Plate 8.

Chapter 5, Plate 9.

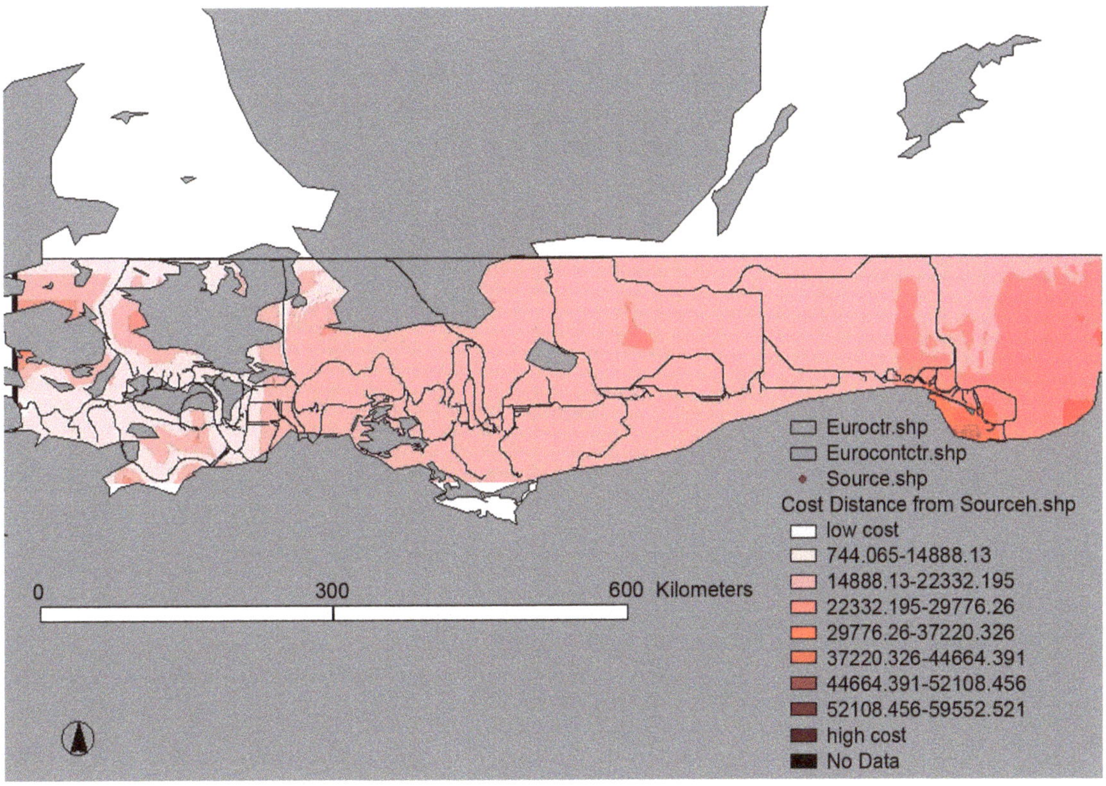

Chapter 5, Plate 10. *Wind direction grid generated by ArcView 3.1.*

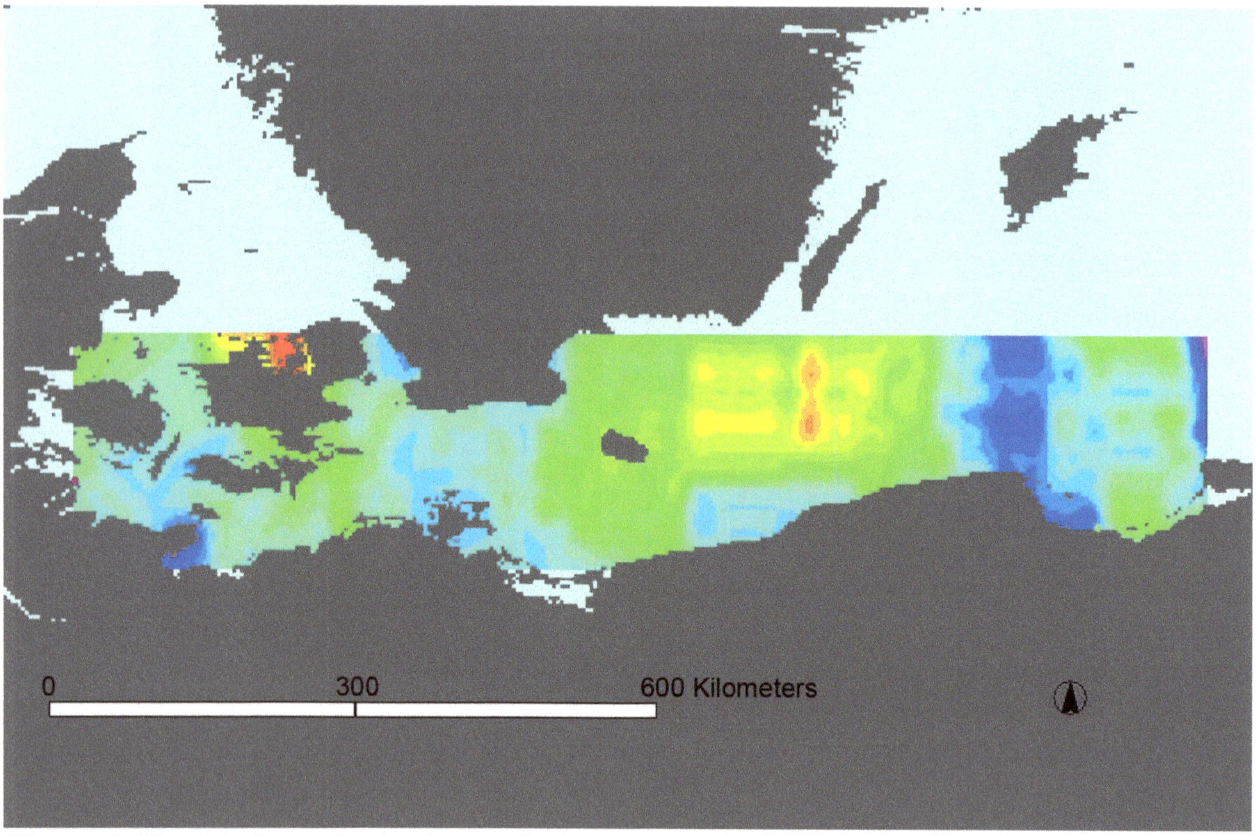

Chapter 5, Plate 11. *Cost surface based on wind velocity generated by the ArcView 3.1 least cost path routine. Lightest is lowest cost and darkest is highest cost.*

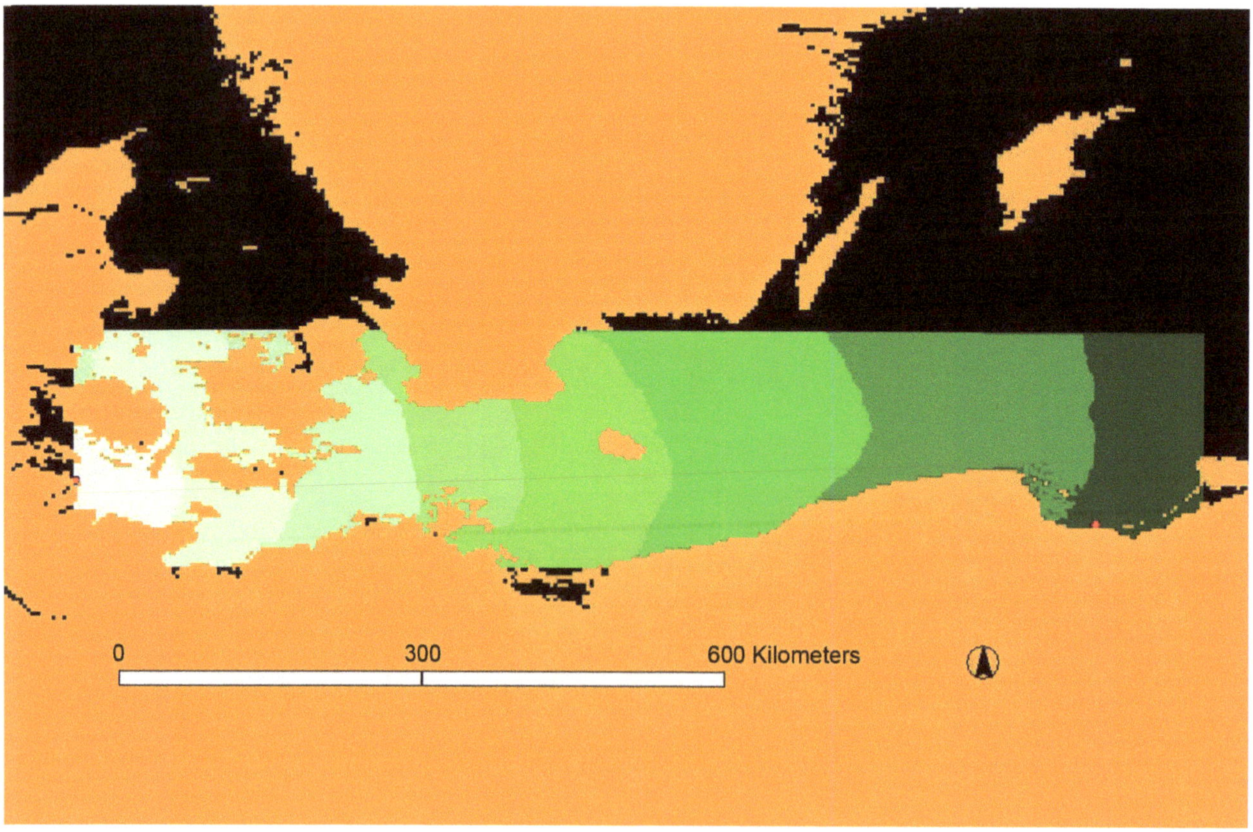

Chapter 5, Plate 12. *Accumulated cost distance grid generated by the ArcView 3.1 least cost path routine. Lightest is lowest cost and darkest is highest cost.*

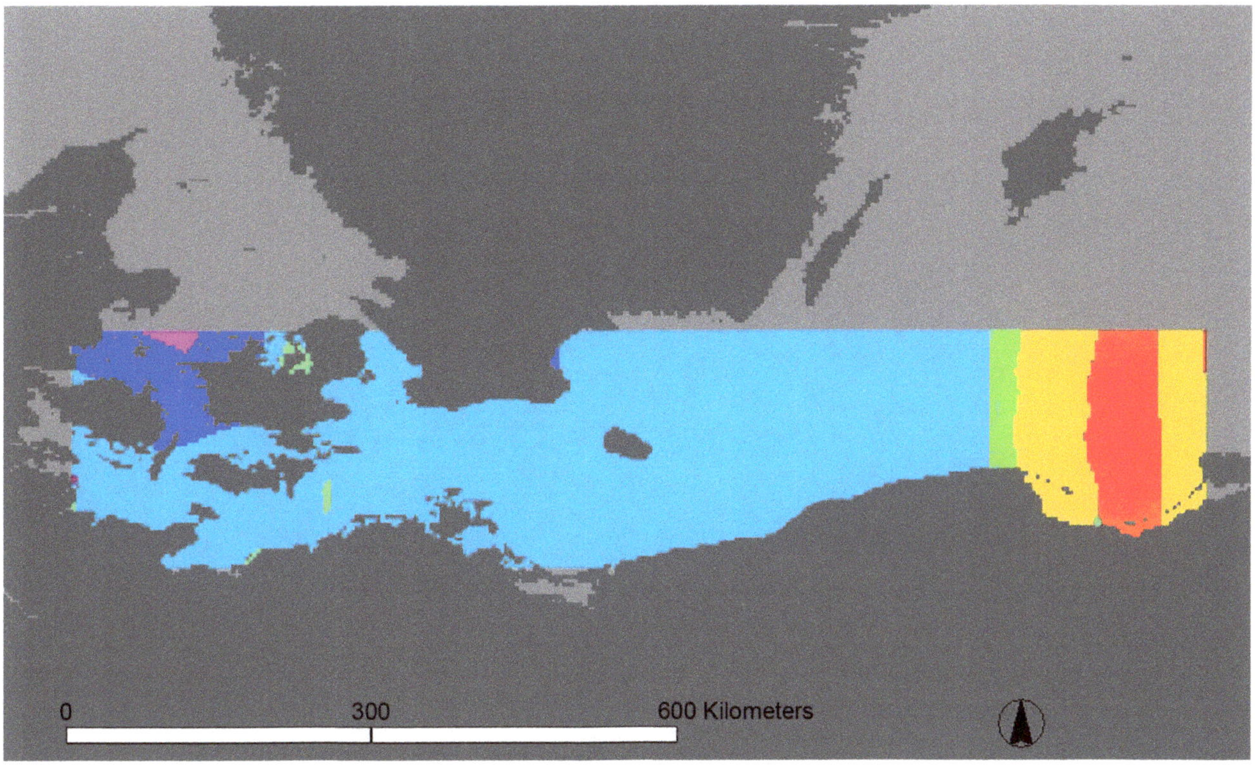

Chapter 5, Plate 13. *Wind direction grid generated by ArcView 3.1.*

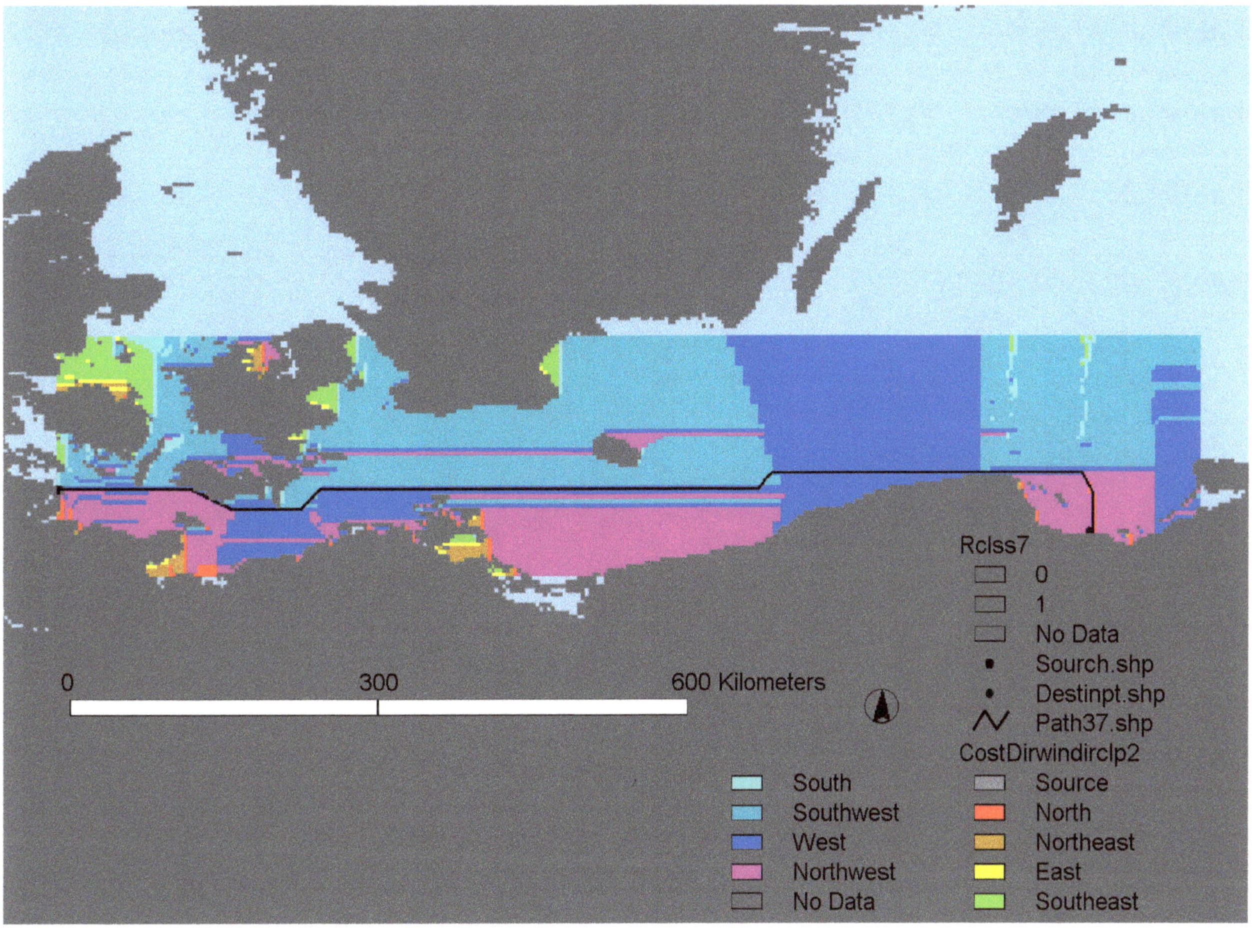

Chapter 5, Plate 14. *Backlink least cost path analysis grid generated by the ArcView 3.1 least cost path routine. White line traces the least cost path from Schlei Fjord to Gdansk.*

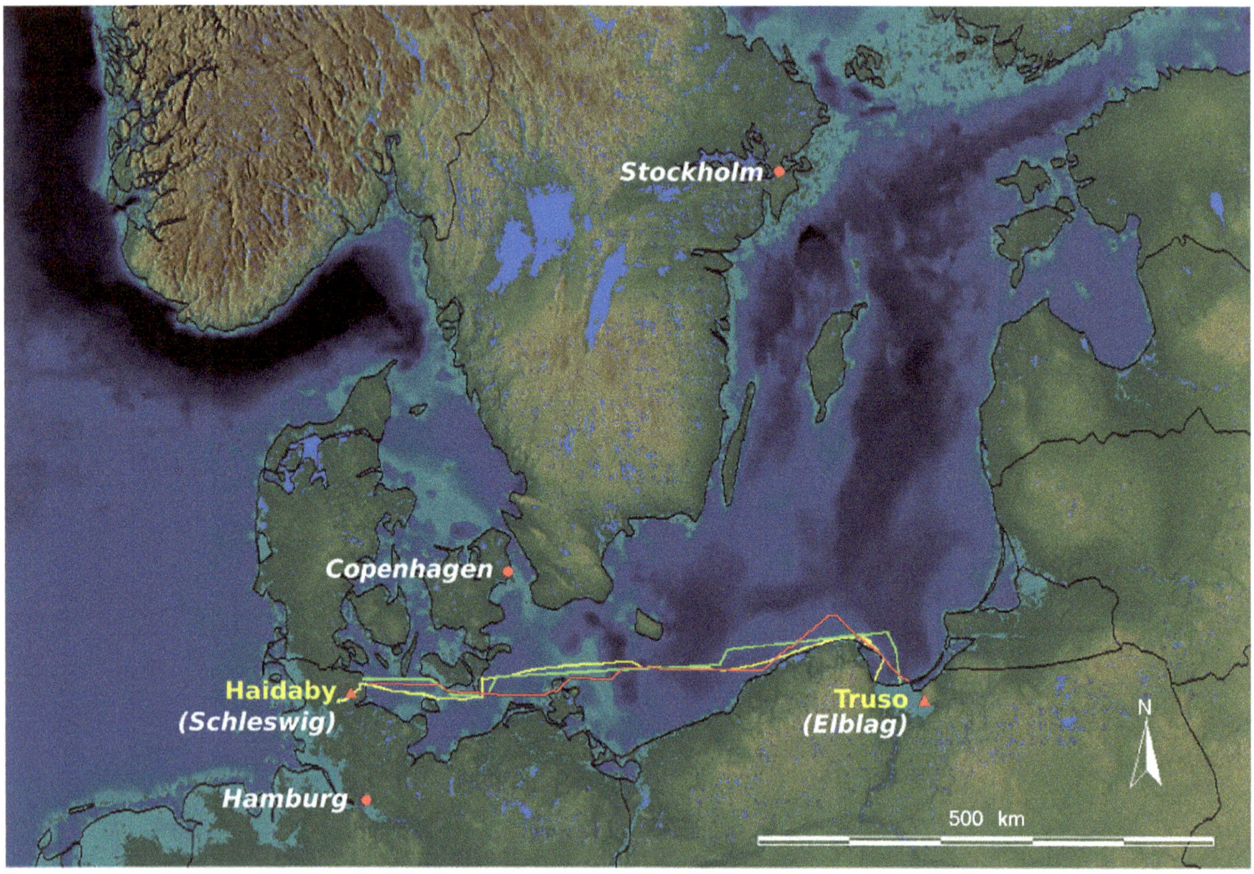

Chapter 5, Plate 15. *Ottar 2004 route (yellow line) and GIS modeled routes. Most probable spread path from Schlei Fjord to Gdansk generated by the GRASS 6 anisotropic wildfire spreading module is shown in red. The green line traces the best least cost path generated in ArcView 3.1.*

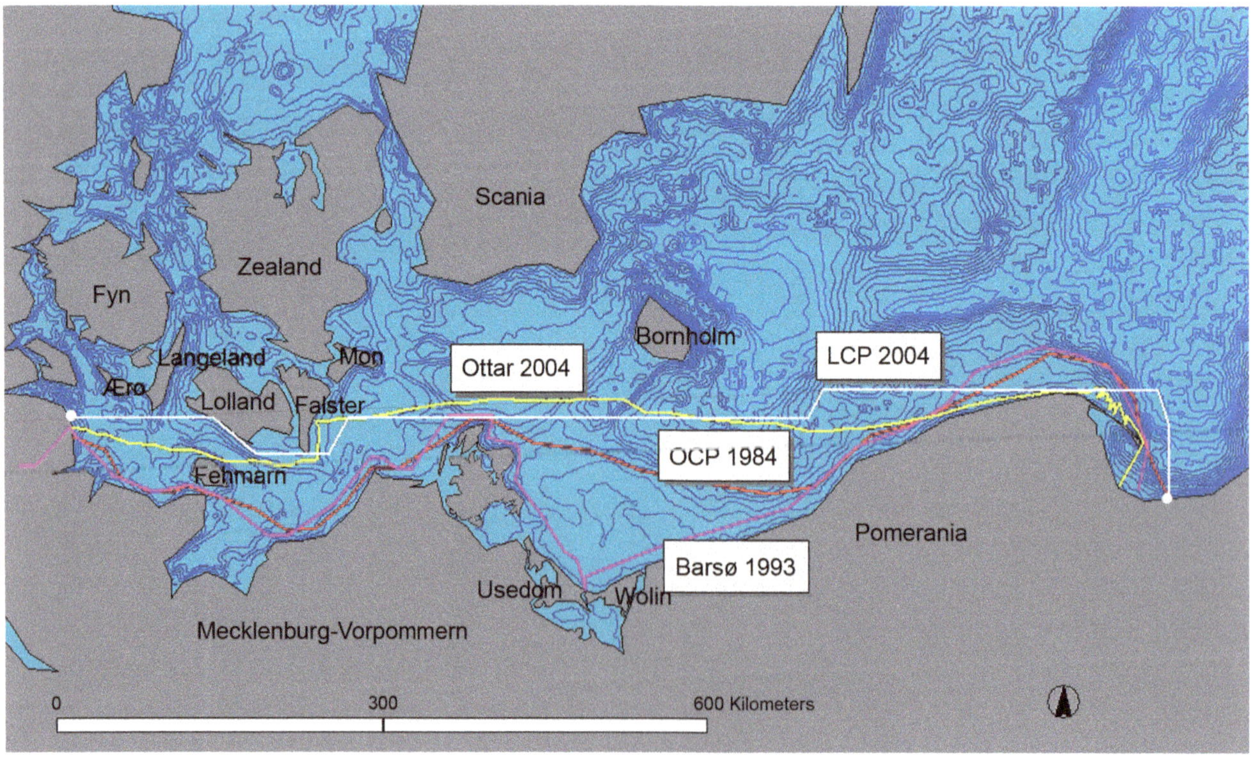

Chapter 5, Plate 16. *Routes of the Ottar in 2004, the Barsø in 1993, and Crumlin-Pedersen's proposed route (see text for explanation). Arcview-generated least cost path shown for comparison.*

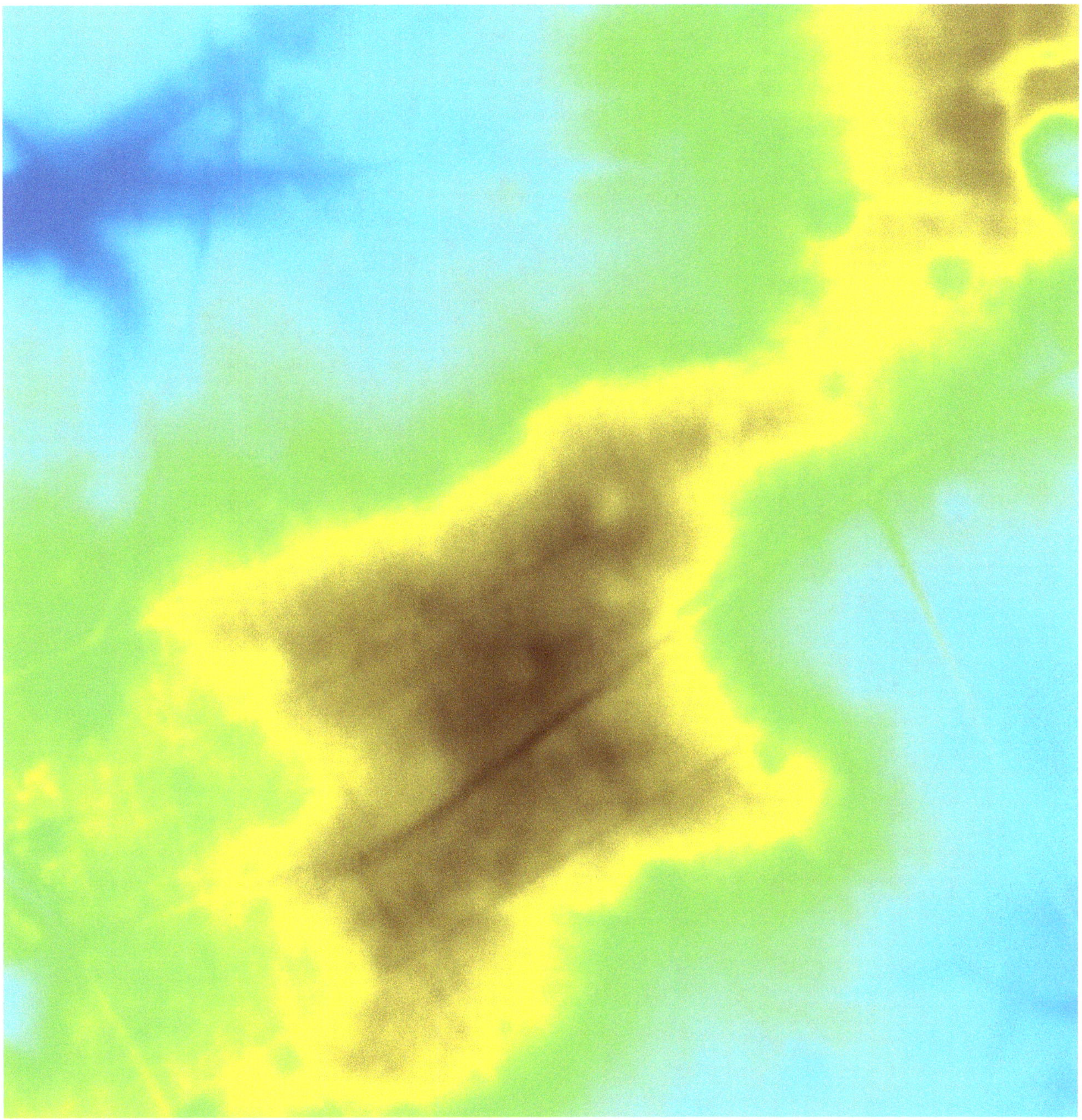

Chapter 6, Plate 1. *Thematic DEM map of elevations covering a 4 square km quadrangle for an agricultural region near Erkelenz, Germany, in the loess landscape of the Rhineland.*

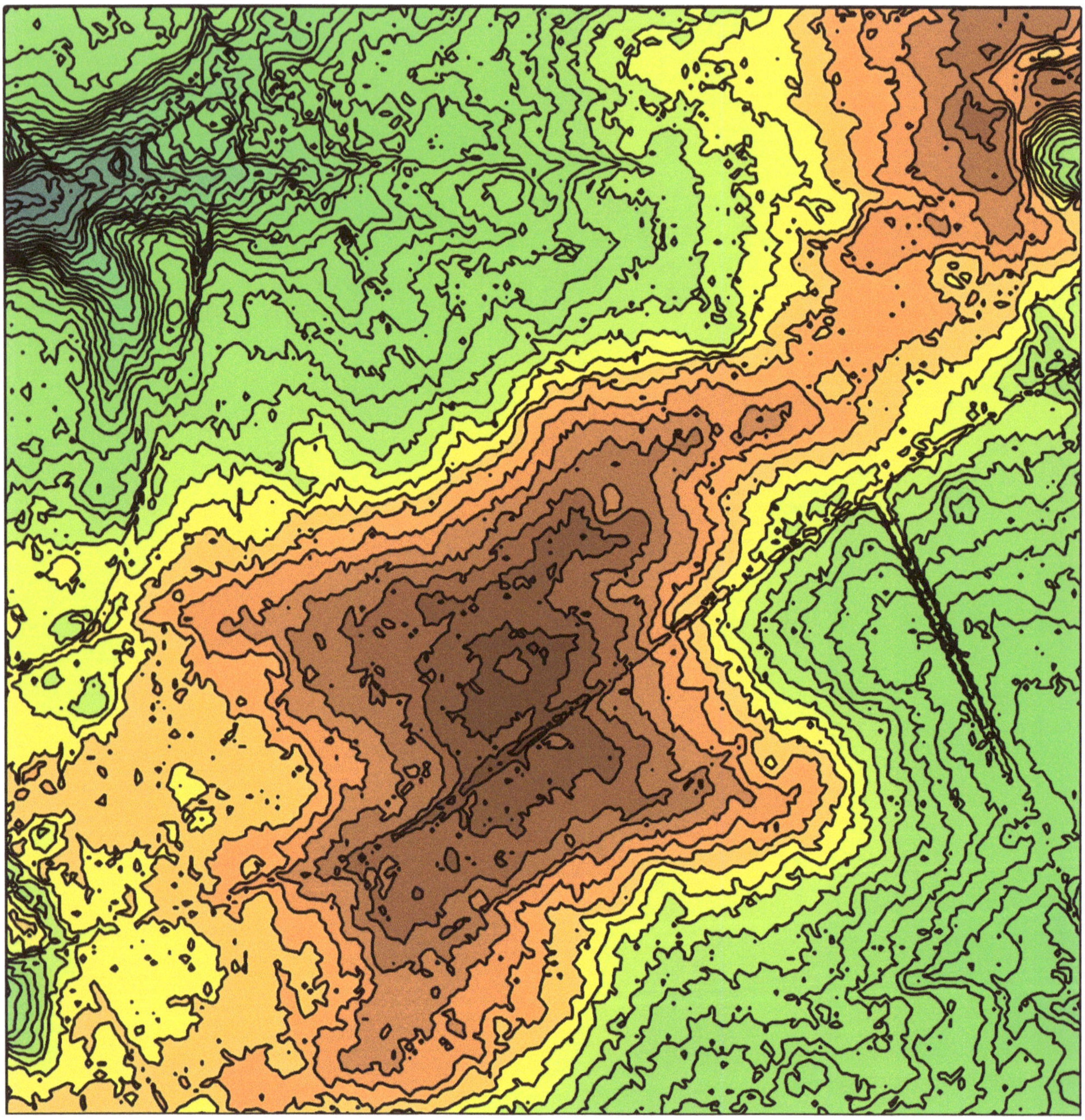

Chapter 6, Plate 3. *Thematic map of the elevations with additional contour lines for the area depicted in Plate 1.*

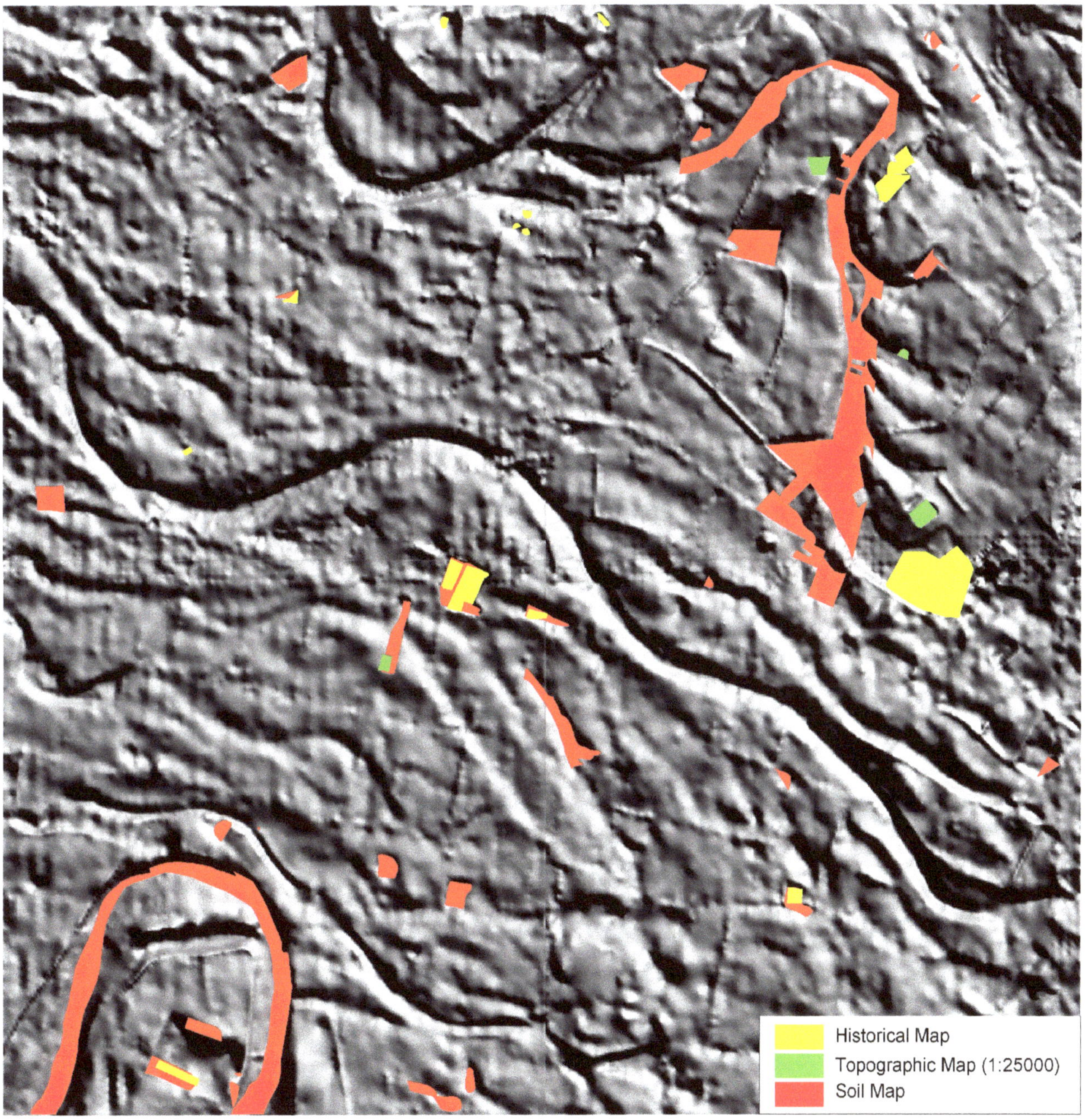

Chapter 6, Plate 4. *16 square km quadrangle on the lower terrace near Goch; 5% of the area featuring altered topsoil.*

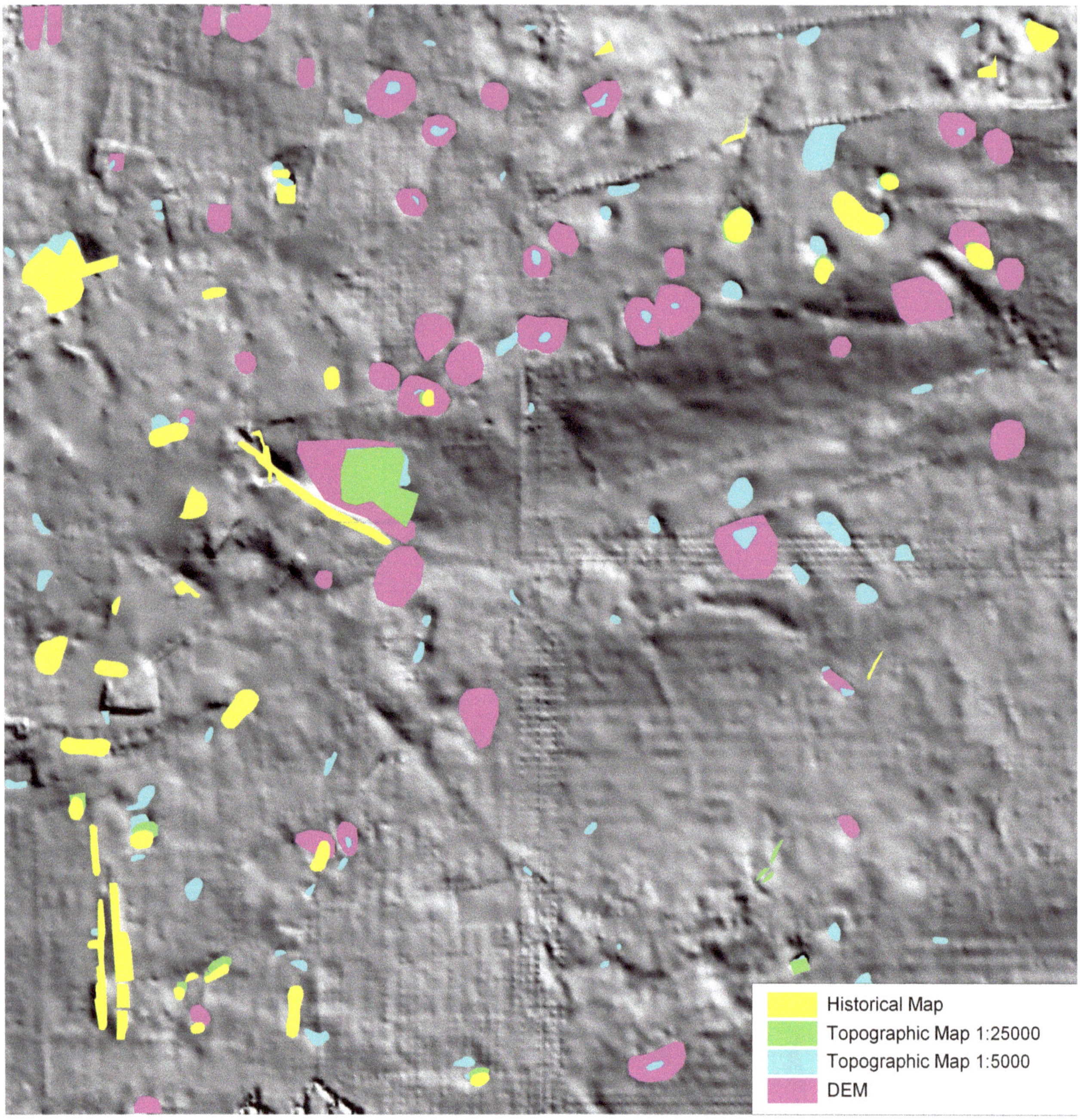

Chapter 6, Plate 5. *16 square km sample area in the loess landscape near Erkelenz; pits covering at least 7.7 % of the area (the bumps in the south-north and east-west axes are an artefact of small errors in the elevation data).*

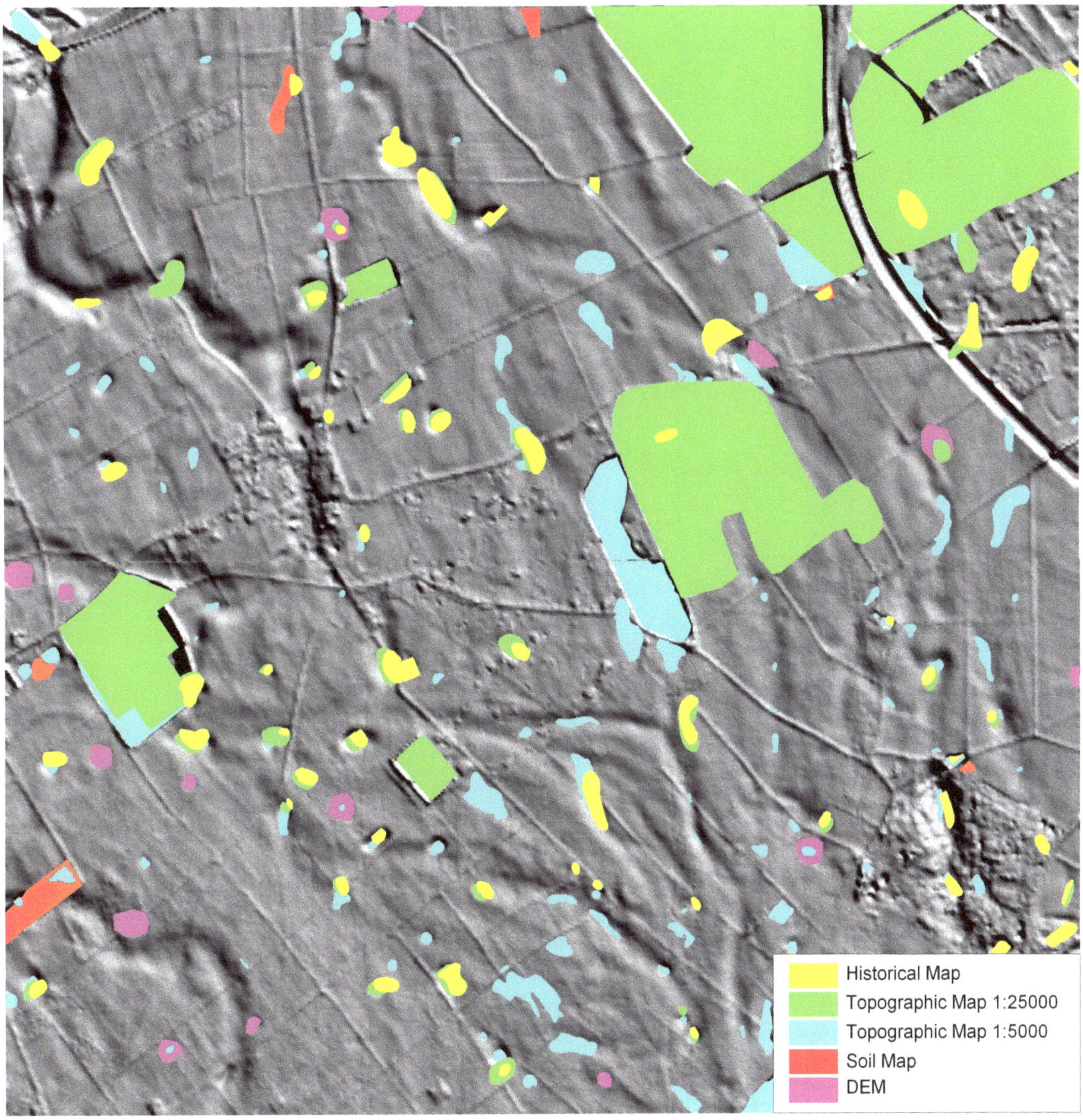

Chapter 6, Plate 6. *16 square km sample area on the lower terrace of the river Rhine between Cologne and Bonn; pits covering at least 16% of the area.*

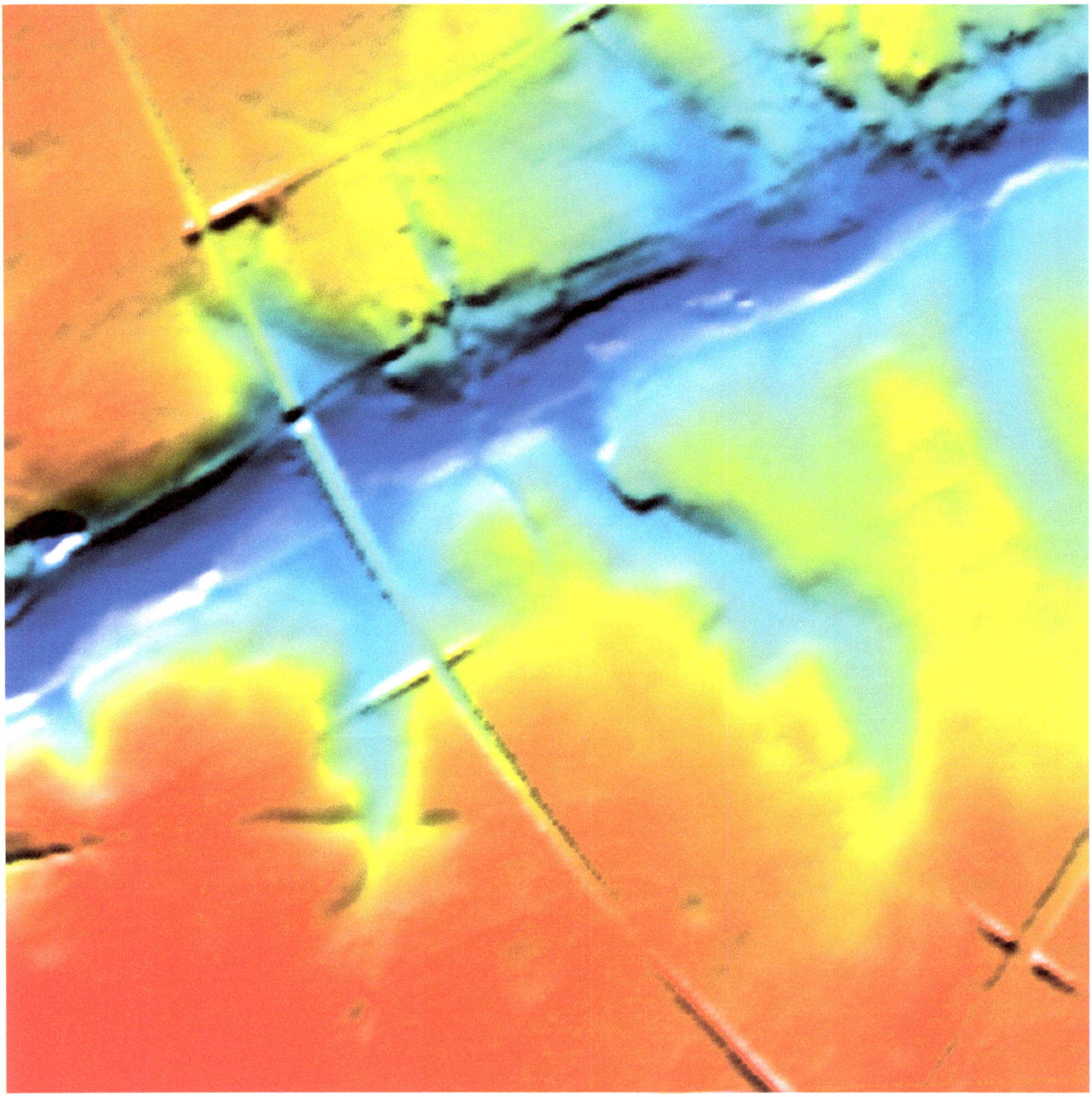

Chapter 6, Plate 7. *DEM covering a 4 square km quadrangle of a rural area in the triangle formed by the German towns Linnich, Jülich, and Titz; modern features, and an old sunken road crossing.*

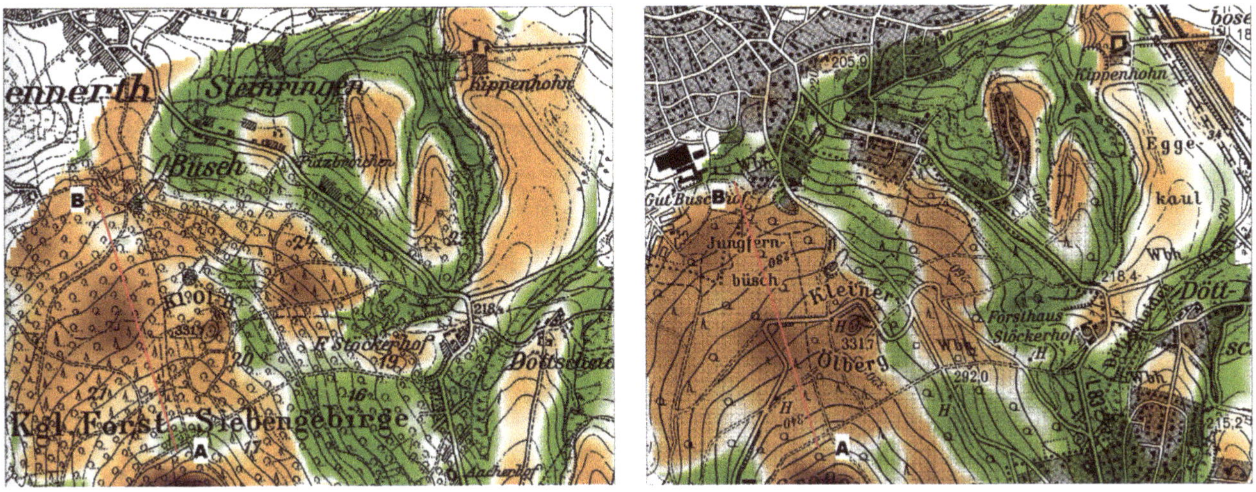

Chapter 7, Plate 2. *Area Siebengebirge. On the left the differences between DGM5 and PN, on the right the differences between DGM5 and TK25.*

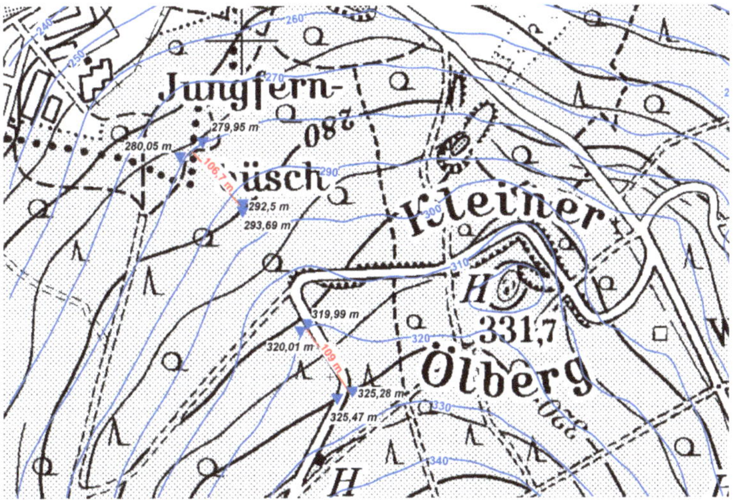

Chapter 7, Plate 4. *Section of the sheet TK25 5309 Königswinter. Aberrations between the contour lines of the DGM5 (blue) and the topographic map 1 : 25,000.*

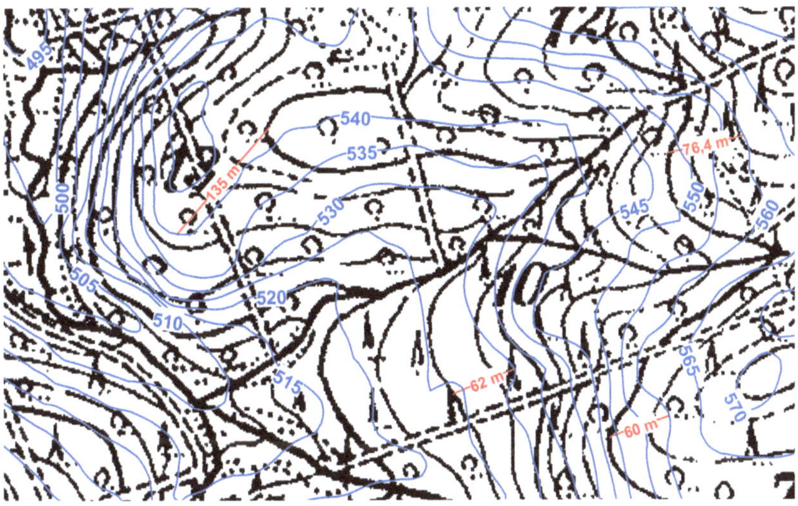

Chapter 7, Plate 5. *Section of the sheet 5505 Blankenheim, PN. Aberrations between the contour lines of the DGM5 (blue) and the topographic map 1 : 25,000.*

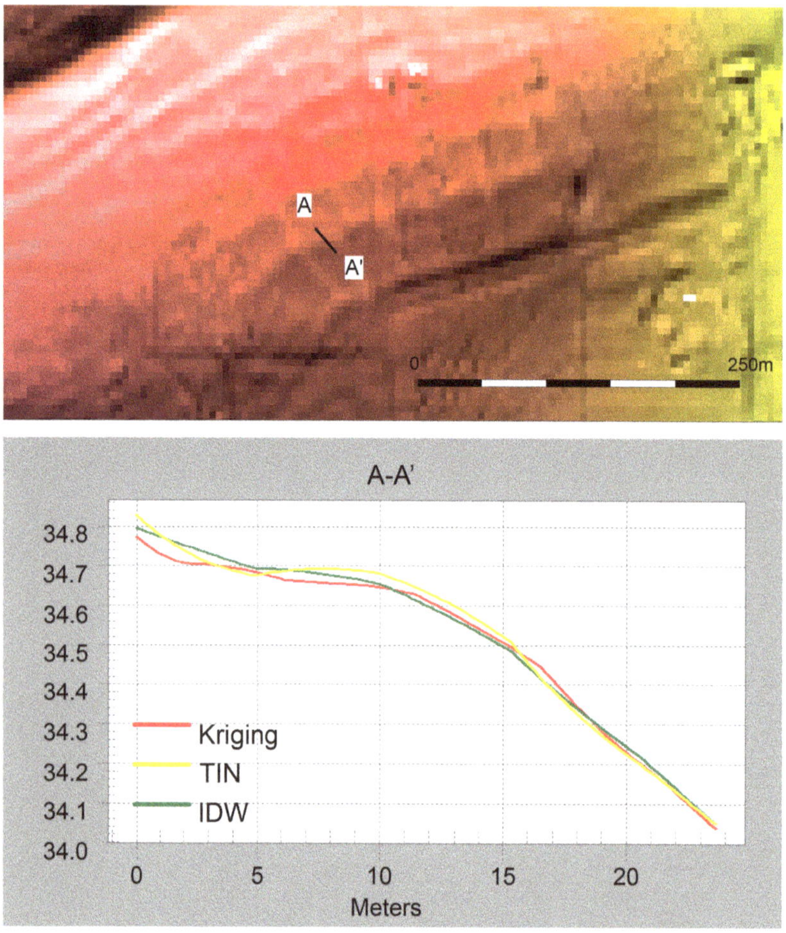

Chapter 8, Plate 1. *Comparison of different interpolation techniques.*

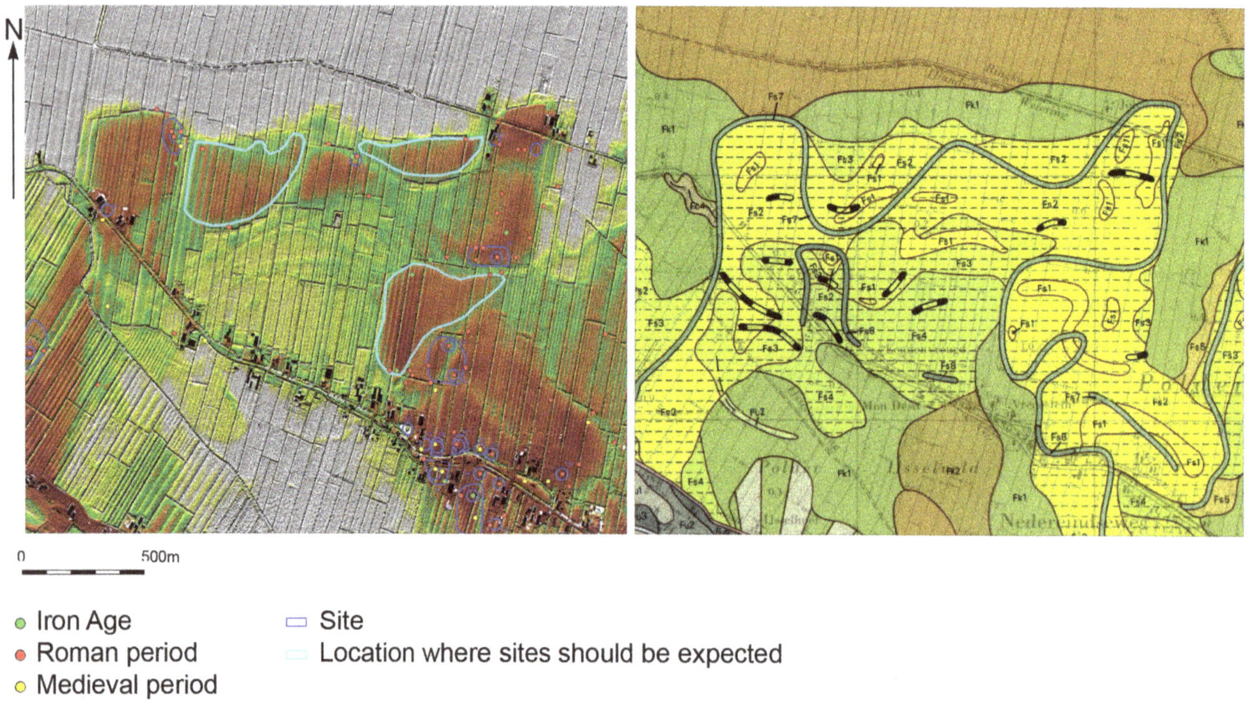

Chapter 8, Plate 2. *Comparison of a geomorphogenic map based on borings (Berendsen 1982, original scale 1: 25,000) and a LIDAR-based DEM.*

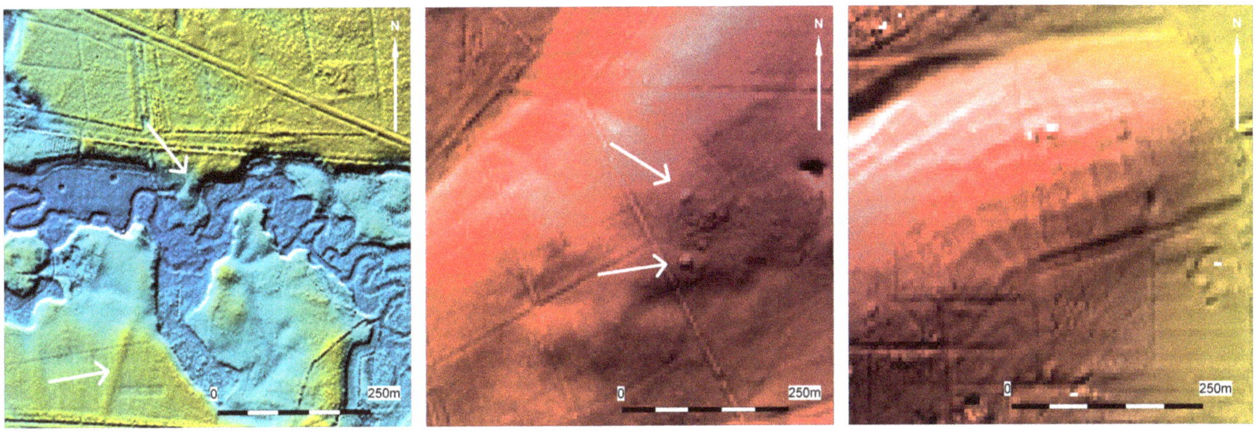

a *b* *c*

Chapter 8, Plate 3. *Examples of tracing individual archaeological monuments by expert scanning: a) Roman road and possible remnants of a bridge; b) burial mounds; c) Celtic fields.*

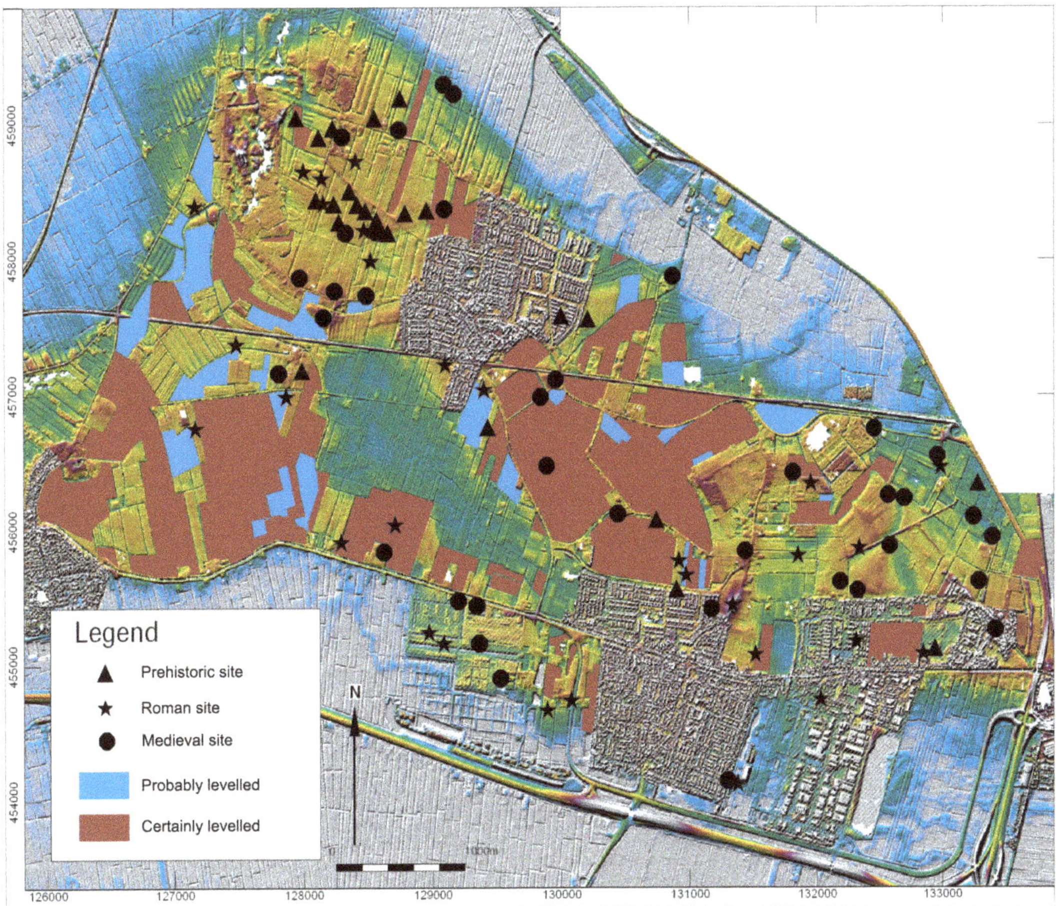

Chapter 8, Plate 5. *Tracing recent disturbances due to subsurface mining of clay.*

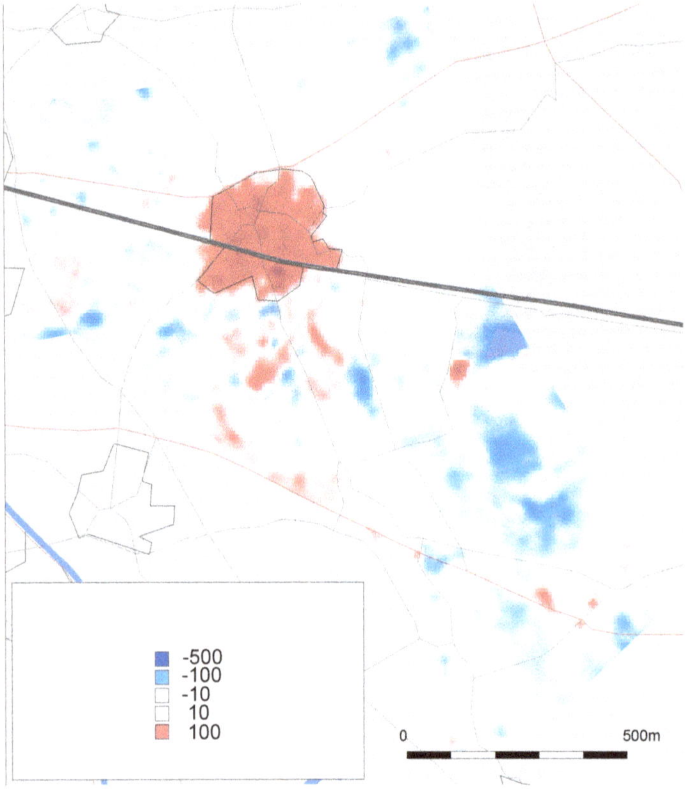

Chapter 8, Plate 4. *Changes in the bare surface height, in centimeters, since 1954 in the municipality of Deurne (after Oudhoff 2003: fig. 3).*

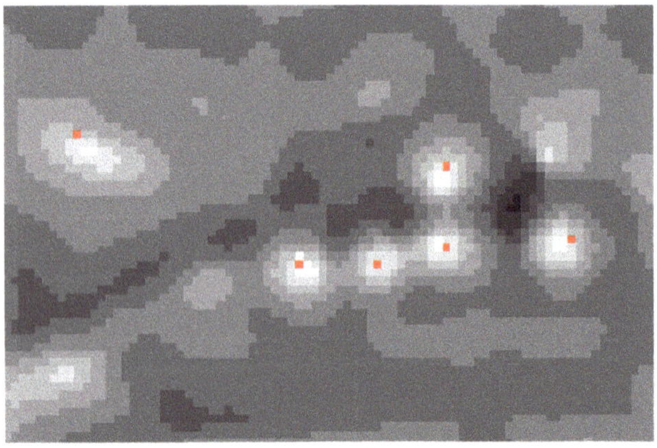

Chapter 8, Plate 8. *Result of a pattern search combined with locations of known burial mounds.*

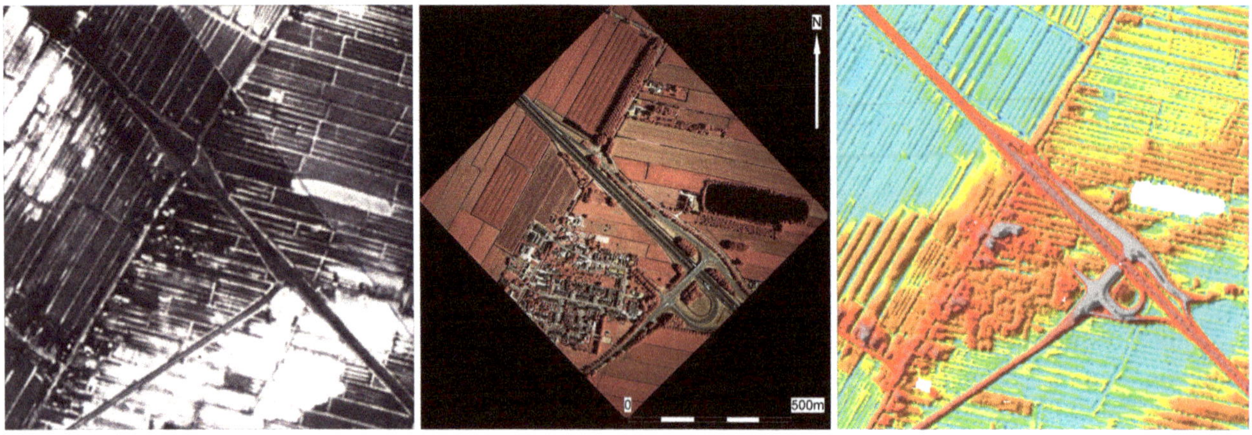

a *b* *c*

Chapter 8, Plate 9. *Comparison of different remote-sensing techniques: A. Black-and-white photograph; B. infra-red photograph; C. LIDAR-based DEMs.*

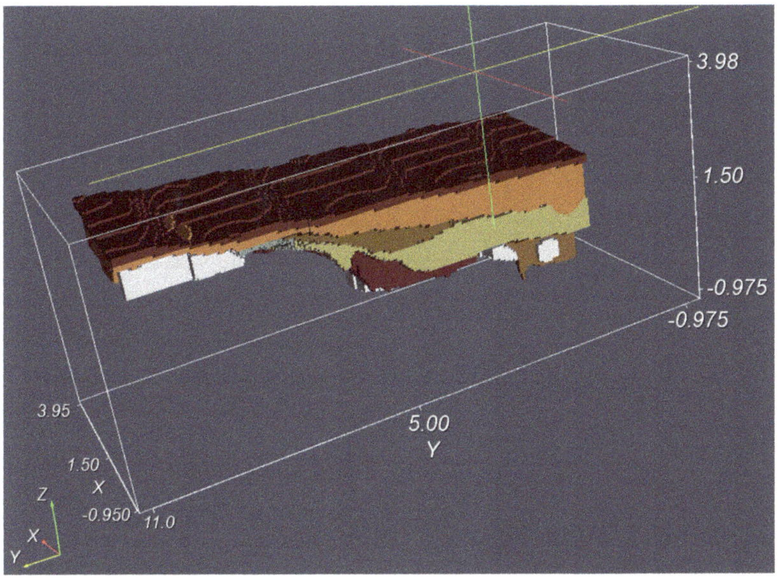

Chapter 9, Plate 11. *Trench IX of the Akroterion excavation at Kythera, stratigraphical units in colour, architectural features in white; generated by GRASS GIS, visualized by ParaView.*

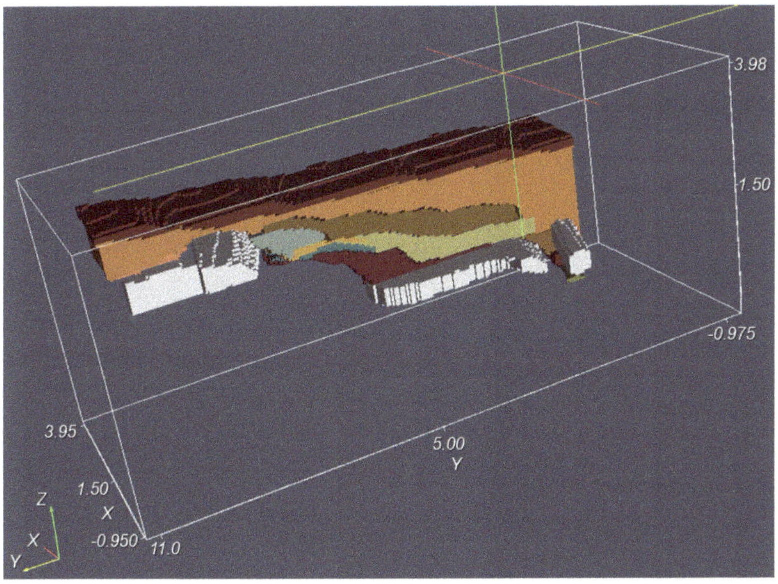

Chapter 9, Plate 12. *Trench IX of the Akroterion excavation at Kythera, vertical slice of all stratigraphical units; generated by GRASS GIS, visualized by ParaView.*

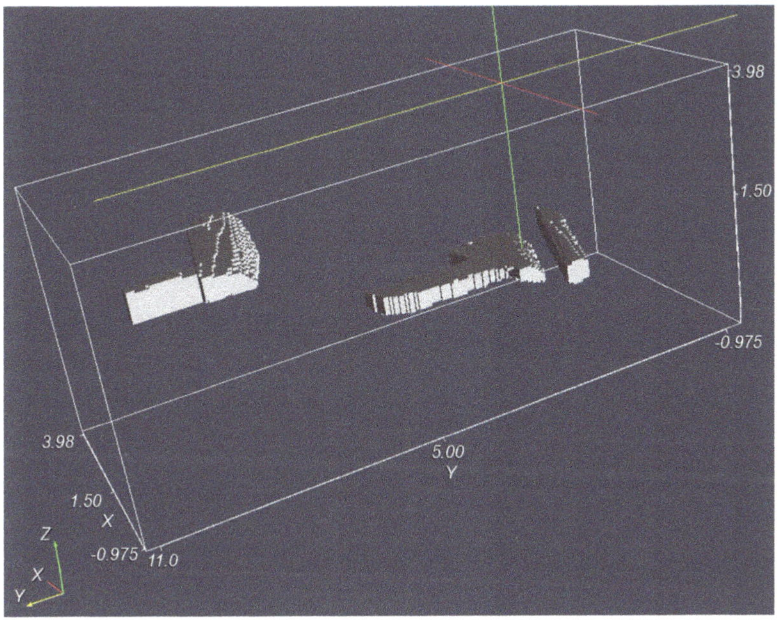

Chapter 9, Plate 13. *Trench IX of the Akroterion excavation at Kythera, depiction of all architectural features; generated by GRASS GIS, visualized by ParaView.*

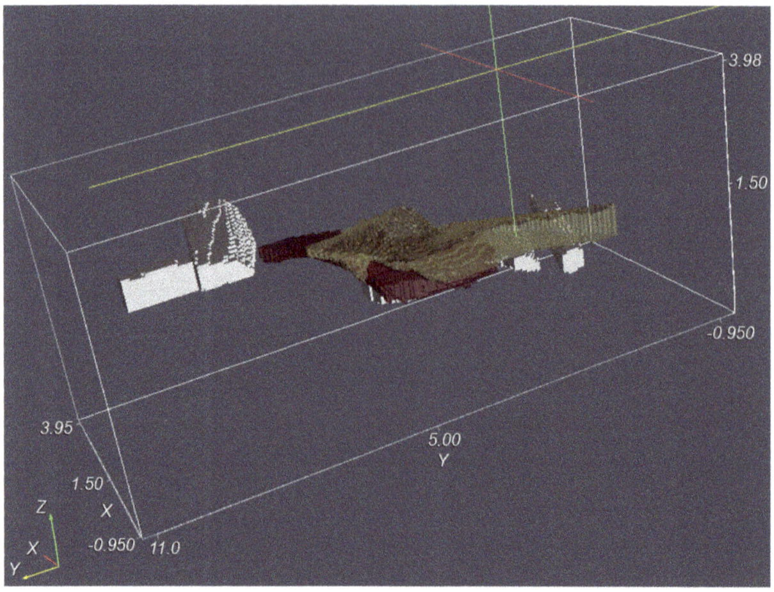

Chapter 9, Plate 14. *Trench IX of the Akroterion excavation at Kythera, 'negative' Unit Surface 4 with transparent Unit 2 above; generated by GRASS GIS, visualized by ParaView.*

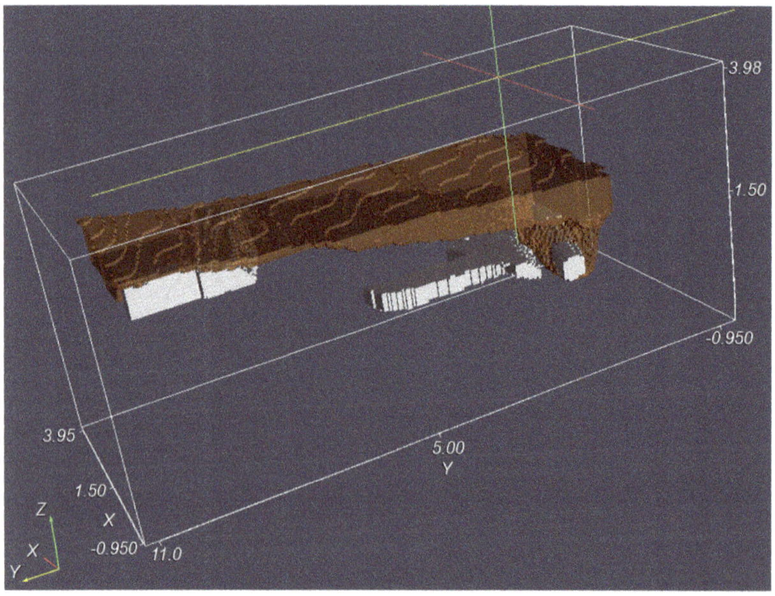

Chapter 9, Plate 15. *Trench IX of the Akroterion excavation at Kythera, Unit 4 (transparent) with 'negative' (dark) and 'positive' surfaces; generated by GRASS GIS, visualized by ParaView.*

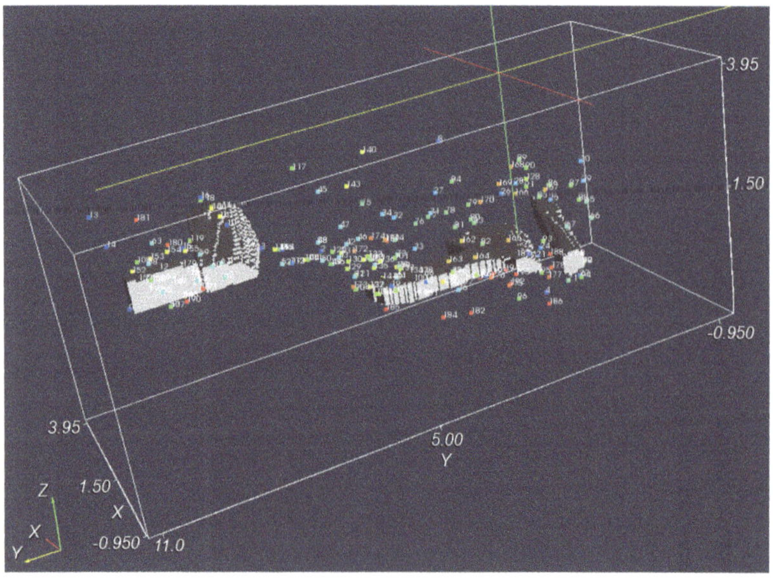

Chapter 9, Plate 16. *Trench IX of the Akroterion excavation at Kythera, depiction of all architectural features with simulated finds as vector points with identification numbers; generated by GRASS GIS, visualized by ParaView.*

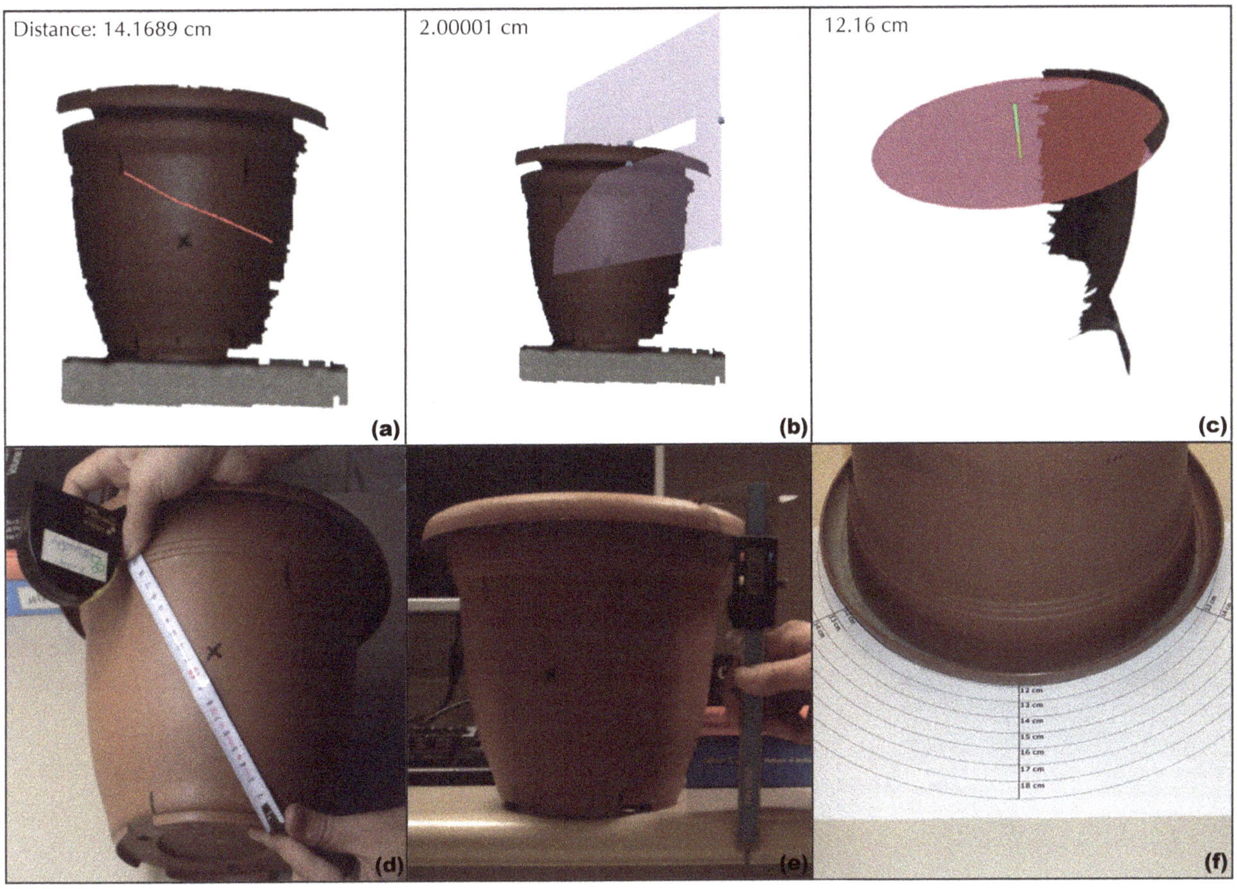

Chapter 10, Plate 1. *a) Screenshot of the virtual tape measure; b) the virtual caliper; c) the virtual radius estimator versus their real-life counterparts; d) a tape measure; e) a caliper; f) a rim chart.*

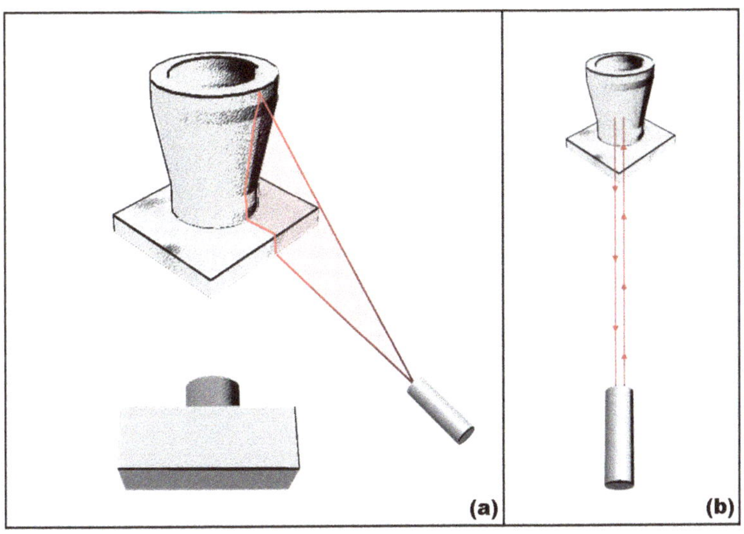

Chapter 10, Plate 2. *a) Triangulation-based scanning works by analysing the captured projection of a defined pattern, here a straight line; b) TOF-based scanning works by measuring the time it takes for a reflected laser beam to travel back to the source.*

Chapter 10, Plate 3. *System setup showing the spaceball on the left (non-dominant hand) and the mouse on the right (dominant hand).*

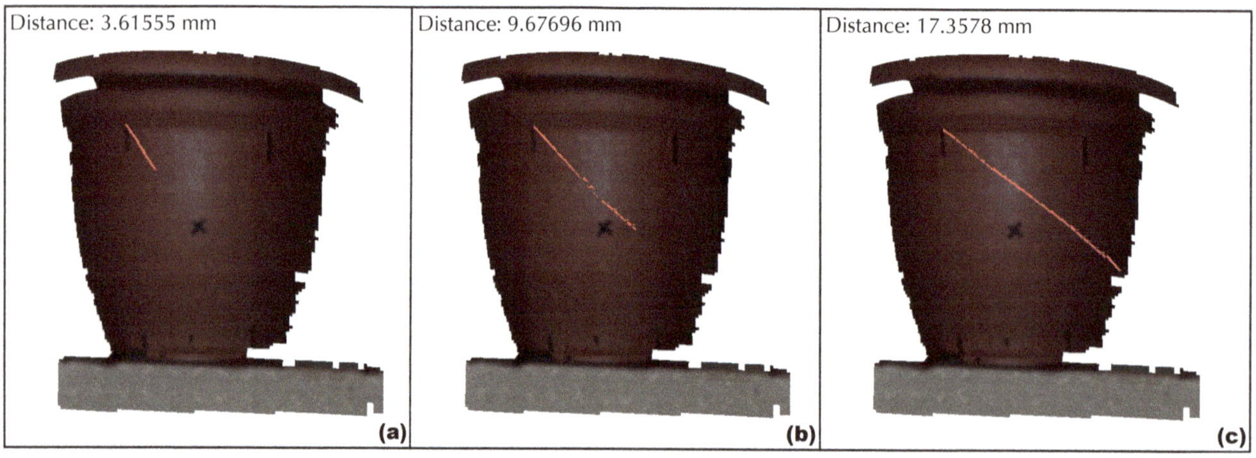

Chapter 10, Plate 4. *a) The virtual tape measure is used by fixing the starting point; b-c) moving the end point with the mouse.*

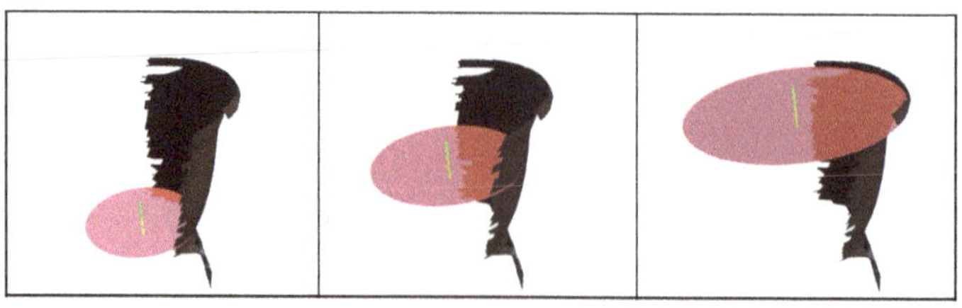

Chapter 10, Plate 6. *Screenshot of the virtual bordimeter in action.*

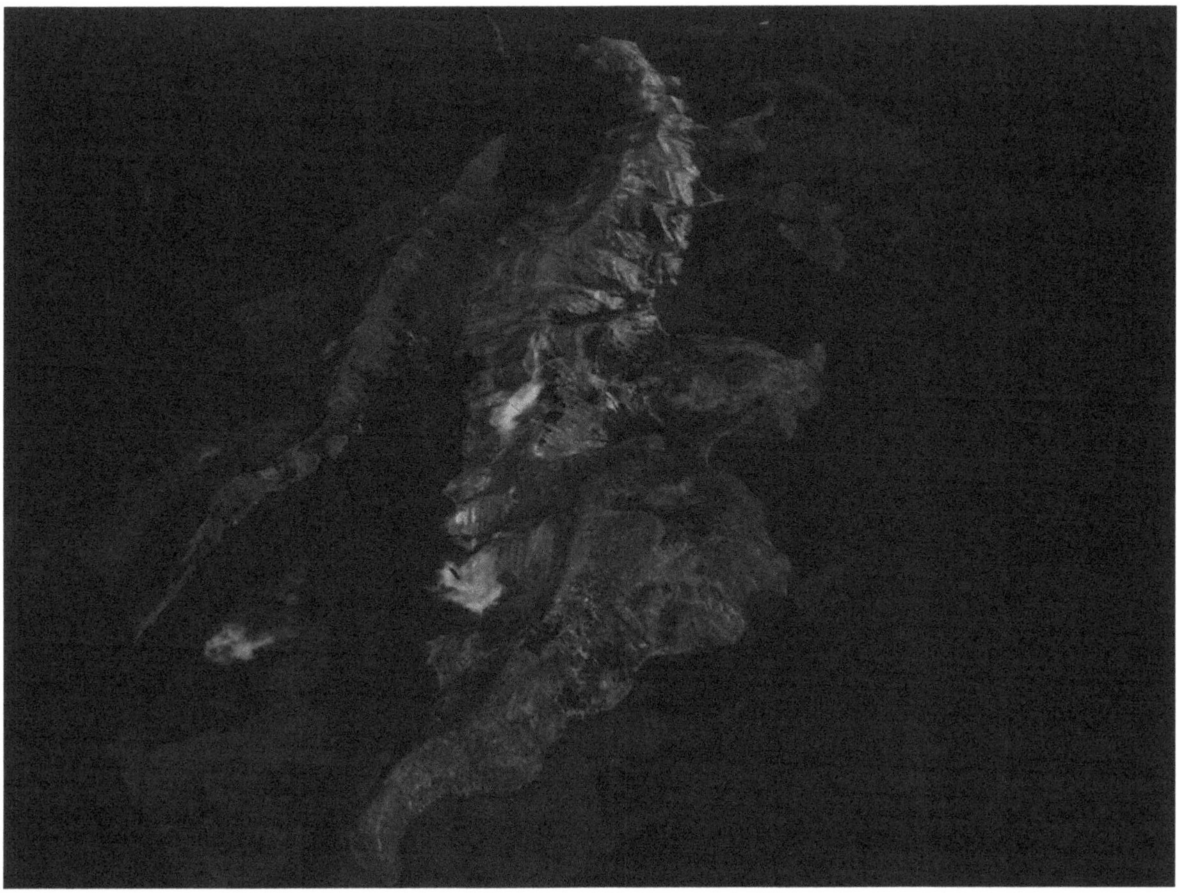

Chapter 11, Plate 1. *The Island of the Sun.*

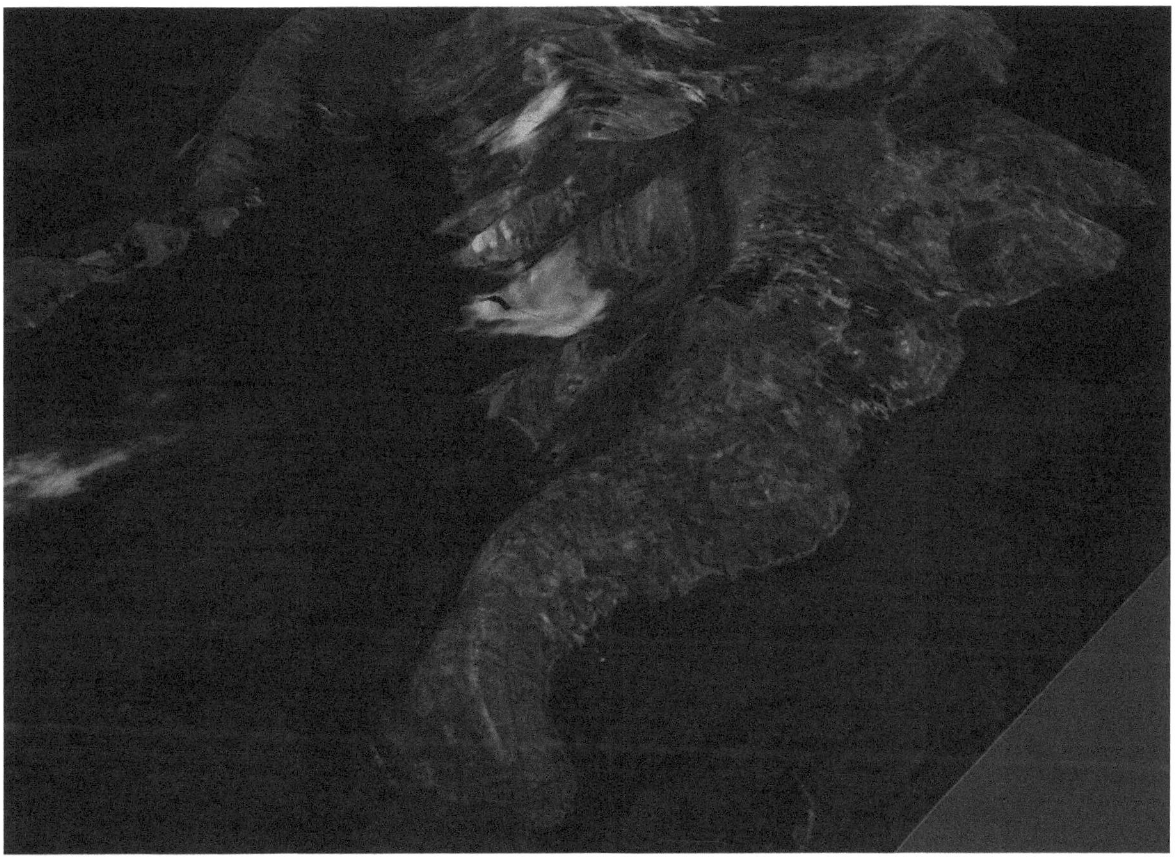

Chapter 11, Plate 2. *The southern tip of the island.*

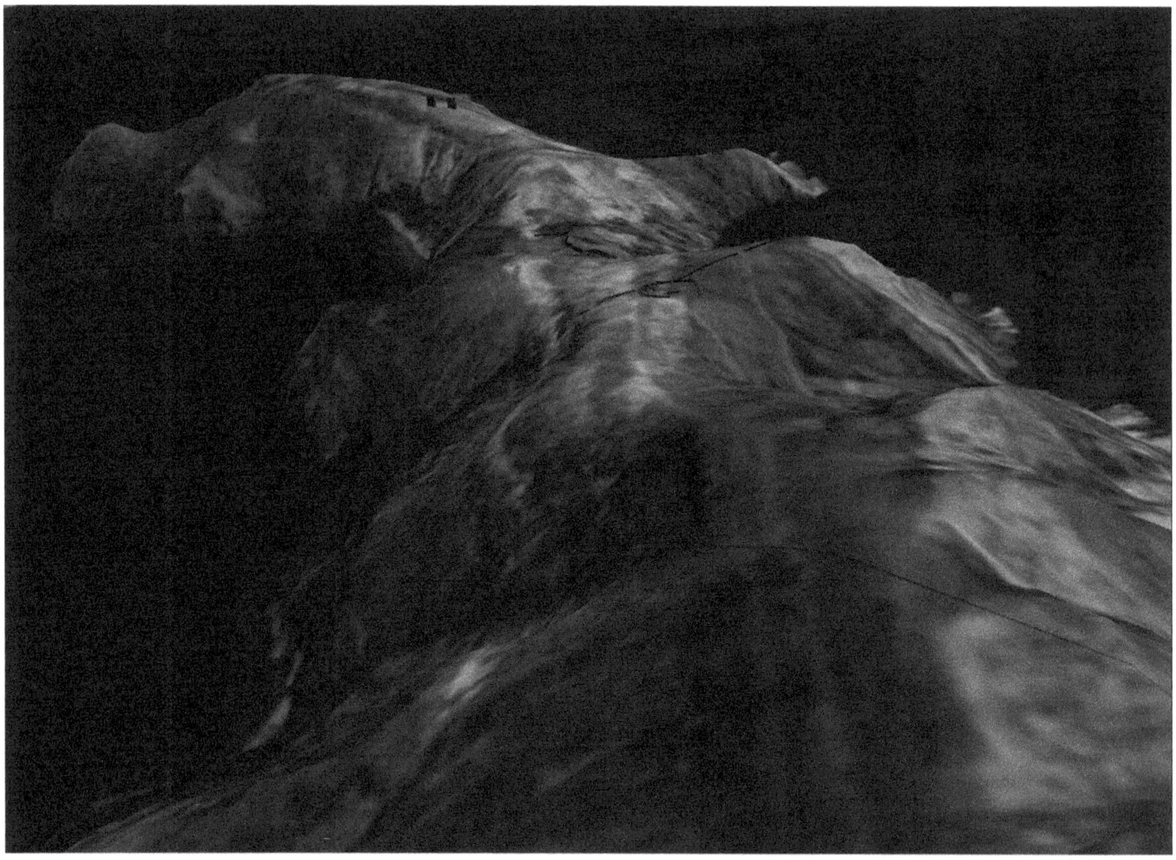

Chapter 11, Plate 3. *Approaching the first precinct.*

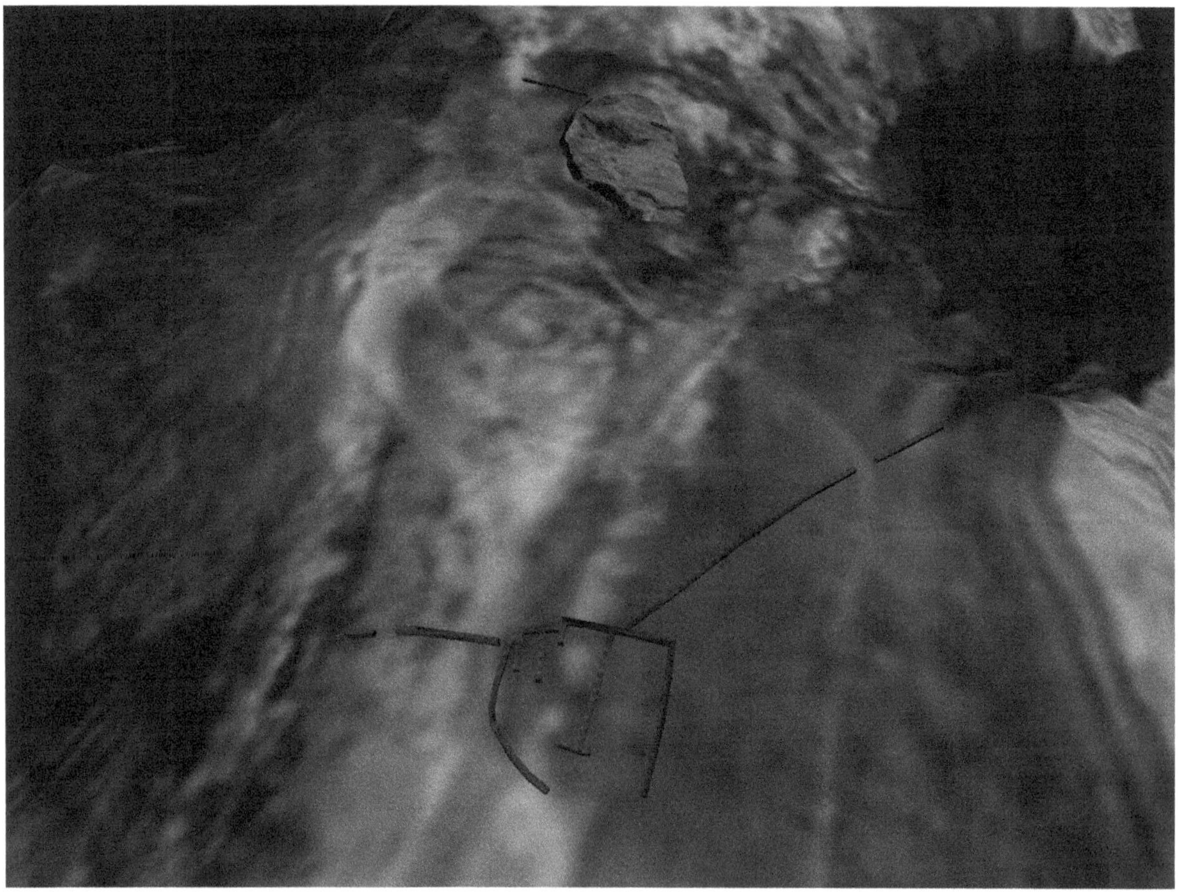

Chapter 11, Plate 4. *The first precinct (bottom) and the sacred rock (top).*

Chapter 11, Plate 5. *The Sacred Rock at winter solstice.*

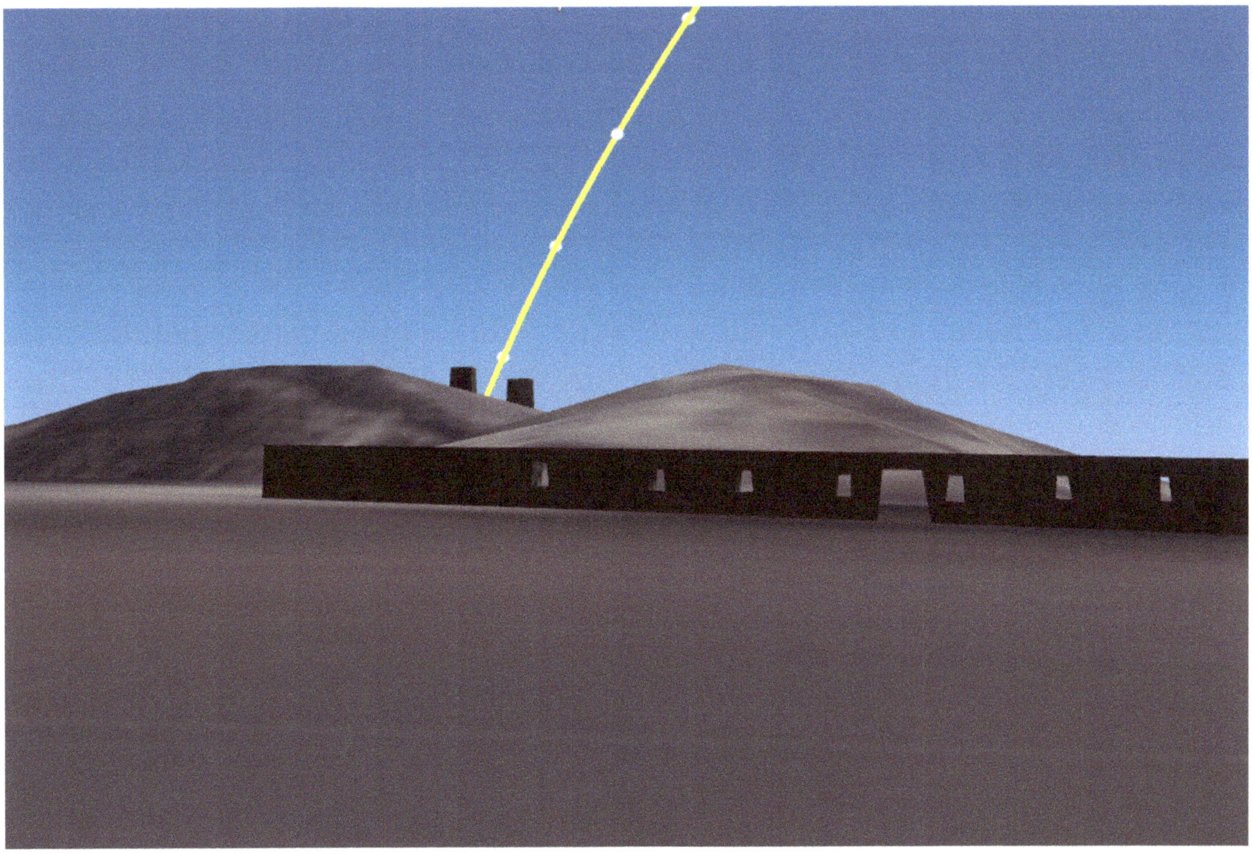

Chapter 11, Plate 6. *The solar markings at the winter solstice.*

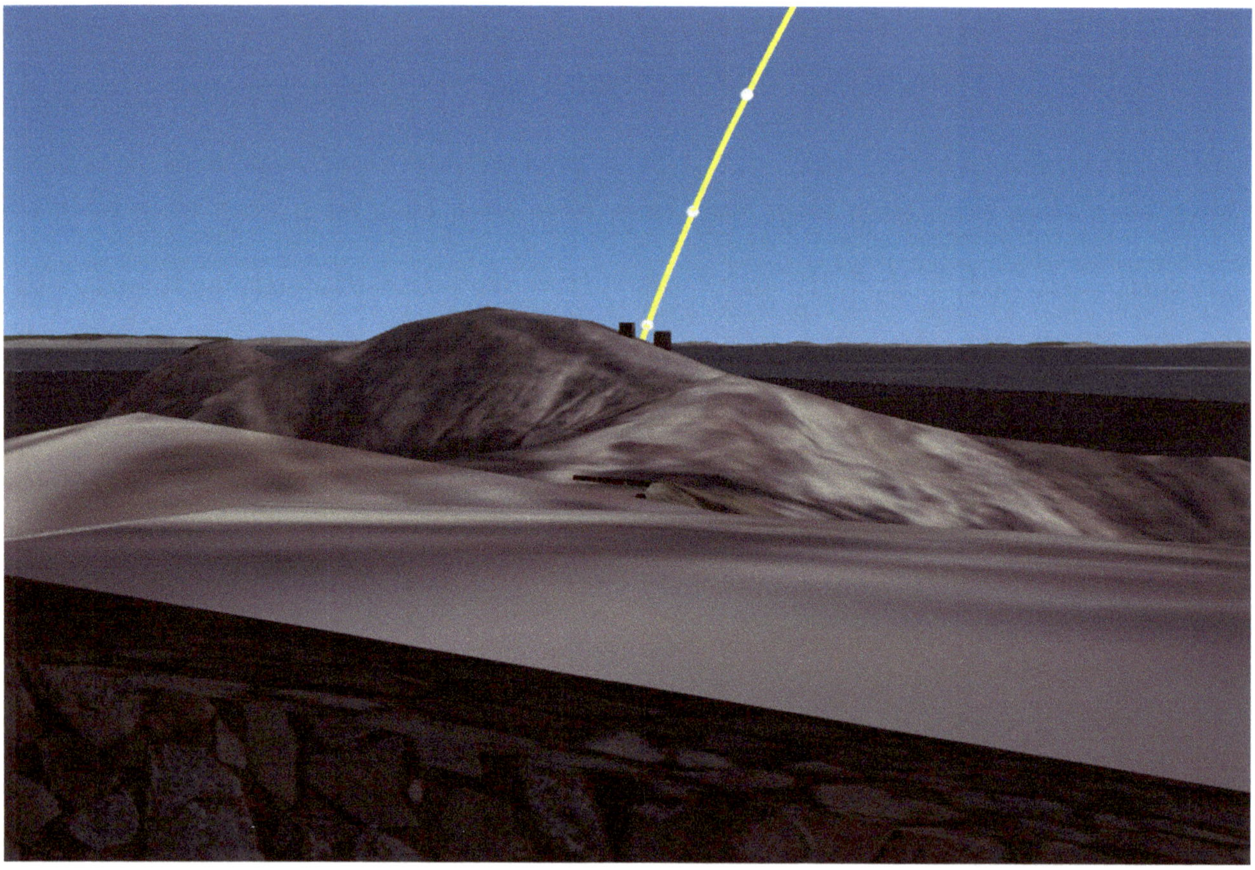

Chapter 11, Plate 7. *The viewing precinct at the winter solstice.*

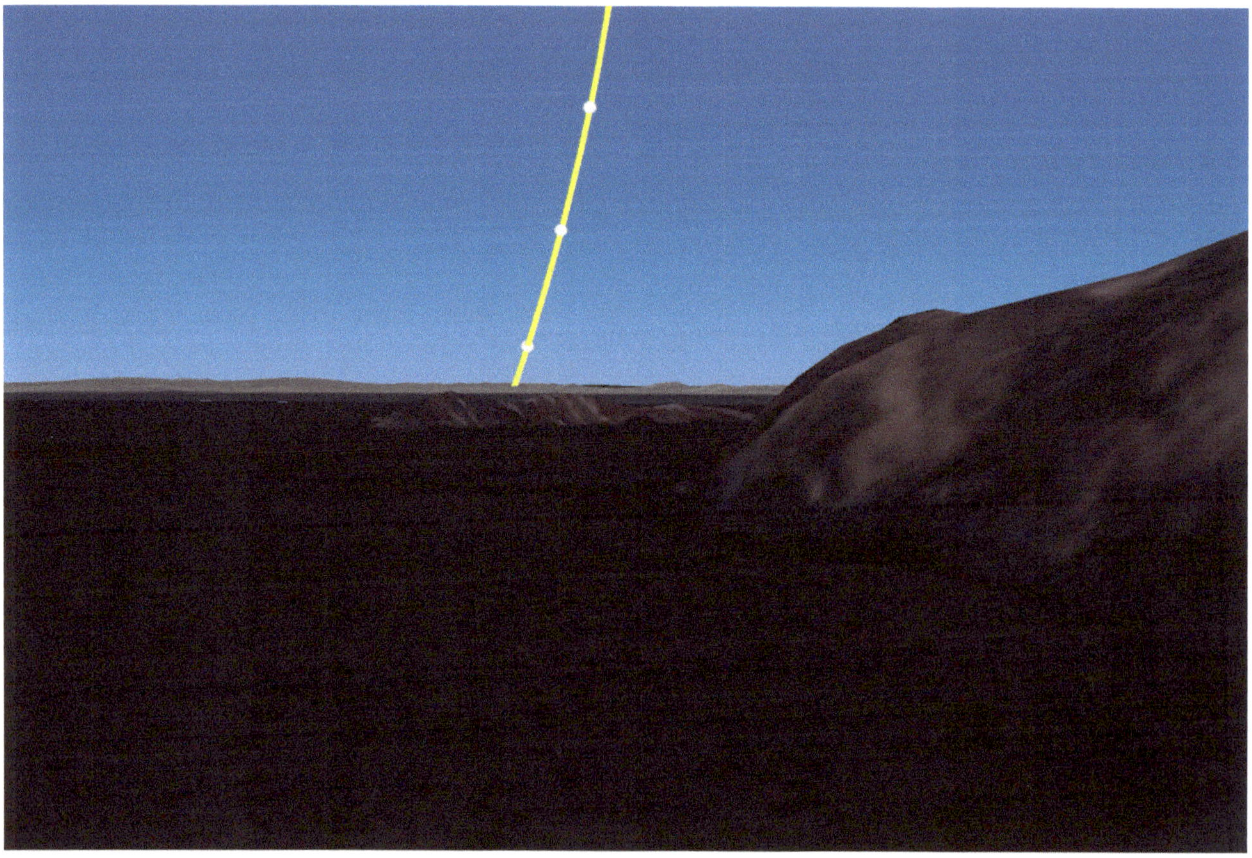

Chapter 11, Plate 8. *The summer solstice sun.*

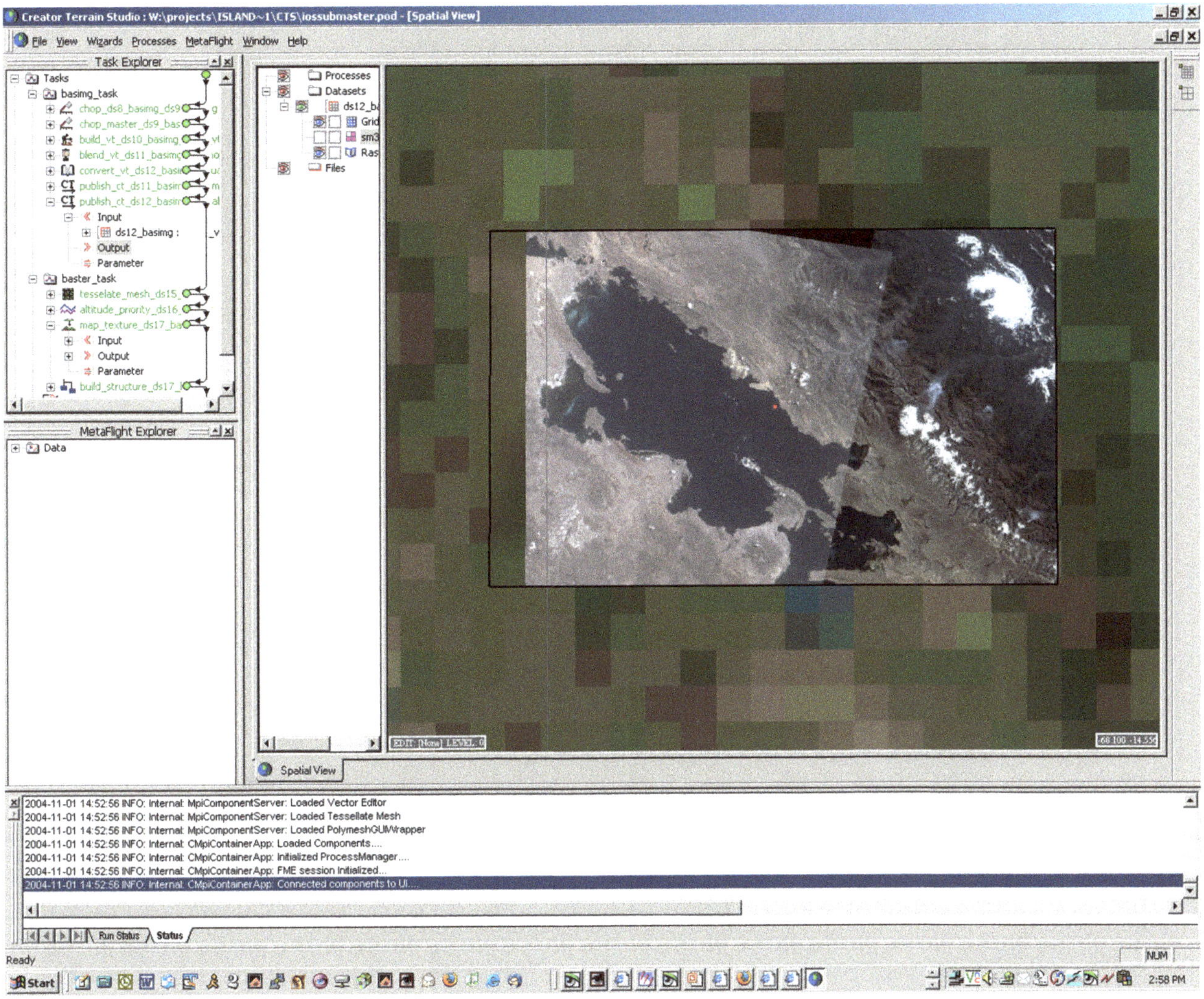

Chapter 11, Plate 9. *Merging satellite and DEM data in Creator Terrain Studio.*

Chapter 11, Plate 10. *Tiled geometry.*

Chapter 11, Plate 11. *The 2D sun.*

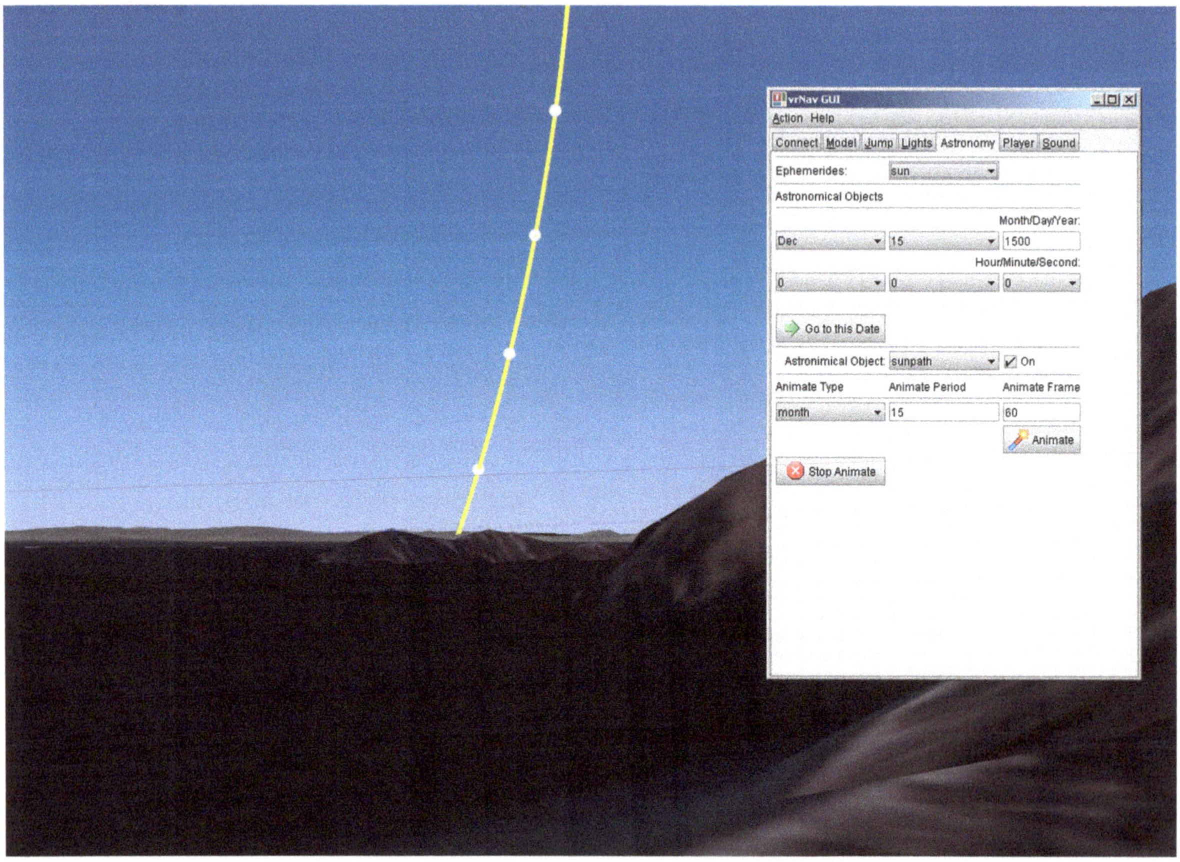

Chapter 11, Plate 12. *Manipulating time with the vrNav GUI.*

Stanford Digital Forma Urbis Romae Project

• Home • Project • Map • Database • Slab Map • Glossary • Bibliography • People • Links •

Page 16 of 433

◀Prev Next▶

ID AND LOCATION

Stanford #	8h(*)
AG1980 #	8h
PM1960 #	8 h
Slab #	VIII-5
Adjoins	none

CONDITION

Located	true
Incised	true
Surviving	true
Subfragments	1
Plaster Parts	0
Back Surface	smooth
Thickness	not yet available
Slab Edges	1
Clamp Holes	1
Tassello	no

TECHNICAL INFO

Scanner	model15

Search by:
All
where value is:
NOT
AND OR
Search by:
All
where value is:
NOT

Search

View All Fragments

BIBLIOGRAPHY

- AG 1980, pp. 30, 74-5, fig. 5, pls. 5, 14
- LTUR I: Circus Maximus (P.C. Rossetto), pp. 272-277
- LTUR IV: Sol [et Luna], aedes, templum (P.C. Rossetto), pp. 333-334
- PM 1960, pp. 66-67, pls. 17, 62
- Reynolds 1996, pp. 85-86, 101-102 (Circus Maximus)
- Richardson 1992, pp. 84-87 (Circus Maximus)

Photograph (43 KB)
Full resolution photo

PM 1960 Plates: 17 62
AG 1980 Plates: 5 14

IDENTIFICATION

Circus Maximus (*circus Maximus*)

INSCRIPTION Epigraphic conventions used

- **Transcription**

[---][.]C[---] (vertical)

- **Renaissance Transcription**

None

- **Reconstruction**

C[IR]C[VS] [M]AX[IMVS]
(with frs. 8c, h, 9: PM 1960; AG 1980)

3D Model Full model | PLY(13 MB)
Download the viewer | Note about 3D models

ANALYSIS

Description The fragment was part of a slab edge; a clamp hole is visible on the side. A large inscribed C takes up roughly half of the surface area. Above, traces of the legs of another letter are visible. To the right, two straight, vertical lines traverse the fragment. A third line, parallel to these two, perhaps runs very close along the edge. Between them, two separate staircases are represented by sets of short, parallel lines.

Identification: *Circus Maximus* The C on this fragment is the second C of the label CIRCUS MAXIMUS which was inscribed vertically down the arena of the *circus Maximus*. Other parts of the building and the inscription are visible in frs. 7abcd, 7e, 8bde, 8c, 8fg, and 9. Situated in the valley between the Palatine and the Aventine Hills, the *circus Maximus* played a central role in Rome's earliest history. Sources attribute its conception to the Etruscan kings and relate it to the rise of the *ludi Romani* (LTUR I, p. 272). For centuries, the Circus was nothing but an open space with wooden partitions and seating; more permanent walls were not constructed until the 2nd c. BCE. Julius Caesar is credited with giving the building the shape and enormous size it was to retain for centuries: According to Dionysius of Halicarnassus (3.68.1-4), the Circus had a length of 421 m. and a width of 118 m., and the *cavea* held 150,000 spectators (LTUR I, p. 273). The structure was destroyed by fire several times and it collapsed occasionally, but it underwent several reconstructions by various emperors and remained in use until the 6th c. In Medieval times, the area was mainly used for agriculture, and in the following centuries it was gradually encroached upon by various forms of construction until it was cleared in the beginning of the 20th c. (LTUR I, pp. 274-75).

Evidence gathered from excavations, written sources, coins, and standing remains reveals the architecture of the Circus Maximus in the imperial period: Raised above the surrounding area, the building measured

Chapter 13, Plate 3. *Screenshot of the database page for a fragment.*

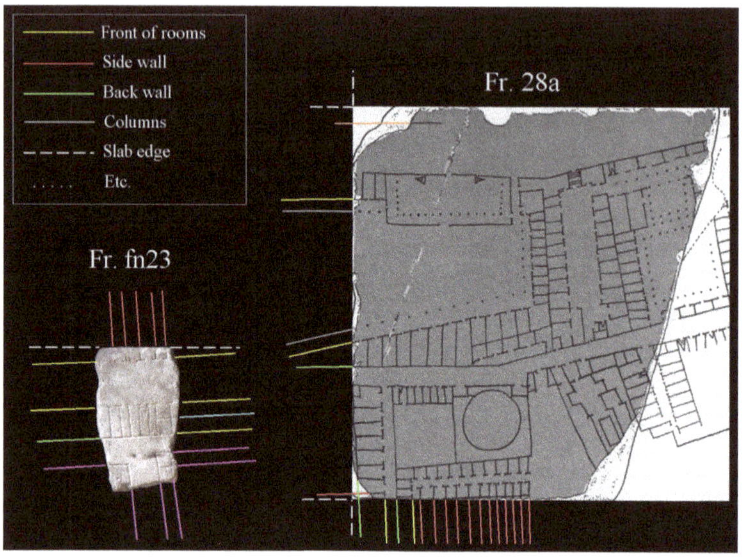

Chapter 13, Plate 4. *Fragments fn23 and 28a with their boundary incision annotations indicated. The different colors correspond to different feature type labels (fr. 28a illustration from Rodríguez-Almeida 1981).*

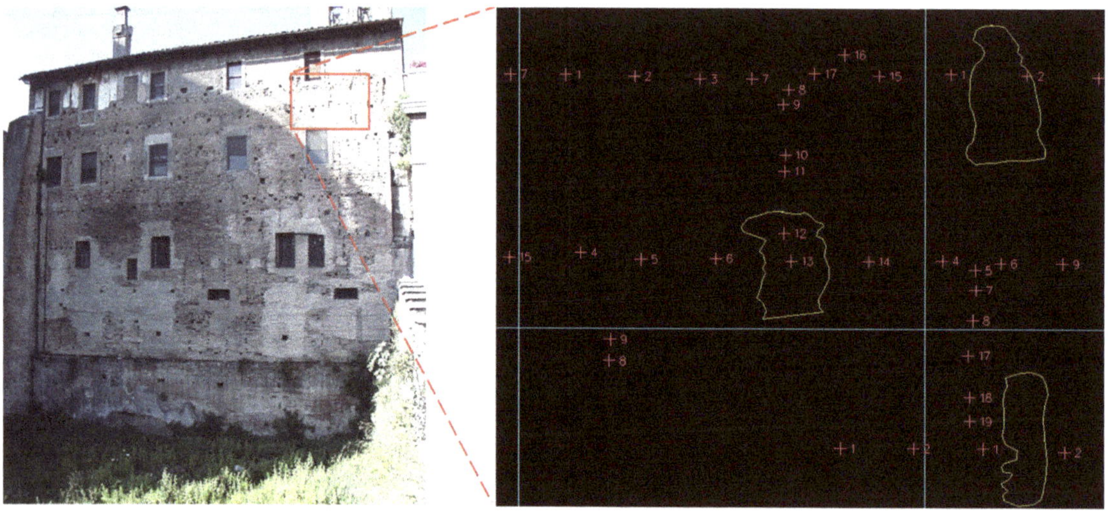

Chapter 13, Plate 9. *Modern photograph of the surviving aula wall on which the Marble Plan was mounted (left), and a section of the digitized wall features (right) with clamp hole locations indicated in red and masonry patches in yellow.*

www.ingramcontent.com/pod-product-compliance
Lightning Source LLC
Chambersburg PA
CBHW041716180926
51615CB00022B/3077